MW00825005

War by Numbers

WAR BY NUMBERS

Understanding Conventional Combat

CHRISTOPHER A. LAWRENCE

Potomac Books

AN IMPRINT OF THE UNIVERSITY OF NEBRASKA PRESS

© 2017 by Christopher A. Lawrence

Appendixes 1, 2, and 3 appear courtesy Arnold Dupuy.

All rights reserved. Potomac Books is an imprint of the
University of Nebraska Press.
Manufactured in the United States of America.

Names: Lawrence, Christopher A., author.
Title: War by numbers: understanding conventional
combat / Christopher A. Lawrence.
Description: Lincoln: Potomac Books, an imprint
of the University of Nebraska Press, 2017. | Includes
bibliographical references.
Identifiers: LCCN 2017022872 (print)
LCCN 2017023706 (ebook)
ISBN 9781612348865 (paperback: alkaline paper)
ISBN 9781612349152 (epub)
ISBN 9781612349169 (mobi)
ISBN 9781612349176 (pdf)
Subjects: LCSH: Warfare, Conventional—History. |
Combat—History. | Warfare, Conventional—
Philosophy. | Military art and science—History. |
BISAC: HISTORY / Military / United States. |
HISTORY / Modern / 21st Century.
Classification: LCC U39 (ebook) |
LCC U39 .L375 2017 (print) | DDC 355.02—dc23
LC record available at https://lccn.loc.gov/2017022872

Set in Minion Pro by Rachel Gould.

This book is dedicated to Trevor N. Dupuy (Col. USA),
as it is a continuation of his life's work.

Contents

Preface

Out of World War II, initially as part of the effort to integrate UK radar systems within UK air defense efforts, a new discipline came into being called *operational research* (*operations research* in the United States). As a result of the use of these more quantitative analytical efforts in the UK and U.S. war efforts, a series of analytical centers was established after the war. This included the Operations Evaluation Group (OEG) in 1945 for the U.S. Navy, Project RAND ("research and development") in 1946 for the U.S. Air Force, Operations Research Office (ORO) in 1948 for the U.S. Army, and the Weapons Systems Evaluation Group (WSEG) in 1956 for elements of the Department of Defense.[1]

In the 1960s Secretary of Defense Robert McNamara instituted systems analysis as the basis for Pentagon decision making on force requirements, weapons systems, and other such matters. This led the Defense Department to better incorporate into their analysis the new operations research methodologies and directly led to the growth and influence of various studies and analysis centers, like RAND, Research Analysis Corporation (RAC, the replacement for ORO), the Center for Naval Analyses (CNA, the renamed OEG), and the Institute for Defense Analysis (IDA, the descendant of WSEG). It led to the incorporation of the new discipline of operations research and the use of civilian defense planners as an integral part of the U.S. defense planning process. It also led to computerized combat models.[2]

These computerized combat models first appeared in 1953 at ORO as a simple tank-versus-tank model. By 1965 they had expanded the models to be able to fight entire campaigns. By the early 1970s the models were being used to war game a potential war in Europe for the sake of seeing who would win, for the sake of determining how we could structure our forces better, and for the sake of determining what supplies and other support were needed to sustain this force on the other side of the Atlantic Ocean.

This development of models created a need to understand the quantitative aspects of warfare. While this was not a new concept, the United States suddenly found itself with combat modeling structures that were desperately in need of hard data on how combat actually worked. Surprisingly, even after 3,300 years of recorded military history, these data were sparse.

It was this lack of hard data on which to base operational analysis and combat modeling that led to the growth of the organizations run by Trevor N. Dupuy, such as the Historical Evaluation and Research Organization (HERO). They attempted to fill the gap between the modeling communities' need for hard data on combat operations and the actual data recorded in the unit records of the combatants, which required some time and skill to extract. It was an effort to integrate the work of the historians with these newly developed complex models of combat.

In 1987 Dupuy's book *Understanding War: History and Theory of Combat* was released to almost no fanfare and almost no critical attention, even though this was probably the single most important book of the more than ninety books he authored or coauthored. This was a unique, comprehensive theoretical work that tied together all his previous work and expanded it into a cohesive theory of combat. *Understanding War* was fundamentally Clausewitzian in nature, in that it was an attempt to discuss the basic nature and shape of warfare in general, as was previously done in the 1820s by the Prussian theorist Gen. Carl von Clausewitz.

Dupuy's previous works with a theoretical bent had received some attention, including *Evolution of Weapons and Warfare*; *A Genius for War: The German Army and the General Staff, 1807–1945*; and *Numbers, Predictions and War.* But for some reason, the overarching theoretical work that tied all these other works together passed by without much comment.[3]

While this book is not an attempt to resurrect *Understanding War*, which is still in print, it does directly build on it, test it, and challenge it. Just as many scientists build their work on the work of their predecessors, this work is built on Dupuy's work, which is built on the work of Clausewitz, Jomini, Fuller, and others.[4] As such, I am not presenting an overarching theory of warfare; instead this is a further testing and refinement of what is already known or has been discussed by other theorists. In many cases it is simply an attempt to prove whether the theory was right or wrong. In many cases this proof is in the form of a more rigorous quantitative analysis to supplement what those theorists had originally proposed.

Acknowledgments

I would like to thank all the people who eventually led me to this line of work, which I have enjoyed doing over the past twenty years. First and foremost is Trevor N. Dupuy, who ran the various organizations I worked for during the first eight years of my career. Not only was he an author whom I started reading at twelve years old, he was also the starting point for all my work on conventional warfare since I first went to work for him in 1987.

Next is my predecessor at the Dupuy Institute (TDI), Maj. Gen. Nicholas Krawciw (USA, ret.), who helped keep the Institute alive through some difficult budgetary times and gave me the academic and managerial freedom to follow my own nose. He helped save the Institute after Trevor passed away.

I would be remiss not to mention those who originally led me to this career, hired me, and helped train me in my early years. This would include my own father, Col. William A. Lawrence; his friends Col. John R. Brinkerhoff and Andrew Wittner; and most important, Curt Johnson, my boss at Dupuy's earlier company, Data Memory Systems Incorporated (DMSI).

Most of this work came about as a result of a series of government contracts and commercial contracts. Therefore, of equal importance are E. G. Vandiver, director of the Center for Army Analysis (CAA), Andrew Marshall (Office of the Secretary of Defense, Net Assessment), Walt Hollis (Deputy Undersecretary of the Army, Operations Research), Dr. Ron Bellamy (Col. USA, ret.), Mark Perry (Vietnam Veterans of American Foundation), William Beuttel (Boeing), and many others.

This work could not have been done without the able assistance of the staff and consultants of the Dupuy Institute. These include Richard Anderson, L. Jay Karamales, Susan Sims, and Dr. Shawn Woodford. As this book was based on a series of reports that we did, almost by default some sections were effectively coauthored by our staff, especially Richard Anderson. (The third phase of chapter 16 was his work, as were most significant parts of chapter 17.)

I would also like to thank some others who helped along the way, including Dr. Andrew Birtle, the late Dr. George Daoust (Col. USA), the late John D. Kettelle, Dr. Brian McCue, Lt. Col. Bruce Shahbaz, and Dr. James Taylor.

Abbreviations

AMSAA	Army Material Systems Analysis Activity
ARVN	Army of the Republic of Vietnam
ATCAL	Attrition Calibration
BaDB	Battles Data Base
BLODB	Battalion-Level Operations Data Base
CAA	Center for Army Analysis
CaDB	Campaign Data Base
CEM	Concepts Evaluation Model
CEV	combat effectiveness value
CI	civilian internees
CIA	captured in action
CNA	Center for Naval Analyses
COSAGE	Combat Sample Generator
DLEDB	Division-Level Engagement Data Base
DMSI	Data Memory Systems Incorporated
DOD	Department of Defense
DOW	died of wounds
EF	Eastern Front
EPW	enemy prisoner of war
ETO	European Theater of Operations
FCO	Future Combat System
HDQA	Headquarters Department of the Army
HERO	Historical Evaluation and Research Organization
IDA	Institute for Defense Analyses
IED	improvised explosive device
ISIL	Islamic State of Iraq and the Levant
ISIS	Islamic State of Iraq and Syria
JICM	Joint Integrated Contingency Model
KIA	killed in action
LADB	Large Action Data Base
LSSAH	Leibstandarte ss Adolf Hitler
LWDB	Land Warfare Data Base
MBT	main battle tank
MIA	missing in action

NATO	North Atlantic Treaty Organization
NVA	North Vietnamese Army
OLI	operational lethality index
OEG	Operations Evaluation Group
ORO	Operations Research Office
POL	petroleum, oil, and lubricants
PRO	Public Records Office
PTO	Pacific Theater of Operations
QJM	Quantified Judgment Model
QJMA	Quantified Judgment Method of Analysis
RAC	Research Analysis Corporation
RMA	revolution in military affairs
SABD	Small Action Data Base
SSCO	Small Scale Contingency Operations
SSPK	single shot probability of kill
TAA	Total Army Analysis
TNDA	Trevor N. Dupuy and Associates
TNDM	Tactical Numerical Deterministic Model
USAAF	U.S. Army Air Forces
USMC	U.S. Marine Corps
VC	Viet Cong
WIA	wounded in action
WSEG	Weapons Systems Evaluation Group

1. Understanding War

My personal feeling is that if I have done anything worthwhile, it is in military
theory and the relationship of the elements of historical experience to theory.

—TREVOR N. DUPUY, quoted in Susan Rich, "TDI Profile: Trevor N. Dupuy"

In March 1973 the U.S. Army ended its eight-year war in Vietnam. At the time
this was longest war in U.S. history. It was a large, grinding guerrilla war that
included many battalion-level actions. In the northern part of the I Corps operational area, near the border with North Vietnam, the conflict was almost a
conventional war. Nonetheless this was a brushfire war, or counterinsurgency,
not a conventional war like World War I, World War II, or the Korean War. As
the Vietnam War ended, U.S. Army officials appear to have decided that they
were never going to fight that type of war again. They did not analyze the war
in depth, they did not further study it, and they did not plan for engagement
in any other guerrilla wars.[1] This was an army that felt its primary mission was
to fight and win conventional wars.

Throughout the Vietnam War the U.S. Army maintained a major conventional warfare mission: to defend Western Europe from the sizable conventional threat posed by the Soviet Union and the Warsaw Pact.[2] In 1974 the Soviet
Union had a 1.8 million–man army, with thirty-one divisions (including sixteen tank divisions) and 9,025 medium tanks in Eastern Europe threatening
Western Europe with invasion.[3] Backing this up were another sixty-three divisions in the European part of the Soviet Union. These included around twenty
tank divisions and probably more than 10,000 tanks. Their allies, the Warsaw
Pact, consisting of East Germany, Poland, Czechoslovakia, Hungary, Romania,
and Bulgaria, were armed and ready to join them with armies totaling 826,000
men and thousands more tanks.[4]

The United States maintained four divisions in Europe in 1974, along with
2,100 tanks ready or stockpiled there. Out of sixteen total divisions (including three marine divisions) another three stood ready to reinforce the Sev-
enth Army in Europe and at least four divisions were held in strategic reserve.
These were ably supported by U.S. allies in the North Atlantic Treaty Organization (NATO) with combined armies of around 2 million men, at least forty-
five divisions, and at least 10,000 tanks.[5] The balance of power, or balance of
terror, in such a large conventional conflict pitted Soviet and Warsaw Pact

ground armies of at least 2.6 million men and 30,000 tanks against a defending force of at least 2.3 million men and 12,000 tanks. This was the primary mission of the U. S. Army and would define its structure, planning, and focus for the next two decades.

As the Vietnam War continued without U.S. ground involvement, the United States seemed to retreat into itself, absorbed in its domestic conflicts and civil demonstrations. In the wake of a president who resigned under the threat of impeachment, the nation was divided as to the utility of the war in Vietnam or any such armed action. The U.S. defense budget was cut repeatedly over the years, in part because there was no need to maintain an expensive force in Vietnam, and in part because America's focus had retreated inward after the depressing experience of fighting a large guerrilla war for eight years and walking away with nothing. In 1975 South Vietnam was conquered through a conventional ground campaign by North Vietnam, and the nation we had invested two decades in supporting and lost almost sixty thousand American lives fighting for disappeared without looking like it had even put up a decent fight.

The 1970s was the decade of the hollow army, when the budget was cut, manpower declined, and morale was low. A sense existed that the U.S. Army was at its weakest in decades. It still had a mission to defend Western Europe, though there was a fear that if the Soviet Union and its Warsaw Pact allies attacked, it would be only a matter of weeks before the attacking army was across the Rhine and our defense would completely collapse. For example, in 1978 the book *Imbalance of Power: Shifting U.S.-Soviet Military Strengths* stated that in NATO's Central Sector (meaning Germany) "NATO is quantitatively outclassed by the Warsaw Pact in almost every category, and is losing its qualitative edge in several respects that count."[6] This imbalance was the scenario that the defense analytical community needed to properly address.

Conventional combat and the war in Europe remained the focus of much of the U.S. Army analytical and modeling efforts through the 1980s, and it was the primary focus until the Soviet Union and the Warsaw Pact collapsed suddenly. This rapidly hemorrhaging series of events began with Mikhail Gorbachev becoming head of the Soviet Union in March 1985 and his first reforms (called *perestroika*) in 1986; they continued with the opening of the Soviet Union in 1988 (the policy called *glasnost*), the tearing down of the Berlin Wall on 9 November 1989 by the people of East Germany, the dissolution of the Warsaw Pact on 1 July 1991, and finally the dissolution of the Soviet Union on 25 December 1991. Suddenly the basis for the previous four decades of U.S. defense planning had disappeared.

But the U.S. Army had two more major conventional warfare missions to complete. In August 1990 the Iraqi dictator Saddam Hussein invaded and occupied Kuwait. The United States and its allies deployed significant forces to halt any farther expansion and in February 1991 drove Hussein's forces out of Kuwait with a corps-size armor sweep. Many of these forces deployed directly from their previous assignment in Germany, where they had been facing down the Soviet Union. The United States limited its actions at the time to simply freeing Kuwait and did not push on farther into Iraq.

On 11 September 2001 the United States was attacked by Islamic extremists, leaving over three thousand American civilians dead. In response, in December 2001 the U.S. armed forces entered Afghanistan to support factions wishing to overthrow the government, which had provided shelter and support to the terrorist organization that attacked the United States. In March 2003 the United States invaded Iraq with a more conventional operation for the sake of eliminating that country's weapons of mass destruction. This was a surprisingly easy operation and the last major conventional operation of the U.S. Army. It was completed in April 2003, with the United States and its allies conquering the entire country.

The overthrow of two third-world governments, the U.S. occupation of these countries, and the establishment of new democratic governments in these countries presented the U.S. Army with a very different set of missions than the conventional war mission it had considered its primary job for the previous thirty years. As insurgencies developed in both Afghanistan and Iraq against our allied governments and armed forces, the U.S. Army suddenly found itself back to fighting the type of war it thought it had left behind in 1973. In 2005 the missions facing the U.S. Army were commonly thought to be new, but in fact they were the same type of missions the U.S. Army has conducted since the days of the frontier.[7]

During that time the study of conventional war had taken a backseat to the study of insurgencies. Our work at the Dupuy Institute shifted to reflect this emphasis so that all of our work after 2006 was related to studying and analyzing insurgencies. Much of that work is covered in my book *America's Modern Wars: Understanding Iraq, Afghanistan and Vietnam*.

But conventional warfare has not been replaced entirely by counterinsurgency, counterterrorist operations, and air strikes and drone strikes. It is not something antiquated that will never be encountered again. Just as the U.S. Army was not able to avoid engaging in insurgencies, the armies in the future will not always be able to pick and choose the types of wars they fight.

To start with, the United States throughout this period has maintained overt conventional missions. First, the United States still has the mission to assist South Korea in case of an invasion by North Korea, a threat that has existed for over sixty years. The U.S. Army still maintains the better part of the 2nd Infantry Division in South Korea as a defensive reserve for the Korean Army. This is very clearly a conventional warfare mission, although many people suspect that the conflict will not end with the war between the two Koreas but with the collapse of the North Korean government and subsequent efforts by South Korea to deal with any disorder related to that collapse.

Second, though not often discussed, is a possible conventional mission in Asia based in a conflict over Taiwan, which is still claimed by the People's Republic of China. China is poised with large conventional forces across the strait from this small democracy, ready to cross and occupy it. This could be a classic conventional amphibious operation and conventional conquest. Helping to defend Taiwan—or, worse, reclaim Taiwan—could force the United States back into another conventional war.

The United States has spent the past ten years involved in fighting two large insurgencies. All insurgencies contain a conventional aspect, but the size of the operations tends to be smaller. So while there may be no division-on-division conventional combat, there are certainly large numbers of company-on-company and smaller conventional fights in many insurgencies. The tendency for many recent conventional warfare situations to be battalion-level and company-level actions is what led to our research on smaller unit actions, discussed in chapter 12.

Events in Iraq in 2014 have also driven home that there are still conventional combat missions for the U.S. armed forces. Mao Zedong, the Chinese communist revolutionary leader, postulated that "revolutionary wars" have three stages. The first stage is the organization, consolidation, and preservation of base areas, usually in difficult and isolated terrain. The second stage is the progressive expansion by terror and attacks on isolated enemy units to obtain arms, supplies, and political support. The third stage is the destruction of the enemy in battle.[8] This means, in many cases, conventional warfare.

In many respects this is how the Chinese Civil War ended in 1948–49, with the Communist Chinese armies shifting over to more conventional operations, greatly assisted by the large infusion of weapons and aid provided by the Soviet Union. But we also saw significant conventional operations late in the Indo-China War. The Battle of Dien Bien Phu in 1954 was a three-month siege of a trapped division-size French force. The Vietnam War always had significant conventional elements to it; for example, the offensive in 1972 that almost collapsed the South Vietnamese included significant conventional forces fielded by North Vietnam, and it was a large conventional offensive by North Vietnam in 1975 that ended the bloodiest guerrilla war in modern history. So while most guerrilla wars do not enter that third stage postulated by Chairman Mao, some do, and this is conventional warfare.

In fact this is in part what occurred in Iraq in 2014, when the guerrilla group ISIL swept across the northwestern third of Iraq, occupying it and taking Mosul, the second largest city in the country.[9] Though a guerilla force, ISIL had developed a conventional combat capability, arming itself with more traditional weapons, including tanks and other heavy equipment. Suddenly ISIL had the ability to move, engage, and defeat major elements of the Iraqi Army. Being a conventional force, it also provided the U.S. Air Force with prime targets to attack. As such, the U.S. Air Force developed a role in the Iraq War that it did not have before. Aerial bombardment is of limited value in a guerrilla war, but if those guerrilla forces become more conventional, then aerial bombardment has greater purpose. While you cannot defeat an insurgency with air power, you can certainly whittle away its ability to conventionally take and hold ground. Now the Iraq War has developed more conventional warfare elements, similar to some other insurgencies.

So the conventional warfare mission for the United States armed forces remains. Furthermore, other conventional missions are appearing on the horizon. A conventional threat appears to be developing in Eastern Europe, where conflicts between Ukraine and Russia led to Russia annexing the Crimean peninsula in March 2014 and directly supporting rebels who have seized parts of Donetsk and Luhansk provinces in eastern Ukraine. More to the point, NATO members are now concerned that their mutual defense mission, which was thought to be over in 1991, has not entirely ended. In response NATO is now looking at basing more conventional defensive forces in Eastern Europe.

Finally, there are conventional missions that one does not plan for. Since the fall of the Berlin Wall in 1989, several of these conventional operations have suddenly cropped up, unheralded and not part of any U.S. defense planning. The Iraqi invasion and occupation of Kuwait in 1990 and the U.S. major multidivision operations to liberate Kuwait in 1991 are perfect examples of these unheralded conventional warfare missions. The United States did not have any defensive treaties with Kuwait before that war. The U.S. invasion and occupation of Iraq in 2003 was one such conventional mission, and there was a smaller conventional operation in Afghanistan in November 2001, when the U.S. Marine Corps was able to insert a battalion from sea directly into Afghanistan. The U.S. entry into Panama in December 1989 (Operation Just Cause) was fundamentally a conventional operation. None of these operations was in discussion or in planning the year before; they all developed on short notice and with actors the United States had not planned on engaging. These four examples are certainly a warning that any number of conventional scenarios can suddenly develop at any time and apparently at almost any place. If such a scenario has happened in the recent past, there is no reason to believe it will not happen again in the near future.

Of course, conventional warfare will never go away. It is the means by which armed forces take and hold ground. There is a still a need to review what we have learned and understand about conventional warfare. The work of the Dupuy Institute throughout the 1990s and up through 2006 was heavily oriented toward examining many of those issues. We feel that this work is still relevant and useful in the modern world and therefore present it in this book.

From 1996 through 2005 the Dupuy Institute did a series of reports primarily for the Department of Defense (DOD) and the U.S. Army on combat mortality, prisoner-of-war capture rates, the utility of lighter-weight armor, the utility of landmines, urban warfare, measuring situational awareness, casualty estimation methodologies, and a range of other subjects primarily related to conventional warfare. While these reports were designed to answer the specific questions and needs of our sponsors, they also contained, as a by-product, analysis and testing of various aspects of warfare, including such issues as force ratios and human factors. As such, buried and scattered in over sixty reports were bits and pieces of analysis that addressed these bigger issues and provided a basis for a quantitative analysis of various aspects of warfare. This book is primarily based on this quantitative analysis.

Much of what has been developed in the past on the theory of warfare is not based on quantitative analysis but is instead based on case studies of history or personal experience. For example, if Clausewitz said defense was the stronger form of combat, this point was established by looking at a range of cases, personal experience, and a good dose of deductive reasoning. Trevor Dupuy's work added an element of quantitative analysis to the theoretical examination of warfare, and the Dupuy Institute has further expanded this analysis. This book will attempt to show that defense is the stronger form of combat based on statistics from a large number of cases. In some instances it is even possible to provide some measure of the degree to which it is the stronger.

One of the primary analytical tools for doing this is a series of databases on combat called the DuWar databases. We relied on a database of 752 division-level engagements from 1904 to 1991 for much of our analysis, but the DuWar databases are a suite of nine databases developed over the years to answer various analytical questions.[10] These are the most extensive set of force-on-force combat databases we are aware of. They mostly consist of sets of engagements that match and compare opposing forces at the same level of combat.

This book does not attempt to modify or develop any existing theory of combat. It does attempt to establish what we actually do know, and why we know it, and perhaps provide some indication of how much impact these factors have. As such, this book supplements Trevor Dupuy's original work and, to some extent, Clausewitz's work. It is the next step in the analysis of combat.

2. Force Ratios

Superior combat power always wins.

—TREVOR N. DUPUY, *Understanding War*

Clausewitz writes in *On War*, "In tactics, as in strategy, superiority of numbers is the most common element in victory."[1] This basic truth has been evident throughout history, although some people resist accepting it.

While the impact of force ratios on combat had already been addressed by Trevor Dupuy in his books, I independently led a group of staff at the Dupuy Institute in further examining force ratios. My first effort to address force ratios was in response to an article published in the *Army Times* in June 1996.[2] In my rebuttal I provided the comparison in table 2.1, based on an analysis of 605 engagements from 1600 to 1973.[3]

Table 2.1. Force Ratio Analysis of 605 Engagements

	Force Ratio Greater than 1 to 1	Force Ratio Equal	Force Ratio Less than 1 to 1	Total Cases
Attacker Won	271	7	89	367
Draw	35	—	6	41
Defender Won	126	4	67	197
Total	432	11	162	605

An examination of table 2.1 shows that the larger side won 56 percent of the time (271 + 67), whereas the smaller side won 36 percent of the time (89 + 126). The sides were equal or the result was a draw in 52 cases (9 percent). Leaving out the draws and battles where the two sides were equal, the larger side won 61 percent of the time over the smaller side.

Looking further into these figures, in the 367 cases where the attacker won, he had superior numbers 74 percent of the time. This would indicate a strong bias in favor of numbers for the attacking force.

Each engagement in this database consisted of an attacker, with a list of its forces and equipment, and a defender, with a list of its forces and equipment. The engagement also had an outcome, indicating whether the attacker won or lost or the engagement was a draw. There is a narrative of the engagement and a range of factors that influenced this engagement. The work was assembled from many different primary and secondary sources; unit records were used extensively for the more recent engagements. Earlier versions of this database have been published.[4]

This comparison looks only at aggregate personnel strengths and whether the unit was the attacker or the defender. It did not look at how the force was armed, trained, deployed, or led. Force ratios were calculated by dividing the defender's strength into the attacker's strength. Therefore a force ratio greater than 1 means the attacker is stronger than the defender, while a force ratio less than 1 means the defender is stronger. This analysis was done on an earlier version of the Dupuy Institute databases, so there were only 605 cases to draw from.[5]

Analysis of these data over time and whether the attacker or the defender won appears in table 2.2.

Table 2.2. Force Ratios over Time with Outcomes

ATTACKER WON

	Force Ratio Greater than or Equal to 1 to 1	Force Ratio Less than 1 to 1	Percentage of Attack Wins: Force Ratio Greater than or Equal to 1 to 1
1600–1699	16	18	47
1700–1799	25	16	61
1800–1899	47	17	73
1900–1920	69	13	84
1937–1945	104	8	93
1967–1973	17	17	50
Total	278	89	76

DEFENDER WON

	Force Ratio Greater than or Equal to 1 to 1	Force Ratio Less than 1 to 1	Percentage of Defense Wins: Force Ratio Greater than or Equal to 1 to 1
1600–1699	7	6	54
1700–1799	11	13	46
1800–1899	38	20	66
1900–1920	30	13	70
1937–1945	33	10	77
1967–1973	11	5	69
Total	130	67	66

The changes over time would indicate the offensive was better able to win at lower odds in 1600–1699 than was the case in the twentieth century. This may have been driven by the selection of the engagements in the database or by the small sample size, or it may be a reflection of the differences in professionalism and training between the armies of that time.[6] Still, the fact that the relationship between attack and defense does change over time was noted but only briefly discussed by Clausewitz.[7] On the other hand, in the almost four hundred years covered by these data, in no case does the winner of any battle have less than one-fourth the strength of the loser. This would clearly indicate that numbers count absolutely when you have less than one-fourth the strength of the enemy.

We later did a series of studies on urban warfare in which we performed a more extensive analysis of force ratios using the additional data developed for these studies. This was a series of division-on-division engagements where the data were drawn almost entirely from the unit records of the opposing sides. Table 2.3 is drawn from a series of 116 engagements in France in 1944 against the Germans.[8]

Table 2.3. European Theater of Operations Data, 1944

Force Ratio	Result	Percentage of Failure	Number of Cases
0.55 to 1.01-to-1.00	Attack fails	100	5
1.15 to 1.88-to-1.00	Attack usually succeeds	21	48
1.95 to 2.56-to-1.00	Attack usually succeeds	10	21
2.71 to 1.00 and higher	Attacker advances	0	42

The results in table 2.3 make the argument concerning force ratios fairly convincingly. The European Theater of Operations (ETO) data are a comparison of mostly U.S. and UK attackers versus Germans, although there are some cases where the Germans are the attackers. As discussed in chapter 4, which analyzes human factors, we consider these forces to be relatively similar in training, morale, and capability. Odds below 1 to 1 (actually at or below 1.01 to 1) always fail, although there are only five cases. Odds above 2.71 to 1 always succeed. This is regardless of fortifications, terrain, and all other factors. In fact out of 116 attacks, only 5 were made at roughly 1 to 1 odds or less, which is probably a strong indication that the people involved in this fighting had already figured out that low-odds attacks were a bad idea.

Tables 2.4 and 2.5 examine data from the fighting around Kharkov in February, March, and August 1943 and the fighting during the Battle of Kursk in July 1943. They cover seventy-three engagements between the German and Soviet armies.[9] These tables still show the same pattern of force ratios mattering, but the force ratios change greatly depending on who is attacking. It is clear that force ratios are making a difference in the outcome. It is also clear that there is a performance difference between the Germans and the Soviets. This is discussed in more depth in chapter 4.

Table 2.4. Germans Attacking Soviets (Battles of Kharkov and Kursk), 1943

Force Ratio	Result	Percentage of Failure	Number of Cases
0.63 to 1.06-to-1.00	Attack usually succeeds	20	5
1.18 to 1.87-to-1.00	Attack usually succeeds	6	17
1.91 to 1.00 and higher	Attacker advances	0	21

Table 2.5. Soviets Attacking Germans (Battles of Kharkov and Kursk), 1943

Force Ratio	Result	Percentage of Failure	Number of Cases
0.40 to 1.05-to-1	Attack usually fails	70	10
1.20 to 1.65-to-1.00	Attack often fails	50	11
1.91 to 2.89-to-1.00	Attack sometimes fails	44	9

Table 2.6, from the Pacific Theater of Operations (PTO) in 1945, rounds out the data and shows some of the few cases of high-odds attacks failing.[10] Still, only four attacks fail at force ratios around 3 to 1 or higher out of forty cases. There is even a single engagement where the attack fails at force ratios above 4 to 1.[11] Almost all of these cases were drawn from U.S. attacks on heavily fortified Japanese positions in Manila and Okinawa. These were not typical combat situations.

Table 2.6. Pacific Theater of Operations Data, U.S. Attacking Japanese, 1945

Force Ratio	Result	Percentage of Failure	Number of Cases
1.40 to 2.89-to-1.00	Attack succeeds	0	20
2.92 to 3.89-to-1.00	Attack usually succeeds	21	14
4.35 to 1.00 and higher	Attack usually succeeds	4	26

All these tables clearly show that force ratios matter. As will be shown in later discussion, there is nothing in the post–World War II data that changes this observation.

Note that among these data are only seven cases of the attacker succeeding when outnumbered, and only one case where he succeeds when outnumbered by a factor of 2. Furthermore the attacker almost always wins when he outnumbers the opponent by at least 2 to 1. Clausewitz also noted this phenomenon:

At Leuthen Frederick the Great, with about 30,000 men, defeated 80,000 Austrians; at Rossbach he defeated 50,000 allies with 25,000 men. *These however are the only examples of victories over an opponent two or even nearly three times as strong.* Charles XII at the battle of Narva is not in the same category. The Russians at that time could hardly be considered as Europeans; moreover, we know too little about the main features of that battle. Bonaparte commanded 120,000 men at Dresden against 220,000—not quite half. At Kolin, Frederick the Great's 30,000 men could not defeat 50,000 Austrians; similarly, victory eluded Bonaparte at the desperate battle of Leipzig, though with his 160,000 men against 280,000, his opponent was far from being twice as strong.

These examples may show that in modern Europe even the most talented general will find it very difficult to defeat an opponent twice his strength. When we observe that the skill of the greatest commanders may be counterbalanced by a two-to-one ratio in the fighting forces, we cannot doubt that superiority in numbers (it does not have to more than double) will suffice to assure victory, however adverse the other circumstances.[12]

He further clarifies this with the statement:

If we thus strip the engagement of all the variables arising from its purpose and circumstance, and disregard the fighting value of the troops involved (which is a given quantity), we are left with the bare concept of the engagement, a shapeless battle in which the only distinguishing factor is the number of troops on either side.

These numbers, therefore, will determine victory. It is, of course, evident from the mass of abstractions I have made to reach this point that superiority of numbers in a given engagement is only one of the factors that determines victory. Superior numbers, far from contributing everything, or even a substantial part, to victory, may actually be contributing very little, depending on the circumstances.

But superiority varies in degree. It can be two to one, or three or four to one, and so on; it can obviously reach the point where it is overwhelming.

In this sense superiority of numbers admittedly is the most important factor in the outcome of an engagement, as long as it is great enough to counterbalance all other contributing circumstances. It thus follows that as many troops as possible should be brought into the engagement at the decisive point.[13]

But Clausewitz also points out the problem of building a model of warfare based solely on numbers:

Numerical superiority was a material factor. It was chosen from all elements that make up victory because, by using combinations of time and space, it could be fitted into a mathematical system of laws. It was thought that all other factors could be ignored if they were assumed to be equal on both sides and thus cancelled one another out. That might have been acceptable as a temporary device for the study of the characteristics of this single factor; but to make the device permanent, to accept superiority of numbers as the one and only rule, and to reduce the whole secret of the art of war to a formula of numerical superiority *at a certain time and a certain place* was an oversimplification that would not have stood up for a moment against the realities of life.[14]

This of course leads us to those other factors, which we will stand up against the realities of life.

3. Attacker versus Defender

Defensive strength is greater than offensive strength.

—Trevor N. Dupuy, *Understanding War*

Defense is the stronger form of combat is a classic Clausewitz quote that even now is sometimes disputed.[1] In the very first chapter of his seminal *On War* he writes:

> As we shall show, defense is the stronger form of fighting than attack. Consequently we must ask whether the advantage of *postponing a decision* is as great for one side as the advantage of *defense* is for the other. Whenever it is not, it cannot balance the advantage of defense and in this way influence the progress of the war. It is clear, then, that the impulse created by the polarity of interests may be exhausted in the difference between the strength of attack and defense, and may thus become inoperative.
>
> Consequently, if the side favored by present conditions is not sufficiently strong to do without the added advantages of the defense, it will have to accept the prospect of acting under unfavorable conditions in the future. To fight a defensive battle under these less favorable conditions may still be better than to attack immediately or to make peace. I am convinced that the superiority of the defensive (if rightly understood) is very great, far greater than it appears at first sight. It is this which explains without any inconsistency most periods of inaction that occur in war. The weaker the motives for action, the more will they be overlaid and neutralized by this disparity between attack and defense, and the more frequently will action be suspended—as indeed experience shows.[2]

Let us return to table 2.1 (page 8), which shows that the attacker won in 367 of 605 cases (61 percent of the time). In the 197 cases where the defender won, 64 percent of the time he was numerically inferior. In the 367 cases where the attacker won, 24 percent of the time he was numerically inferior. This would indicate that defense is the stronger form of combat. For the attacker to win, he had to outnumber the defender 74 percent of the time, while the defender was able to win while outnumbered 64 percent of the time.

I speculate that much of the confusion over the issue comes from the fact that one cannot usually win a war by remaining on the defensive. To win a campaign or war, offensive action at some point is needed. But this does not negate the finding that on the field of battle, a defending force has advantages over an attacker in such a way that attacks at odds of less than 1 to 1 usually fail.

Again, this is not breaking new ground. For example, in *The Conquest of Gaul*, written over two thousand years ago, Caesar clearly understands that his Roman legions were stronger standing uphill from their opponent. So too did his Gallic opponents, and both sides repeatedly refused combat in such circumstances.[3] Clausewitz still felt that this was a factor in the warfare of his own time, which he both studied and actively participated in. Based on the data presented in table 2.1, this is still the case in the days of tanks and airplanes. The World War II data presented in chapter 2 only shows the attacker winning at less than 1 to 1 odds when the Germans were attacking the Soviet forces. The defender wins in thirty-three cases (77 percent) when outnumbered, while the attacker wins in only eight cases when outnumbered. Clearly the changes in warfare over the past two thousand years have not changed this basic relationship, although the value of being on the defense may have changed some from period to period.

The question is this: Has any development in warfare since World War II changed what appears to be a universally held result? The data presented in chapter 2 included only fifty cases from the Arab-Israeli wars from 1967–73, and in 69 percent of the cases where the defender won, he was outnumbered. Despite this very limited selection of data, it would appear that there might be some change for the attacker, although it is almost certainly driven by human factors that resulted in the superior performance of the Israeli Army compared to their Arab opponents. It is impossible to analyze warfare without a full appreciation of the impact that human factors play. Therefore, before we can answer whether these two-thousand-year-old patterns have changed in the past fifty years, we need to examine human factors.

4. Human Factors

The moral is to the physical as three is to one.

—Napoleon Bonaparte, in a letter written August 27, 1808, to his brother Joseph in Spain

Human factors clearly play a part in warfare.[1] Consider again two force ratio tables from chapter 2.

Table 2.4. Germans Attacking Soviets (Battles of Kharkov and Kursk), 1943

Force Ratio	Result	Percentage of Failure	Number of Cases
0.63 to 1.06-to-1.00	Attack usually succeeds	20	5
1.18 to 1.87-to-1.00	Attack usually succeeds	6	17
1.91 to 1.00 and higher	Attacker advances	0	21

Table 2.5. Soviets Attacking Germans (Battles of Kharkov and Kursk), 1943

Force Ratio	Result	Percentage of Failure	Number of Cases
0.40 to 1.05-to-1	Attack usually fails	70	10
1.20 to 1.65-to-1.00	Attack often fails	50	11
1.91 to 2.89-to-1.00	Attack sometimes fails	44	9

The German and Soviet forces had technological parity, and being 1943, both of their armies had at least two years of experience in warfare. In many of these cases both sides had months to rest and prepare before the battles started in July 1943. Yet there was a clear difference in their performance.

Clausewitz's statement, "If we thus strip the engagement of all the variables arising from its purpose and circumstance, and disregard the fighting value of the troops involved (which is a given quantity)," makes clear that he considers the "fighting value of the troops" to be a measurable quantity.[2] Our work at the Dupuy Institute demonstrates the same. We call it "human factors" rather than "fighting value," but we and Clausewitz are clearly discussing aspects of the same phenomenon, which needs to be considered for any proper understanding of combat. As Clausewitz stated:

Everyone knows the moral effect of an ambush or an attack in flank and rear. Everyone rates the enemy's bravery lower once his back is turned, and takes much greater risks in pursuit than while being pursued. Everyone gauges his opponent in the light of his reputed talents, his age, and his experience, and acts accordingly. Everyone tries to assess the spirit and temper of his own troops and of the enemy's. All these and similar effects in the sphere of mind and spirit have been proved by experience: they recur constantly, and are therefore entitled to receive their due as object factors. What indeed would become of a theory that ignored them?[3]

What are human factors? Trevor Dupuy listed them as morale, training, experience, leadership, motivation, cohesion, intelligence (including interpretation), momentum, initiative, doctrine, the effects of surprise, logistical systems, organizational habits, and even cultural differences.[4] Human factors are hard to measure, and as such the analytical community often ignores them.

These factors, added together, made up what Dupuy called the combat effectiveness value (CEV).[5] He could add this value to his combat model to try to represent the differences in relative performance of two opposing armies. For example, he used a force multiplier of 1.2 for instances when the German army faced the U.S. Army in World War II in 1943–44. This indicated the German army (which, when lowercased here, indicates a combination of forces and not only the German Army proper) was 20 percent more effective, given that all other factors were equal. For the Eastern Front in World War II, we have tended to use a combat force multiplier of 3.0 to represent the difference between the German army and the Soviet Army in 1943. This is the same combat force multiplier Dupuy used to represent the differences between the Israeli Army in 1967 and 1973 and the various Arab armies opposing it.

For any student of military history, to state that human factors are really important in warfare is stating the obvious. It is what enables attackers to win when outnumbered. It is what allowed the German army in 1943 to succeed in attacks at or greater than 1.91 to 1 while the Soviet Army still failed 44 percent of the time at those odds.

Human factors also affect casualty exchange rates, not just winning or losing. For example, in our urban warfare studies, we compared engagements from the Eastern Front, where the performance differences between the two armies were very clear. In this case we compared the engagement by outcome. So for example, outcome III means a failed attack. Table 4.1 shows the loss rates in two German failed attacks compared to the loss rates of seven Soviet failed attacks. Outcome IV means attacker advances but without a penetration or envelopment.[6] Again, for outcome IV we compared the loss rates of nine German attacks to three Soviet attacks.

Table 4.1. Losses Compared to Outcome

GERMANS ATTACKING, KURSK	I	II	III	IV	V	VI
Number of cases	4	6	2	9	7	3
Average percentage of attacker losses/day	0.23	0.56	0.68	1.30	1.22	0.75
Average percentage of defender losses/day	0.16	0.70	1.33	5.34	7.92	38.32
SOVIETS ATTACKING, KURSK						
Number of cases	—	5	7	3	—	—
Average percentage of attacker losses/day	—	0.78	3.37	3.54	—	—
Average percentage of defender losses/day	—	0.30	0.86	1.03	—	—

In the case of outcome III, which is coded as "failed attack," when the Germans attacked they suffered 0.68 percent losses, while their opponents suffered 1.33 percent. Yet when the Soviets attacked (and failed), they suffered 3.37 percent losses, while their opponents suffered 0.86 percent losses. In outcome IV cases, where the attack succeeded and the attacker advanced (but did not penetrate the defense or envelop the defense), we see the same pattern. The Germans when attacking lost 1.30 percent, while their opponents lost 5.34 percent. When the Soviets attacked, they lost 3.54 percent, while their German opponents lost only 1.03 percent.

Clearly, no matter whether attacker or defender, the Soviets lose more than the Germans, often more than three times more, as measured as a percentage of force. There is an obvious performance difference between these forces. The next chapter discusses how human factors in combat can be measured.

5. Measuring Human Factors in Combat

Italy, 1943–1944

> If we thus strip the engagement of all the variables arising from its
> purpose and circumstance, and disregard the fighting value of the troops
> involved (which is a given quantity), we are left with the bare concept of the
> engagement, a shapeless battle in which the only distinguishing factor is the
> number of troops on either side.
>
> —CARL VON CLAUSEWITZ, *On War*

Clausewitz clearly believed in a mathematical or quantitative construct of combat, even if he did not do any quantitative analysis himself. His statement in the epigraph is the basis for Trevor Dupuy's theoretical work.[1] This quantitative historical analysis, as I refer to it, was pioneered by Dupuy and continues to be the thrust of the work we do today at the Dupuy Institute. Dupuy himself never gave what he did a name.

This work is sometimes called "historical analysis," a term that has been in use for a while. It describes work that can be either qualitative or quantitative but is oriented toward analyzing why historical events happened. The British operational analysis community has used this term to describe their similar analytical work, considering it a "legitimate branch" of operational analysis and operational research.[2] It is work related to quantitative history; econometrics, which is quantitative analysis of economic data or economic phenomena (the latter phrase is really more correct); and cliometrics, the quantitative study of economic history. For lack of a better term, I prefer to call the work we do "quantitative historical analysis."

Regardless of what it is called, what we have been attempting to do is measure the difficult to measure: human factors. Along with numbers, they are probably one of the most significant factors in combat.[3] To understand the outcomes of combat, one must be able to understand and measure human factors. If one is going to analyze military affairs, do combat modeling, or understand historical combat, at some point one must address human factors. It is necessary to do so if one is going to be entirely scientific about the study of warfare. So how do we measure human factors?

Not all armed forces are the same. Their performance and capabilities in battle vary widely. The differences go far beyond the numbers, mix, and capabilities of the weapons brought onto the field of battle. There is an entire range of force multipliers that are related to the performance of human beings (and groups of human beings) on the battlefield. These force multipliers—what the Dupuy Institute refers to as "combat effectiveness"—include leadership, generalship, training, experience, morale, motivation, cohesion, intelligence (including interpretation), momentum, initiative, doctrine, the effects of surprise, logistical systems, organizational habits, and even cultural differences.

During our studies it was impossible to ignore such issues as morale, motivation, and cohesion. These components of combat effectiveness have an effect on combat capability as well other objects of our analysis like enemy prisoner-of-war (EPW) capture rates. One would expect more personnel surrendering in a force with lower morale, motivation, and cohesion (and less combat effectiveness) than one with higher morale, motivation, and cohesion (and more combat effectiveness). A proper estimation of enemy prisoner-of-war capture rates could not be developed without taking combat effectiveness in account.

As developed by Dupuy, performance differences in opposing combat forces may be measured by mission accomplishment, casualty effectiveness, and spatial effectiveness.

1. Mission accomplishment is a measurement of who won or lost. This can be ascertained either by judgment or by whether or not the attacker advanced. The Dupuy Institute prefers to use judgment, as in some cases the attacker may make limited advances in attacks that are otherwise disastrous. This is not uncommon. In most cases, however, there are no differences between the results made from judgment and those made from a rigid rule based on advance rates. Mission accomplishment can be further refined by scoring mission success on both sides from 0 to 10 based on judgment and using a set of five rules.[4]

2. Casualty effectiveness is the ability of one side to cause enemy casualties relative to its own losses. This is probably the best measure of combat effectiveness, although it has some weaknesses. First, casualty reports are not always as precise as one would hope. Second, not all nations classify or report their casualties in the same way. This is a particular problem in the reporting of wounded and makes comparisons of total casualty figures a little difficult. Total casualties are reported as the number killed in action (KIA), the number wounded in action (WIA), and the number missing in

action (MIA). The Dupuy Institute used these numbers for casualty comparisons even though there was some concern over how the number of WIA was reported.[5] The third weakness is that casualty effectiveness is not always the best measure of combat effectiveness. It is influenced by the doctrine of the army and the actual mission and objective.

3. Spatial effectiveness is the measurement (usually in kilometers per day) of the ability to advance. This is probably the weakest metric and as such is not used in this study. There is clearly a combat effectiveness difference between armies when it comes to their ability to maneuver and exploit opportunities. Still, there are problems with this metric. Opposed advance rates are often surprisingly difficult to measure. Furthermore they are often driven by the availability of gaps in the enemy lines and are heavily influenced by factors like terrain and degree of motorization. Sometimes advance rates are limited by the desire of an attacker to advance or by where his objectives are. In some cases they are limited by the depth of the terrain (for example, battles in the Pacific Atolls in World War II).

When using any of these measurements one must also consider the conditions of combat. These include not only any inherent advantages of being on the defense, but also terrain, weather, and a host of other factors. Furthermore the analyst must consider the mix of weapons and the capabilities of the weapons of each side. Obviously a heavy armor force well supported by artillery will have greater effective combat power than an unsupported mass of infantry. The effects of air power also need to be considered. To address these three factors (conditions, weapons, air power) requires an analytical structure, most likely a combat model. This last ambitious step is what Dupuy attempted to do by comparing the results of his combat model, the Quantified Judgment Model (QJM), to the historical outcome of the engagements and noting the differences.[6]

With these considerations in mind, the Dupuy Institute instead attempted a first-order measurement of the effectiveness of forces by different nations. This was accomplished by attempting to find a simple measurement of mission accomplishment and casualty effectiveness.

Our data are initially from World War II, as this was the better of the data available. It is possible to collect the unit records from both sides of a World War II engagement, which allows for direct comparison of their strengths and losses. For engagements after World War II, invariably the unit records for one side are not available (and often still classified), and in many cases are not available for either side. Therefore, for the sake of illustrating how they can be measured, I will first look at the more reliable World War II data. For the purposes of this discussion, we originally analyzed seventy-six engagements from the Italian Campaign from 1943 and 1944, seventy-one engagements from the Ardennes Campaign from December 1944 to January 1945, and forty-nine engagements from the Battle of Kursk in July 1943. This was work we did for the Capture Rate Study in 2000–2001. Since that time we have researched additional engagements; the updated analysis based on this additional research is presented here.

The Italian Campaign Engagement Comparisons

One of the advantages of studying the Italian Campaign is that it involved combat between forces of different backgrounds and nationalities. A number of situations existed that could be helpful in an analysis of human factors. First and foremost, there were two similarly organized and armed forces (U.S. and UK) fighting side by side, and in some cases cross-attached to each other, against essentially the same opponent in similar terrain and climate conditions. This allows for a comparison to be made between U.S. and UK forces for capture rates. There were forty-five U.S. battles and thirty-one UK battles in our original Capture Rate Study database. This analysis could be extended further to include various Commonwealth units and other allies involved in the Italian Campaign, including Indians, South Africans, Canadians, New Zealanders, Brazilians, French, and French Moroccans.

Dupuy had already explored the Italian Campaign in some depth. He had developed a database of sixty engagements from the Italian Campaign and twenty-one from Northwest Europe that he then modeled using his Quantified Judgment Model. As a result of this effort, he came to the following conclusions concerning human factors:

1. The average CEV of the U.S. forces was 0.84.

2. The average CEV of the UK forces was 0.76.

3. The average CEV of the German forces was 1.10.

This means the Germans had a 20 to 30 percent advantage over the average U.S. division and a 30 to 40 percent advantage over the average UK division. And in fact the U.S. divisions did appear to perform slightly better than the UK divisions.[7]

These conclusions were not always well received by some in the U.S. Army, who dismissed the validity of his methodology in addition to dismissing the results. Curiously, they had no objection to Dupuy's conclusion developed from the same methodology that the Israeli Army was notably better than the Arab armies they faced in 1967 and 1973.[8] There was little criticism of Dupuy's work from the British operational research and historical analytical community.

As part of our Capture Rate Study, we revisited these same engagements and did a simple statistical test instead of using a model structure. We used seventy-six engagements from the Italian Campaign, many of the same engagements that Dupuy used.[9] Our conclusions from this particular part of the study were:

1. Data from mission success may show a 10 to 20 percent advantage on the part of the Germans as they are able to succeed with a lower average force ratio (only seventeen cases).

2. U.S. and UK versus Germans:

 a. German casualty effectiveness advantage of around 30 percent when defending against U.S. attacks.

 b. German casualty effectiveness advantage of around 70 percent when defending against UK attacks.

 c. German casualty effectiveness parity U.S./UK when attacking (seventeen cases).

3. U.S. compared to UK:

 a. Tendency for U.S. forces to take and cause higher casualties.

 b. Casualty effectiveness advantage in the attack of 30 percent by the U.S. over the UK (compared to opposing Germans).

 c. Casualty effectiveness advantage of 4 by U.S. over UK in the defense (seven cases vs. ten cases).

4. U.S. may have been as much as 20 percent less effective than the Germans.

5. Combat performance of UK forces relative to U.S. forces was clearly inferior, probably 20 to 30 percent.

 a. This makes German forces definitely superior to UK forces, by as much as 50 percent.[10]

That these conclusions paralleled Dupuy's work is not surprising. We were using some of the same data; sixty of his engagements were from the Italian Campaign, and most were part of our database of seventy-six Italian Campaign engagements. We were using a different methodology. We did not use a model structure but compared the aggregate statistics from the engagement, sorted by posture and nation. An example of how that work was done is provided below, except using an expanded data set.

Separate from us was an effort by the analyst and historian Niklas Zetterling of Sweden, who tested nineteen engagements, all from Italy in 1943, using the revised version of the QJM model, called the Tactical Numerical Deterministic Model (TNDM). In this case he created the engagements to be analyzed from his own research, although all were engagements that Dupuy had also used. He then independently tested them using the model structure. He concluded, "It is suggested that the German CEV superiority was higher than originally calculated. . . . Rather, the Germans seem to have (in Italy 1943) a superiority on the order of 1.4–1.5, compared to the original figure of 1.2–1.3."[11] Thus not only did he find a notable German superiority in combat effectiveness, he found that superiority to be even higher than Dupuy had.

In the meantime our database of Italian Campaign engagements was greatly expanded as part of other work we were doing. We now have 137 Italian Campaign engagements in our expanded database. For this book we decided to retest them using the same methodology as for the Capture Rate Study, but now based on 137 engagements rather than 76. In this expanded database 40 engagements were from the original database, 22 were revisions of the original engagements, and 75 were additional engagements or ones so heavily revised that the name changed.

Measurement by Mission Accomplishment

In the case of mission accomplishment, we looked only at whether the attack succeeded or failed (draws are considered failures). Of the seventy U.S. attacks, thirty-six were successes and thirty-four were failures (51 percent success). The force ratios for the successes ranged from 1.23 to 4.25 (average of 1.97). The force ratios for the failures ranged from 1.13 to 2.96 (average of 1.62).

In the case of the British, there were forty-nine offensive actions, of which twenty-three were successes and twenty-six were failures (47 percent success). The force ratios for the successes ranged from 1.30 to 4.53 (average of 2.97). The force ratios for the failures ranged from 0.85 to 4.99 (average of 3.03).[12]

Overall the British attacks were conducted at higher ratios than the American attacks. The British average force ratio across their forty-nine offensive engagements was 3.00 (or 2.58 as a weighted average).[13] The American average force ratio across their seventy engagements was 1.80 (or 1.65 as a weighted average). So the United States and the United Kingdom had a similar success rate, but the British were successful at a higher force ratio. When the Americans succeeded they did so with an average force ratio of 1.97. When the British succeeded, they did so with an average force ratio of 2.97. Does this mean that the United States was 51 percent better?[14] Or does it simply mean that the

British were just more cautious and deliberate? This is a database of 119 Allied attacks in Italy from September 1943 through June 1944, so it is probably reasonably representative of combat at that time.[15]

In the case of the Germans, there were only eighteen attacks (eight versus the United States), of which only five were successful (28 percent success). While there are not enough cases to draw any type of reliable conclusion comparing the U.S. and UK defenders, note that only one attack in eight succeeded against the United States (13 percent success), while four attacks in ten succeeded against the United Kingdom (40 percent success). The force ratios for the successes ranged from 1.23 to 3.12 (average of 1.85). The force ratios for the failures ranged from 0.72 to 3.24 (average of 1.28). Out of 137 cases, there is not a single case of any of the three nations succeeding while attacking outnumbered.

Looking at force ratios and success rates alone, there does seem to be a strong indication of significant performance differentials between the U.S. and UK forces. As the number of cases of Germans attacking is low (eighteen examples), one is hesitant to draw conclusions from it. But the data do seem to indicate a possible German combat advantage in the range of 10 percent or more as they were able to succeed with a lower average force ratio.[16]

Measurement by Casualty Effectiveness

Another way to measure the performance difference between armed forces is to look at casualty effectiveness. This tends to produce more clearly defined differences in results. As above, I will look at three different aspects of the subject. First the U.S. attacks, then the UK attacks, then the German attacks. Furthermore we will need to compare those attacks that succeeded with those attacks that failed. As successful attacks that penetrate the defender heavily tilt the casualty exchange ratio in favor of the defender, we will also need to separate these out. Added to that, there are two different nations facing the German attacks, generating additional comparisons. This may take a little patience to read through, but it is simply multiple similar comparisons of the various combat engagements.

First, there are thirty-six examples in the database from Italy in which the United States attacked successfully. In these cases the Americans caused from 40 to 1,617 losses for the Germans (an average of 397 per engagement), while suffering themselves from 26 to 1,524 losses (an average of 353 per engagement). In seventeen of the cases the attacker suffered fewer losses than the defender. These figures point to an American 12 percent casualty effectiveness advantage over the Germans, assuming all other things are not a factor. This difference may be merely a product of the small sample size (thirty-six cases), highly variable data, or other variables.

These results are influenced by thirteen of the attacks being penetrations. It is readily apparent from the data that in a penetration the casualty exchange ratio tilts in favor of the attacker. In the thirteen U.S. attacks that resulted in penetration, the total U.S. casualties were 5,863, while the total German casualties were 8,680, a 48 percent casualty effectiveness advantage for the United States. It also includes nine of the cases where the attacker suffered fewer losses than the defender. Of course the ability to penetrate the enemy may also be a measure of combat effectiveness.

In the case of successful attacks that did not penetrate, the total U.S. casualties were 6,833 (average U.S. losses per attack of 297 vs. 451 for penetrating attacks), while the German losses were 5,616 (an average of 244 vs. 668 for penetrating attacks). The nonpenetrating figure points to a casualty effectiveness advantage of 22 percent for the Germans.

In their thirty-four unsuccessful attacks, the Americans caused from 34 to 1,698 losses for the Germans (an average of 351), while suffering themselves from 7 to 1,374 losses (an average of 262). There were only eleven cases where the attacker's loss was less than the defender's. This would point to a 34 percent casualty effectiveness advantage for Germany.

Therefore for those attacks where the attacker penetrated, the United States showed a 48 percent casualty effectiveness advantage; for those attacks where the attacker succeeded, Germany showed a 22 percent casualty effectiveness advantage; and for those attacks that failed, the casualty effectiveness advantage was 34 percent. In all cases the Americans outnumbered the Germans. The overall exchange rate across all seventy attacks is an average of 352 for the Americans and 332 for the Germans (a 6 percent advantage). When one considers that the United States had the advantage of superior force ratios (and in many cases better logistics and more air support) and the German advantage was terrain and the strength of their defensive posture, this does seem to indicate that the Germans held a small casualty effectiveness advantage over the Americans. Of course not being able to measure or account for all the other factors that influence combat is the reason Dupuy went with a combat model to do his analysis. We chose instead to use more data and hope that the larger number of cases would produce a measurable difference, if such a difference does indeed exist.

The British casualty effectiveness for their attacks was somewhat lower. In the twenty-three cases in which they successfully attacked, they caused from 8 to 850 losses to the Germans (an average of 146) while suffering themselves from 11 to 1,180 losses (an average of 213). In only eight of the cases did they suffer fewer casualties than the defender. There were no penetrating attacks, which is a pretty significant absence for forty-nine engagements, although this does simplify the analysis. The British operations do include six engagements by the 7th Armoured Division and have significant armor.[17] This points to a 46 percent casualty effectiveness advantage for the Germans. If this small data sample (twenty-three cases) is representative, it strongly indicates a performance difference between the Germans and the British and implies a difference between the Americans and the British, as the Americans were much closer statistically to the German levels of performance. It is worth noting that the difference in mission effectiveness between the United States and the United Kingdom was 51 percent. These two pieces of analysis clearly point to a performance difference between the two allies.

In their twenty-six unsuccessful attacks, the British caused from 0 to 478 German losses (an average of 69), while suffering themselves from 6 to 1,213 losses (an average of 137). The totals in this case point to a 99 percent casualty effectiveness advantage for the Germans.

The purpose of this discussion is not to denigrate the performance of our allies in World War II; however, for analytical purposes it is important to understand that there may have been a performance difference. Therefore I will offer a quick and dirty comparison between the U.S. and UK combat performances when it comes to casualty effectiveness. Keep in mind that there was a significant difference when we measured their performance using mission accomplishment.

One can combine the results from engagements in which the outcome was "attack advances" or "failed attack" for each nation.[18] There is not a significant difference in the average casualties of these two outcomes, nor is there a large difference between the attacker and defender casualty ratios for these two outcomes. Therefore these are particularly useful for direct comparison. This removes the "limited action" and "limited attack" engagements from the comparison, which are often very low rates of casualties. It also removes the "defender penetrated" engagements from the comparison, which often produce exchange ratios in favor of the attacker.

There were forty-nine cases in which the United States suffered a total of 17,823 casualties (average of 364 per engagement) compared to 13,874 German casualties (average of 283 per engagement). There were sixteen cases (33 percent) in which the United States suffered fewer losses than the defender. These figures point to a 29 percent casualty effectiveness advantage for the Germans.[19]

In their thirty-nine engagements, the British suffered 8,369 casualties (average of 215 per engagement), while the Germans suffered 4,984 (average of 128 per engagement). There were ten cases (26 percent) in which the British suffered fewer casualties than the defender. In four of these cases, casualties for both sides were quite low (fewer than 100 for either side). Only in two of the U.S. cases were the casualties so low. These figures point to a 68 percent casualty effectiveness advantage for the Germans.[20]

Directly comparing the U.S. and UK figures shows a tendency for the United States to take higher casualties (364 vs. 215) by 69 percent and a tendency to cause higher casualties (283 vs. 128) by 121 percent. If these samples are representative of the Italian Campaign and the U.S., UK, and German army performances in general, this would point to a 30 percent casualty effectiveness advantage for the United States over the United Kingdom.[21]

There is no overwhelming reason to consider the 119 battles used for this comparison to be representative of the Italian Campaign as a whole, although they make up much of the significant fighting in Italy between September 1943 and June 1944. Similarly there is no overwhelming reason not to consider them representative. The casualty reporting systems in both allied armies were similar, and the two tended to generate similar killed-to-wounded ratios. The differences in performance could be explained by a biased selection of the battles, by random differences due to a statistically insignificant number of battles, by differences in the battle conditions between the two sections of the front, by a difference in the opposing German forces in the two sectors of the front, or by the absence or presence of air power. This clearly needs to be studied further, but there is a strong reason to believe that there was a performance difference between the U.S. and UK forces.

In contrast, we have only eighteen examples of the Germans attacking. There were only five cases of successful German attacks (one was a penetration). These attacks caused 54 to 1,639 losses to the Allies (an average of 697) and from 110 to 1,721 losses to the Germans themselves (an average of 588). There were ten cases (56 percent) in which the attacker lost less than the defender. These casualty figures indicate a 19 percent casualty effectiveness advantage over the Germans by the Allies. Keep in mind the Allies here have the advantage of defense, in addition to their other advantages.

For their thirteen unsuccessful attacks, the Germans caused 54 to 1,639 losses (an average of 654), while themselves suffering between 110 and 1,129 losses (an average of 467). There were seven cases (54 percent) in which they suffered fewer casualties than the defender. These casualty figures point to a 40 percent casualty effectiveness advantage for the Germans even though they were the attacker and they lost the fight!

If one considers all eighteen German attacks together, not including the one penetrating attack, the result is seventeen attacks causing 11,810 Allied losses (an average of 695) and 10,299 German losses (an average of 606). There were nine cases (53 percent) in which the attacker suffered fewer casualties than the defender. There were no cases where both sides took fewer than 100 casualties. This still shows a 15 percent casualty effectiveness difference between the Germans and the Allies when the Germans were attacking.

Regardless, over half the time the attacking Germans caused more casualties than the defending Allies. They appear to have a casualty effectiveness advantage of between 15 and 40 percent when attacking. As "defense is the stronger form of combat," this could lead one to conclude that the Germans had a very real combat effectiveness advantage.

Unfortunately, when trying to compare the United States and the United Kingdom on defense, the number of examples is quite small. There were only eight examples of the United States in defense and ten of the United Kingdom. Still, in light of the discussion of performance differences, it was felt worthwhile to examine these cases as well. In the eight U.S. defensive cases, the Germans caused 5,572 casualties (an average of 697) and suffered 5,140 losses (an average of 643). There were four engagements in which the Germans lost fewer than the defender, and only one attack was successful. The figures indicate a casualty effectiveness difference of 8 percent in favor of the Germans. These engagements contain two cases in which the Germans attacked while outnumbered.

In the ten UK cases, the Germans caused 6,959 casualties (an average of 696) and suffered 5,436 casualties (an average of 544). This is a significant performance difference, as the Germans caused a similar number of casualties per engagement (697 U.S., 696 UK) but suffered fewer losses per engagement (643 vs. U.S., 544 vs. UK). This is a difference in casualty effectiveness of 18 percent between the United Kingdom and the United States.[22] There were seven engagements in which the Germans lost less than the defender. These engagements also included five instances in which the Germans attacked while outnumbered (and they lost in every case).

While the two data sets are extremely small and not quite equivalent, they clearly support the contention that there was a performance difference between the United States and the United Kingdom and between the Allies and the Germans.

Other than calculating averages, the Dupuy Institute did not conduct any other statistical analysis of this data. As the largest data set is seventy and the smallest is eight, and the data are highly variable, it was felt that not much more could be learned from such analysis. Furthermore, even if one does achieve a statistical fit, the most important question—whether this is an unbiased sample (meaning it really does represent the data)—cannot be answered by statistics. We do feel that the data point in a very definite direction. The data do appear to be typical of the Italian Campaign battles at this stage, and there is no reason to believe that they are not.

In addition, the conditions of combat, the weapons used, and air power should be addressed. No attempt was made to examine these conditions except to separate attacker from defender. In many respects this separation also somewhat addressed the effects of terrain, as terrain usually favors the defender. All the forces were in the same theater, so there were no drastic differences in climate, although weather certainly differed from engagement to engagement. In many cases the engagements in question featured the Americans and the British fighting side by side. This occurred in the engagements at Salerno and Anzio. In some cases the U.S. and UK divisions were fighting different elements of the same German division. In those cases many of the conditions of combat would be similar. Overall there was no sense that the mix of terrain, weather, opponent, or other factors biased the outcome of one side over the others.

It is also not a case of one particularly good or bad unit influencing the outcome. The 137 battles included seven different American divisions, five different British divisions, and twelve different German divisions. The greatest number of battles fought by any formation was the German 15th Panzer Grenadier Division, which fought in thirty-nine engagements. Among the Allies the UK 56th Infantry Division fought in the greatest number of battles, twenty-four. All the battles involving UK units occurred while they were under command of the U.S. Fifth Army. Thus the British were fighting near the U.S. units to which they were being compared and often opposed the same enemy formations.

The mix, number, and type of weapons used by the U.S. and UK forces were similar. The divisions were similar in size and weapon assortment. The German divisions were also similar in organization to the U.S. and UK divisions. The technology and quality of weapons were similar among all three armies. While force mix (armor vs. infantry) certainly favored one side or the other in individual battles, there is no reason to believe that there were any significant advantages to any army from its mix and type of weapons.

Air power was not considered in this analysis. It certainly should be. Both the United States and the United Kingdom had a considerable air presence and air superiority over most of the battlefield, but the Germans did have some air support. Still, the advantage in air power was certainly with the Allies. However, there is no reason to believe that it favored the United States over the United Kingdom.

Besides lack of air support, the Germans probably suffered from having some logistical limitations as to the availability of artillery ammunition and, early in the campaign, shortages of nondivisional (corps and army) artillery assets.

The tentative conclusion from these comparisons is that the German forces were 20 percent better than the U.S. forces in combat capability.[23] This ignores the favorable impact on the United States of its air support and the negative impact on the Germans of their logistical restrictions. Furthermore the Germans often counted wounded differently, which could result in fewer wounded being reported. This could easily make the overall reported German casualties 20 percent lower than a U.S. or UK unit that had suffered the same number and type of losses. Given that, it would still appear that the combat effectiveness of the German forces was slightly superior to the Americans, by at least 20 percent. It appears that it took 120 Americans to match 100 Germans in combat.

The combat performance of the UK forces relative to the U.S. forces was clearly inferior, probably by around 30 percent. This makes the German forces definitely superior to the UK forces, by as much as 60 percent.[24] It appears that it took 160 British to match 100 Germans in combat.

This is measuring the differences between forces that are roughly similar in capability. A 20 percent difference in combat effectiveness is not overwhelmingly significant; we have seen much worse (for example, Israeli Army vs. Arab armies; the United States vs. the Iraq Army). Still, with enough cases and some simple statistics, one can certainly ferret out those differences. This chapter shows how it can be done. If there were more cases in the database and more engagements researched, even more analysis could be done. Certain other elements, like airpower, could be factored out. This all takes time and money of course.

We have examined Italy in depth and have done it four times by three different groups of people: (1) by Dupuy and his staff using the QJM and 81 cases, (2) by Zetterling using the TNDM and 19 cases, (3) by the Dupuy Institute using 76 cases, and (4) by the Dupuy Institute using 137 cases (resulting in the discussion above).[25] All examinations come to the same or similar conclusions. Having discussed Italy extensively, it is time to look at the U.S. Army versus the German army in Northwest Europe some six to fifteen months after the comparisons used for the Italian Campaign analysis.

6. Measuring Human Factors in Combat

Ardennes and Kursk, July 1943

> We can still lose this war. . . . The Germans are colder and hungrier than we are, but they fight better.
>
> —GEN. GEORGE S. PATTON, January 4, 1945, in Dupuy et al., *Hitler's Last Gamble*

Needless to say, the conclusion that the German army in World War II was more combat effective than the U.S. Army was met with some resistance in the United States. Through multiple iterations by multiple people and by using different methodologies, I think we have clearly established that this was the case for Italy in 1943–1944. Only one engagement in our Italian Campaign data was after June 1944.

In June 1944 the Allies landed in France at Normandy and began the long fight into Germany. This was an extended campaign that was larger, but not longer, than the Italian Campaign. It included landings in the south of France in August 1944 by some of the forces that had been involved in Italy. The Allied forces then conducted an extended fight along the borders near Germany in late fall of 1944 and winter of 1944–45. This included the German counteroffensive of the famous Battle of the Bulge, also known as the Ardennes Offensive or the (Second) Ardennes Campaign.

Some argue that the Italian data were exceptional or not typical, and others examine actions from October 1944 to January 1945 to try to refute the claim that the German army was more combat effective. These arguments led us to examine engagements from the Ardennes Campaign.

The Ardennes Campaign engagements are problematic in that they reflect the German army as it was in the final six months of an almost six-year war. Some of the German units had somehow maintained their capabilities and combat effectiveness under the serious state of duress they faced, but many others, particularly the infantry, were poorly recruited and trained compared to German infantry divisions earlier in the war. As this stage, six months away from the end of the war, parts of the German army were in significant decline. This produced some very inconsistent results in our analysis, depending on which German units were being examined.

Research on engagements from this period also suffers because the German record-keeping system was now failing. The unit records were usually wrapped up and shipped to the rear every six months (after June and after December). But because the Third Reich ceased to exist in May 1945, many of the records after June 1944 are simply missing or incomplete. This has made researching two-sided data during this period much less productive than before July 1944. The quality of data for the Italian Campaign is much better than for Ardennes. This is part of the reason Dupuy originally used the Italian Campaign for his analysis of human factors and that all but one engagement is from June 1944 or earlier.

In our analysis of the Ardennes Campaign engagements, our original Capture Rate Study used 71 engagements.[1] Our expanded database now includes 141 engagements from Northwest Europe, but still only 57 division-level engagements from the Ardennes.[2] Most of the additional engagements from Northwest Europe, representing the fighting around places like Brest and Aachen, were developed for our urban warfare studies. Therefore I will simply present the results from our original work without revision.

Ardennes Campaign Engagements

All of the Ardennes engagements involve the U.S. Army and the German army. There were situations in which UK and other Allied forces fought alongside the Americans, but we didn't use any of these cases. As such, one can only look at whether there is a measurable performance difference between the U.S. and German armies.

The German army in the Ardennes was less consistent in morale, motivation, and unit cohesion than it had been in Italy. At this late stage of the war, it was evident to many German soldiers that Germany was losing. This certainly had some effect on the motivation of some units. Furthermore many of the infantry units had been raised from the extreme ends of the manpower pool, consisting of the very young and very old. Many of these units (mostly Volksgrenadier units) had undergone only minimal training. In contrast, there were a number of ss units that, while perhaps not more competent at warfare than regular German Army units, were more politically motivated. As such they may have had a higher morale in the face of a very difficult situation. Some of the ss and army units were veteran formations that had seen years of combat on the Eastern Front. The Ardennes offensive included some of the most experienced units in the German army, while other units were newly raised. This further magnifies the performance differences between individual units. Finally, the Germans were making an even greater use of foreign nationals at this time.

The Ardennes data encompass seven battles with ss armor units, fifteen battles with German Army armored units, thirty battles with Volksgrenadier units, and nineteen battles with other units (regular infantry and parachute formations).[3]

Regarding mission accomplishment, we looked at whether the attack succeeded or failed (draws were considered failures). Of the forty-one U.S. attacks, twenty-eight were successes and thirteen were failures (68 percent success). The force ratios for the successes ranged from 1.15 to 7.83 (average of 2.24). The force ratios for the failures ranged from 1.23 to 2.24 (average of 1.57).

In the case of the Germans there were thirty attacks, of which eleven were successful and nineteen failed (37 percent success). The force ratios for the successes ranged from 1.05 to 36.36 (average of 7.22). The force ratios for the failures ranged from 0.34 to 12.80 (average of 1.85). The German data clearly had some outliers. In the attack the highest force ratio was 36.36 and the second highest was 9.14. Excluding the highest ratio, the average was 3.92. In the case of the German attacks that failed, the highest force ratio was 12.80, while the second highest was 2.40. Excluding the highest force ratio, the average was 1.17.

As with the Italian data, there were no cases in which any unit succeeded while attacking outnumbered (out of a total of 208 cases!). In contrast, there were 65 cases (47 percent) in the Italian Campaign and 25 cases (35 percent) in the Ardennes where the attacker failed though he outnumbered the defender.

Table 6.1 compares U.S. and German data from the Ardennes and Italian Campaigns.

Table 6.1. U.S. and German Data from Ardennes and Italian Campaigns

	Ardennes	Italy
U.S. SUCCESSFUL ATTACKS		
Number of cases	28	36
Percentage of success	68	51
Lowest force ratio	1.15	1.23
Highest force ratio	7.83	4.25
Average force ratio	2.24	1.97
U.S. FAILED ATTACKS		
Number of cases	13	34
Lowest force ratio	1.23	1.13
Highest force ratio	2.24	2.96
Average force ratio	1.57	1.62
GERMAN SUCCESSFUL ATTACKS		
Number of cases	11	5

Percentage of success	37	28
Lowest force ratio	1.05	1.23
Highest force ratio	9.14	3.12
Average force ratio	3.92	1.85
GERMAN FAILED ATTACKS		
Number of cases	19	13
Lowest force ratio	0.34	0.72
Highest force ratio	2.40	3.24
Average force ratio	1.17	1.28

It appears that the U.S. Army performed better on the attack in the Ardennes engagements than it did in the Italian engagements. The average ratio for a successful attack in the Ardennes was 2.24 compared to 1.97 in Italy, while the average ratio for a failed attack was 1.57 in the Ardennes and 1.62 in Italy. Yet the United States won in 68 percent of the Ardennes attacks compared to 51 percent in Italy.

While the Americans clearly had air supremacy in the Ardennes Campaign, they certainly had air superiority through most of the Italian Campaign as well. As there is no other clear pattern of differences (technological, terrain, etc.) in the two sets of engagements, this would indicate either an improvement in the U.S. Army in the second half of 1944 compared to the U.S. Army in Italy in late 1943 and the first half of 1944, or a decline in the overall performance of the German army, or both.

Unfortunately there are only eighteen examples of German attacks in the Italian data, including only eight examples of Germans attacking Americans and ten examples of Germans attacking the British. As it appears that the performance of UK forces involved was worse than the U.S. performance, this biases the data somewhat.

The Ardennes data for the Germans on the attack are more difficult to interpret. In the Ardennes the Germans outnumbered the defenders by 3.92 to 1, compared to 1.85 to 1 in Italy. The Ardennes figure may not be indicative of the change in force ratios required by the Germans to win, as many of the German attacks in the Ardennes data set are from the early days of the offensive, when three armies attacked a single corps in an effort to breach the U.S. lines. As a result the statistics are skewed. In the case of the failed German attacks, there is not much difference. In the Ardennes the Germans failed on an average ratio of 1.17, while the average ratio of failures in Italy is slightly higher, at 1.28. No conclusions can be drawn from this small sample.

Considering casualty effectiveness, in the twenty-eight cases in the Ardennes data in which the United States attacked successfully, the Americans caused from 18 to 3,616 German losses (an average of 541 per engagement) while suffering themselves from 1 to 1,477 losses (an average of 207 per engagement). In twenty-three of the cases the attacker suffered fewer losses than the defender.

These data are heavily influenced by the number of successful penetrations and envelopments in the Ardennes. The United States staged thirteen attacks that penetrated and one in which the defender was enveloped. This is a higher percentage (50 percent) of penetrations and envelopments than in the Italian data (39 percent). In the fourteen U.S. attacks that penetrated or enveloped, the total U.S. casualties were 2,963 (average of 212 per engagement) while the total German casualties were 8,484 (average of 606). This was a much better U.S. performance than in Italy, where U.S. casualties averaged 435 per engagement, while the Germans averaged 624.[4]

In the case of successful attacks that did not penetrate or envelop, the total U.S. casualties were 2,839 (average of 203 per attack, 212 for a penetrating attack), while the German losses were 6,662 (average of 476 losses per attack, 606 for a penetrating attack).

This indicates a performance difference relative to the U.S. versus the German army in the Ardennes when compared to Italy. Overall, in the Ardennes the United States caused 2.61 casualties for every 1 it received during a successful attack. In Italy the ratio was 1.13 to 1. When penetrating, the ratio was 2.86 to 1 versus 1.48 to 1 for Italy. When not penetrating, the exchange ratio was still a significant 2.34 to 1 in the Ardennes compared to 0.82 to 1 in Italy. This suggests a shift in casualty effectiveness by a factor of 2 between Italy and the Ardennes.

The same pattern appears in the unsuccessful U.S. attacks. In the thirteen unsuccessful attacks, the United States caused from 29 to 2,028 losses to the Germans (an average of 502 losses per engagement), while suffering themselves from 6 to 1,096 losses (an average of 223 per engagement). There were eight cases in which the attacker lost fewer than the defender. These data are heavily influenced by one very lopsided battle (4th Armored Division Attack IV), in which the United States suffered 125 casualties while Germany lost 2,028. Excluding this battle, the average German loss was 375 and the average U.S. loss was 231.[5] The data show a significant difference in result from the Italian Campaign engagements, where over the course of thirty-four unsuccessful U.S. attacks, the Americans suffered an average of 351 casualties while the German average was only 262. The Italian data show the Germans losing 0.75 men for every U.S. loss, while the Ardennes data show the Germans losing 1.62 men for every U.S. loss. Again the casualty effectiveness of the U.S. forces in the Ardennes is twice that of Italy.

Combining all the "attack advances," "failed attacks," and "limited attacks" into one category and excluding the one outlier results in twenty-six cases in which the United States suffered a total of 5,616 casualties (average of 216 per engagement) compared to 11,161 German casualties (average of 429 per engagement). There were twenty cases (77 percent) in which the United States suffered fewer losses than the defender. These figures point to a 99 percent casualty effectiveness advantage on the part of the United States. Table 6.2 compares these Ardennes data directly with the Italian data. It shows that U.S. casualty effectiveness increased from 0.78 German losses per U.S. loss to 1.99 German losses per U.S. loss, a casualty effectiveness improvement of 155 percent.

Table 6.2. All Attack Advances, Failed Attacks, and Limited Attacks

	Ardennes	Italy
Number of cases	26	56
Average U.S. loss	216	331
Average German loss	429	259
Percentage of cases in which U.S. suffered less	77	34

Grouping the data from all successful U.S. attacks produced similar figures. The total across all forty-one U.S. attacks was 8,704 U.S. casualties (average of 212) and 21,673 German casualties (average of 529). There were thirty-one cases (76 percent) in which the United States suffered fewer losses than the defender. These figures indicate a 150 percent casualty effectiveness advantage on the part of the United States. Table 6.3 compares this directly with the Italian data.

Table 6.3. Successful U.S. Attacks

	Ardennes	Italy
Number of cases	41	70
Average U.S. loss	212	352
Average German loss	529	332
Percentage of cases in which U.S. suffered less	77	40

These aggregate figures show that U.S. casualty effectiveness increased from 0.94 German losses per U.S. loss in Italy to 2.50 German losses per U.S. loss in the Ardennes, a casualty effectiveness improvement of 166 percent.

Unfortunately the Ardennes data may be biased. They include thirty-five engagements drawn from the U.S. III Corps attack on the German southern flank (part of General Patton's offensive in late December 1944). In this case the initial U.S. attack benefited from surprise, and the German opposition was dispersed and out of position. This made it an unusually successful offensive that may not be typical. A mixture of other U.S. attacks in the Ardennes would need to be analyzed to have complete confidence in these data.

While the data for the German attacks in Italy are less satisfactory due to the small number of examples and because only eight of the cases feature the United States as defender, they still need to be looked at to see if differences of the same order of magnitude are detected when the Germans are attacking and the Americans are defending.

There are thirty examples in the Ardennes data of German attacks, eleven successful and nineteen unsuccessful. Of the eleven successful attacks (as rated by the mission accomplishment scores) two were "failed attacks," two were "attack advances," three were "penetrations," and four were "defender enveloped." These attacks caused 89 to 3,535 U.S. losses (an average of 1,185) and 4 to 1,237 German losses (an average of 428). There were eight cases in which the attacker lost fewer than the defender.

For the nineteen unsuccessful attacks, there were one "limited action," two "limited attacks," nine "failed attacks," and seven "attack advances." These attacks caused from 15 to 888 U.S. casualties (average of 222) and 4 to 824 German casualties (an average of 253). There were seven cases in which the attacker lost fewer than the defender.

Comparing these data to the Italian data is a little more difficult. In the case of the successful attacks, the Italian data contain only five cases, of which only one was a penetration, while seven of the eleven Ardennes attacks were penetrations. Comparing only the four "attack advances" results from the Ardennes data to the four from the Italian data is probably irrelevant as the number of examples is too small. Therefore nothing can be concluded from these data.

In the case of the unsuccessful attacks, in the Ardennes engagements the Germans caused 0.88 casualties for every 1 they suffered, while in the Italian engagements the Germans caused 1.34 casualties for every 1 they suffered. Assuming all other factors are equal, this implies degradation in relative casualty effectiveness of the German forces of some 52 percent from Italy to the Ardennes. Table 6.4 compares the performance of the U.S. and German forces in Ardennes and Italy.[6]

Table 6.4. Performance Comparison of U.S. and German Forces

	Ardennes	Italy
U.S. SUCCESSFUL ATTACKS		
Number of cases	28	36
Average U.S. losses	207	353
Average German losses	541	397
Times U.S. losses lower	23	17
No. of type V+ outcomes	14	14
Average U.S. losses, type V+	212	435
Average German losses, type V+	606	624
Average U.S. losses, type IV	203	291
Average German losses, type IV	476	227
U.S. FAILED ATTACKS		
Number of cases	13	34
Average U.S. losses	223	351
Average German losses	502	262
Times U.S. losses lower	8	11
Average U.S. losses, less outlier	231	—
Average German losses, less outlier	375	—
GERMAN SUCCESSFUL ATTACKS		
Number of cases	11	5
Average German losses	428	902
Average U.S. losses	1,185	807
Times German losses lower	8	3
GERMAN FAILED ATTACKS		
Number of cases	19	13
Average German losses	253	467
Average U.S. losses	222	654
Times German losses lower	7	8

Based on the data from the U.S. attacks, one can conclude that the relative performance difference between the two armies had changed by as much as a factor of 2. This conclusion may be influenced by the Ardennes data set being biased due to a group of unusually successful attacks by the United States. The data from the German attacks do not support that contention, although they do seem to indicate some change. The difference between the German performance when attacking as opposed to their later performance when defending could also be caused by three other factors: better U.S. air and artillery support, declining German morale after the Ardennes offensive had failed, or random variations or biased data.

To address the first point, only thirteen of the U.S. attacks in the Ardennes occurred in good weather with extensive air support and good artillery observation. Most of the German attacks occurred in bad weather and the United States had little air support. The Germans did not have any effective air support throughout the Ardennes Campaign. Still, this does not explain the difference in the results from the U.S. attacks in Italy and in the Ardennes. Many of the U.S. attacks in Italy were also conducted with air support and in favorable weather. Without looking extensively at the air support for each individual attack, which was well beyond the budget of the contract this work was done for, this issue cannot be definitively answered. There were improvements in U.S. close air support doctrine and tactics from early 1944 to late 1944; however, such improvements would not account for what appears to be a 2-to-1 increase in casualty effectiveness. Command of the air is certainly a factor in explaining the differences in the relative effectiveness of the two forces when the Americans are attacking as opposed to when the Germans are attacking.

Most of the U.S. attacks in the data set took place after the first five days of the Ardennes Campaign, when the German offensive had failed, the weather had cleared (although only for four days), and the Germans were under attack on the ground and sometimes from the air as well. The perceived decline in German defensive capabilities may have been due to declining morale and motivation stemming from either the situation on the ground or from aerial bombardment. To make such a determination of cause would require more research. Still, at this point Germany was only five months away from complete collapse and conquest.

Finally, one cannot rule out the possibility that the data are simply biased or the results are within the random variation of the data. As the data selected were not a true random sampling, the data selection could have resulted in a bias in one direction or the other. However, the data do not seem abnormal to us and the engagements were not selected to any specific criteria, so we do not expect the data to show a strong bias.

Of course all these data exhibit quite wide statistical variability. For example, the standard deviation of the twenty-eight successful attacks for the attacker (average losses of 207) is 304.22. For the defender (average losses of 541) the standard deviation is 701.15. This means that if the data are truly unbiased and truly representative of the combat in the Ardennes as a whole, then the 80 percent confidence interval for the attacker losses is between 131 to 283, while the 80 percent confidence interval for the average defender losses is between 366 to 715.[7]

Dupuy also conducted an analysis of the Ardennes Campaign engagements, published in his book *Hitler's Last Gamble*.[8] He and his coauthors used his combat model. Unfortunately it was limited to only eleven cases, with the United States on the attack in only one of those cases. Of those eleven cases the Germans had a superior CEV in seven (ranging from 1.03 to 1.43), while the Americans had a superior CEV in four (ranging from 1.10 to 1.48). This is not out of line with what our data are showing.

One must concede that there is a possibility that the relative performance between the U.S. and German forces in the Ardennes was different (in favor of the United States) than in Italy. It would appear that when the Germans were on the attack, mostly early in the Battle of the Bulge, the differences were not that significant. After the German offensive had failed and the United States was able to get air support and start attacking back, there was a noticeable difference in relative combat performance. It does not appear that the mix of units was a factor. The Volksgrenadier divisions were the primary units involved in fifteen of the thirty attacks and fifteen of the forty-one defensive efforts. While there clearly was a difference between many of these newly raised infantry units and the more veteran ss and regular army armored units, it does not appear that they performed much differently in the offense than in the defense.[9] Of course capabilities between individual units can vary considerably.

While being able to determine that the German army was in decline by December 1944 is not particularly surprising to many familiar with the history of that period, it is surprising that it is fighting from this time (in particular the Vosges Campaign from October to December 1944) that has been used as an argument against Dupuy's claim that the German army was better than the American Army in Italy. It is clear from an examination of the large number of cases studied here that the relative effectiveness of the two forces had shifted over time, most likely due to a decline in German capabilities.

The Battle of Kursk

Few people disagree that the German army's combat performance was better than the Soviet Army's combat performance on the Eastern Front. That was certainly the case in the disastrous 1941 campaign, where Germany destroyed large parts of the Russian Army and overran half of European Russia. It was also the case in 1942, when the Germans were able to push all the way to Stalingrad and the Caucasus Mountains. By the middle of 1943 the front had stabilized, and after several months of rest and buildup, the German army launched a large armored offensive into Soviet-prepared defenses around the Kursk salient. Not only was this the first time the Soviets fought the Germans to a standstill in the summer, it was also the first time they were able to take the offensive in the summer. Strategically the tide was shifting in favor of the Soviet Union, but tactically it appeared that Germany still held a significant edge.

The most salient point of the Kursk data is that they show the significance of the nation on exchange rates. These differences appear in both the casualty rates and the capture rates and are so apparent that we can simply dispense with the detailed analysis as provided for the Italian and Ardennes data. A look at the force ratios for the Soviet and German attacks compared to the casualty exchange ratios for these attacks shows the combat effectiveness differences at Kursk (see table 6.5). Looking separately at low-odds (low force ratios) attacks is also illustrative.[10]

Table 6.5. German and Soviet Casualty Effectiveness at Kursk

Battle of Kursk Data	Average Force Ratio	Average Loss Ratio
All Soviet attacks (18)	1.42 to 1	5.63 to 1
Soviet low-odds attacks (12)	1.00 to 1	4.83 to 1
0.51 TO 1.34 TO 1		
All German attacks (31)	1.66 to 1	0.30 to 1
German low-odds attacks (21)	0.93 to 1	0.41 to 1
0.63 TO 1.42 TO 1		

Table 6.5 shows a very significant casualty effectiveness advantage for the Germans. When the Soviets attacked, they lost an average of 5.63 men for every German lost. When the Germans attacked, they lost 0.30 men for every Soviet lost, or inflicted 3.33 casualties for every 1 they lost. The difference between the effectiveness of the Germans when attacking versus defending is probably explained by the advantages of defense, terrain, and so on. When the odds are even, which is roughly approximated by the low-odds attacks, the Soviets attacked at average odds of 1 to 1, yet lost almost 5 men for every 1 the Germans lost. The Germans attacked at less than 1 to 1 and caused almost 2.5 losses per 1 of their own.

If the Italian data are analyzed the same way, the result is a similar tendency, although much more subtle (see table 6.6).

Table 6.6. American, British, and German Casualty Effectiveness in Italy

Italian Campaign Data	Average Force Ratio	Average Loss Ratio
All U.S. attacks (70)	1.80 to 1	2.41 to 1
U.S. low-odds attacks (13)	1.35 to 1	3.95 to 1

	Average Force Ratio	Average Loss Ratio
1.20 TO 1.50 TO 1		
All UK attacks (49)	3.00 to 1	3.17 to 1
UK low-odds attacks (7)	1.29 to 1	2.20 to 1
0.85 TO 1.50 TO 1		
All German attacks (18)	1.44 to 1	1.14 to 1
German low-odds attacks (13)	1.02 to 1	0.92 to 1
0.72 TO 1.48 TO 1		

In this case, when the Americans attacked, they lost more than 2 men for every 1 the defending Germans lost. The British lost about 3 men in the attack for every German loss. When the Germans attacked, they lost about 1 for 1. This was true even though the average force ratios of the U.S. and UK attacks were higher than for the German attacks.

The low-odds attack data just reinforce this impression. When the Americans attacked, they lost 4 men for every defending German lost. The British low-odds attacks were little better, losing 2 men for every defending German lost. When the Germans attacked at low odds, they lost fewer than 1 for 1. Significantly this pattern does not carry through to the Ardennes data (see table 6.7).

Table 6.7. American and German Casualty Effectiveness in Ardennes

Ardennes Campaign Data	Average Force Ratio	Average Loss Ratio
All U.S. attacks (41)	2.03 to 1	0.24 to 1
U.S. low-odds attacks (12)	1.31 to 1	0.65 to 1
1.15 TO 1.48 TO 1		
All German attacks (30)	3.33 to 1	0.70 to 1
German low-odds attacks (13)	0.80 to 1	0.38 to 1
0.34−1.37 TO 1		

In the case of the Ardennes data, when the United States attacked, Germany lost about 4 men to each American lost. When the Germans attacked, the Americans lost about 1.5 men to each German lost. This contrast between Germans attacking and defending is notable.

Taken at face value, these data argue for a casualty effectiveness of the Germans over the Soviets by a factor of around 4 to 1 and over the Americans and British in Italy by a factor of around 2 to 1, and for the Americans having a casualty effectiveness advantage over the Germans in the Ardennes of around 2 to 1, with some notable exceptions (especially when the Germans were on the offensive). This implies a significant shift in capability by the U.S. Army or decline of the German army by late 1944.

For several reasons these numbers are not completely acceptable. The calculation of the averages of combat effectiveness becomes somewhat convoluted.[11] In the case of the Kursk data, and to a lesser extent with the Italian data, most of the force ratios tend to be low and the casualty exchange ratios are not widely divergent. In the case of the Ardennes data, we have battles at 40 to 1 odds and several cases in which the casualty exchange ratios are around 25 to 1. These lopsided exchanges heavily influence the mathematics, but they are on both sides. A more useful comparison may be to look at the total casualties.

In table 6.8 the force ratio is the sum of the strength of all the cases compared to the sum of the strength of the opposing forces, while the losses are the total losses for each side compared to the losses on the opposing side.

Table 6.8. German and Soviet Casualty Effectiveness at Kursk

Kursk Campaign Data	Total Force Ratio	Total Loss Ratio
All Soviet attacks (18)	1.43 to 1	6.04 to 1
Soviet low-odds attacks (12)	1.02 to 1	3.92 to 1
0.51 TO 1.34 TO 1		
All German attacks (31)	1.34 to 1	0.30 to 1
German low-odds attacks (21)	0.99 to 1	0.27 to 1
0.63 TO 1.42 TO 1		

Notice that using weighted averages did not change the numbers much. These figures still support the contention that there is a casualty effectiveness difference between the Germans and the Soviets of around 4 to 1.

Table 6.9. American, British, and German Casualty Effectiveness in Italy

Italian Campaign Data	Total Force Ratio	Total Loss Ratio
All U.S. attacks (70)	1.65 to 1	1.06 to 1
U.S. low-odds attacks (13)	1.36 to 1	1.43 to 1
1.20 TO 1.50 TO 1		
All UK attacks (49)	2.58 to 1	1.63 to 1
UK low-odds attacks (7)	1.24 to 1	1.92 to 1
0.85 TO 1.50 TO 1		
All German attacks (18)	1.27 to 1	0.84 to 1
German low-odds attacks (13)	1.03 to 1	0.63 to 1
0.72 TO 1.48 TO 1		

The Italian data, based on weighted averages, show a different picture (see table 6.9). Most significant is the casualty effectiveness of the U.S. attacks. The shift in the loss ratio from 2.41 to 1 down to 1.06 to 1 is caused by a number of smaller engagements having very lopsided exchange ratios. For example the casualty ratio for one of the Rapido River operations was 48.12 to 1. These engagements clearly skewed the statistics. In fact there is only one other engagement that has a casualty exchange ratio greater than 10.

Using these weighted statistics, it is harder to discern any difference in casualty effectiveness between the United States and Germany. The United States had a 1.06 to 1 loss ratio when it attacked (average force ratio of 1.65 to 1), while Germany had a 0.84 to 1 loss ratio with lower average odds (1.27 to 1). This supports the contention that combat effectiveness favored the Germans by 20 to 30 percent. These figures show the British slightly worse than the Americans, with a casualty effectiveness ratio some 50 percent worse.

With little difference in the Ardennes data between U.S. and German relative casualty effectiveness, this leads us to consider whether there was a relative shift between the U.S. and German armies by the time of the Ardennes Campaign. Table 6.10 examines this question.

Table 6.10. American and German Casualty Effectiveness in Ardennes

Ardennes Campaign Data	Total Force Ratio	Total Loss Ratio
All U.S. attacks (41)	1.69 to 1	0.40 to 1
U.S. low-odds attacks (12)	1.29 to 1	0.69 to 1
1.15 TO 1.48 TO 1		
All German attacks (30)	1.52 to 1	0.55 to 1
German low-odds attacks (13)	0.85 to 1	0.38 to 1
0.34 TO 1.37 TO 1		

The use of weighted averages does not change the Ardennes data much. The most significant change is in the overall U.S. casualty effectiveness, which is lower, while the Germans improve. This moves the overall casualty effectiveness of the two forces closer to each other, with the United States having the edge in overall attacks, while Germany has the edge in low-odds attacks. This indicates that there was, at best, a limited change in relative performance between the U.S. and German forces from Italy to the Ardennes.

The figures on Kursk clearly make the case that there was a performance difference between the German and Soviet forces. Still, it is worthwhile to look at some other casualty measurements for Kursk. A summary of the total casualty statistics is presented in table 6.11.[12]

Table 6.11. Summary of Total Casualty Statistics for Kursk

	German	Soviet	Ratio
Total casualties	10,233	40,644	1 to 3.97
WHEN ATTACKING	7,963	13,703	1 to 1.72
WHEN DEFENDING	2,270	26,941	1 to 11.87
Total bloody casualties	9,936	27,046	1 to 2.72
Total KIA	1,523	8,008	1 to 5.26
WIA to KIA ratio	5.52 to 1	2.38 to 1	
WHEN ATTACKING	5.63 to 1	2.90 to 1	
WHEN DEFENDING	5.16 to 1	2.06 to 1	
Total MIA	297	13,598	1 to 45.78
WHEN ATTACKING	190	1,909	1 to 10.05
WHEN DEFENDING	107	11,689	1 to 109.24
Total CIA*	227	12,436	1 to 54.78
PERCENTAGE OF MIA THAT IS CIA	76.43	91.45	
TOTAL DESERTERS	4	599	1 to 149.75
PERCENTAGE OF CIA DESERTERS	1.76	4.82	

*captured in action

The data in table 6.11 come from forty-nine engagements, in which the Germans were considered attackers in thirty-one cases and the Soviets were the attackers in eighteen cases. Converting the gross casualty figures into casualty by engagement results in table 6.12. These data again make the point that the Germans enjoyed a relative performance advantage in both the attack and the defense. This advantage was clearly not related to posture, but appears regardless of posture.

Table 6.12. Casualties by Engagement for Kursk

	German	Soviet	Ratio
Average casualties	209	829	1 to 3.97
WHEN ATTACKING	257	761	1 to 2.96
WHEN DEFENDING	126	869	1 to 6.90

Another fact to note in table 6.12 is that for both sides the wounded-to-killed ratio is higher for the attacker than for the defender. This is as expected and reflects both the higher MIA for the defender and that there is a difference in the ratio of KIA/WIA simply because someone is on the defense versus the attack. This difference in the wounded-to-killed ratio between attacker and defender has shown up in some of our other work, but to date the Dupuy Institute has not published a paper on the subject, although I discuss it in more depth in chapter 15.[13]

The significant figure is the large number of Soviet MIAs, confirmed by the large number of Soviet captured in action (CIA) reported by the Germans. There is clearly a correlation between MIA and CIA, although we do have a number of cases in which the number of MIAs is lower than the number of CIAs reported by the other side.

The deserter figure is the most interesting. There is probably also a correlation between the number of deserters and the number of captured. A force with a higher number of deserters will probably have a correspondingly higher number of CIAs. It is felt that such measurement of deserters and AWOL (absent without leave) is probably a reflection of the general state of a unit's morale and cohesion.[14] The Soviets' high desertion rate reflects their lower morale and cohesion and their higher capture rate.

Also at Kursk the measurement of mission accomplishment is clearly very different. In the thirty-one German attacks, nineteen were successful (61 percent). Of the eighteen Soviet attacks, only three were successful (17 percent). The average force ratio for a German attack, however, was much lower than in the Italian and Ardennes data, being only 1.34 to 1. The average force ratio of the Soviet attacks was effectively the same as for the Germans, 1.43 to 1. Still, numbers matter. There were only two cases in which the Germans were successful while attacking outnumbered. In fact these were the only two such cases out of the 257 attacks reviewed, of which 31 were at odds of 1 to 1 or less. In contrast there was only one case (odds of 1.09 to 1) in which the Germans failed when attacking while outnumbering the Soviets. In the other eleven failed German attacks, the defenders matched or outnumbered them. The Soviets, on the other hand, failed eleven times in the attack even though they outnumbered the defenders.

The terrain in this part of the Battle of Kursk was generally rolling with mixed cover, making it easier to attack than the usual terrain in the Italian and Ardennes engagements. Technology and weapons for the two sides were similar, although one could certainly make the argument that the Soviets were the technologically superior force. The mix, number, and types of weapons in the two forces were different. The Soviets had many more guns on the battlefield, but they tended to be of smaller caliber. The Germans far outnumbered the Soviets in field artillery and large-caliber guns. The German Air Force, although it was numerically outnumbered, was soon able to establish a stronger presence over the battlefield than were the Soviets, and therefore air power favored the

Germans. Still, this establishment of air superiority was achieved by a force that was outnumbered and downed enemy airplanes at a rate of greater than five for every one they lost! The ground formations involved tended to be typical of their armies and in many cases were some of the better-equipped and more experienced forces of their respective armies. Most of the divisions on both sides had seen extensive combat, and most had a period of almost three months to prepare for the upcoming battle. Both sides were initially well supplied and supported, although some Soviet units suffered logistical problems as the battle developed.

We conclude from the Kursk comparison that the Germans had a clear advantage in combat capability that showed itself in both offensive and defensive casualty effectiveness and mission accomplishment. The difference appears to be a factor of 3. This difference appears in the middle of 1943, after the Soviet Army had two years of wartime experience, was using experienced units, and had time to rest, train, and rebuild before the German offensive. Yet there was still a very clear performance difference between these armies. If this noticeable performance difference between otherwise experienced, well-developed, and well-equipped armies existed in World War II, it should be no surprise that an examination of the armies of the postwar period also finds such differences.

7. Measuring Human Factors in Combat

Modern Wars

> This example suggests that it behooves the Israelis to seek a lasting peace
> while their military quality is still preeminent. If they wait too long it may be
> too late.
>
> —TREVOR N. DUPUY, *Elusive Victory* (1978)

At the Dupuy Institute we chose to focus first on World War II division-level
data because we can get accurate data from both sides, division-level is the
lowest level where a researcher can consistently collect good unit data, and we
have a large number of cases to work from. When we look at post–World War
II data, we rarely can get accurate data from both sides and often cannot get
unit records from either side. There are also a limited number of division-level
engagements. As such, the quality of data for post–World War II engagements
is noticeably inferior. For many of the engagements the losses for one or both
sides were determined by informed estimates in the absence of unit reporting. The modern engagements also suffer from there being a much smaller
number of cases to choose from. Still, we have done some work examining the
engagements of the Arab-Israeli fighting in 1956–73, the Vietnam War in 1963–
68, the fighting in the Falklands Islands in 1982, Grenada in 1983, the fighting
in Angola in 1987–88, and the 1991 Gulf War, among others. With the caveat
that the quality of data is lower and the number of cases is less than what we
had for our analysis of World War II, let us look at what these data indicate.

Arab-Israeli Wars, 1956–1973

The Arab-Israeli data parallel the cases and the work Dupuy did, although some
of the data have been revised and updated. We were able to assemble fifty-one
division-level engagements from the Arab-Israeli fighting of 1956, 1967, 1968,
and 1973. There are two engagements from 1956, sixteen from 1967, one from
1968, and thirty-two from 1973 (the Yom Kipper or Ramadan War). Our database also contains numerous brigade, battalion, and company engagements
from this period, but for the sake of consistency we analyzed only the division-
level engagements. For the sake of brevity, I will follow the approach I used
for the Kursk data in chapter 6. Table 7.1 presents the ratios for the fifty-one

division-level engagements from the Arab-Israeli fighting. There are probably performance differences between the Egyptian, Syrian, Jordanian, Iraqi, and Palestinian forces, but for the sake of simplicity, all the Arab armies were lumped together. All the Arab attacks, with the exception of Mitla Pass in 1967, are from the 1973 war.

Table 7.1. Force Ratios from Arab-Israeli Engagements

	Average Force Ratio	Average Loss Ratio	Total Force Ratio	Total Loss Ratio
All Israeli attacks (33)	1.29 to 1	0.46 to 1	1.04 to 1	0.31 to 1
Israeli low-odds attacks (26)	0.92 to 1	0.43 to 1	0.89 to 1	0.28 to 1
0.54 TO 1.47 TO 1				
All Arab attacks (18)	4.09 to 1	3.65 to 1	3.02 to 1	2.81 to 1
Arab low-odds attacks (2)	0.96 to 1	4.91 to 1	0.95 to 1	3.87 to 1
0.87 TO 1.09 TO 1				

This fighting has the advantage that technologically there was not much difference between the opposing forces. The units were well armed, and both sides had considerable armor. The Israelis had air superiority, although in 1973 the Egyptians had very good air defense. It would appear that the major difference between the two armies was combat effectiveness.

One cannot help but note that the relative combat performance of the Israelis and the Arabs in 1956–73 was similar in disparity to that between the Germans and the Soviets in 1943 (see table 6.5).[1] This is not to say that the Germans and the Israelis performed at similar levels, as we measured only the relative combat performance between the two opposing forces. The German army in 1943 could have been superior to the Israeli Army of 1956–73, which means that the Soviet Army in 1943 was superior to the Arab armies in 1956–73. We do not know if this is the case.

Dupuy's analysis, using his model structure but much of the same data, came to the following conclusion: "The average Israeli combat effectiveness value (CEV) with respect to the Egyptians in 1967 was found to be 1.75; in other words, a combat effectiveness superiority of almost two-to-one. Following an identical procedure for the 1973 war, the average Israeli CEV with respect to the Egyptians for that war was 1.98."[2]

As Dupuy's combat effectiveness value is a force multiplier in his model of combat power, it is not directly comparable to exchange ratios, although it is related. In general, a force multiplier of 2 in his models will produce a casualty exchange rate of greater than 2.[3] For all practical purposes, we are showing the same effect and the same results at roughly the same values.

These are forces that are at least competent or motivated enough to fight each other in a back-and-forth conventional engagement. Some of our next examples are truly one-sided, which seems to be typical of many operations in the post–World War II world.

Vietnam, 1963–1968

Our database contains eleven smaller unit actions from the Vietnam War. Although it was a guerrilla war, it did generate thousands of more conventional company- and battalion-level actions. These actions have never been analyzed in any depth. A preliminary study conducted by HERO on conventional actions in guerrilla wars generated a small database of engagements from Vietnam. Working from that and additional research, we then created the eleven Vietnam engagements used for our battalion-level validation of the TNDM. Due to the availability of records at the time, the U.S. figures were developed from reliable secondary sources, while the Viet Cong losses were simply drawn from educated guesses. This is probably the least reliable data presented in this book. It is clearly an area where more research is necessary.[4]

Of these eleven engagements, the two earliest are the Viet Cong (VC) versus the South Vietnamese Army (Army of the Republic of Vietnam, ARVN) in 1963. The other nine are against the United States in 1966–68. In seven of these the Viet Cong or the North Vietnamese Army (NVA) are the attackers. Many of them are night engagements. Air support is a factor in five of the engagements. These are battalion-level actions; the average attacker strength is 891, and the average defender strength is 431. The figures for the two ARVN cases are presented in table 7.2.

Table 7.2. ARVN vs. VC Exchange Ratios, 1963

	Force Ratio	Loss Ratio	Note
One ARVN attack	8.33	0.08	Cau Lanh, 28 August 1963
One ARVN defense	3.33	0.27	Cai Nuoc, 10 September 1963

Not much can be determined from these two cases. In both, the attacker got the better of the exchange. In the case of Cau Lanh, the ARVN had air support (eight sorties). In the case of Cai Nuoc, the provincial capital was overrun by the Viet Cong night attack.

Table 7.3. U.S. vs. VC/NVA Exchange Ratios

	Average Force Ratio	Average Loss Ratio	Total Force Ratio	Total Loss Ratio
All VC/NVA attacks (7)	3.35 to 1	9.15 to 1	2.12 to 1	8.64 to 1
All U.S. attacks (2)	2.30 to 1	0.13 to 1	1.33 to 1	0.13 to 1

The analysis of the nine U.S. engagements is shown in table 7.3. We can see in the VC/NVA attacks the U.S. advantage in superior combat performance in addition to prepared positions and superior firepower (artillery and air). There are lots of factors at play here, but, not surprisingly, a guerrilla army that is conducting conventional attacks is not as capable as a modern, well-armed (including artillery) conventional force. The two engagements where the U.S. forces are on the attack also generate a 7.97 to 1 exchange ratio in favor of the United States. This is similar to the exchange ratio obtained when they were attacked. In conventional combat the Americans thoroughly overpowered their opponents. How much of that is superior combat effectiveness and how much is superior firepower is hard to tell from this small sample. In six of the seven engagements, the United States had considerable artillery, ranging from four to thirty tubes (average of thirteen per engagement). The United States also had considerable air support in four of the engagements, ranging from twenty-three to fifty-four sorties in three of them. This is clearly a case where a much larger number of cases is needed and the artillery and air support need to be addressed before anything definitive can be determined. Most likely the very favorable U.S. exchange rates were due to both factors (superior performance and superior firepower).

An exchange ratio between 3 to 1 and 9 to 1 is probably the norm for conventional actions by first-world armies against guerrilla forces. For the record, the United States lost 58,153 in the Vietnam War (47,357 of them combat losses), while the ARVN lost at least 196,863 killed in action, and their military losses may have been as high as 254,257 dead. The allied forces (South Korea, Thailand, Australia, New Zealand, and the Philippines) lost at least 5,193. The official opposing forces' count of losses from the Viet Cong and North Vietnamese Army from 1961–73 was 927,124; adding in the last two years of the war the official total is 1,027,085. This is an estimate by their opponents and could be inflated by a third or more. The total may be closer to 731,000.[5] Still, this is a 2.4 to 1 exchange ratio in favor of the allied forces.[6] The exchange ratio between the United States and the VC/NVA was probably above 3 to 1.[7]

Falkland Islands, 1982

The Falklands data are also built primarily from battalion-level engagements.

It was a smaller campaign, with battalion- and company-level actions. We have a database of six battalion-level engagements to work with that covers most of the major actions of the war. The average strength of the British in these engagements was 550, while the Argentines' average strength was 637. Because of their much smaller size, these actions are very different than the 10,000- to 20,000-troop division-level engagements we have been looking at. These battalion-level engagements pretty much encompass all the major fighting in the Falklands in 1982.[8] It was a very one-sided affair; all six attacks were conducted by the British and resulted in the defender being defeated and penetrated. All the engagements were low-odds attacks; one was at 0.41 to 1, while the rest were around 1.1 to 1. Results of our analysis are shown in table 7.4.

Table 7.4. UK vs. Argentine Exchange Ratios

	Average Force Ratio	Average Loss Ratio	Total Force Ratio	Total Loss Ratio
All British attacks (6)	0.99 to 1	0.24 to 1	0.86 to 1	0.26 to 1

It would appear that the relative performance difference between the British and the Argentines was even greater than what we see between the Germans and the Soviets or the Israelis and the Arabs. We do have other post–World War II brigade- and battalion-level engagements in our databases, and many of them also show similarly lopsided results.

Grenada, 1983

The British were able to obtain a 4 to 1 exchange ratio in their six battalion-level fights in the Falklands. In 1983 the United States overran the tiny, poor island nation of Grenada with overwhelming force. Surprisingly the defending Grenadian and Cuban troops put up some real resistance. The results from these two engagements are shown in table 7.5.

Table 7.5. U.S. vs. Grenadian and Cuban Exchange Ratios

	Average Force Ratio	Average Loss Ratio	Total Force Ratio	Total Loss Ratio
U.S. attacks (2)	7.54 to 1	0.25 to 1	1.39 to 1	0.10 to 1

Overall U.S. losses from the operation were 19 killed and 125 wounded; Grenadian and Cuban combat losses were 487.[9] This is a 3.38 to 1 loss ratio in favor of the United States, not counting captured. The United States also conducted an operation in Panama in 1989 that overwhelmed the opposition with 27,500 troops and produced a 2.5 to 1 exchange ratio.[10] Such loss ratios are to be expected given the preponderance of firepower and superior training and effectiveness of many first-world armies and should not be particularly surprising in any such intervention.

South Africa in Angola, 1987–1988

South Africa fought a number of engagements with UNITA, a separatist force located in southern Angola, and later with the Angola Army. These three large brigade-size engagements are notable in that the UNITA and Angola forces had more equipment, including main battle tanks, and had air superiority. Yet South Africa, outnumbered and fighting with jeeps and trucks, managed to defeat these well-armed forces. It was a very lopsided exchange, in which all the advantages of terrain, posture, firepower, armor, and air support lay in the hands of opposing side, while the South Africans had only superior combat effectiveness. This is a case where other factors are not in play to explain South Africa's success in these engagements. The South Africans were simply so good, or their opponents were so bad, that they were able to succeed in the face of overwhelming odds and firepower. Table 7.6 presents an examination of the combined statistics from these three engagements.

Table 7.6. South African vs. UNITA and Angolan Exchange Ratios

	Average Force Ratio	Average Loss Ratio	Total Force Ratio	Total Loss Ratio
South African attacks (3)	0.74 to 1	0.08 to 1	0.75 to 1	0.06 to 1

The research on these engagements came from the post-apartheid South African Defense Force, including secondary sources and personal accounts of the participants. Obviously the UNITA and Angolan losses are intelligence estimates and could be well off the mark. The outcome, on the other hand, is not in doubt. But this is significant, for even with almost all factors against them, the South Africans were able to inflict a 17 to 1 loss rate (34 total South Africa casualties versus 570 UNITA and Angolan) that can only be the result of combat effectiveness differences.[11] This is a point worth remembering whenever a modern first-world force is deployed in conventional operations against combat forces from less-developed nations.

Gulf War, 1991

For the U.S. actions in the Gulf War we were able to obtain accurate information on U.S. strength and losses. We mostly used estimates based on U.S. intelligence records for the Iraqi numbers. This is a questionable source for any research but is effectively the only source available. We were able to assemble fifteen division-level engagements for this analysis. There were eight American attacks, two British attacks, and one French attack. Every coalition attack was a success, with the outcome being either defender penetrated or defender enveloped. There were four Iraqi attacks, all against the United States, and all failed. The data for this very lopsided campaign appears in table 7.7.

Table 7.7. U.S., UK, and French vs. Iraqi Exchange Ratios

	Average Force Ratio	Average Loss Ratio	Total Force Ratio	Total Loss Ratio
All coalition attacks (11)	2.09 to 1	0.03 to 1	1.76 to 1	0.01 to 1
Coalition low-odds attacks (4)	0.96 to 1	0.00 to 1	1.00 to 1	0.00 to 1
0.67 TO 1.16 TO 1				
All Iraqi attacks (4)	1.01 to 1	31.26 to 1	0.51 to 1	20.20 to 1
Iraqi low-odds attacks (3)	0.35 to 1	39.43 to 1	0.35 to 1	64.53 to 1
0.20 TO 0.64 TO 1				

This is probably one of the most extreme cases of mismatched combat performance. Of course the United States was helped in this operation by a massive air campaign that considerably attrited and demoralized the Iraqi army before the ground campaign began. Yet there is no reason to assume that the Iraqi army (lowercase indicating a force consisting of both the Iraqi Army proper and the Republican Guard) was reasonably capable and that it suffered attrition and demoralization only because of coalition air power. In one of our Arab-Israeli engagements (Tel el Hara on 13 October 1973) the Iraqi army attacked at a force ratio of 0.87 to 1 and suffered losses at a ratio of 8.02 to 1.

We also have five brigade-level engagements from the Gulf War (the average strength of the attackers was 5,300). They are similar to the Falklands engagements in that they were all U.S. attacks resulting in U.S. victories and with the outcome in three of the cases being defender penetrated. They show the patterns presented in table 7.8.

Table 7.8. U.S. Brigade-Level Engagements Exchange Ratios

	Average Force Ratio	Average Loss Ratio	Total Force Ratio	Total Loss Ratio
All American attacks (5)	3.25 to 1	0.03 to 1	2.72 to 1	0.02 to 1

The United States did conduct another conventional campaign against Iraq, this one in 2003 using two divisions. It was also a mismatch in capabilities that resulted in the entire country being overrun in less than four weeks. U.S. problems in Iraq developed in the ensuing guerrilla war, which is analyzed in my book *America's Modern Wars: Understanding Iraq, Afghanistan and Vietnam.*

Casualty Effectiveness versus Combat Effectiveness

Much of the above analysis was based on a measurement of casualty effectiveness, but casualty effectiveness is an outcome. The actual factor we are trying to measure is combat effectiveness. We have no means of directly measuring combat effectiveness. For his combat models, Dupuy was able to produce a combat effectiveness value based on comparing the results of the model runs to the historical outcomes. The CEV served as a force multiplier for one side: if a force with the CEV of 2 was attacking at even odds, for example, it would be treated the same as if it was attacking at 2 to 1 odds. This would result in better outcomes, more favorable casualty exchange ratios, and higher advance rates. While there was not a direct linear relationship in the model between combat effectiveness and casualty effectiveness, a higher combat effectiveness value improved casualty effectiveness. Casualty effectiveness was usually higher than the combat effectiveness value.

There is a sense that one can calculate combat effectiveness as the square root of casualty effectiveness. In this construct a casualty effectiveness of 4 would mean a combat effectiveness value of 2. In effect, being twice as good as your opponent results in a favorable casualty exchange being four times better. This method has not been systematically tested.[12]

In addition some armies are "casualty insensitive." This certainly describes the Soviet Army in World War II, which was more than willing to take casualties for the sake of completing the mission or fulfilling orders. The failure to encourage individual initiative at the lower levels and the insistence that orders must be followed regardless amplified this tendency. It appears that the Soviet Army rather needlessly suffered additional casualties above and beyond that which other armies would suffer in the same scenario and that this "casualty insensitive" regime also influenced the casualty effectiveness figures. This assessment also certainly applies to the Japanese Army in World War II, especially with their "banzai charges" and tendency to fight until exterminated.

Still, casualty effectiveness is an important metric and one that gets the analyst closer to combat effectiveness; it is just not a perfect measure.

The Data Used for This Analysis

Many of the data used for this analysis have been published in various forms over the years. The QJM analysis using the original engagements was published in detail in the eight volumes of the *Combat Data Subscription Service*, the twelve issues of *History, Numbers and War*, and in other HERO and DMSI reports. Some of the data used for the Ardennes engagements were published in Dupuy et al.'s book on Ardennes, *Hitler's Last Gamble*. The Ardennes Campaign Simulation Data Base (ACSDB) has been publicly available for a while through the U.S. government, as is the Kursk Data Base.[13] All 192 engagements created from the Kursk data are described in depth in my book *Kursk: The Battle of Prokhorovka*. The data specifically used for the Dupuy Institute's capture rate studies, urban warfare studies, and situational awareness studies were included in the appendixes of these reports.[14] The Arab-Israeli engagements are described in depth in Dupuy's book *Elusive Victory*. The data for the other post–World War II engagements came from a variety of sources, with good detailed secondary sources available for the United Kingdom in the Falklands, the United States in Grenada, and South Africa in Angola. Their opponent strengths and losses are estimates, although we gather they are fairly accurate for the Falklands and Grenada. The U.S. Gulf War data are from primary sources, including the estimates of Iraqi strengths and losses (many were prisoners of war). So while our databases remain corporate proprietary, it is possible to check and validate much of the data used for this analysis. Our experience is that few actually do this, especially our critics.

Certainly we expect someone to take umbrage at or even be outraged by some of the conclusions presented here, possibly because of some slight to national honor. We have seen from past discussions that even the most intelligent and educated people are not immune to nationalistic bias. I request only that those who take exception to the findings I have presented do the legwork required to research operations, assemble the databases, and test the factors across a large number of cases. Only arguments based on a solid foundation of data should have any validity. Sadly I do not expect anyone else to actually do this, as it has rarely been done in the past.

Application to Analysis

Having established the obvious conclusion that human factors exist and having shown that they can indeed be measured (at least after the fact and relative to each other), the question becomes: Why do need to know this?

First, the Department of Defense combat modeling community needs to address these human factors. Most combat models ignore them and simply assume parity. If you assume parity, then at the most basic level you are saying the U.S. armed forces, with their higher levels of education (most enlisted are high school graduates; most officers are college graduates), higher levels of training, greater number of career professionals, higher selection criteria, and common sense of mission should be rated the same as the Iraqi army in the Gulf War. In 1991 the Iraqi army had politically appointed officers, and it drafted troops that served for only a few years, in some cases with almost no training for the draftees. Further there were many last-minute emergency call-ups and a much lower average level of education in a country that was internally divided among various religious factions.

The United States spends a considerable amount of money to maintain its all-volunteer professional army. Our troops are paid well. If one assumes that the Iraqi army, full of short-term draftees paid a fraction of our troops, is the equal of the U.S. army, then why pay additional money for a high quality all-volunteer force?

In almost any conflict the U.S. Army is sent to, it will face armies of draftees, who are not as well trained, not as professional, and therefore not of equal caliber. At some point, this has to be accounted for. An assumption of parity in performance is simply ignoring the real world.

Throughout history unmatched forces are as common as or more common than forces that are equal in ability. For example, there was a mismatch between the Germans and Soviets in tactical competence in 1943, just as there was between the Israelis and the Arabs in 1967 and 1973 and between the United States and Iraq in 1991. The argument that you should play parity simply ignores this large and very clear reality. And these differences can be measured, at least relative to each other.

Second, human factors need to be understood for certain types of analysis. For example, we needed to address the subject in our analysis of urban terrain; it was needed for our capture rate studies and for our work on measuring information advantages. A significant element of work we did on the combat effectiveness of Soviet and Chinese armies was based on this.[15] It needs to be understood wherever one uses data from the past to try to address or analyze the issues of today.

Third, understanding human factors is essential to future planning efforts and operations. The United States could not have undertaken the invasion of Iraq in 2003 with such limited forces unless there was some understanding of the human factors involved. The invasion was very successful, even if the subsequent occupation of Iraq was not initially well handled. With a primary strike force of 75,000 ground troops, the United States conquered a country with an armed force that may have consisted of 400,000 troops and Republican Guards. The entire operation resulted in only 687 casualties.[16]

The United States knew it could conduct such a lopsided offensive because of its experience in the Gulf War in 1991, where it was able to defeat the Iraqi army with only 1,143 casualties.[17] In fact those models and analysts that measure human factors as part of their analysis of warfare were able to predict before the Gulf War in 1991 that U.S. casualties would be relatively low, while some of those who did not address human factors produced estimates that diverged wildly from what actually occurred.[18]

Most U.S. operations in the future are going to be against opponents who are not as highly trained and capable as the U.S. military. To be able to understand, plan, model, and prepare for such operations, we need to understand how human factors affect warfare and how we can measure them in the future.

8. Outcome of Battles

Casualty rates of winners are lower than those of losers.

—TREVOR N. DUPUY, *Understanding War*

Around 2000 the Dupuy Institute conducted a series of studies for the Center for Army Analysis on determining enemy prisoner-of-war capture rates.[1] The subject matter was at CAA's request, although the approach and methodology was left completely up to us. These capture rate studies were intended to develop estimates of capture rates for enemy prisoners of war and civilian internees (CI). It was intended that these rates would be incorporated into the Headquarters Department of the Army (HQDA) Total Army Analysis (TAA) process.

The old capture rates the CAA was using for modeling and planning were based primarily on World War II data. These were contained in a look-up table listing the number of U.S. troops, the type of unit (i.e., infantry regiment, front line division, corps troops), and their posture (i.e., attack or defense, meeting engagement, inactive, pursuit, retirement or delaying action). From just those factors one could estimate how many enemies would be captured. The conditions of combat did not matter, nor did the outcome of the engagements, the unit size (army or division or battalion), human factors, or enemy strength. There were several conceptual issues here, but one that truly bothered us was that the capture rate was completely unrelated to opposing force strength.

So instead of just updating these tables with more recent data, we decided to create a new set of tables based on two-sided data, where we compared the United States versus Germany and Germany versus the Soviet Union. We also decided to measure our capture rates based on division-level combat so we would have a consistent basis for comparison. Later, we determined that the capture rates were heavily influenced by the outcome (some of this is alluded to earlier in this book) and that this needed to be included in our capture rate results. We therefore decided to define a series of engagement outcomes and classified all of the engagements according to those definitions. Seven engagement outcomes were defined:

1. *Limited action*: an engagement characterized by limited activity by either side. In this case the category of attacker and defender may be arbitrary but

is usually determined by the side on the strategic or operational offensive during the period of the engagement.

For much of the time in most military operations, the majority of units are primarily engaged in limited action. This is the norm of warfare. Therefore these "engagements" needed to be either ignored or coded as such. In the case of the Kursk engagements, we assembled the data for every pair of opposing division-size forces over two weeks facing three German corps. We naturally ended up with a number of limited action engagements and therefore needed to address them.

2. *Limited attack*: an engagement where the attacker's offensive activity is characterized by patrols, raids, or attacks with limited objectives. Limited attacks include feints and secondary attacks that are part of larger battles.

As we were collecting division-level data, we often found a number of operations where the only action of the day was a battalion-level or company-level action for the purpose of reconnaissance or taking a limited objective. In some cases these smaller actions could be quite intense, but when compared to the division-level data, the percentage-of-loss statistics were lower. This category serves to codify these types of engagements.

3. *Failed attack*: an engagement where the attacker attempts to mount a significant attack with the intention of dislodging the enemy but does not make a significant advance and does not achieve its objective.

4. *Attack advances*: an engagement where the attacker advances but does not achieve a clear-cut penetration of the defender's position. Depending on the degree to which the attack achieved its objective, the attacker may or may not be the winner.

5. *Defender penetrated*: an engagement where the attacker achieves a penetration of the defender's position. In this case the attacker is almost invariably the winner.

6. *Defender enveloped*: An engagement where the attacker achieves a penetration or breakthrough of the defender's position and successfully envelops or surrounds major parts of the defending force.

7. *Other*: any outcome that cannot be described by the other six categories. These are rare cases.

Note that these categorizations were applied based on careful analysis of the course of the engagement and its result. They were not simply based on "winners" and "losers" or the assigned mission accomplishment scores of the participants.

The following were determined to have had an effect on capture rates: (1) posture (whether attacking or defending), (2) outcome of the engagement, (3) force mix (armor to troop strength ratios), and (4) combat effectiveness (being Soviet). Combat effectiveness was examined only for the Kursk engagements, as the U.S., German, and UK forces were close enough in combat capabilities that we were comfortable lumping their data together. Obviously there are lots of other factors that influence the capture rates, including terrain, but these were the four that made a notable, measurable difference.

We ended up generating six tables from the data sets (Italy, Ardennes, and Kursk), and then created three other tables that looked at the same data in different ways. Table 8.1 covers the seventy-five engagements (except Avellino) from the Italian Campaign divided into the six outcome categories and posture (whether attacker and defender).[2] Table 8.2 reveals the same data for the seventy-one Ardennes engagements, and table 8.3 reveals the same data for the forty-nine Kursk engagements. Tables 8.4 and 8.5 show the Kursk data separated according to who was the attacker, the Germans or the Soviets. Table 8.6 summarizes final figures based on all three data sets.

Table 8.1. Italian Campaign (75 Engagements)

	No Attack	Limited	Failed	Advances	Penetrated	Envelopment
	I	II	III	IV	V	VI
Number of engagements	0	0	30	32	13	0
Attacker percentage casualties per day	—	—	1.67	1.21	0.96	—
Defender percentage casualties per day	—	—	1.47	1.90	3.08	—
Attacker percentage CIA per day	—	—	0.49	0.15	0.16	—
Defender percentage CIA per day	—	—	0.23	0.65	1.35	—
Attacker percentage losses that are CIA	—	—	18.39	11.89	6.63	—
Defender percentage losses that are CIA	—	—	16.55	41.86	49.55	—

Table 8.2. Ardennes Campaign (71 Engagements)

	No Attack	Limited	Failed	Advances	Penetrated	Envelopment
	I	II	III	IV	V	VI
Number of engagements	1	7	15	27	16	5
Attacker percentage casualties per day	0.03	0.86	5.56	0.90	0.71	1.47
Defender percentage casualties per day	0.45	1.21	5.85	3.63	8.80	34.60
Attacker percentage CIA per day	0.10	0.02	0.51	0.08	0	0.09
Defender percentage CIA per day	0.02	0.31	0.72	1.29	4.33	26.58
Attacker percentage losses that are CIA	100	6.17	19.06	10.90	0	4.33
Defender percentage losses that are CIA	4.49	24.61	9.65	33.46	47.96	79.95

Table 8.3. Battle of Kursk (49 Engagements)

	No Attack	Limited	Failed	Advances	Penetrated	Envelopment
	I	II	III	IV	V	VI
Number of engagements	8	13	9	12	4	3
Attacker percentage casualties per day	0.27	0.77	3.04	1.86	0.91	0.75
Defender percentage casualties per day	0.17	0.58	1.04	4.27	7.59	38.32
Attacker percentage CIA per day	0.04	0.05	0.10	0.09	0	0.01
Defender percentage CIA per day	0.04	0.20	0.06	0.83	2.86	36.85
Attacker percentage losses that are CIA	7.23	11.38	4.17	4.25	0.47	0.93
Defender percentage losses that are CIA	30.32	23.83	6.62	25.21	36.54	79.28

Table 8.4. Battle of Kursk (Germans Attacking)

	No Attack	Limited	Failed	Advances	Penetrated	Envelopment
	I	II	III	IV	V	VI
Number of engagements	7	7	1	9	4	3
Attacker percentage casualties per day	0.16	0.73	0.83	1.30	0.91	0.75
Defender percentage casualties per day	0.13	0.84	1.74	5.35	7.59	38.32
Attacker percentage CIA per day	0	0	0.01	0.01	0	0.01
Defender percentage CIA per day	0.04	0.37	0.24	1.09	2.86	36.85
Attacker percentage losses that are CIA	3.50	1.09	0.79	1.52	0.47	0.93
Defender percentage losses that are CIA	34.00	42.22	13.64	30.95	36.54	79.28

Table 8.5. Battle of Kursk (Soviets Attacking)

	No Attack	Limited	Failed	Advances	Penetrated	Envelopment
	I	II	III	IV	V	VI
Number of engagements	1	6	8	3	0	0
Attacker percentage casualties per day	1.01	0.81	3.32	3.54	—	—
Defender percentage casualties per day	0.40	0.28	0.95	1.03	—	—
Attacker percentage CIA per day	0.34	0.10	0.12	0.31	—	—
Defender percentage CIA per day	0.02	0.01	0.04	0.06	—	—
Attacker percentage losses that are CIA	33.33	23.38	4.60	12.45	—	—
Defender percentage losses that are CIA	4.55	2.37	5.74	8.00	—	—

Table 8.6. Summation (195 Engagements)

	No Attack	Limited	Failed	Advances	Penetrated	Envelopment
	I	II	III	IV	V	VI
Number of engagements	9	20	54	71	33	8
Attacker percentage casualties per day	0.24	0.80	2.98	1.20	0.83	1.20
Defender percentage casualties per day	0.20	0.80	2.62	2.96	6.40	36.00
Attacker percentage CIA per day	0.05	0.04	0.43	0.11	0.02	0.06
Defender percentage CIA per day	0.04	0.24	0.34	0.92	2.98	30.43
Attacker percentage losses that are CIA	17.54	9.56	16.21	10.22	2.67	3.06
Defender percentage losses that are CIA	27.45	24.10	12.98	35.85	47.20	79.70

The Italian Campaign engagements data show a consistent pattern. As the outcome becomes more successful for the attacker, his casualties, measured as a percentage of strength per day, declines, while the defender's casualties increase. The average CIA, measured as a percentage of strength per day, decreases from effective parity in the "failed attack" results for both the attacker and defender to almost nothing as the attacker succeeds. In contrast, the defender's CIA rate increases as the attacker succeeds. The percentage of losses that are CIA also shows the same pattern. While this is not unexpected, it is convenient that it fits so well into the expected pattern.

The "limited action" and "limited attack" engagements are not present in the Italian Campaign data set, but the data from the Ardennes closely matches that from the Italian Campaign, with two major exceptions. The first is that the casualty rates for failed attacks are much higher, although the capture rates are similar. Part of this difference is caused by the smaller forces involved. Seven of the fourteen brigade-size engagements in the Ardennes data are failed attacks. These smaller engagements, which make up some 20 percent of the Ardennes engagements, constitute almost 50 percent of the failed attacks. The average attacker strength for the fifteen failed attacks is 9,845, compared to the database average of 15,024. The average defender strength for these engagements is 8,798, compared to the database average of 9,311. This is a case where the biased selection of the data influenced the results. But this is not the only reason for the difference, as the Italian "failed attack" data also have a number of small and low-odds attacks. The other main difference is that defender casualties are simply higher. For example, in the Italian data, the defender suffered losses of 1.90 percent in "attack advances" results, while in the Ardennes the defender lost 3.63 percent. For "defender penetrated" results, the difference is 3.08 percent versus 8.80 percent. The percentages of captures per day also differ accordingly. This difference, which is also reflected in the "failed attack" results, is caused by a mixture of the selection of engagements, more intense fighting, a larger number of small engagements, and the nature of the operations themselves.

The Kursk data show the same pattern, but again with higher casualty rates than in Italy. The casualty rates at Kursk tended to be closer to that of the Ardennes, but some of this is driven by the high loss rates for the Soviets. The one figure that is different for Kursk is the defender's casualties per day for "failed attack." This is almost entirely due to most of the failed attacks being Soviet attacks against German positions, resulting in fairly high losses for the attacker and low losses for the defender. When separated into German attacks and Soviet attacks, the data show very different results (provided in tables 8.4 and 8.5). Unfortunately we probably need to analyze about one hundred Kursk engagements to firmly establish these points.[3] But the German attack figures seem to be in line with the Italian and Ardennes data: the defender's losses are high. A very different pattern is evident in the Soviet attacks. While measuring the statistical significance of this small number of cases (maximum of nine in any category) may be academic, the contrasting and consistent patterns tend to make a very strong case.

Table 8.6 shows the summation of all 195 points of data into one table. As different as these three operations were, when the engagements are divided into outcomes, the results are surprisingly similar. The mix of different campaigns, different size units, and different nations muddies the results a little, but the sheer number of cases helps establish a very clear and consistent pattern.

While the purpose of the CAA study was to determine enemy prisoner-of-war capture rates, the real value for the general reader is in the top three lines of table 8.6, where it is obvious that outcome determined loss rates in World War II division-level combat.

Research on combat after World War II suffers from a number of problems. First, the sources are often poor. We are lucky if we have primary source data from one side. Often we lack access to such data, or the data are not publicly available. Second, there is a limited number of conventional war examples to draw from, especially those with data. For example, we have yet to see a comprehensive and reliable quantitative discussion of the eight-year war between Iran and Iraq in 1980–88.[4] This was the largest conventional war in recent times.

We ended up assembling a database of sixty-one post–World War II engagements. This included six engagements from the 1956 Suez War, the Battle at Kerama in 1968 from the War of Attrition (1967–73), and twenty-seven engagements from the Ramadan or Yom Kipper War of 1973, for a total of thirty-four engagements from the Arab-Israeli wars. We also had seven engagements from the Falkland Islands War of 1982 and twenty engagements from the 1991 Persian Gulf War, for a grand total of sixty-one post–World War II engagements. As these took place mostly around three to five decades after World War II, it is worth comparing them to World War II data to see what remains the same and what has changed. To that end the data were laid out in the same format.

Table 8.7. Post–World War II (61 Engagements)

	No Attack	Limited	Failed	Advances	Penetrated	Envelopment
	I	II	III	IV	V	VI
Number of engagements	0	1	14	8	33	5
Attacker percentage casualties per day	—	0.26	3.20	1.60	1.36	2.54
Defender percentage casualties per day	—	0.12	2.80	4.83	15.10	49.48
Attacker percentage CIA per day	—	0.01	1.28	—	—	—
Defender percentage CIA per day	—	0.01	0.46	1.01	9.85	39.86
Attacker percentage casualties that are CIA	—	4.29	29.83	—	—	—
Defender percentage casualties that are CIA	—	10.82	9.83	23.34	60.61	87.10

The results, seen in table 8.7, are clearly far more similar to than different from the World War II data. The World War II data on 195 engagements is based mostly on primary sources (the unit records). The post–World War data on 61 engagements comes mostly from secondary sources and mostly where unit records still cannot be accessed.

But the post–World War II data suffer from there being no evenly matched forces facing each other. Just as there was a difference between the Germans and the Soviets, so too was there a difference between the Arabs and Israelis, between the British and the Argentine armies, and between the Americans and the Iraqis. For example, table 8.8 presents a simple comparison of the Germans attacking the Soviets and the Israelis attacking the Arabs.

Table 8.8. Germans vs. Soviets Compared to Israelis vs. Arabs

	No Attack	Limited	Failed	Advances	Penetrated	Envelopment
	I	II	III	IV	V	VI
No. of German-Soviet engagements	7	7	1	9	4	3
No. of Arab-Israeli engagements	—	—	4	3	7	1
ATTACKER PERCENTAGE CASUALTIES PER DAY						
German	0.16	0.73	0.83	1.30	0.91	0.75
Israeli	—	—	2.88	2.98	1.82	0.43
DEFENDER PERCENTAGE CASUALTIES PER DAY						
Soviet	0.13	0.84	1.74	5.35	7.59	38.32
Arab	—	—	2.73	4.03	7.37	50.00
	No Attack	Limited	Failed	Success	Penetrated	Envelopment
	I	II	III	IV	V	VI
No. of German-Soviet engagements	1	6	8	3	—	—
No. of Arab-Israeli engagements	—	1	6	2	3	1
ATTACKER PERCENTAGE CASUALTIES PER DAY						
Soviet	1.01	0.81	3.32	3.54	—	—
Arab	—	0.26	2.66	0.24	0.87	10.00
DEFENDER PERCENTAGE CASUALTIES PER DAY						
German	0.40	0.28	0.95	1.03	—	—
Israeli	—	0.12	1.03	2.08	4.34	80.00

The patterns for both mismatched forces are the same, even if the Arab-Israeli fights provide higher loss percentages. These higher loss percentages are almost entirely driven by the unit sizes in the different databases: the Arab-Israeli engagements contained a lot of brigade-size engagements, while all the Kursk engagements were division-size or even larger.

There are three outliers in these data. All are smaller brigade- or battalion-size engagements. They include an Israeli low-odds attack that failed (Mt. Hermon II, 500 attacking 1,000), an Israeli attack that penetrated (Mt. Hermon III, 2,500 attacking 1,000), and a successful encirclement by the Syrians (Syrian Assault on Mt. Hermon, 500 attacking 55). The statistics change somewhat if these three Mt. Hermon engagements are left out of the data.

Overall the results were not significantly changed by removal of the outliers, except for the percentage of casualties per day. Comparing the Soviet-German and the Arab-Israeli data still shows some differences. First, the casualty rates for the Arab-Israeli data tend to be higher when the Israelis are the attacker. This is in line with the smaller unit sizes in these engagements. The casualty rate for the Arabs when they attack tends to be lower. This supports the hypothesis that the Arab armies tended to be less stubborn when attacking, as analyzed in other parts of our work.[5] Still, the percentage of Arab casualties who surrender is lower than that of the Soviet casualties who surrender. While there are some very clear differences between these two armies, they are roughly comparable in performance. All the data are combined in tables 8.9 and 8.10.

Table 8.9. Germans/Israelis Attacking (46 Cases)

	No Attack	Limited	Failed	Advances	Penetrated	Envelopment
	I	II	III	IV	V	VI
Number of engagements	7	7	5	12	11	4
Attacker percentage casualties per day	0.16	0.73	2.47	1.72	1.49	0.66
Defender percentage casualties per day	0.13	0.84	2.53	5.02	7.45	41.24
Attacker percentage CIA per day	0.00	0.00	0.08	0.01	0.00	0.01
Defender percentage CIA per day	0.04	0.37	0.69	0.92	1.66	39.10
Attacker percentage casualties that are CIA	3.50	1.09	2.35	1.14	0.17	0.70
Defender percentage casualties that are CIA	34.00	42.22	12.50	25.93	22.85	82.38

Table 8.10. Soviets/Arabs Attacking (31 Cases)

	No Attack	Limited	Failed	Advances	Penetrated	Envelopment
	I	II	III	IV	V	VI
Number of engagements	1	7	14	5	3	1
Attacker percentage casualties per day	1.01	0.73	3.04	2.22	0.87	10.00
Defender percentage casualties per day	0.40	0.26	0.98	1.45	4.34	80.00
Attacker percentage CIA per day	0.34	0.09	11.00	0.19	0.00	0.00
Defender percentage CIA per day	0.02	0.01	0.03	0.08	0.70	36.36
Attacker percentage casualties that are CIA	33.33	20.65	3.97	7.47	0.00	0.00
Defender percentage casualties that are CIA	4.55	3.58	3.43	6.70	14.59	45.45

Note that we have lumped together data from a period scanning thirty years. There does not seem to be a strong argument against doing so (which is a significant finding into and of itself).

While the rest of our work on this project was oriented toward estimating capture rates, which is not of interest to most readers, the tables presented in this chapter were very helpful in establishing expected loss rates dependent on outcome. Keep in mind that these are division loss rates, so a 1 percent loss rate across a force of 15,000 men represents 150 killed, wounded, or missing. This becomes pretty significant, especially if you are anywhere near or among those 150 men.

These outcome tables establish several points. First, loss rates are tied to outcome. The percentage of loss rates for both sides tends to be about the same for outcomes I through III. The highest loss rate for an attacker is a failed attack (outcome III). Starting with a successful attack (outcome IV), the percentage of loss rate favors the attacker, and continues to decline for the attacker through penetration (outcome V) and envelopment (outcome VI). The opposite is true for the defender, for whom the rate gets worse in each category.

Basically, if the attack fails, the attacker will lose more than the defender. Even though the percentage of loss is the same, the attacker usually outnumbers the defender, often resulting in absolute losses being twice or more than that of the defender. If the attack succeeds, the two sides tend to suffer about the same absolute losses. These tables show that the attacker had a lower loss percentage than the defender, but as the attacker usually outnumbered the defender, the actual losses between the opposing forces were similar. If the defender is penetrated or enveloped, he will usually lose more than the attacker.

These patterns remain the same even when forces are mismatched in capability. This is important to note, as it further reinforces the idea that losses are a result of outcome rather than force ratios or combat effectiveness. That said, higher force ratios and combat effectiveness also lead to more successful outcomes, so these three issues become interrelated. But clearly the relationship is more complex than simple cause and effect (i.e., higher force ratio = higher casualties for the defender).

The second major point, one I will revisit, is that statistically the patterns of modern combat are not radically different from those in World War II. Even with modern and more lethal weapons, the pattern of losses and the relationships between losses, force ratios, outcomes, posture, and human factors remain relatively similar from 1943 to 1973. In that thirty-year period military technology and the art of war certainly improved rapidly. In 1943 many of the infantry units were still using horse-drawn artillery! The armies fighting in 1973 tended to be vastly more mechanized. One could argue that the differences between the armies of 1943 and 1973 were greater than they were between 1973 and 2013. We have not tested this last point, but if the patterns between 1943 and 1973 remained relatively constant amid all the technology changes, then one should not expect to see a radical change between 1973 and 2013 unless there has been some kind of "revolution in military affairs." That last phrase, abbreviated RMA, was a popular topic of discussion inside the Pentagon until the United States got tangled up simultaneously in guerrilla wars in Iraq and Afghanistan. The RMA advocates are no longer beating their drums as loudly as they used to. We have data up to 1991 for division-level combat and up to 2001 for company-level combat, and we have yet to see anything in modern combat that obviates the results we obtained from these earlier historical data.

9. Exchange Ratios

> There is no direct relationship between force ratios and casualty rates.
>
> —TREVOR N. DUPUY, *Understanding War*

As part of the *Casualty Estimation Methodologies Study* the Dupuy Institute looked at comparing force ratios to casualty exchange ratios.[1] Ever since combat models were first created, analysts have tried to directly connect force ratios to exchanges of losses, usually with defenders' losses increasing as the force ratio increases. Therefore this methodology needed to be addressed.

For these tests we used a further development of the 605-case Land Warfare Data Base (LWDB). Instead of having one big database of over 600 battles that took place between 1600 and 1973, from very small engagements to massive World War I engagements that lasted for six months and included hundreds of thousands of men, we decided to break the database into component parts based on the period of the battle (pre- or post-1904), the size of the battle (whether a small action, a battalion-level operation, a division-level engagement, or a larger action), and the duration (whether a few days or operations lasting weeks). We thus broke the older LWDB into seven different databases. These seven databases, along with some others, make up our DuWar suite of databases. We then added to each database and further expanded it. The exception was our Battles Data Base (BaDB) of 243 cases, which covered 1600–1900 and remained the same as the earlier part of the original LWDB. All the post-1900 databases were expanded considerably.

For our analysis, we used two databases, the BaDB of 243 cases and the new Division-Level Engagement Data Base (DLEDB) of 675 division-level engagements from 1904 to 1991. About half the engagements in this database were from the original LWDB, and the other half were new division-level engagements that we added, primarily from Kharkov in 1943, Kursk in 1943, the Ardennes Campaign in 1944–45, and the Gulf War in 1991. Many of the older LWDB engagements were also revisited, checked, and corrected, in particular the British engagements from Italy in 1943–44, which were originally based on secondary sources. These were revised based on our research into unit records from the British Public Records Office (PRO). The new engagements were created almost exclusively from primary sources (unit records), so the database was now a more precise analytical tool. This gave us a strong, well-developed, con-

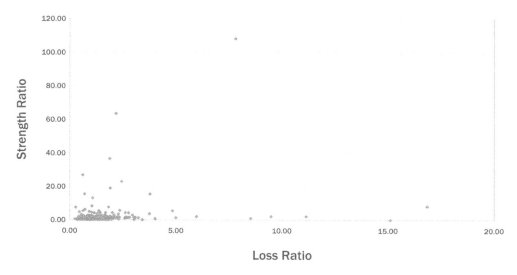

Fig. 9.1. Strength ratio vs. loss ratio. Source: Dupuy Institute, Battles Data Base.

sistently defined database for analysis, the best developed database for analysis of combat that we are aware of.

Comparing Force Ratios to Casualty Exchange Ratios

There are three versions of force ratio versus casualty exchange ratio rules, such as the 3 to 1 rule as it applies to casualties. The earliest version of the rule as it relates to casualties that we have been able to find appears in the 1958 edition of the U.S. Army *Maneuver Control* manual, which states, "When opposing forces are in contact, casualties are assessed in inverse ratio to combat power.

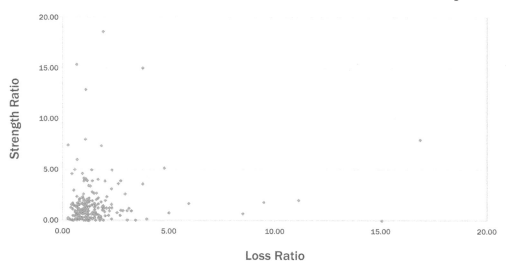

Fig. 9.2. Strength ratio vs. loss ratio (maximum 20 to 1).
Source: Dupuy Institute, Battles Data Base.

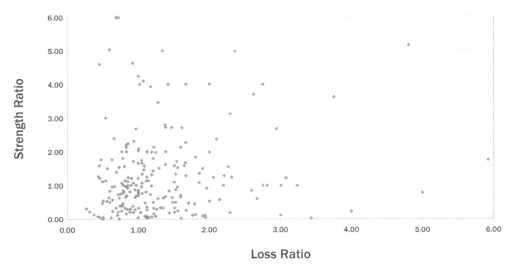

Fig. 9.3. Strength ratio vs. loss ratio (maximum 6 to 1).
Source: Dupuy Institute, Battles Data Base.

For friendly forces advancing with a combat power superiority of 5 to 1, losses
to friendly forces will be about 1/5 of those suffered by the opposing force."[2]

RAND also has a version (1992) of "the famous '3:1 rule,' according to which
the attacker and defender suffer equal fractional loss rates at a 3:1 force ratio
if the battle is in mixed terrain and the defender enjoys 'prepared' defenses."[3]

Finally there is a version of the rule that dates from the 1967 *Maneuver Control* manual that only applies to armor (see table 9.1).

Table 9.1. 3 to 1 Rule (*Maneuver Control*)

Combat Ratio		Tank Losses (per platoon of 5 tanks) per hour	
ATTACKER	DEFENDER	ATTACKER	DEFENDER
1	1	2	1
2	1	2	1
3	1	1	1
4	1	1	2
5	1	1	3

As the RAND construct also applies to equipment losses, this formulation is
directly comparable to the RAND construct.

Therefore we have three contradictory versions of the 3 to 1 rule as it applies
to casualties and/or equipment losses. One version states that there are even
fractional loss rates at 3 to 1 (the RAND version), a second version states that at 3
to 1, the attacker will suffer one-third the losses of the defender, and a third version states that at 3 to 1, the attacker will suffer the same losses as the defender.

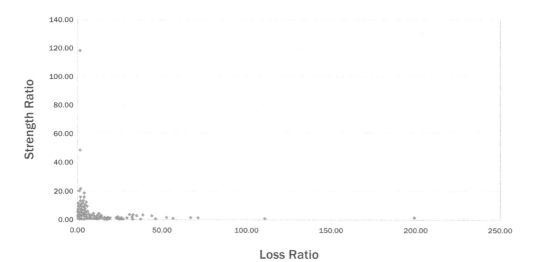

Fig. 9.4. Strength ratio vs. loss ratio. Source: Dupuy Institute, Division-Level Engagement Data Base.

In this chapter I will examine the relationship between force ratios and exchange ratios. First we will first look at the Dupuy Institute's BADB, which covers 243 battles from 1600 to 1900. I will chart on the y-axis the force ratio (called "strength ratio" in the figure) as measured by the number of people on each side of the forces deployed for battle. The force ratio is the number of attackers divided by the number of defenders. On the x-axis is the exchange ratio (or "loss ratio" in the terminology of the figure), which is the number of people on each side who were killed, wounded, missing, or captured during that battle. It does not include disease and other nonbattle injuries. Again, it is calculated by dividing the total attacker casualties by the total defender casualties. The results are provided in figure 9.1.

As is clear, there are a few extreme outliers among these 243 data points. The most extreme is the Battle of Tippermuir (1 September 1644), in which an English Royalist force under Montrose routed an attack by Scottish Covenanter militia, causing about 3,000 casualties to the Scots in exchange for a single (allegedly self-inflicted) casualty to the Royalists.[4] Because this 3,000 to 1 loss ratio was deemed too great an outlier to be of value in the analysis, it was removed from the chart.

As it is, the vast majority of cases are clumped into a corner of the graph, with only a few scattered data points outside. If one did try to establish some form of curvilinear relationship, one would end up drawing a hyperbola. It is worthwhile to look inside that clump of data to see what it shows. Therefore, figure 9.2 offers a truncated version of the graph showing only force ratios (strength ratios) at or below 20 to 1 and exchange ratios (loss ratios) at or below 20 to 1.

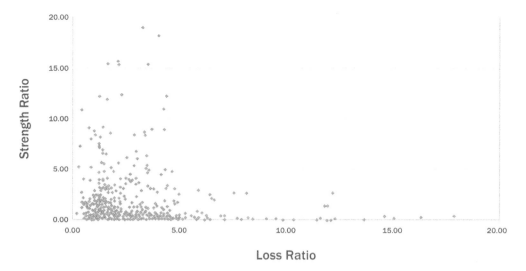

Fig. 9.5. Strength ratio vs. loss ratio (maximum 20 to 1). Source: Dupuy Institute, Division-Level Engagement Data Base.

Again the data remain clustered in one corner, and the outlying data point to a hyperbola as the only fitting curvilinear relationship. Figure 9.3 looks a little deeper by truncating the force ratios and exchange ratios at 6 to 1.

If the RAND version of the 3 to 1 rule is correct, then the data should show a 3 to 1 force ratio and a 3 to 1 casualty exchange ratio. However, there is only one data point that comes close to this out of the 243 points we examined!

If the U.S. Army's 1967 version of the rule as it applies to armor is correct, then the data should show that at a 3 to 1 force ratio there is a 1 to 1 casualty exchange

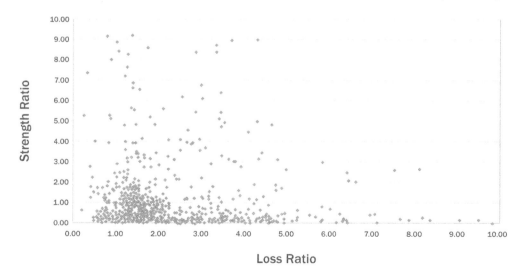

Fig. 9.6. Strength ratio vs. loss ratio (maximum 10 to 1). Source: Dupuy Institute, Division-Level Engagement Data Base.

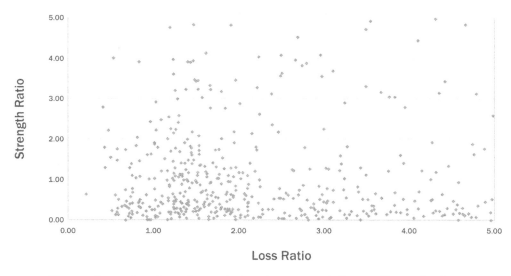

Fig. 9.7. Strength ratio vs. loss ratio (maximum 5 to 1). Source: Dupuy Institute, Division-Level Engagement Data Base.

ratio; at a 4 to 1 force ratio a 1 to 2 casualty exchange ratio; and at a 5 to 1 force ratio a 1 to 3 casualty exchange ratio. Of course there is no armor in these pre–World War I engagements, but in any case no such exchange pattern appears.

If the U.S. Army's 1958 version of the rule as it applies to casualties is correct, the data should show that at a 3 to 1 force ratio there is a 0.33 to 1 casualty exchange ratio; at a 4 to 1 force ratio a 0.25 to 1 casualty exchange ratio; and at a 5 to 1 force ratio a 0.20 to 5 casualty exchange ratio. There is not much indication of this pattern either.

Still, such a construct may not be relevant to data before 1900. For example, F. W. Lanchester claimed in in his 1914 book *Aircraft in Warfare* that greater advantage is to be gained in modern warfare from concentration of fire.[5] Therefore I will tap the more modern DLEDB of 675 engagements, of which 628 had force ratios and exchange ratios calculated.[6] Figure 9.4 shows these 628 cases on a scattergram, which enables us to detect any similar patterns.

Even though these data cover the period 1904–91, with the vast majority from engagements after 1940, the same pattern appears as in the data from 1600–1900. If there is a curvilinear relationship, it is again a hyperbola. As before, it is useful to look into the mass of data clustered into the corner by truncating the force and exchange ratios at 20 to 1. This produces the scattergram in figure 9.5.

Again the data are clustered in the corner and the curvilinear relationship is a hyperbola. A look at the data further truncated to a 10 to 1 force or exchange ratio does not yield anything more revealing (fig. 9.6).

Truncating these data to show only 5 to 1 force and exchange ratios produces the scattergram in figure 9.7.

Once again the data appear to be mostly just noise, with no clear patterns supporting any of the three constructs. In the case of the RAND version of the 3 to 1 rule, there is again only one data point (out of 628) that is anywhere close to the crossover point (even a fractional exchange rate) that RAND postulates. In fact it almost looks like the data conspire to leave a noticeable hole at that point. The other two postulated versions of the 3 to 1 rule are also given no support in these charts.

Also of note, the relationship between force ratios and exchange ratios does not appear to significantly change for combat during 1600–1900 when compared to the data from combat from 1904–91, an almost four-hundred-year span of data. This does not provide much support for any intellectual construct developed from Lanchester to argue for his N-square law.

While we can attempt to torture the data to find a better fit or argue that the patterns are obscured by various factors that have not been considered, I do not believe such a clear pattern and relationship exist. More advanced mathematical methods may show such a pattern, but to date such attempts have not been successful. For example, see Janice Fain's article on the Lanchester equations, the Dupuy Institute's *Capture Rate Study, Phases I & II*, or any number of other studies that have looked at Lanchester.[7]

The fundamental problem is that a direct cause-and-effect relationship between force ratios and exchange ratios does not appear to exist. Instead there is an indirect relationship in the sense that force ratios are one of several independent variables that determine the outcome of an engagement, and the nature of that outcome helps determine the number of casualties. As such, there is a more complex set of interrelationships that have not yet been fully explored in any study that we know of, although it is briefly addressed in the Dupuy Institute's *Capture Rate Study, Phases I & II*.

10. The Combat Value of Superior Situational Awareness

> The Army doctrine of force multipliers is based upon a simple mathematical concept, but it is mathematics without numbers or scale. The doctrine does not define, list, or quantify these multipliers, and it does not suggest the quantity or value of the multiplicand, nor the size or the nature of the product.
>
> —TREVOR N. DUPUY, *Understanding War*

Situational awareness is not a new concept; it has existed since ancient times when generals took vantage points on hills and surveyed the battlefield. In many cases, from this height, given the small forces arrayed before them, these generals effectively had complete situational awareness. Since battles were first recorded in detail, beginning around 1274 BC with the Battle of Kadesh, complete situational awareness has been a documented factor in warfare. In the almost 3,200-year period between 1274 BC to around 1904, one can regularly find situations in which one or even both sides of a battle have complete situational awareness.[1]

Over time, as the forces a general deployed became larger and more dispersed, it became harder to view them all across the width and depth of the battlefield. Terrain, weather, and smoke could interfere with observation. Still, there were numerous battles in the Crimean War (1853–56), the U.S. Civil War (1861–65), and the Franco-Prussian War (1870–71) where complete, or at least close to complete, situational awareness existed, even if the means for command and control of those armies were less than perfect.

The development of large armies and continuous fronts created the modern "fog of war" problem. The continuous front was foreshadowed by the extended siege lines of 53 miles at Petersburg in the U.S. Civil War and in the 68-mile-long lines during the Russo-Japanese War of 1904–5. By World War I (1914–18) the continuous front had become the rule of modern warfare, and complete situational awareness had essentially disappeared. Not only was it impossible to have a vantage point to see the entire battlefield, but all armies made extensive use of cover and concealment in an attempt to minimize casualties and gain advantage. Even the tradition of wearing brightly colored uniforms, which allowed for visual identification of your own and enemy units, had disappeared. It was now difficult for a general to tell what he might be facing, who he was facing, and how many enemies there were. Even knowing the status of friendly units was more difficult as the general's command post was now well to the rear so as to be safe from artillery fire.

It is at this time that we see extraordinary attempts to restore the bird's-eye view of the battlefield. In World War I the battlefield sprouted observation balloons across the entire front, while an invention hardly a decade old, the airplane, regularly flew overhead. There was even extensive aerial photography of the World War I battlefield. A lack of situational awareness was a major problem, and considerable resources were spent to get information on the enemy. To date this situation has not been corrected, although the development of existing and new technologies potentially offers the United States the opportunity to return to a situation where complete situational awareness can again exist.

Despite its importance, to our knowledge no extensive historical analysis of situational awareness has been done. Unfortunately, history does not always support such analysis. For one thing, to be able to measure the effects of such awareness one needs accurate data on the strengths and losses of both sides, data that do not systematically exist for both sides until the advent of professional armies in modern warfare. Effectively data do not exist until after 1700 AD, and even those data are mostly for European and American wars. Still, this is a fertile area of research and could lead to a useful understanding of the advantages of complete situational awareness.

Most people conceive of modern warfare as employing tanks, planes, and indirect artillery fire, yet these elements do not regularly appear in combat until 1917. Unfortunately, that is also the period when complete situational awareness effectively disappeared from the battlefield, although a total lack of situational awareness almost never exists. While the modern period is a very productive area of research, unfortunately records for both sides become inaccessible in all but a few cases after 1945 (at the end of World War II). The need for accurate two-sided data limits analysis of situational awareness to World War I and World War II engagements. World War II, being the more modern of the two, is usually the preferred choice (unless one needs to examine the effects of chemical warfare).

At the Dupuy Institute we assembled a large number of real-world engagements from World War II for which we had reasonably good data for both sides. We then coded each engagement as to the degree of situational awareness for each side. There are few cases of complete situational awareness and there are also few cases of effectively no situational awareness. Most cases in the real world seem to fall between these two extremes. The degree of situational awareness in each of these cases was determined by analyst judgment based on an examination of the unit records of both sides, including their intelligence reports on the enemy. These were coded as "considerable," "some," and "little," which along with "complete" and "none" give us five levels of situational awareness. We then compared the level of situational awareness to the results of the battles. We examined the casualties received, casualties inflicted, casualty exchange ratios, outcomes, distance advanced, and whether or not surprise was achieved.

Finally, using situational awareness as the independent variable (cause) and the other factors as dependent variables (effect), we hoped to get simple quantitative measurements of the effect of superior situational awareness on each of these factors.

We developed a database of 295 engagements from existing and new research. The data used consisted of 149 division-level engagements from the Western Front and 146 division-level engagements from the Eastern Front.[2] The database contained quantitative descriptions of the casualties and advance rates and a determination of outcome.

We then needed to develop some means to measure situational awareness. Any complex quantifiable methodology was rejected, as it was simply not going to be consistently supported by the unit records in existence. Instead we decided to use a simple descriptive code. (A detailed definition of each category in this code is provided at the end of this chapter.) This coding was done for each side in each engagement and was primarily based on an examination of the intelligence reports for both sides, along with an examination of the opposing battle narratives. Although we created a set of rules for coding situational awareness, ultimately the actual application of the code was left to the judgment of the analyst. The five choices, as mentioned above, were (1) complete, (2) considerable, (3) some, (4) little, and (5) none. We expected that instances of situational awareness in which one side's knowledge was "complete" or "none" would be rare. We further expected that there would essentially be only three choices for each side in each engagement.

These three codes create nine permutations of situational awareness. In total there are twenty-five permutations if one considers "complete" and "none," but there were only four cases where "complete" situational awareness was coded and only two where "none" was coded (although in a number of other cases, knowledge of the enemy was pretty sparse). In table 10.1 "complete" situational awareness is included with "considerable," and "none" is included with "little."

Table 10.1. Combinations of Situational Awareness

Attacker	Defender	Number of Cases
Considerable	Considerable	81
Considerable	Some	21
Considerable	Little	22
Some	Considerable	24
Some	Some	66
Some	Little	27
Little	Considerable	4
Little	Some	13
Little	Little	37

One concern with any system that relies on the judgment of the analyst is the consistency of that judgment. Obviously judgment will vary from individual to individual, but it is hoped that with experienced personnel such variation will be minimal. The personnel used for this work were certainly the most experienced available; both analysts have worked with versions of this database since 1987. Richard C. Anderson coded all the Italian Campaign and other Western Front engagements, and I coded all the Eastern Front engagements. A comparison of the coding is presented in tables 10.2 and 10.3.

Table 10.2. Western Front Engagements (149 Cases)

Attacker	Defender	Number of Cases
Considerable	Considerable	68
Considerable	Some	11
Considerable	Little	2
Some	Considerable	23
Some	Some	32
Some	Little	3
Little	Considerable	4
Little	Some	1
Little	Little	5

Table 10.3. Eastern Front Engagements (146 Cases)

Attacker	Defender	Number of Cases
Considerable	Considerable	13
Considerable	Some	10
Considerable	Little	20
Some	Considerable	1

Some	Some	34
Some	Little	24
Little	Considerable	—
Little	Some	12
Little	Little	32

There are both striking similarities and striking differences here. The first major difference is that the Western Front engagements tend to have many more cases of "considerable" information for both sides and far fewer cases of "little" information. Out of 298 cases (counting both sides), there were 176 cases (59 percent) where one side had "considerable" information regarding the other side, 102 cases (34 percent) where they had "some" information regarding the other side, and 20 cases (7 percent) where they had "little" information regarding the other side.

In the case of the Eastern Front engagements, the relationship is very different. Out of 292 cases (counting both sides), there were 58 cases (20 percent) where one side had "considerable" information regarding the other side, 114 cases (39 percent) where they had "some" information regarding the other side, and 120 cases (41 percent) where they had "little" information regarding the other side.

The Eastern Front engagements were from four very different sets of operations. All the engagements from the Battle of Kursk started as a set-piece operation and developed from there in a fairly linear fashion. The three different sets of Kharkov engagements occurred in the middle of a mobile operation centered on Kharkov that was already in progress. At that stage operations were fairly confused for both sides, and then developed from there. Therefore it is useful to look at the mix and coding of the engagements from these different operations (tables 10.4 and 10.5).

Table 10.4. Kursk Engagements (91 Cases)

Attacker	Defender	Number of Cases
Considerable	Considerable	13
Considerable	Some	9
Considerable	Little	20
Some	Considerable	1
Some	Some	19
Some	Little	12
Little	Considerable	—
Little	Some	5
Little	Little	12

Table 10.5. Kharkov Engagements (55 Cases)

Attacker	Defender	Number of Cases
Considerable	Considerable	—
Considerable	Some	2
Considerable	Little	—
Some	Considerable	—
Some	Some	14
Some	Little	12
Little	Considerable	—
Little	Some	7
Little	Little	20

We probably want to compare the more set-piece Kursk engagements with the set-piece Italian Campaign engagements. For the Kursk engagements, out of 182 cases (counting both sides), there were 56 cases (31 percent) where one side had "considerable" information about the other side, 65 cases (36 percent) where they had "some" information about the other side, and 61 cases (34 percent) where they had "little" information.

There is no similar noticeable division found in the Western Front engagements, although engagements before the Italian Campaign tend to display low situational awareness. In part this is probably because those particular engagements were cherry-picked to make sure we had more cases where situational awareness was crucial to the outcome. Looking just at the Italian Campaign engagements results in the numbers in table 10.6.

Table 10.6. Italian Campaign Engagements (137 Cases)

Attacker	Defender	Number of Cases
Considerable	Considerable	66
Considerable	Some	10
Considerable	Little	1
Some	Considerable	23
Some	Some	30
Some	Little	1
Little	Considerable	2
Little	Some	—
Little	Little	4

Even when comparing the more set-piece Italian Campaign engagements with the more set-piece Battle of Kursk engagements, there is clearly a higher percentage of cases recorded as "considerable" (57 percent compared to 31 percent) than cases recorded as "little" information (4 percent compared to 34 percent). We are left to determine whether this is caused by differences between the two operations or differences between the two analysts.

There are probably a number of reasons the Italian Campaign has many more cases of "considerable" and far fewer cases of "little" information. First, the Allies committed just seventeen divisions to Italy in the first months of fighting.[3] There were only limited changes in the order of battle through June 1944. As a result the number of formations the Germans had to keep track of was well defined and limited. By the same token, the number of defending formations in 1943 was essentially only eleven divisions.[4]

While the southern portion of the Battle of Kursk had a similar number of attacking divisions (seventeen), the Germans had held back their nine armored divisions from the offensive until the day before the attack began. This left the Soviets in considerable doubt as to who was located where until the day of engagement. Then a quick German breakthrough of the first two Soviet defensive lines and a subsequent chaotic feeding of forces by the Soviets into the battle created a confused melee that left neither side with a clear picture of exactly where the forces of the enemy were. The Soviets would eventually commit some forty-seven division-size formations to the battle. Thus the sheer number of Soviet units in the battle often left the Germans not knowing the location of one or more of their division-size opponents.

Second, the Italian Campaign was a series of battles starting in September 1943 and continuing for months on end between basically the same opponents. Thus over time both sides developed a reasonable picture of each other's forces. This was reinforced by the extended periods of stalemate that characterized this campaign.

On the other hand, the Kursk offensive in the south was over in two weeks. The operation never reached a stable or static point except for a few days in some sectors. The German forces were withdrawn once the offensive had failed.

A third but less significant reason was that the front line of the Italian Campaign remained fairly restricted, no more than about 120 to 140 kilometers in width overall across the Italian peninsula. Furthermore the center of the line was very mountainous and therefore not under attack, and operations in the eastern part were limited. The active operations for the units in the database occurred in a narrow band stretching little more than 40 kilometers inland from the coast.

In contrast, the defensive front at Kursk for the three armies primarily engaged (40th, 6th Guards, and 7th Guards) covered some 164 kilometers, the majority of that area used for offensive operations. The frontage of the battlefield expanded as the fighting continued.

Nevertheless these two sets of set-piece battles are similar in attacker size (although not in defender size) and frontage. The main difference is that the Italian Campaign was a more defined and limited theater, and the forces were in contact with each other for a longer duration. This may provide most of the explanation for the difference. The engagements in the first fifteen days of the Italian Campaign (matching the time scale of the Battle of Kursk engagements) contain only fourteen cases (28 data points). Of those cases, 25 percent are coded "considerable" (versus 31 percent for Kursk), 54 percent are coded "some" (versus 36 percent for Kursk), and 21 percent are coded "little" (versus 34 percent for Kursk).

There is no clear way to determine or measure how much of this difference is caused by differences in analyst judgment. Discussions between the analysts regarding this subject did not result in any significant changes to the database or the feeling by the analysts that something was amiss with these findings. While one cannot rule out coding differences as a problem, the analysts had the sense that the differences in coding were a reasonable reflection of the differences in these two campaigns.

There are also some interesting similarities in the coding of situational awareness. First, the number of cases where both sides had a similar level of information about each other vastly exceeded the number of cases where there was a noticeable difference in knowledge. Table 10.7 summarizes this analysis.

Table 10.7. Cases of Different Levels of Knowledge

Knowledge	Western Front	Eastern Front	Total
Attacker much more knowledgeable	2	20	22
Attacker more knowledgeable	13	35	48
Same for both sides	106	78	184
Defender more knowledgeable	24	13	37
Defender much more knowledgeable	4	0	4

Table 10.8 converts it into percentages of the whole set of data.

Table 10.8. Percentage of Cases of Different Levels of Knowledge

Knowledge	Western Front	Eastern Front	Total
Attacker much more knowledgeable	1	14	7
Attacker more knowledgeable	9	24	16
Same for both sides	71	53	62
Defender more knowledgeable	16	9	13
Defender much more knowledgeable	3	0	1

These data take on the shape of a bell curve, with similar levels of situational awareness holding the dominant central point. In the end the attacker had a knowledge advantage only 23 percent of the time, while the defender had a knowledge advantage only 14 percent of the time. Note that these percentages are different and opposite for the Western Front compared to the Eastern Front. The Western Front defender was more knowledgeable than the Western Front attacker. On the other hand, the Eastern Front attacker was often more knowledgeable than the Eastern Front defender.

The differences between the shapes of the curves (the Eastern Front curve is flatter) is probably due to the more freewheeling and rough-and-tumble (mobile and improvised) nature of the Eastern Front operations that were examined, especially those around Kharkov. The defender being more knowledgeable more often than the attacker in the Italian Campaign engagements probably reflects in part the nature of the fighting and the terrain.

The Combat Value of an Information Advantage

Our analysis proceeded based on the assumption that our data were reasonably unbiased. Two separate but closely related subjects were analyzed: What is the combat value of an information advantage? What is the combat value of situational awareness? In the case of an information advantage, we attempted to measure the value of superior or inferior knowledge of the enemy. In the case of situational awareness, we attempted to measure the value of knowledge of one side's knowledge of the other. I will discuss information advantage in this section and situational awareness in the next section. These are simply two different ways of looking at the same phenomenon, but each requires a separate analysis.

For most of the cases in the database, the attacker and the defender have similar knowledge of each other. However, there are enough cases where one side had greater knowledge than the other for us to draw some comparisons. We looked at the effect of information advantage on mission accomplishment, casualty effectiveness, and spatial effectiveness. The database had 32 cases of surprise out of 295 total cases (10.85 percent). As surprise clearly changed the outcome of the battles, our analysis used only those cases where there was not surprise. Table 10.9 summarizes the data on surprise by category.

Table 10.9. Total Cases of Surprise

Knowledge	Cases	Surprise	Percentage
Attacker much more knowledgeable	22	5	22.73
Attacker more knowledgeable	48	7	14.58
Same for both sides	184	17	9.24
Defender more knowledgeable	37	1	2.70
Defender much more knowledgeable	4	—	—

Surprise is coded in the databases for each of these engagements. Again coding was based on analyst judgment. In the case of the Western Front engagements, some of the coding was done in the 1970s and 1980s by analysts with the Historical Evaluation and Research Organization and was based on their assessment of the battle.[5] For the rest of the Western Front and all the Eastern Front engagements, surprise was coded at the time the engagement was created, which was well before we did this situational awareness study or knew we were going to do such a study. As such, surprise was coded well before and completely independent of the coding for situational awareness. As one side achieving surprise often greatly unbalances the results of the battle, these cases were excluded from this analysis. Surprise is discussed in depth in chapter 11.

Mission Accomplishment

Mission accomplishment is measured by a determination of the winner or loser, the outcome (one of seven categories), or the mission accomplishment score. Table 10.10 presents a summary.

Table 10.10. Western Front: Information Advantage and Mission Accomplishment

	Attacker Much More Knowledgeable	Attacker More Knowledgeable	Same for Both Sides	Defender More Knowledgeable	Defender Much More Knowledgeable
Number of cases	22	48	184	37	4
Cases without surprise	17	41	165	36	4
Winner					
ATTACKER	8	25	81	17	0
DRAW	7	3	25	2	0
DEFENDER	2	13	59	17	4
Percentage of attacker wins	47	61	49	47	0
LESS DRAWS	80	66	58	50	0
OUTCOMES					
I Limited action	6	1	13	3	—
II Limited attack	—	2	26	4	—
III Failed attack	2	13	32	5	4
IV Attack advances	5	12	75	22	—
V Defender penetrated	4	12	16	1	—
VI Defender enveloped	1	1	1	—	—
VII Other	—	2	33	—	—
PERCENTAGE OF OUTCOMES					
IV, V, and VI	53	61	56	67	0
III	12	32	19	14	100
Ratio: IV, V, and VI vs. III	4.50 to 1	1.92 to 1	2.88 to 1	4.80 to 1	0 to 1
Scoring					
ATTACKER	5.65	5.63	5.52	5.20	2.50
DEFENDER	4.47	4.69	5.06	5.06	7.55
Ratio of attacker vs. defender score	1.26 to 1	1.20 to 1	1.09 to 1	1.03 to 1	0.33 to 1

There are three items in table 10.10 that should draw our attention. First is the percentage of attacker wins, less draws. The rate declines from 80 percent wins when the attacker is much more knowledgeable to 50 percent when the defender is more knowledgeable. Note that the mission accomplishment scoring the outcome, not surprisingly, follows the same pattern. Second, there are no attacker wins when the defender has much more knowledge.

Casualty Effectiveness

Casualty effectiveness is a more objective metric but one that we had trouble fitting in the various categories of information advantage. When we looked at the complete set of data, we were not left with a very clear pattern. There were some problems with the data in that over half of the high-loss cases were from the Soviet side in the fighting at Kursk, and there were several extremely high casualty cases also from the Soviet side. There was a noticeable difference in casualty effectiveness in the Eastern Front engagements between the Germans and the Soviets. Therefore the data needed to be separated into Western Front and Eastern Front engagements if we were going to get any significant results. Furthermore, because of the performance differences, we needed to separate the Eastern Front engagements into those with German attackers and those with Soviet attackers. Table 10.11 looks just at the Western Front.

Table 10.11. Western Front: Information Advantage and Casualty Effectiveness

	Attacker Much More Knowledgeable	Attacker More Knowledgeable	Same for Both Sides	Defender More Knowledgeable	Defender Much More Knowledgeable
Number of cases	22	48	184	37	4
Cases without surprise	17	41	165	36	4
Western Front	1	8	92	23	4
Average attacker strength	11,679	12,612	20,088	18,131	17,362
Average defender strength	16,047	12,350	10,893	8,504	16,962
Average attacker armor	52	63	77	73	107

Average defender armor	42	70	35	16	126
Average attacker casualties	122	614	257	166	711
Average defender casualties	323	973	261	79	85
Average attacker armor loss	0.00	18.63	2.32	3.48	22.25
Average defender armor loss	0.00	8.25	1.20	0.30	3.00
Average attacker percentage loss	0.52	1.43	0.59	0.41	6.46
Average defender percentage loss	1.01	2.67	1.06	0.41	0.46
Average attacker armor percentage loss	0.00	10.31	1.01	1.69	24.32
Average defender armor percentage loss	0.00	6.78	1.47	0.61	3.10

Table 10.11 shows a very clear pattern with the overall casualties, in that the exchange ratio favors the attacker when he knows more and favors the defender when he knows more. On the other hand, there is not a clear pattern with the armor losses, but this is not surprising and not unexpected. Armor losses tend to be far more variable than personnel losses and very situation-specific. Table 10.12 looks a little further into the casualty data.

Table 10.12. Western Front: Information Advantage and Casualty Exchange Ratio

	Casualty Exchange Ratio	Highest Attacker Losses	Highest Defender Losses
Attacker much more knowledgeable	0.34 to 1	122	323
Attacker more knowledgeable	0.63 to 1	1,612	1,639

Same for both sides	0.99 to 1	1,304	1,379
Defender more knowledgeable	2.09 to 1	759	290
Defender much more knowledgeable	8.34 to 1	1,251	217

This is a pretty noticeable and consistent pattern. Obviously, though, with three of the five bins of data having fewer than ten cases, one may question its significance. The question remains whether the German versus Soviet (Eastern Front) data follow the same pattern. Since there is a significant difference between Soviet and German performance, the engagements had to be further divided into "German attacker" and "Soviet attacker" (tables 10.13 and 10.14).

Table 10.13. Eastern Front: Information Advantage and Casualty Effectiveness (German Attacker)

	Attacker Much More Knowledgeable	Attacker More Knowledgeable	Same for Both Sides	Defender More Knowledgeable	Defender Much More Knowledgeable
Number of cases	22	48	184	37	4
Cases without surprise	17	41	165	36	4
Eastern Front	16	33	73	13	0
German attacker	16	19	51	11	—
Average attacker strength	24,649	20,187	21,752	22,794	—
Average defender strength	8,080	8,649	14,549	19,018	—
Average attacker armor	135	92	75	86	—
Average defender armor	14	59	51	112	—
Average attacker casualties	396	229	164	216	—
Average defender casualties	597	561	451	1,007	—

Average attacker armor loss	15.75	15.89	7.59	11.00	—
Average defender armor loss	6.56	16.00	9.22	22.45	—
Average attacker percentage of loss	1.59	1.04	0.71	0.76	—
Average defender percentage of loss	7.69	9.36	3.43	4.23	—
Average attacker armor percentage of loss	8.39	10.92	6.31	12.27	—
Average defender armor percentage of loss	8.67	9.51	10.93	12.94	—

Table 10.14. Eastern Front: Information Advantage and Casualty Exchange Ratio (German Attacker)

	Casualty Exchange Ratio	Highest Attacker Losses	Highest Defender Losses
Attacker much more knowledgeable	0.66 to 1	1,663	2,197
Attacker more knowledgeable	0.41 to 1	581	1,442
Same for both sides	0.36 to 1	695	2,412
Defender more knowledgeable	0.21 to 1	639	3,079
Defender much more knowledgeable	—	—	—

No clear conclusion could be drawn from these data, unless one accepts the probably illogical conclusion that less of an information advantage leads to a more favorable casualty ratio.

Tables 10.15 and 10.16 examine the cases when the Soviets were the attackers.

Table 10.15. Eastern Front: Information Advantage and Casualty Effectiveness (Soviet Attacker)

	Attacker Much More Knowledgeable	Attacker More Knowledgeable	Same for Both Sides	Defender More Knowledgeable	Defender Much More Knowledgeable
Number of cases	22	48	184	37	4
Cases without surprise	17	41	165	36	4
Eastern Front	16	33	73	13	0
Soviet attacker	0	14	22	2	—
Average attacker strength	—	29,469	18,509	14,793	—
Average defender strength	—	17,174	16,343	9,806	—
Average attacker armor	—	62	38	0	—
Average defender armor	—	51	41	10	—
Average attacker casualties	—	960	386	195	—
Average defender casualties	—	159	82	55	—
Average attacker armor loss	—	6.36	1.59	0	—
Average defender armor loss	—	6.07	2.00	0	—
Average attacker percentage loss	—	2.61	2.07	1.29	—
Average defender percentage loss	—	0.94	0.52	0.57	—
Average attacker armor percentage loss	—	6.86	3.10	0	—
Average defender armor percentage loss	—	6.83	2.64	0	—

Table 10.16. Eastern Front: Information Advantage and Casualty Exchange Ratio (Soviet Attacker)

	Casualty Exchange Ratio (Attacker vs. Defender)	Highest Attacker Losses	Highest Defender Losses
Attacker much more knowledgeable	—	—	—
Attacker more knowledgeable	6.03 to 1	4,431	313
Same for both sides	4.69 to 1	1,551	215
Defender more knowledgeable	3.55 to 1	266	55
Defender much more knowledgeable	—	—	—

Again these data point to the probably illogical conclusion that less of an information advantage leads to a more favorable casualty exchange ratio. The Eastern Front casualty effectiveness data do not support the argument that an information advantage helps in combat.

With a clear and expected pattern in the casualty exchange ratio in the Western Front engagements, and the reverse pattern in the Eastern Front engagements, one is forced to either draw conclusions about the differences in the value of information between the two fronts or accept that the data do not point to a clear conclusion. Therefore, we accept the finding that an information advantage does not lead to a more favorable casualty exchange ratio. Considering that our tests on achieving surprise (discussed in chapter 11) showed that it did not seem to have an effect on the casualty exchange ratio, it is not entirely surprising that having an information advantage also does not have a measurable effect on the casualty exchange ratio.

Spatial Effectiveness

Spatial effectiveness is measured as the advance rate in kilometers per day. Again we looked at the Western and Eastern Front engagements separately, with the Kharkov engagements in particular being heavily influenced by a series of sweeping maneuvers that had high rates of advance (tables 10.17–10.19).

Table 10.17. Western Front: Information Advantage and Spatial Effectiveness

	Attacker Much More Knowledgeable	Attacker More Knowledgeable	Same for Both Sides	Defender More Knowledgeable	Defender Much More Knowledgeable
Number of cases	22	48	184	37	4
Cases without surprise	17	41	165	36	4
Western Front	1	8	92	23	4
Average attacker strength	11,679	12,612	20,088	18,131	17,362
Average defender strength	16,047	12,350	10,893	8,504	16,962
Average attacker armor	52	63	77	73	107
Average defender armor	42	70	35	16	126
Average daily advance rate (in kilometers)	0.00	1.03	1.23	0.94	0.43

Table 10.18. Eastern Front: Information Advantage and Spatial Effectiveness (German Attacker)

	Attacker Much More Knowledgeable	Attacker More Knowledgeable	Same for Both Sides	Defender More Knowledgeable	Defender Much More Knowledgeable
Number of cases	22	48	184	37	4
Cases without surprise	17	41	165	36	4
Eastern Front	16	33	73	13	0
German attacker	16	19	51	11	0

Average attacker strength	24,649	20,187	21,752	22,794	—
Average defender strength	8,080	8,649	14,549	19,018	—
Average attacker armor	135	92	75	86	—
Average defender armor	14	59	51	112	—
Average daily advance rate (in kilometers)	3.36	8.61	4.79 4.65	—	—

Table 10.19. Eastern Front: Information Advantage and Spatial Effectiveness (Soviet Attacker)

	Attacker Much More Knowledgeable	Attacker More Knowledgeable	Same for Both Sides	Defender More Knowledgeable	Defender Much More Knowledgeable
Number of cases	22	48	184	37	4
Cases without surprise	17	41	165	36	4
Eastern Front	16	33	73	13	0
Soviet attacker	0	14	22	2	0
Average attacker strength	—	29,469	18,509	14,793	—
Average defender strength	—	17,174	16,343	9,806	—
Average attacker armor	—	62	38	0	—
Average defender armor	—	51	41	10	—
Average daily advance rate (in kilometers)	—	3.96	0.30 14.00	—	—

These data do not lead to a firm conclusion. There does seem to be a tendency in some cases for the attacker with information advantage to advance more, but this effect does not appear with any consistency and does not appear at all in the Italian Campaign engagements. Since advance rates are often determined by outcome, one would expect the advance rates to correlate with the outcomes. This does occur to some extent, as shown in table 10.20.

Table 10.20. Advance Rates Compared to Outcomes

	Attacker Much More Knowledgeable	Attacker More Knowledgeable	Same for Both Sides	Defender More Knowledgeable	Defender Much More Knowledgeable
Percentage of attacker wins	47	61	49	47	0
LESS DRAWS	80	66	58	50	0
Average daily advance rate (in kilometers)	3.16	5.54	2.21	2.80	0.43

In this case, though, the outcome appears to be correlated with "Percentage of attacker wins," which is often influenced by the selection of the engagements. Therefore we are not seeing any effect for spatial effectiveness that is not directly a result of winning or losing.

To summarize the effects of an information advantage on mission accomplishment, casualty effectiveness, and spatial effectiveness:

1. Information advantage has some effect on mission accomplishment. The rate of attacker wins, less drawn engagements, declines from 80 percent when the attacker is much more knowledgeable to 50 percent when the defender is more knowledgeable.

2. There are no cases of attacker wins when the defender has much greater knowledge. However, this conclusion is based on only four cases. The casualty exchange ratio is also very favorable to the defender.

3. An information advantage does not lead directly to a more favorable casualty exchange ratio. Considering that achieving surprise did not seem to have an effect on the casualty exchange rates, it is not entirely surprising that having an information advantage also does not have an effect on the casualty exchange rates.

4. Spatial effectiveness (advance rates) appears to be correlated with the "Percentage of attacker wins," which is often influenced by the engagements selected. Therefore we are seeing no effect for spatial effectiveness that is not directly a result of winning or losing.

The Combat Value of Situational Awareness

The first part of this chapter examined the combat value of an information advantage. This second part explores the actual combat value of good versus poor information regarding an enemy. As I have already suggested, one expects that poor situational awareness of the enemy will be a significant factor in combat. For the sake of consistent analysis, I will present the data in a manner similar to that done for measuring an information advantage, using three measurements: (1) mission accomplishment, (2) casualty effectiveness, and (3) spatial effectiveness. As we are looking independently at the data from both sides, this gives us 590 cases to examine, as categorized in table 10.21.

Table 10.21. Cases of Knowledge

Knowledge	Total Cases
Attacker has considerable knowledge	124
Attacker has some knowledge	117
Attacker has little knowledge	54
Defender has considerable knowledge	109
Defender has some knowledge	100
Defender has little knowledge	86

Mission Accomplishment

The area of mission accomplishment provided clear results when we looked at information advantage, and it continued to do so when examined as an element of situational awareness. Looking at all the engagements by attacker or defender provides the data presented in tables 10.22 and 10.23.

Table 10.22. Situational Awareness (Attacker)—All Engagements

	Considerable	Some	Little
Number of cases	124	117	54
Cases without surprise	113	106	44
Percentage without surprise	91	91	81
Winner			
ATTACKER	46	53	32
DRAW	27	9	1
DEFENDER	40	44	11
Percentage of attacker wins	41	50	72

LESS DRAWS	53	54	74
OUTCOMES			
I Limited action	17	6	—
II Limited attack	14	13	2
III Failed attack	25	26	8
IV Attack advances	43	46	25
V Defender penetrated	13	10	6
VI Defender enveloped	—	1	2
VII Other	1	4	1
PERCENTAGE OF OUTCOMES			
IV, V, and VI	50	54	75
III	22	25	18
Ratio: IV, V, and VI vs. III	2.24 to 1	2.19 to 1	4.13 to 1
Scoring			
ATTACKER	5.23	5.03	5.41
DEFENDER	4.98	4.77	4.20
Ratio of attacker vs. defender score	1.05 to 1	1.05 to 1	1.29 to 1

Table 10.23. Situational Awareness (Defender)—All Engagements

	Considerable	Some	Little
Number of cases	109	100	86
Cases without surprise	106	89	68
Percentage without surprise	97	8%	79
Winner			
ATTACKER	40	41	50
DRAW	19	10	8
DEFENDER	47	38	10
Percentage of attacker wins	38	46	74
LESS DRAWS	46	52	83
OUTCOMES			
I Limited action	13	4	6
II Limited attack	15	13	1
III Failed attack	23	26	10
IV Attack advances	45	42	27

V Defender penetrated	9	3	17
VI Defender enveloped	—	1	2
VII Other	1	—	5
PERCENTAGE OF OUTCOMES			
IV, V, and VI	51	52	68
III	22	29	15
Ratio: IV, V, and VI vs. III	2.35 to 1	1.77 to 1	4.60 to 1
Scoring			
ATTACKER	5.20	4.98	5.41
DEFENDER	5.33	4.93	3.68
Ratio of attacker vs. defender score	0.98	1.01	1.47

The outstanding salient feature is that the attacker does better when either attacker or defender has little situational awareness. This seemingly illogical mirror-image result is due to the fact that in the majority of the engagements where the attacker had "little" situational awareness the defender also had "little" situational awareness. In the forty-four cases without surprise where the attacker had "little" situational awareness, the defender had "little" situational awareness in twenty-seven cases (61 percent). In the nine cases where the attacker had surprise with "little" situational awareness, the defender had "little" situational awareness in nine cases (100 percent). In contrast, in the sixty-eight cases without surprise where the defender had "little" situational awareness, the attacker had "little" situational awareness in twenty-seven of those cases (40 percent). In the eighteen cases where the attacker had surprise, the defender had "little" situational awareness in nine cases (50 percent).

In general the attacker and the defender are sharing the same data set, with "little" (for both attacker and defender) making up 61 percent of the cases of "little" situational awareness for the attacker and 40 percent of the cases of "little" situational awareness for the defender. This is what is actually causing the attacker with "little" situational awareness not only to have better resulting statistics compared to when the attacker has "some" or "considerable" situational awareness, but even to do better when the defender has "little" situational awareness. Tables 10.24 and 10.25 look at these two categories in more depth.

Table 10.24. Attacker Has "Little" Situational Awareness (without Surprise)

	Defender Has Considerable	Defender Has Some	Defender Has Little
Number of cases	4	13	37
Cases without surprise	4	13	27
Percentage without surprise	100	100	73
Winner			
ATTACKER	0	9	23
DRAW	0	0	1
DEFENDER	4	4	3
Percentage of attacker wins	0	69	85
LESS DRAWS	0	69	88
OUTCOMES			
I Limited action	—	—	—
II Limited attack	—	1	1
III Failed attack	4	1	3
IV Attack advances	—	9	16
V Defender penetrated	—	1	5
VI Defender enveloped	—	1	1
VII Other	—	—	1
PERCENTAGE OF OUTCOMES			
IV, V, and VI	0	85	81
III	100	8	11
Ratio: IV, V, and VI vs. III	0 to 1	9 to 1	5.33 to 1
Scoring			
ATTACKER	2.50	5.31	5.89
DEFENDER	7.75	4.00	3.78
Ratio of attacker vs. defender score	0.32 to 1	1.33 to 1	1.56 to 1

Table 10.24 shows the value of the defender's situational awareness in those cases where the attacker had "little" situational awareness. The attacker definitely wins more often when the defender has "little" situational awareness and also obtains surprise more often. There is no such clear pattern when the attacker has "some" or "considerable" situational awareness.

Table 10.25. Defender Has "Little" Situational Awareness (without Surprise)

	Attacker Has Considerable	Attacker Has Some	Attacker Has Little
Number of cases	22	27	37
Cases without surprise	17	24	27
Percentage without surprise	77	89	73
Winner			
ATTACKER	8	19	23
DRAW	7	—	1
DEFENDER	2	5	3
Percentage of attacker wins	47	79	85
LESS DRAWS	80	79	88
OUTCOMES			
I Limited action	6	—	—
II Limited attack	—	—	1
III Failed attack	2	5	3
IV Attack advances	5	6	16
V Defender penetrated	4	8	5
VI Defender enveloped	—	1	1
VII Other	—	4	1
PERCENTAGE OF OUTCOMES			
IV, V, and VI	53	63	81
III	12	21	11
Ratio: IV, V, and VI vs. III	4.50 to 1	3.00 to 1	7.33 to 1
Scoring			
ATTACKER	5.65	4.71	5.89
DEFENDER	4.47	3.00	3.78
Ratio of attacker vs. defender score	1.26	1.57	1.56

Table 10.25 does not show much of a difference in results whether the attacker has "considerable," "some," or "little" situational awareness. If this pattern holds in the tests for casualty effectiveness and spatial effectiveness, then one will be left to conclude that only the defender's knowledge of the attacker's situation is critical to the results of the battle.

Casualty Effectiveness

Casualty effectiveness did not yield meaningful results when we examined it in light of having an information advantage. For the cases of overall situational awareness, the results were also limited. Again we divided the data into Western and Eastern Front engagements. Table 10.26 presents the results for Western Front attackers.

Table 10.26. Casualty Effectiveness (Attacker)—Western Front Engagements

	Considerable	Some	Little
Number of cases	124	117	54
Cases without surprise	113	106	44
Western Front cases	74	49	5
Average attacker strength	19,741	18,323	17,693
Average defender strength	10,911	9,943	17,170
Average attacker armor	76	74	100
Average defender armor	35	32	110
Average attacker casualties	278	228	720
Average defender casualties	341	174	86
Average attacker armor loss	3.93	2.73	21.20
Average defender armor loss	1.32	1.73	2.40
Average attacker percentage loss	0.56	0.67	5.36
Average defender percentage loss	2.21	0.82	0.39
Average attacker armor percentage loss	1.64	1.78	20.65
Average defender armor percentage loss	1.32	2.16	2.48

Weighted attacker percentage loss	1.41	1.24	4.07
Weighted defender percentage loss	3.12	1.75	0.50
Weighted attacker armor percentage loss	5.17	3.67	21.28
Weighted attacker armor percentage loss	3.78	5.39	2.19

Looking at the casualty exchange ratios, as was done when measuring an information advantage, one again sees a clear relationship, provided in table 10.27. Note that the "little knowledge" category came from only five engagements. Not surprisingly, the range of results is similar to those obtained from our examination of casualty effectiveness based on information advantage for those cases on the Western Front.

Table 10.27. Western Front: Attacker Knowledge Compared to Casualty Exchange Ratios

	Casualty Exchange Ratio (Attacker vs. Defender)	Highest Attacker Losses	Highest Defender Losses
Attacker has considerable knowledge	0.82 to 1	1,612	1,639
Attacker has some knowledge	1.31 to 1	1,213	802
Attacker has little knowledge	8.36 to 1	1,251	217

In table 10.12, provided earlier, the bottom category ("little knowledge" and "defender much more knowledgeable") consists of effectively the same data, with the four cases of "defender much more knowledgeable" being four of the five cases of "little knowledge." Of course the problem with comparing the information advantage of Western Front data with Eastern Front data (Germans or Soviets attacking) was that the Eastern Front data showed the exact opposite trend (the attacker performed better as his information advantage declined). Therefore we would expect to see a similarly confused message in these data (table 10.28).

Table 10.28. Casualty Effectiveness (Defender)—Western Front Engagements

	Considerable	Some	Little
Number of cases	109	100	86
Cases without surprise	106	89	68
Western Front cases	92	34	2
Average attacker strength	19,812	17,817	9,340
Average defender strength	10,253	12,230	10,675
Average attacker armor	78	74	53
Average defender armor	31	54	28
Average attacker casualties	235	394	161
Average defender casualties	215	398	425
Average attacker armor loss	3.22	6.85	1.00
Average defender armor loss	0.60	4.00	2.00
Average attacker percentage loss	0.71	1.00	0.98
Average defender percentage loss	0.90	1.25	2.99
Average attacker armor percentage loss	1.85	4.09	0.93
Average defender armor percentage loss	0.93	3.99	7.69

In the case of the defender data, we do not see as clear a pattern emerging (table 10.29).

Table 10.29. Western Front: Defender Knowledge Compared to Casualty Exchange Ratios

	Casualty Exchange Ratio (Attacker vs. Defender)	Highest Attacker Losses	Highest Defender Losses
Defender has considerable knowledge	1.09 to 1	1,304	1,379
Defender has some knowledge	0.99 to 1	1,612	1,639
Defender has little knowledge	0.38 to 1	200	527

The last data point (the defender has little knowledge) is based on only two cases. In light of the clear pattern for the attacker and a clear pattern for information advantage, the lack of any pattern here is troubling.

The Eastern Front data, of course, have to be divided into those cases with German attackers and those cases with Soviet attackers. Table 10.30 presents the results for the German attackers on the Eastern Front.

Table 10.30. Casualty Effectiveness (Attacker)—Eastern Front Engagements (German Attacker)

	Considerable	Some	Little
Number of cases	124	117	54
Cases without surprise	113	106	44
Eastern Front cases	39	57	39
German attacker	32	32	33
Average attacker strength	20,265	21,046	24,729
Average defender strength	10,969	11,162	16,316
Average attacker armor	74	87	107
Average defender armor	7	75	77
Average attacker casualties	268	205	190
Average defender casualties	412	532	730

Average attacker armor loss	9.06	10.91	12.82
Average defender armor loss	3.28	15.53	15.88
Average attacker percentage loss	1.13	0.91	0.74
Average defender percentage loss	4.91	7.16	4.13
Average attacker armor percentage loss	5.85	8.17	10.64
Average defender armor percentage loss	4.34	10.09	16.90

With each bin in table 10.31 having thirty-two to thirty-three cases, this is a nicely balanced set of data. As before, these data show the opposite trend found for the Western Front. Here the attacker does better the less knowledge he has of the enemy. This is of course counterintuitive but not unexpected in light of the results from our analysis of information advantage. Compare these results below with the results in table 10.14 earlier.

Table 10.31. Eastern Front: Attacker Knowledge Compared to Casualty Exchange Ratios (German Attacker)

	Casualty Exchange Ratio (Attacker vs. Defender)	Highest Attacker Losses	Highest Defender Losses
Attacker has considerable knowledge	0.65 to 1	1,663	2,197
Attacker has some knowledge	0.39 to 1	695	2,412
Attacker has little knowledge	0.26 to 1	639	4,012

In keeping with our pattern of separating the Eastern Front engagements by German or Soviet attacker, tables 10.32 and 10.33 examine the casualty effectiveness based upon defender knowledge for those cases where the Germans were the attackers.

Table 10.32. Casualty Effectiveness (Defender)—Eastern Front Engagements (German Attacker)

	Considerable	Some	Little
Number of cases	109	100	86
Cases without surprise	106	89	68
Eastern Front cases	14	55	66
German attacker	10	36	51
Average attacker strength	15,934	20,282	24,481
Average defender strength	17,740	13,631	11,343
Average attacker armor	1.90	67	123
Average defender armor	5.70	66	53
Average attacker casualties	62	218	254
Average defender casualties	74	646	594
Average attacker armor loss	0.10	6.72	16.06
Average defender armor loss	0.00	12.22	13.45
Average attacker percentage loss	0.28	0.93	1.05
Average defender percentage loss	0.25	4.46	7.04
Average attacker armor percentage loss	0.53	7.87	10.02
Average defender armor percentage loss	0.00	7.90	14.41

Table 10.33. Eastern Front: Defender Knowledge Compared to Casualty Exchange Ratios (German Attacker)

	Casualty Exchange Ratio (Attacker vs. Defender)	Highest Attacker Losses	Highest Defender Losses
Defender has considerable knowledge	0.84 to 1	159	158
Defender has some knowledge	0.34 to 1	695	3,079
Defender has little knowledge	0.43 to 1	1,663	4,012

The problems with the "considerable knowledge" bin remain, except it is now missing the four cases where the Soviets were conducting limited actions or limited attacks. The rest of the data establishes nothing.

The same examination was done for those cases when the Soviets were the attackers, with tables 10.34 and 10.35 examining the cases based upon attacker knowledge and tables 10.36 and 10.37 examining the cases based upon defender knowledge.

Table 10.34. Casualty Effectiveness (Attacker)—Eastern Front Engagements (Soviet Attacker)

	Considerable	Some	Little
Number of cases	124	117	54
Cases without surprise	113	106	44
Eastern Front cases	39	57	39
Soviet attacker	7	25	6
Average attacker strength	14,861	24,713	21,249
Average defender strength	13,019	15,300	24,325
Average attacker armor	12	49	65
Average defender armor	3	44	88
Average attacker casualties	208	731	433

Average defender casualties	93	116	99
Average attacker armor loss	0.00	4.28	2.83
Average defender armor loss	0.00	4.28	3.67
Average attacker percentage loss	1.19	2.66	1.67
Average defender percentage loss	0.68	0.74	0.45
Average attacker armor percentage loss	0.00	4.76	7.56
Average defender armor percentage loss	0.00	5.08	4.44

Unfortunately the data in table 10.34 are clumped around a center point, leaving a very small number of data points in the "considerable" and "little" bins. There are certainly many more cases of Soviet offensive actions that can be drawn from the Eastern Front data to add to this.

Compare the data in table 10.35 on situational awareness to the data in table 10.16 on information advantage.

Table 10.35. Eastern Front: Attacker Knowledge Compared to Casualty Exchange Ratios (Soviet Attacker)

	Casualty Exchange Ratio (Attacker vs. Defender)	Highest Attacker Losses	Highest Defender Losses
Attacker has considerable knowledge	2.22 to 1	523	217
Attacker has some knowledge	6.29 to 1	4,431	313
Attacker has little knowledge	4.37 to 1	1,551	215

None of this points to any clear conclusions.

Table 10.36. Casualty Effectiveness (Defender)—Eastern Front Engagements (Soviet Attacker)

	Considerable	Some	Little
Number of cases	109	100	86
Cases without surprise	106	89	68

Eastern Front cases	14	55	66
Soviet attacker	4	19	15
Average attacker strength	14,834	17,064	31,052
Average defender strength	14,323	12,072	22,196
Average attacker armor	15	22	82
Average defender armor	0	23	80
Average attacker casualties	142	368	984
Average defender casualties	54	87	152
Average attacker armor loss	0	0.95	7.07
Average defender armor loss	0	1.16	7.13
Average attacker percentage loss	0.67	2.30	2.56
Average defender percentage loss	0.24	0.73	0.73
Average attacker armor percentage loss	0	1.21	9.42
Average defender armor percentage loss	0	1.65	8.15

Again the "considerable" bin in table 10.36 has only four cases, and all the other bins of data have too few cases.

Table 10.37. Eastern Front: Defender Knowledge Compared to Casualty Exchange Ratios (German Attacker)

	Casualty Exchange Ratio (Attacker vs. Defender)	Highest Attacker Losses	Highest Defender Losses
Defender has considerable knowledge	2.61 to 1	224	110
Defender has some knowledge	4.22 to 1	1,275	217
Defender has little knowledge	6.48 to 1	4,431	313

The data in table 10.37 show a counterintuitive result. In some of these cases, the German defender had little knowledge of the Soviet attacker because of the number of Soviet units that were massing for the attack, although in most cases the Germans knew the attack was coming.

As with the previous information advantage data, data on situational awareness show contradictory results. A clear pattern emerged for the Western Front attacker in which better results were obtained when it had more knowledge, but no such trend is shown in the Eastern Front data for when the Germans attacked and when the Soviets attacked. In fact the reverse trend was found. Therefore it does not appear that any conclusion about casualty effectiveness can be reached from these data. This parallels what we've already seen from the examination of surprise and information advantage.

Spatial Effectiveness

Spatial effectiveness is measured as the daily advance rate in kilometers. While we obtained a clear pattern with these data, it is counterintuitive. The reason is probably related to the mixture of engagements in each category and the high advance rates that tend to appear in the mobile operations around Kharkov, where both sides had little situational awareness. In fact we may be examining this issue incorrectly. It may not be whether or not good situational awareness improves advance rates, but rather that poor situational awareness may be more typical of scenarios with high advance rates. Therefore there may not be a direct link between situational awareness as the cause and advance rate as the result (effect).

Again, using the same pattern as in the previous two discussions, we will first look at the impact of situational awareness on spatial effectiveness on the Western Front in table 10.38. We will then look at the cases where the Germans were the attacker on the Eastern Front in table 10.39 and finally at the cases where the Soviets were the attacker in table 10.41.

Table 10.38. Spatial Effectiveness on Western Front

	All Cases without Surprise—Attacker		
	Considerable	Some	Little
Number of cases	124	117	54
Cases without surprise	113	106	44
Western Front	74	49	5

Average attacker strength	19,741	18,323	17,693
Average defender strength	10,911	9,943	17,170
Average attacker armor	76	74	100
Average defender armor	35	32	110
Average daily advance rate (in kilometers)	1.31	0.94	0.34

	All Cases without Surprise—Defender		
	Considerable	Some	Little
Number of cases	109	100	86
Cases without surprise	106	89	68
Western Front	92	34	2
Average attacker strength	19,812	17,817	9,340
Average defender strength	10,253	12,230	10,675
Average attacker armor	78	74	53
Average defender armor	31	54	28
Average daily advance rate	1.25	0.79	1.50

As in the previous cases, the Western Front data behave themselves, displaying a higher advance rate when the attacker has better information. But there is no particular pattern for the defender data. On the other hand, as has been the case throughout this study, the Eastern Front data contradict the Western Front data (see table 10.39).

Table 10.39. Spatial Effectiveness on Eastern Front (German Attacker)

	All Cases without Surprise—Attacker		
	Considerable	Some	Little
Number of cases	124	117	54
Cases without surprise	113	106	44
Eastern Front (German attacker)	32	32	33

	Considerable	Some	Little
Average attacker strength	20,265	21,046	24,729
Average defender strength	10,969	11,162	16,316
Average attacker armor	74	87	107
Average defender armor	7	75	77
Average daily advance rate (in kilometers)	2.41	7.53	5.91

All Cases without Surprise—Defender			
	Considerable	Some	Little
Number of cases	109	100	86
Cases without surprise	106	89	68
Eastern Front (German attacker)	10	36	51
Average attacker strength	15,934	20,282	24,481
Average defender strength	17,740	13,631	11,343
Average attacker armor	1.90	67	123
Average defender armor	5.70	66	53
Average daily advance rate (in kilometers)	0.48	4.59	6.72

The attacker data in table 10.39 effectively contradict the Western Front data. Even though the advance rate under "some" is actually higher than under "little," the weighted force ratios for these two engagements (1.89 to 1 vs. 1.52 to 1) probably explain most of this difference. In the defender case, the less information the defender has, the greater the advance rate.

The Soviets' attacks show the same counterintuitive tendency for advance rates to increase with less attacker situational awareness. This is also the case with the defender (table 10.40).

Table 10.40. Spatial Effectiveness on Eastern Front (Soviet Attacker)

	All Cases without Surprise—Attacker		
	Considerable	Some	Little
Number of cases	124	117	54
Cases without surprise	113	106	44
Eastern Front (Soviet attacker)	7	25	6
Average attacker strength	14,861	24,713	21,249
Average defender strength	13,019	15,300	24,325
Average attacker armor	11.71	49	65
Average defender armor	2.86	44	88
Average daily advance rate (in kilometers)	0.06	2.43	4.78

	All Cases without Surprise—Defender		
	Considerable	Some	Little
Number of cases	109	100	86
Cases without surprise	106	89	68
Eastern Front (Soviet attacker)	4	19	15
Average attacker strength	14,834	17,064	31,052
Average defender strength	14,333	12,072	22,196
Average attacker armor	15	22	82
Average defender armor	0	23	80
Average daily advance rate (in kilometers)	0.15	1.74	3.75

As was the case for measuring information advantage, these data on situational awareness do not lead to a clear conclusion. While the Western Front data show a higher advance rate with more situational awareness, both of the Eastern Front data sets (German attacker and Soviet attacker) show the reverse.

There is no discernible pattern in the Western Front defender data. The Eastern Front defender data for both cases of Germans and Soviets attacking show a tendency for cases of less information on the part of the defender to produce higher advance rates, as was the case for the attacker (where with less information, the higher the attacker advance rate). These confusing results parallel the information advantage analysis and certainly exist for the same reasons.

We again found no effect for spatial effectiveness that was not a direct result of the issue of winning or losing or because of the selection of engagements. Many of the engagements with "little" situational awareness are from the very mobile and fluid Kharkov operations. This certainly results in higher advance rates. Of the forty-four cases in which the attacker had little information, twenty-two (50 percent) were from the Kharkov battles. Of the sixty-eight cases in which the defender had little information, twenty-six (38 percent) were from the Kharkov battles. The Kharkov battles make up 19 percent of the database. The average advance rate of the Kharkov battles is 7.00 kilometers per day, while the average advance rate for the Western Front engagements is 1.43 kilometers per day, and for the Kursk engagements 3.41 kilometers per day.

To summarize the effects of situational awareness on mission accomplishment, casualty effectiveness, and spatial effectiveness:

1. In the case of measuring mission accomplishment, we are left to conclude that only the defender's knowledge of the attacker's situation is critical to the results of the battle.

2. It does not appear that any conclusion about casualty effectiveness can be reached from these data. This parallels what we've already seen in the examination of surprise and information advantage.

3. We again find no effect on spatial effectiveness that is not a direct result of the issue of winning or losing or because of the selection of engagements

This differs little from what we found for information advantage.

The Effect of Further Dividing the Data

In this chapter I examined the data measured for information advantage (five categories) and situational awareness (six categories, counting attacker and defender). This analysis did not generate very satisfactory results or firm answers. Nine other permutations of the comparisons of situational awareness could be used, but we avoided using them partly because even with a massive database of 295 engagements (263 without surprise), sectioning it nine ways would leave an average of 33 engagements in each data set. This might be enough to establish some useful conclusions if the engagements were roughly evenly distributed and the selection were unbiased; unfortunately that is not the case. To begin with, we already know that we need to analyze the Western Front data separately from the Eastern Front data. On top of that, we must separate the Eastern Front data by German attacker and Soviet attacker because of the performance difference in the opposing forces. That leaves 295 engagements separated into 27 categories, or an average of 11 engagements in each category. Of course they are not evenly distributed across the bins. As can be seen in table 10.41, such a comparison would generate only two bins of data with more than thirty cases and only six bins of data (out of twenty-seven) with more than fourteen cases. None of these is grouped in a manner that would allow any form of significant testing. Therefore, it would appear that we have reached the natural end of the useful analysis we can do without additional data or a different methodology.

Table 10.41. Comparison of Number of Engagements Using Nine Permutations of Situational Awareness

Attacker	Defender	Western Front	German Attacker Eastern Front	Soviet Attacker Eastern Front
Considerable	Considerable	68	9	4
Considerable	Some	11	7	3
Considerable	Little	2	20	—
Some	Considerable	23	1	—
Some	Some	32	20	14
Some	Little	3	12	12
Little	Considerable	4	—	—
Little	Some	1	10	2
Little	Little	5	25	7

There is a second reason not to further divide these data: there is no clear ranking among the nine categories. While "considerable" is better than "some," and "some" is better than "little," there is no way to compare and order categories like "considerable/considerable" and "some/some" relative to each other or the other seven categories. We can discern a pattern with groups of three bins ("considerable," "some," or "little"), but it is difficult to do more than that with this categorization system.

Therefore the data analysis probably needs to stop at this point. Perhaps more can be learned by performing a more sophisticated numerical analysis of the data, but we will leave that to others. Our conclusion is not that the data need more analysis but that we indeed need more data. If enough data are collected, any trend that exists should become apparent.

Endnote: Definitions of Situational Awareness

For the purposes of this database situational awareness is defined as a measure of the ability of the attacker and the defender to correctly gauge the strength, size and capability, and location and intention of his opposition. Like intangible factors and factors affecting outcome and resolution, these are at least in part judgment calls, although they are based on data drawn from the original intelligence available to the respective opposing forces. The coding is based on a 5-point scale, as follows:

None

1. Although the presence of opposing enemy forces may be known, there is little or no intelligence as to their strength, size, and capability other than of those forces in direct contact. The presence of significant enemy formations capable of participating or influencing the outcome of the engagement, including units similar in size to that of the primary friendly formation involved in the engagement, is unknown, the formations have not been properly located, and/or they have not been identified.

2. There is limited intelligence as to the positions held by enemy forward elements.

3. There is limited intelligence as to the intentions of the enemy.

Little

1. The presence of opposing enemy forces is known, but more than one significant enemy formation capable of participating or influencing the outcome of the engagement has not been identified or located.

2. There is limited intelligence as to the positions held by enemy forward elements.

3. There is limited intelligence as to the intentions of the enemy.

Some

1. The presence of opposing enemy forces is known, but at least one significant enemy formation capable of participating or influencing the outcome of the engagement has not been identified or located or its location has been significantly misidentified.

2. Intelligence as to the positions held by enemy forward elements is fairly complete. Positions of enemy supporting elements may be roughly understood, but deceptions may be accepted as real positions.

3. There is some understanding of the enemy's intent.

Considerable

1. All significant enemy formations capable of participating or influencing the outcome of the engagement have been identified and at least roughly located. Assessments of enemy strengths and capabilities are at least roughly correct.

2. Intelligence as to the positions held by enemy forward and supporting elements is fairly complete, and many enemy deceptions may be identified as such.

3. The enemy's intent is correctly understood.

Complete

1. All significant enemy formations capable of participating or influencing the outcome of the engagement have been identified and at least roughly located. Assessments of enemy strengths and capabilities are complete and substantially correct.

2. Intelligence as to the positions held by enemy forward and supporting elements is complete and accurate. Enemy deception methods and positions are identified.

3. The enemy's intent is correctly understood or may even be known through communications intercepts.

A "significant formation" is one size smaller organizationally (thus company to battalion, brigade to division, etc.), the same size, or larger than the opposing formation. Note that this may include opposing formations that are of similar strength and capability as well in those cases where there are significant differences between the two sides with regard to organizational size and hierarchy. Thus a World War II–style Soviet tank corps was more similar organizationally to a Western-style division, and so its comparable equivalent opposing significant formation is a division rather than a corps. On the other hand, many Soviet infantry divisions late in the war were more similar to brigades in strength and capability and so may be considered equivalent to opposing regiments or brigades.

11. The Combat Value of Surprise

Surprise substantially enhances combat power.

—Trevor N. Dupuy, *Understanding War*

Surprise is one of J. F. C. Fuller's eight principles of war and is listed among the nine principles of war in the various editions of the U.S. Army's *Field Manual 100-5: Operations*.[1] It is also extensively discussed by Clausewitz, who calls it the "most powerful medium in the art of war."[2] It is almost universally recognized that achieving surprise against an enemy force can serve as a powerful force multiplier. The engagements in the Dupuy Institute's division-level database were already coded for surprise. This was a four-tier coding based on a choice of "no surprise," "minor surprise," "considerable surprise," and "complete surprise," and either side could achieve surprise. Therefore an examination of surprise was possible as part of our study of situational awareness, and we took advantage of that existing coding to see what could be determined from it. I will first discuss the frequency of surprise and what is causing it and then the combat value obtained from surprise.

Incidence of Surprise

In the case of the 295 engagements in our sample, surprise was a fairly rare occurrence. It appears in only 11 percent of the engagements, as seen in table 11.1.

Table 11.1. Incidences of Surprise

	Attacker	Defender
Minor surprise	17	3
Considerable surprise	12	0
Complete surprise	0	0

Table 11.2 presents the data in terms of percentages (based upon 295 cases each of attacker and defender).

Table 11.2. Incidence of Surprise as a Percentage

	Attacker	Defender
No surprise	90	99
Minor surprise	6	1
Considerable surprise	4	0
Complete surprise	0	0

As the number of cases of surprise is fairly low (32), a list is provided in table 11.3.

Table 11.3. Cases of Surprise (32 Cases)

Engagement	Start Date	Surprise	Attacker Situational Awareness	Defender Situational Awareness	Notes
WESTERN FRONT					
Flavion	15 May 1940	Substantial	Some	Little	German attack vs. France
Maleme-Retimo-Heraklion	20 May 1941	Minor	Little	Little	German airborne attack vs. United Kingdom
Sidi Bou Zid	14 February 1943	Substantial	Considerable	None	German attack vs. United States
El Guettar	23 March 1943	Substantial	Some	Some	German attack vs. United States
Paestum Beachhead	9 September 1943	Minor	Little	Little	U.S. amphibious landing
Amphitheater beachhead	9 September 1943	Minor	Little	Little	UK amphibious landing
Port of Salerno beachhead	9 September 1943	Minor	Little	Little	UK amphibious landing
Triflisco	13 October 1943	Minor	Some	Some	U.S. attack
Monte La Difensa II	3 December 1943	Substantial	Some	Little	U.S. attack
Aprilia I	25 January 1944	Minor	Little	Little	UK attack
Isola Bella I	25 January 1944	Minor	Some	Some	U.S. attack
Cisterna I	30 January 1944	Minor (Defender)	Some	Considerable	U.S. attack, German surprise
Bowling Alley II	16 February 1944	Substantial	Considerable	Some	German attack vs. United States
Moletta River II	16 February 1944	Substantial	Considerable	Some	German attack vs. United Kingdom
Bowling Alley III	16 February 1944	Substantial	Some	Some	German attack vs. United States
Bowling Alley I	16 February 1944	Substantial	Some	Some	German attack vs. United States
San Martino	12 May 1944	Minor	Some	Some	U.S. attack
Santa Maria Infante	12 May 1944	Minor	Considerable	Considerable	U.S. attack
Anzio breakout	23 May 1944	Substantial	Considerable	Some	U.S. attack
Cisterna	23 May 1944	Substantial	Considerable	Some	U.S. attack

Velletri	26 May 1944	Minor (Defender)	Considerable	Considerable	U.S. attack, German surprise

		KURSK			
Attack on Outpost Line I	4 July 1943	Minor	Considerable	Little	German limited attack
Attack on Outpost Line II	4 July 1943	Minor	Considerable	Little	German limited attack
Gertsovka-Setnoye I	7 July 1943	Substantial	Some	Some	German attack
LSSAH clears Outpost Line	4 July 1943	Minor	Considerable	Little	German limited attack
Totenkopf prepares to attack	4 July 1943	Minor	Considerable	Little	German limited attack

		KHARKOV			
Prudyanka-Dergachi	12 February 1943	Minor	Little	Little	Soviet attack
North of Kharkov III	15 February 1943	Minor	Some	Little	Soviet attack
West of Kharkov I	16 February 1943	Minor	Little	Little	Soviet attack
West of Kharkov II	17 February 1943	Minor (Defender)	Little	Little	Soviet attack, German surprise
Pereshchnaya	9 March 1943	Substantial	Little	Little	German attack
Advance through Derarchi	10 March 1943	Minor	Little	Little	German attack

Surprise in these 32 cases was determined by the analyst and is not based on any hard and fast set of rules. Thus not only is the level of surprise a judgment call, but even the existence of surprise is a judgment call. However, in general these judgments tend to err on the conservative side.

For example, the engagement "Counterattacks around Verkhopenye" on 12 July 1943 is rated as "no surprise" even though the Soviets managed to effectively drive a tank corps over an undefended hill in a gap between two German divisions and into the flank of the XLVIII Panzer Corps. In this case the Germans did know that there was armor on that flank as they had pushed it back the previous day (although they may not have been entirely aware that reinforcing armor had arrived). They had observed the Soviets preparing to attack all along the front. Still, the Germans also wanted to attack to the north this day and were waiting for elements of the 332nd Infantry Division to relieve parts of the 3rd Panzer Division holding height 258.5. When those elements did not arrive by 1000 in the morning, the corps' chief of staff, Major General Mellenthin, ordered the 3rd Panzer Division to move from the height anyway, leaving the flank to the protection of the "attack" of the 332nd Infantry Division. This contravened the advice of the 3rd Panzer Division commander, Major General Westhoven, who had recommended holding a regiment in the area. The Soviet attack then rolled over the empty hill and through the gap that day, putting a halt to any German attempts to attack to the north.

This case could be labeled "minor" or even "substantial" surprise by the Soviet attacker. But it appears that the primary problems were a discounting of the enemy threat, too much focus on attacking when under attack, and a command error on the part of the Germans. As a result this was judged not to be a situation with surprise. In this engagement the situational awareness of the Soviet attacker was "some" and that of the German defender was "little."

The 32 cases of surprise (29 by the attacker) that are recorded in the database make up only 10 percent of attacks (and 1 percent of the defense). This is not out of line with the rest of the database. The DLEDB at the time of this study consisted of 642 engagements, of which 295 were used for this study. Of the 347 other engagements in the database, there are 63 cases of attacker surprise (18 percent) and 2 cases (1 percent) of defender surprise. Of these, 14 cases are from the 1991 Gulf War and 8 are from the first day of the Ardennes Offensive. There are more cases of cherry-picking among these other engagements than there were with the 295 engagements used for this study. Analysts other than the two involved in this study coded most of these other engagements. Of the dozen cherry-picked engagements used in this study, 4 included surprise (33 percent).

Surprise is rare, and as such, even with a robust database of 295 engagements, we ended up with just a small number of cases. This small number is influenced by analyst judgment as to whether there is surprise, the degree of surprise, and the degree of information advantage. Therefore there simply might not be enough data points here to reach a solid determination from such fuzzy data. Still, we have the data in hand, and to our knowledge it is the most extensive collection of engagements comparing situational awareness to chance of surprise. So I will assume that it is both representative and reasonably accurate and continue the analysis from this point.

Incidence of Surprise

Surprise occurs around 10 percent of the time for the attacker: 29 incidents out of 295 attacks (9.83 percent). If the 12 cherry-picked cases are removed from the data, we end up with 25 incidents of surprise in 283 attacks, or 8.83

percent. If we look only at the Italian Campaign cases, we have 17 incidents of surprise in 137 cases, or 12.41 percent. If we look only at the Eastern Front cases, we have 10 incidents of surprise in 146 cases, or 6.85 percent. If we look at all the "other" engagements in the DLEDB, we end up with 63 cases in 347 engagements, or 18.16 percent. If we look at all 642 engagements in the DLEDB together, we have 92 cases of surprise, or 14.33 percent.

We have other databases that are not division-level that are also coded for surprise. The Small Action Data Base (SADB) of 5 engagements includes 3 cases of surprise (60 percent). The Battalion-Level Operations Data Base (BLODB) of 127 engagements includes 37 cases of attacker surprise (29.13 percent) and 1 case of defender surprise (0.79 percent). The Large Action Data Base (LADB) records 55 battles larger than division level and includes 13 cases of attacker surprise (23.64 percent) and 1 case of defender surprise (1.82 percent). The Campaign Data Base (CADB) of 196 campaigns includes 42 cases where surprise influenced the resolution in favor of the attacker (21.43 percent) and 5 cases where surprise influenced the resolution in favor of the defender (2.55 percent). This database codes surprise differently than the previously listed databases. The Small Scale Contingency Operations (SSCO) Data Base of 203 operations includes 6 cases where surprise influenced the resolution in favor of the attacker (2.96 percent) and 3 cases where surprise influenced the resolution in favor of the defender (1.48 percent). This database is only partially completed, and not all surprise fields may have been properly coded. Finally, the Battles Data Base, covering 243 battles from 1600 to 1900, includes 61 cases of attacker surprise (25.10 percent) and 12 of defender surprise (4.94 percent). If we add together all the data from these seven different databases, we end up with 1,471 cases, for which surprise was a factor for the attacker in 255 (17.34 percent).

Surprise occurs 1.02 percent of the time for the defender, based on 3 incidents among 295 defenses. In the Italian Campaign there were 2 incidents of surprise in 137 cases, or 1.46 percent. At the Eastern Front there was 1 incident of surprise in 146 cases, or 0.68 percent. Among all the "other" engagements in the DLEDB were 2 cases in 347 engagements, or 0.58 percent. In all 642 engagements in the DLEDB there were 5 cases of surprise, or 0.78 percent.

Among our other databases we find 1 case of defender surprise (0.79 percent) in the Battalion-Level Operations Data Base of 127 engagements. In the Large Action Data Base (LADB) of 55 engagements there was 1 case of defender surprise (1.82 percent). In the Campaign Data Base (CADB) of 196 campaigns surprise influenced the resolution in favor of the defender in 5 cases (2.55 percent). In the Small Scale Contingency Data Base (SSCO) of 203 operations surprise influenced the resolution in favor of the defender in 3 cases (1.48 percent).

The Battles Data Base found defender surprise in 12 cases (4.94 percent). Combining all the data from the seven different databases, surprise was a factor for the defender in 27 cases (1.84 percent).

One must keep in mind that many of the engagements in these databases are cherry-picked to some extent and therefore are not always representative of combat as a whole. The engagements used in this study, with 12 exceptions, are effectively not cherry-picked, although they are biased toward periods when there were extensive combat actions.

If I had to provide a single value for the chance of obtaining surprise for the attacker in modern division-level combat (say 1940 to present), I would say 9 to 10 percent. If I had to provide a single value for the chance of obtaining surprise for the defender in modern division-level combat, I would say around 1 percent. It may be higher for more recent combat—meaning the last fifty or so years (1967 to present)—it may have been higher for combat before 1900, and it may be higher for lower levels of combat. It is hard to say with certainty without a more focused research and analytical effort.

Surprise Compared to Situational Awareness

Table 11.4 shows a simple top-level comparison between cases of attacker surprise and cases of defender surprise.

Table 11.4. Permutations of Attacker and Defender Knowledge Compared to Cases of Surprise

Attacker	Defender	Number of Cases	Number of Cases of Attacker Surprise
Considerable	Considerable	81	1
Considerable	Some	22	4
Considerable	Little	22	5
Some	Considerable	24	—
Some	Some	65	7
Some	Little	27	3
Little	Considerable	4	—
Little	Some	13	—
Little	Little	37	9
Attacker	Defender	Number of Cases	Number of Cases of Defender Surprise
Considerable	Considerable	81	1
Considerable	Some	22	—
Considerable	Little	22	—

Some	Considerable	24	1
Some	Some	65	—
Some	Little	27	—
Little	Considerable	4	—
Little	Some	13	—
Little	Little	37	1

Effects of an Information Advantage on Surprise

In this data collection of 295 engagements, the attacker was adjudged to have an information advantage 24 percent of the time, while the defender had an information advantage 14 percent of the time. The question becomes: Did this information advantage result in an increased chance of surprise?

Comparing the mixture of knowledge advantage to the incidence of surprise achieved is revealing (table 11.5).

Table 11.5. Information Advantage Compared to Incidences of Surprise

Knowledge	Western Front	Eastern Front	Total	Surprise Western Front	Surprise Eastern Front	Total
Attacker much more knowledgeable	2	20	22	1	4	5
Attacker more knowledgeable	13	35	48	6	1	7
Same for both sides	106	78	184	12	5	17
Defender more knowledgeable	24	13	37	—	—	—
Defender much more knowledgeable	4	0	4	—	—	—

To summarize:

1. In 23 percent of the cases in which the attacker had much more knowledge than the defender, the attacker achieved surprise.

2. In 15 percent of the cases in which the attacker had more knowledge than the defender, the attacker achieved surprise.

3. In 9 percent of the cases in which both sides had similar levels of knowledge, the attacker achieved surprise.

4. In no case did the attacker achieve surprise when the defender was more knowledgeable.

Similar rules can be developed for the defender, except they are based on only three cases of defender surprise. Still, just for completeness, they are:

1. In none of the cases in which the defender had much more knowledge than the attacker did the defender achieve surprise. Since this was only four cases, there are not enough data to draw any conclusions.

2. In 3 percent of the cases in which the defender had more knowledge than the attacker, the defender achieved surprise.

3. In 1 percent of the cases in which both sides had similar levels of knowledge, the defender achieved surprise.

4. In no case did the defender achieve surprise when the attacker was more knowledgeable.

Even with the limited size of the data set on surprise and despite other imperfections, one does see a consistent pattern in this data: the side with an information advantage achieves surprise more often. Although it is built only on thirty-two cases, the converse, which is that no surprise is achieved against an enemy with an information advantage, may also be a very significant finding.

Knowledge and Surprise

Since the database is coded as to levels of knowledge about the enemy, it is worth examining whether there is a difference in chances for surprise based on knowledge (table 11.6).

Table 11.6. Attacker's Knowledge Level Compared to Incidences of Surprise

Attacker's Knowledge Level	Number of Cases	Cases of Surprise	Percentage
Considerable	125	10	8.00
Some	116	10	8.62
Little	54	9	16.67

These results are, of course, counterintuitive. Perhaps the driving factor is the defender's knowledge level (table 11.7)?

Table 11.7. Defender's Knowledge Level Compared to Incidences of Surprise

Defender's Knowledge Level	Number of Cases	Cases of Surprise	Percentage
Considerable	109	1	0.92
Some	100	11	11.00
Little	86	17	19.77

One is left with the impression that the defender's knowledge of the attacker creates the possibility of surprise, not the attacker's knowledge of the defender.

Examination of the three cases where the defender achieved surprise is not very telling. In two cases the defender had considerable knowledge, and in one case little knowledge. The opposing side's knowledge in these three cases covered each of the three possibilities (considerable, some, little). There is simply not enough data here to draw a conclusion.

We have drawn two conclusions from looking at these data: an information advantage gives an increased chance of surprise (table 11.8), and the defender's lack of situational awareness gives the attacker an increased chance of surprise (table 11.9). In this second formulation, obscuring one's intent from the defender is important to achieving surprise. The question is, which of these is the dominant factor? Or are they both simply reflecting the same limited data selection?

Table 11.8. Information Advantage Achieves Surprise

Knowledge	Total Cases	Cases of Surprise	Percentage
Attacker much more knowledgeable	22	5	22.73
Attacker more knowledgeable	48	7	14.58
Same for both sides	184	17	9.24
Defender more knowledgeable	37	—	—
Defender much more knowledgeable	4	—	—

Table 11.9. Poor Enemy Situational Awareness Achieves Surprise

Defender's Knowledge Level	Number of Cases	Cases of Surprise	Percentage
Considerable	109	1	0.92
Some	100	11	11.00
Little	86	17	19.77

An examination of the seventeen cases in which both sides have similar knowledge may be useful in determining which is the dominant effect (table 11.10).

Table 11.10. Seventeen Cases of Surprise, Both Sides Similar Knowledge

Situational Awareness	Number of Cases	Case of Surprise	Percentage
Considerable vs. considerable	81	1	1.23
Some vs. some	65	7	10.77
Little vs. little	37	9	24.32

It would appear that the defender's knowledge level is the dominant factor. Table 11.11 examines a few other cases to see if we get consistent results (even if they are not statistically significant).

Table 11.11. Twelve Additional Cases of Surprise (Attacker)

Situational Awareness	Number of Cases	Cases of Surprise	Percentage
Considerable vs. some	22	4	18.18
Considerable vs. little	22	5	22.73
Some vs. little	27	3	11.11

It would appear from table 11.11 that there is an advantage in achieving surprise if one has considerable situational awareness. Still, the data are not very consistent, for "Some vs. little" has an 11 percent chance of achieving surprise, while "Little vs. little" (in table 11.10) has a 24 percent chance of achieving surprise. This could lead one to conclude that an attacker who knows less about the enemy has a better chance of achieving surprise.

It is probably worthwhile to look more closely at the thirty-seven engagements that make up the "Little vs. little" group and the twenty-seven that make up the "Some vs. little" group. The "Some vs. little" group includes two of the cherry-picked engagements (one with surprise), one engagement from the Italian Campaign (with surprise), twelve from the Battle of Kursk (no surprise), and twelve from the fighting around Kharkov (one with surprise). The "Little vs. little" group includes four amphibious or airborne operations (all with surprise), one from the Italian Campaign (with surprise), twelve from the Battle of Kursk (no surprise), and twenty from the fighting around Kharkov (four with surprise).

This still does not provide a perfectly clear picture of what may be driving these results. However, it is the nature of amphibious and airborne operations that they begin with little knowledge of either side and that they often achieve surprise. If those cases are removed, then twenty-four of the remaining thirty cases include only five cases of surprise (15.15 percent). This figure brings these small data sets closer together, and yet the data subsets are so small now that drawing further conclusions from them is probably not valid.

It would appear that both information advantage and poor enemy situational awareness play a role in the attacker achieving surprise. Of those, poor enemy situational awareness appears to be more important, allowing one to achieve surprise in about 20 percent of the cases. Having an information advantage appears less important, but still at least doubles one's chances of achieving surprise. Having an information advantage also protects one from being surprised.

Statistical Significance

With good, tight data, one can achieve statistically representative results with fifteen cases, although a minimum of thirty is usually recommended. Looser fitting data require at least thirty cases, and sixty are usually recommended. Since much of this analysis is based on a comparison of twenty-nine cases in which the data are highly variable, we have doubt that statistical testing will result in tight confidence intervals or good fits. In fact we felt no need to actually test the data since that had been done before.[3]

The fact that these data may not achieve a good fit does not mean that drawing a null conclusion (no results) is correct. The data clearly show patterns and trends, and these seem logical. They are real-world combat data, and they are consistent across a range of cases, different campaigns, and engagements. They do point to a set of conclusions, or at least provide the basis for a good working hypothesis. More data will certainly increase the confidence in these results.

The Value of Surprise

All we have determined so far is that an information advantage and poor enemy situational awareness increase the chance of surprise. It is assumed that achieving surprise is a good thing (in other words, it is a force multiplier) for the force achieving surprise based on a mass of writing and theory over the past two centuries. We know of no theorist who believes that achieving surprise is not a combat advantage.

The only measured value of surprise comes from Dupuy's work as documented in two of his books. The first measurement is found in his combat model and analysis methodology, which was validated (fitted) to historical data. The earliest version of that model, the Quantified Judgment Model (QJM), is described in *Numbers, Predictions and War: The Use of History to Evaluate and Predict the Outcome of Armed Conflict*, first published in 1979. Dupuy postulated that the force multiplier value of surprise influenced the mobility factor in the model, as well as the vulnerability of the surprising force and the surprised force. He postulated three levels of surprise: complete, substantial, and minor. This somewhat complex computation basically produced values for surprise as a combat multiplier with a value starting around 1.10 and maximizing around 2.24. Looking at just the multiplier for mobility, the value for "minor surprise" is 1.14, for "substantial surprise," 1.73, and for "complete surprise," 2.24. In the examples Dupuy provides, the value for "minor surprise" is 1.10, for "substantial surprise," 1.60 to 1.70, and for "complete surprise," 2.24.[4] The effects of surprise did decline for subsequent days of combat (but are a factor for up to three days, after which the value of the effect drops to zero).

The second measurement of surprise is contained in a further development of the model, as discussed in Dupuy's book *Attrition: Forecasting Battle Casualties and Equipment Losses in Modern War*.[5] There he gives a multiplier for the effects of differing levels of surprise to operational factors, casualty rates, and armored attrition and postulates that the effects would be felt for up to three days. In the case of the multiplier for casualties, the factors for the first day are 1.50 for "minor surprise," 2.00 for "substantial surprise," and 2.50 for "complete surprise." There are no cases of "complete surprise" in the thirty-two cases of surprise we have examined. The values for operational factors are, respectively, 1.40, 1.80, and 2.20 and for armored attrition 1.30, 1.50, and 1.80.

The factors were entirely based on analyst judgment (in this case Dupuy's judgment). As such, the values Dupuy inserted in his models were untested, and this effort is the first test of the value of surprise.

The question, then, is whether in the twenty-nine engagements in which the attacker achieved surprise it resulted in significantly different (better) results for the surprising force than in the engagements where surprise was not achieved. If Dupuy's factors have any validity, we would expect to see a value for surprise as a multiplier of between 1.40 and 2.00.

Measuring the Value of Surprise

The value of surprise was measured in three different ways. First we examined "mission accomplishment": Did forces who achieved surprise also achieve a higher percentage of wins, or better wins, than those who did not? Second we examined "casualty effectiveness": Did forces who achieved surprise also achieve a more favorable casualty exchange than those who did not? Third we examined "spatial effectiveness": Did forces who achieved surprise advance or seize more ground than those who did not?

MISSION ACCOMPLISHMENT

Mission accomplishment is usually based on a "winner," that is, a judgment call as to which side is the winner or loser. An additional field in our databases tracks the "outcome" of an engagement and categorizes engagements as to whether they are:

I. Limited action
II. Limited attack
III. Failed attack
IV. Attack advances
V. Defender penetrated
VI. Defender enveloped
VII. Other (rarely used)

Outcome III (failed attack) is invariably a defender win, while outcomes V (defender penetrated) and VI (defender enveloped) are invariably attacker wins, as are most incidents (but not all) of outcome IV (attack advances). Outcome I and II engagements do not, by definition, indicate a winner or loser, but outcome I (limited action) is usually coded as a draw, while the winner or loser of outcome II engagements depends on the specifics of the engagement. The database is scored for the attacker and defender mission accomplishment (higher is better). This score, based on a judgment call, can also be used to measure mission accomplishment.

. Thus there are three measurements of mission accomplishment in the database. All are fundamentally based on analyst judgment, and all are somewhat complementary. We have not made a judgment as to which is the best measurement of mission accomplishment. It could also be claimed that spatial effectiveness is the best measurement of mission accomplishment. The data are presented in table 11.12.

Table 11.12. Engagements with Surprise: Mission Accomplishment

	Engagements with No Surprise	Engagements with Attacker Surprise
Number of Engagements	263	29
Winner		
ATTACKER	132	25
DRAW	36	—
DEFENDER	95	4
OUTCOMES		
I Limited action	22	—
II Limited attack	30	4
III Failed attack	59	4
IV Attack advances	114	12
V Defender penetrated	33	9
VI Defender enveloped	3	—
VII Other	2	—
Scoring		
ATTACKER	5.45	6.93
DEFENDER	5.02	3.97

Converted into percentages, the results appear in table 11.13.

Table 11.13. The Value of Surprise: Mission Accomplishment

	Engagements with No Surprise	Engagements with Attacker Surprise
Percentage of attacker wins	50	86
Percentage of outcomes IV, V, and VI	57	72
Percentage attacker average score is higher	—	27
Percentage defender average score is lower	—	21
Multiplier for attacker higher than defender	1.0857	1.7456

It appears that the benefit of surprise increases the chance of success by more than 50 percent (up to 72 percent based on the scoring of wins) and increases the scoring of success by at least 50 percent (up to 61 percent based on the difference between attacker/defender scoring for surprise and no surprise).

The question remains: In the twenty-nine engagements where surprise was a factor, was it being driven by the selection of engagements or by other external factors? Table 11.14 combines the two databases (less the three cases of defender surprise). Nothing stands out that is particularly anomalous regarding the location or nation of the forces in the engagements that would bias the results. Note that the Germans achieve surprise 11.45 percent of the time (15 cases out of 131 attacks) but are themselves surprised only 8.70 percent of the time (14 out of 161 attacks).

Table 11.14. Surprise by Campaign and Nation

	Engagements with No Surprise	Engagements with Attacker Surprise	Percentage
Number of cases	263	29	9.93
Pre-Italian engagements	8	4	33.33
Italian Campaign engagements	120	15	11.11
Kursk engagements	86	5	5.49
Kharkov engagements	49	5	9.26
U.S. attacker	61	8	11.59
UK attacker	48	3	5.88
French defender		1	100.00
U.S. defender	6	5	45.45
UK defender	13	2	13.33
Soviet attacker	38	3	7.32
Soviet defender	97	7	6.73

The most commonly used metric of combat effectiveness is casualty effectiveness, which is the ability of one side to cause losses of another compared to their own losses. Other than interpreting the occasionally inconsistent or incomplete records, this metric is not based on subjective judgment but rather on measurable counts of losses. For casualties, we included all combat losses: killed, wounded, and missing. No attempt was made to adjust for the various casualty recording systems in use by the different nations, even though we are aware that some differences existed between U.S., British, German, and Soviet methodologies.

Table 11.15. Engagements with Surprise: Casualty Effectiveness

	Engagements with No Surprise	Engagements with Attacker Surprise	Percentage
Number of cases	263	29	9.93
Average attacker strength	20,663.00	18,668.00	90.34
Average defender strength	12,345.00	12,020.00	97.37
Average attacker armor	77.00	98.00	127.28
Average defender armor	44.00	39.00	88.67
Average attacker casualties	301.00	659.00	219.35
Average defender casualties	352.00	1,486.00	421.83
Average attacker armor loss	6.53	8.45	129.40
Average defender armor loss	5.51	9.83	178.40
Average attacker percentage loss	1.05 per day	1.61 per day	153.33
Average defender percentage loss	2.58 per day	4.51 per day	174.81
Average attacker armor percentage loss	4.85 per day	5.40 per day	111.34
Average defender armor percentage loss	5.28 per day	9.50 per day	179.92

Table 11.15 demonstrates a pretty noticeable effect from surprise. For the engagements without surprise, the defender loses 1.17 men per attacker loss. With surprise, the defender loses 2.25 men per attacker loss. In effect, the loss exchange is almost doubled (1.92 to 1). A similar shift occurs in armor losses, although not of the same magnitude (1.38 to 1).

One does need to examine these data to determine if there is anything anomalous in the engagements that may be causing such results. The twenty-nine engagements include one eight-day engagement where losses were very high. The Maleme-Retimo-Heraklion engagement, with 6,453 attacker casualties and 28,647 defender casualties, is cherry-picked. No other engagement has more than 1,721 casualties for a side. If this one engagement is removed as an outlier, the comparison in table 11.16 is produced.

Table 11.16. Engagements with Surprise: Casualty Effectiveness Less Outlier

	Engagements with No Surprise	Engagements with Attacker Surprise	Percentage
Number of cases	263	28	9.62
Average attacker strength	20,663.00	18,549.00	89.77
Average defender strength	12,345.00	10,891.00	88.23
Average attacker armor	77.00	101.00	129.34
Average defender armor	44.00	39.00	89.91
Average attacker casualties	301.00	453.00	150.53
Average defender casualties	352.00	516.00	146.39
Average attacker armor loss	6.53	8.75	135.45
Average defender armor loss	5.51	9.36	169.87
Average attacker percentage loss	1.05 per day	1.54 per day	146.67
Average defender percentage loss	2.58 per day	4.38 per day	169.77
Average attacker armor percentage loss	4.85 per day	5.59 per day	116.46
Average defender armor percentage loss	5.28 per day	9.40 per day	178.03

With the outlier removed, most of the effects from surprise disappear. For the engagements without surprise, the defender loses 1.17 men per attacker loss. With surprise, the defender loses 1.14 men per attacker loss. In effect, the loss exchange remains the same, although total losses for both sides are higher. There is a slight shift for armor, as the attacker loses 1.19 tanks for every defender tank without surprise, and with surprise the attacker loses 0.93 tanks, for an overall shift in effectiveness of 1.27 to 1.

The end result appears to be that while surprise does increase the chance of a successful outcome, it does not increase the casualty exchange ratio.

SPATIAL EFFECTIVENESS

Spatial effectiveness is measured as the daily advance rate in kilometers. The results in table 11. 17 are not unexpected. If surprise generates more successful outcomes (including 28 percent of the results being "defender penetrated" vs. 11 percent without surprise), then one is naturally going to get greater spatial effectiveness. This does not tell us much more than an examination of mission accomplishment reveals; the difference is that spatial effectiveness is not a metric based on judgment (except for the technical details of measuring distance advanced) but on a measurable result.

Table 11.17. Engagements with Surprise: Spatial Effectiveness

	Engagements with No Surprise	Engagements with Attacker Surprise	Percentage
Number of cases	263	29	9.93
Average attacker strength	20,663.40	18,667.66	90.34
Average defender strength	12,344.81	12,019.62	97.37
Average attacker armor	76.62	97.52	127.28
Average defender armor	43.70	38.72	88.60
Average daily advance rate	2.84 km	5.44 km	191.55
Less Maleme-Retimo-Heraklion	N/A	5.85 km	—

Summation of the Effects of Surprise

To summarize the relationship between situational awareness and surprise:

1. An information advantage leads to a doubling of the chance of surprise.

2. Poor enemy situational awareness leads to a 20 percent chance of surprise.

3. Surprise increases the chance of a favorable outcome by at least 50 percent.

4. Surprise doubles the opposed advance rate, in part due to the increase in favorable outcomes.

One could therefore conclude that poor enemy situational awareness, and to a lesser extent information advantage on the part of the attacker, results in a 20 percent chance of surprise and that surprise leads to at least a 50 percent chance of a favorable outcome. Therefore the real value of poor enemy situational awareness as a force multiplier is somewhere around 10 percent (up to a maximum of around 20 percent). This is without considering its value outside of surprise.

On the other hand, an information advantage secures the defender against surprise, preventing the enemy attacker from gaining an advantage over the defender due to poor situational awareness.

Surprise over Time

Surprise is more common in the most recent engagements found in the database (table 11.18). This is something that needs to be studied further.

Table 11.18. Surprise over Time

War/Campaign	Years	Total Cases	Cases of Surprise	Percentage
Russo-Japanese War	1904–5	3	0	0
Balkan Wars	1912	1	0	0
WWI vs. United Kingdom	1916	2	1	50
WWI vs. United States	1918	5	1	20
WWI vs. Russia	1914	1	1	100
WWI vs. Turkey	1915–18	8	3	38
Total	1904–18	20	6	30
Manchuria	1938	1	0	0
France	1940	2	2	100
North Africa	1941	5	0	0
Crete	1941	1	1	100
Tunisia	1943	5	2	40
Italy	1943–44	141	17	12
Eastern Front	1943	155	11	7
ETO	1944–45	141	18	13
Eastern Front	1943–45	11	0	0
Pacific	1941–45	33	4	12
Manila	1945	61	0	0
Total	1938–45	556	55	10
Arab-Israeli	1956	2	0	0
Arab-Israeli	1967	16	9	56
Arab-Israeli	1968	1	0	0
Arab-Israeli	1973	32	13	41
Total	1956–73	51	22	43
Gulf War	1991	15	14	93
Grand Total	1904–91	642	97	15

Overall Conclusions

I have now presented four tests of the data. The first was to determine if an information advantage resulted in an advantage in combat other than from surprise. The second was to determine if situational awareness resulted in an advantage in combat other than from surprise. The third was to see if an information advantage or situational awareness increases the chance for surprise. The fourth was to obtain a measure of the combat value of that surprise. To briefly summarize the results:

Nature of the Data

1. Both sides in the engagements examined had the same level of situational awareness over 60 percent of the time.

2. In addition to many units having similar levels of situational awareness, the attacker and the defender had a similar number of cases in which they held the information advantage.

3. Having a significant information advantage was not common (less than 10 percent of the cases).

4. The nature of the operation really does influence the degree of situational awareness.

Value of Information Advantage

5. Three items should draw our attention in the data on mission effectiveness.

    a. In the case of attacker wins, less draws, the rate declines from an 80 percent chance of a win when the attacker is much more knowledgeable to a 50 percent chance when the defender is more knowledgeable.

    b. Not surprisingly, the scoring follows the same pattern.

    c. There are no attacker wins when the defender has much more knowledge.

6. An information advantage does not lead to a more favorable casualty exchange ratio. This is not surprising, considering that achieving surprise did not have an effect on the casualty exchange rates.

7. There is no effect on spatial effectiveness that is not a direct result of the issue of winning or losing.

Value of Situational Awareness

8. When measuring mission accomplishment, only the defender's knowledge of the attacker's situation is critical to the results of the battle.

9. As with surprise and information advantage, no conclusion about casualty effectiveness can be reached from these data.

10. There is no effect on spatial effectiveness that is not a direct result of the issue of winning or losing or because of the selection of engagements.

Effect of Situational Awareness on Force Ratios

11. The actual aggregate force ratio for those engagements where the attacker has "considerable" or "some" situational awareness is consistently higher than for the "little" category. This is demonstrated in table 11.19. However, this is not a definitive result.

Table 11.19. Aggregate Force Ratios Based on Attacker Knowledge

	Considerable	Some	Little
All engagements	1.77	1.78	1.34
Western Front	1.81	1.84	1.03
Eastern Front (German attacker)	1.85	1.89	1.52
Eastern Front (Soviet attacker)	1.14	1.62	0.87

12. There is not much evidence to support the notion that the defender having good situational awareness reduces (moves in his favor) the force ratios for division-level combat.

Chance of Surprise

13. Surprise is not common, occurring in about 10 percent of the attacker cases and 1 percent of the defender cases.

14. Having an information advantage increases the chance of surprise.

a. In 23 percent of the cases in which the attacker had much more knowledge than the defender, the attacker achieved surprise.

b. In 15 percent of the cases in which the attacker had more knowledge than the defender, the attacker achieved surprise.

c. In 9 percent of the cases in which both sides had similar levels of knowledge, the attacker achieved surprise.

d. In no case did the attacker achieve surprise when the defender was more knowledgeable.

15. One is left with the impression that the defender's knowledge of the attacker (or lack thereof) creates the possibility of surprise, not the attacker's knowledge of the defender.

Value of Surprise

16. It appears that the benefit of surprise increases the chance of success by more than 50 percent (up to 72 percent based on the scoring of wins) and increases the scoring of success by at least 50 percent (up to 61 percent based on the difference between attacker/defender scoring for surprise and no surprise).

17. While surprise does increase the chance of a successful outcome, it does not necessarily create a more favorable casualty exchange ratio.

18. One achieves better spatial effectiveness with surprise. This is not a surprising result, for if surprise generates more successful outcomes (including

28 percent of the results being "defender penetrated" vs. 11 percent without surprise), one is naturally going to achieve better spatial effectiveness.

19. To summarize the relationship between situational awareness and surprise:

a. An information advantage leads to a doubling of the chance of surprise.

b. Poor enemy situational awareness leads to a 20 percent chance of surprise.

c. Surprise increases the chance of a favorable outcome by at least 50 percent.

d. Surprise doubles the opposed advance rate, in part due to the increased favorable outcomes.

20. One could conclude that poor enemy situational awareness, and to a lesser extent an information advantage, results in a 20 percent chance of surprise. One could also conclude that surprise leads to at least a 50 percent chance of a more favorable outcome. Therefore the real value of poor enemy situational awareness as a force multiplier is somewhere around 10 percent (up to around 20 percent). This is without considering its value outside of surprise.

21. On the other hand, an information advantage secures the defender against surprise, preventing the enemy from gaining an advantage due to poor enemy situational awareness.

Further Analysis

22. Our conclusion is not that the data need more analysis, but that we indeed need more data. If enough data are collected, then if there is a trend, that trend should become clear.

Measuring the Effects of Surprise, Information Advantage, and Situational Awareness

All effective measurement of these three factors ended up being primarily based on mission accomplishment. From this we can get a measurement of just how much of an advantage this provides. Tables 11.20–11.23 compare these data.

Table 11.20. Surprise

	Engagements with No Surprise	Engagements with Attacker Surprise
Percentage of attacker wins	50	86
Percentage of outcomes IV, V, and VI	57	72
Percentage attacker average score is higher	—	27
Percentage defender average score is lower	—	21
Multiplier attacker higher than defender	1.0857	1.7456

Table 11.21. Information Advantage (without Surprise)

	Attacker Much More Knowledgeable	Attacker More Knowledgeable	Same for Both Sides	Defender More Knowledgeable	Defender Much More Knowledgeable
Percentage of attacker wins	47	61	49	47	0
LESS DRAWS	80	66	58	50	0
Percentage of outcomes: IV, V, and VI	53	61	56	67	0
Scoring					
ATTACKER	5.65	5.63	5.52	5.20	2.50
DEFENDER	4.47	4.69	5.06	5.06	7.55
Ratio of attacker vs. defender score	1.26 to 1	1.20 to 1	1.09 to 1	1.03 to 1	0.33 to 1

Table 11.22. Situational Awareness (Attacker)—All Engagements

	Considerable	Some	Little
Percentage of attacker wins	41	50	72
LESS DRAWS	53	54	74
Percentage of outcomes IV, V, and VI	50	54	75
Scoring			
ATTACKER	5.23	5.03	5.41
DEFENDER	4.98	4.77	4.20
Ratio of attacker vs. defender score	1.05 to 1	1.05 to 1	1.29 to 1

Table 11.23. Situational Awareness (Defender)—All Engagements

	Considerable	Some	Little
Percentage of attacker wins	38	46	74
LESS DRAWS	46	52	83
Percentage of outcomes IV, V, and VI	51	52	68
Scoring			
ATTACKER	5.20	4.98	5.41
DEFENDER	5.33	4.93	3.68
Ratio of attacker vs. defender score	0.98	1.01	1.47

Surprise results in a more effective outcome by 26 to 72 percent.[6] The range of favorable outcomes for an information advantage (without surprise) is from effectively 22 percent to 60 percent greater.[7] As discussed in chapter 10, the results for the attacker with good situational awareness are the reverse of what would be expected and contradict the other trends. This result is not considered relevant.[8] The results for the defender with considerable situational awareness are from 33 to 80 percent greater.[9] The averages of the outcomes of the three relevant tests are, respectively, 1.53, 1.20, and 1.54.

Therefore achieving surprise serves as a considerable force multiplier, and having an information advantage or poor defender situational awareness increases the chance of surprise. Even without achieving surprise, having a large information advantage or having a defender suffering poor situational awareness gives an advantage of the same order of magnitude. Having either an information advantage or poor defender situational awareness appears to serve as a force multiplier of around 50 percent from the two extremes (from "little" to "considerable" or from "defender more knowledgeable" to "attacker much more knowledgeable").

The advantage of surprise is above and beyond the advantage gained for information advantage or poor defender situational awareness. Surprise serves as a force multiplier of 50 percent and is achieved at least twice as often (from around 10 percent to around 20 percent) due to information advantage, and from about 1 percent to around 20 percent of the time due to poor enemy situational awareness. Therefore, on the average, surprise serves as an additional 10 percent force multiplier, appearing in only 20 percent of the cases with an information advantage and giving around a 50 percent advantage.

The advantage gained from an information advantage and poor defender situational awareness thus appears to be an average force multiplier of 60 percent or greater. In those cases where surprise is achieved, it can easily become a "doubling" force multiplier.

The Advantage Gained from Complete Situational Awareness

The force multiplier estimate just cited is based on the difference between "little" to "considerable" or "defender more knowledgeable" to "attacker much more knowledgeable." As such, neither serves to fully measure the advantage gained from complete situational awareness. Also the differences within those two extremes is obviously less, leaving much smaller gains to be made in combat power from incremental gains in situational awareness.

The real difference in most cases is at the lowest level (i.e., "little" to "some"). In some cases the combatants in the "considerable" cases pretty much knew what they were facing and roughly where. They made up for any shortfalls with battlefield reconnaissance. Therefore we do not expect that there will be a big difference between "considerable" and "complete."

On the other hand, if one can provide complete situational awareness at all times and relay that in a usable format to the lower-level tactical units involved in the engagements, there may be an additional multiplier effect beyond what we are measuring here. The values provided here represent the advantage gained if that information is available to the decision makers at brigade, division, and corps headquarters. We cannot say if the values would remain the same if that information was available to the leadership at battalion headquarters or below, or if it was in the hands of every soldier.

Information Advantage versus Poor Situational Awareness

The best and clearest results we obtained, and with the greatest difference, were due to poor defender situational awareness (when the defender has "little" situational awareness). We conclude that if all things are equal, it is more important to have poor situational awareness than to have good situational awareness on your own or even superior situational awareness. In other words, obscuration (poor enemy situational awareness) is more important than knowledge for the attacker.

While the attacker obviously would prefer to both obscure his forces and have more knowledge, it may be worth making trade-offs in battle. By the same token, when funding new systems and technology, there may also be a need to make some trade-offs, and certainly there are always trade-offs to be made within what is always a finite budget. One needs to at least consider that obscuration is as important as improved situational awareness.

Defender Favored by Good Situational Awareness

The defender is favored by good situational awareness. He is never surprised when he has an information advantage over the attacker and, of course, is very vulnerable if he has "little" situational awareness. The attacker and defender benefit differently from differences in situational awareness. The most important element for the attacker is enemy situational awareness. Having good situational awareness helps, as does having an information advantage. The most important element for the defender is not having poor situational awareness or having an information advantage (which could be the same as poor enemy situational awareness).

The most lopsided combat results would be expected in a situation where the attacker had good situational awareness while being obscured from the defender so the defender has poor situational awareness. Such a scenario certainly describes most of the actions in the 1991 Gulf War.

Final Observations

Obscuration is as important for the attacker as having good situational awareness. This comparison, which was never the intent of this study, came about because of the patterns observed in the data.

The same may be true for the defender. Certainly the defender is seriously disadvantaged by having "little" situational awareness. Having good situational awareness or an information advantage is important for the defender and may be more important than for the attacker.

The value of good situational awareness as a force multiplier is around 50 percent or greater. This figure appears to be, on the face of it, less than what we have inferred from other literature on the subject. There is an additional value gained from surprising the enemy, but this is not the primary value of having good situational awareness. Having good situational awareness also has a security value in that it helps protect you from surprise.

These are tentative results. Even though this study used far more real-world data than anyone else has attempted to use, more research needs to be done. This is the first study we are aware of that has attempted to measure the combat value of situational awareness using real-world combat data.

There is definitely a need for analysis of situational awareness in operations below division level. This study can be viewed as an analysis of the advantage of improved situational awareness in the corps, division, and brigade headquarters. A similar analysis should be done using battalion-level data to see if there is a difference in results.

While there have been historical analyses and studies based on a few examples of information advantage (case studies), there are no other broad-ranging studies similar to ours. We have seen in our casual reading measurements of situational awareness that are based on abstract games. This may be fine as an intellectual construct, but it is not by any stretch of the imagination a measurement of the advantage of situational awareness in the real world. We suspect that some studies may also have been done using data from war games and exercises, but again, as these are not data derived from real combat, they are fundamentally different from what we are analyzing.

12. The Nature of Lower Levels of Combat

Casualty rates of small forces are higher than those of large forces.
—Trevor N. Dupuy, *Understanding War*

Most of the Dupuy Institute's past analysis has been based around division-level combat.[1] There are two reasons for this. First, much of the U.S. defense community's previous focus was on higher levels of combat operations. This was certainly the case during the Cold War and was still the nature of combat in the Gulf War of 1991. The division is often the first real level of combined arms operations and often the first level of a unit that is structured to fight independently. As a result much of the analysis done in the U.S. defense community has been focused on comparing and modeling divisions. Second, the division level has good supporting data. This point is more significant than it may appear to the casual observer. Divisions have extensive staffs that regularly maintain records on all aspects of operations. Headquarters for units smaller than the division usually have minimal staff. In addition to maintaining records on operations, the division level regularly saves these records. For example, in the case of the U.S. Army in the Gulf War of 1991, 86 or 87 percent of the battalion daily journals were not preserved.[2] Also, to do two-sided analysis of combat you need the unit records for the opposing force. Sometimes these records are available for opposing divisions, but they rarely are for lower-level units.

Force-on-force comparisons below the division level are more difficult to research: the data are sparser, and opposing forces are harder to match up. These problems are reflected in the Dupuy Institute databases. We have three databases of combat that are sorted by unit size. Our largest is a division-level database of 752 cases. Our battalion-level database has only 127 cases, and our company-level database has 98 cases. This is a reflection of where our customers' focus has been in the past and what research the records support. It gets difficult (and more expensive) to do research at the lower levels, especially as our requirement at the Dupuy Institute is to base our work on two-sided data. Still, we have begun looking at lower levels of combat, and I will share some of that work here.

In this chapter I will look at the nature and patterns of the data from combat and see how they differ according to level of combat. Dupuy found a relationship between unit size and average daily casualty rates, as demonstrated in table 12.1.

Table 12.1. Relationship of Unit Size to Casualty Rates

	U.S. Experience in World War II	
Unit	Approximate Strength	Average Casualty Daily Engagement Rates, Percentages
Company	200	21.0 (estimated)
Battalion	800	9.5
Brigade (Regiment)	3,000	2.6
Division	15,000	1.0
Corps (3 divisions)	65,000	0.6
Corps (4 divisions)	90,000	0.4
Army (3 corps)	250,000	0.3

Dupuy based these numbers on reports and research the Historical Evaluation and Research Organization conducted in the 1980s.[3] He used two hundred engagements (four hundred attrition cases) of moderate- to high-intensity combat in World War II (1939–45). The company figures were estimated, as the database he used did not contain many, if any, company-level actions.[4] This relationship is best illustrated by figure 12.1.[5]

As noted in a 1980s HERO report, there is a difference between casualty rates in World War II and in post–World War II contingency operations (roughly equivalent to what is now referred to as "irregular warfare").[6] This is demonstrated in table 12.2.

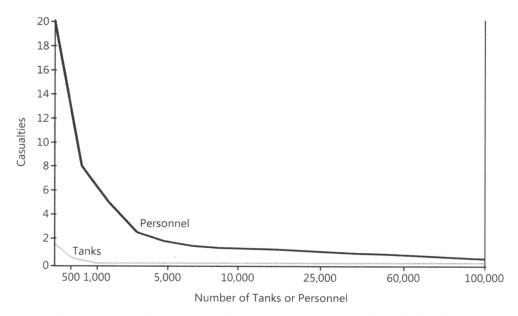

Fig. 12.1. Strength/size attrition factors (tz). Source: Perez, "Exactly How," 22. Graph redrawn by Jay Karamales.

Table 12.2. Comparison of World War II and Minor Conflict Casualty Rates

Unit Size	World War II Percentage	Minor Contingencies Percentage
Company	—	5.0
Battalion	5.5	2.3
Brigade	3.6	1.3
Division	2.1	—

An effort specifically looking at casualties in contingency operations provided the data in table 12.3.[7]

Table 12.3. Total Battle Casualties by Unit Strength

Unit Strength Class	Number of Engagements	Mean Daily Casualty Rate	Standard Deviation
Fewer than 300	14	50	72
301–600	15	32	38
601–1,000	13	23	20
1,001–2,500	17	13	12
Over 2,500	14	12	20

The figures for casualty rates are per 1,000. So a figure of 50 would be 50 casualties per 1,000 troops, or 5 percent. These are the same data as in table 12.2, but now one can see the genesis of that table. For minor contingencies, company data came from the "Fewer than 300" category, battalion data came from the "601–1,000" category, and brigade data came from the "1,001–2,500" category. No data from the "301–600" category were used nor from the "Over 2,500" category. As the data are in casualties per 1,000, later tables converted the results to percentages by simply moving the decimal point one place, so 50 per 1,000 in 1985 was reported as 5 percent in 1986.[8]

This issue is further amplified in a report on low-intensity conflict that looked at fourteen Vietnam-era engagements (table 12.4).[9]

Table 12.4. Data from Fourteen Vietnam Engagements

	Troop Strength		Historical Casualties			
	ATTACKER	DEFENDER	ATTACKER		DEFENDER	
Averages	782	386	188	21.2%*	90	32.4%*
				24.0%**		23.3%**

*Average of percentages

**Percent of Averages

This appears to be the entire collection of analysis done for casualty rates by unit size by HERO and related organizations. We are not aware of any other studies that address this subject by the U.S. Department of Defense, its contractors, its federally funded research and development centers such as RAND and the Center for Naval Analyses, or by the United Kingdom or other foreign operational research establishments. The data set consists of over four hundred World War II data points from army level to battalion level (we do not believe there was any systematically collected company-level data) and seventy-three post–World War II data points, from below 300 troops to above 2,500. That is all that has been done in the past fifty years![10]

For a comparison, we assembled a database of around one hundred company-level actions. There were eighty-nine actions in which both sides had six hundred troops or fewer. For another nine actions one side had greater than six hundred troops. These actions came from a number of distinct conflicts over the past hundred years and were chosen because of ease of data collection and virtually no other criteria. The ninety-eight actions were from the wars and theaters of war listed in table 12.5.

Table 12.5. Sources of Company-Level Actions

	Total Cases	Conventional	Guerrilla	Intervention	Raid
World War I and interwar	26	11	15	—	—
World War II	20	13	7	—	—
Post–World War II (to 1978)	47	6	29	10	2
Recent (1981 to present)	5	2	2	1	—

For convenience, the engagements were organized by period: those from 1900 to 1938 were listed under "World War I," those from 1939 to 1945 were listed under "World War II," those from 1946 to 1980 were listed under "Post–World War II," and those from 1981 to the present were listed under "Recent." The statistics are broken out by period in table 12.6.

Table 12.6. Company-Level Action Statistics

	World War I	World War II	Post–World War II	Recent
Number of cases	26	20	47	5.
Average attacker strength	236	417	257	162
Average defender strength	123	299	169	294
Weighted force ratio	1.92	1.39	1.52	0.55
Duration (hours)	10.42	14.56	5.10	0.93
Front (km.)	—	0.61	0.075	—

Attacker density (men per km.)	—	810.40	1140	—
Average attacker casualties	21	49	36	5
Average defender casualties	14	72	43	109
Weighted percentage of losses for attacker	8.74	11.75	14.19	3.09
Weighted percentage of losses for defender	11.16	23.91	25.25	37.19
Distance advanced (in km.)	0.48	0.67	1.24	2.84
Attacker wins	12	11	33	4

The differences by period in these statistics are clearly being driven by the choice of engagements, as opposed to any historical trends. For example, the World War I engagements consist of two collections of engagements that are not very indicative of the trench warfare in Flanders Fields. The first group of eleven engagements is from fighting between colonial forces in West Africa. These were European-officered local forces and the fighting was a kind of warfare very different from that being fought in northern Europe. The other fifteen engagements are fights between the U.S. Marines and the Sandinistas in 1927–28, which was a classic modern guerrilla war. As such, it probably has more in common with Vietnam than with classic World War I or II conventional engagements. Table 12.7 compares the statistics on the two.

Table 12.7. Comparison of Colonial West Africa Actions and Sandinistas Actions

	Colonial West Africa	Sandinistas
Number of cases	11	15
Average attacker strength	375	134
Average defender strength	185	77
Weighted force ratio	2.03	1.73
Duration (hours)	4.91	14.47
Front (km.)	—	—
Attacker density (men per km.)	—	—
Average attacker casualties	35	10
Average defender casualties	24	6
Weighted percentage of losses for attacker	9.31	7.57
Weighted percentage of losses for defender	13.04	7.85
Distance advanced (in km.)	0.22	0.67
Attacker wins	7	5

Table 12.7 shows a clear difference between the two sets of data. The first set of World War I data, while certainly not Flanders Fields, is from more traditional conventional combat, for it is showing larger units suffering higher losses in engagements with shorter durations. In contrast, the Sandinistas' engagements are more typical of guerrilla warfare. So even though these are small-unit engagements, as the original HERO research pointed out, there is a difference between the casualty rates in engagements from the major conventional wars (e.g., World War I and World War II) and those from insurgencies and other contingency operations.

The World War II data group is also not typical of the range of conflicts in Europe during that war. To start with, fifteen of the cases are engagements with the Japanese, an unusual army noted for their suicide charges and fights to the death. The five European engagements are mostly commando raids. As such, this does not provide a good comparison with the World War I cases. On the other hand it is probably worthwhile to look at the data from the fifteen Japanese engagements separate from the five European engagements. Also, an incomplete data set of four ETO conventional fights from the Battle of the Bulge was appended to this database. Although the data on these four engagements are incomplete and have not been fully proofed, it is useful for analysis to look at them here (table 12.8).

Table 12.8. World War II Company-Level Actions

	Pacific Engagements	European Engagements	ETO 1944 Engagements
Number of cases	15	5	4
Average attacker strength	457	295	260
Average defender strength	351	144	225
Weighted force ratio	1.30	2.05	1.15
Duration (hours)	15.27	12.45	24
Front (km.)	0.70	0.35	1.08
Attacker density (men per km.)	708.66	1115.63	389.17
Average attacker casualties	52	41	40
Average defender casualties	71	72	21
Weighted percentage of losses for attacker	11.30	13.85	15.51
Weighted percentage of losses for defender	20.29	50.42	9.44
Distance advanced (in km.)	0.48	1.24	0
Attacker wins	7	4	1

Oddly enough, the differences among these three groups of engagements are not as great as one would think, considering that one engagement was mostly jungle fighting against the Japanese, one was mostly commando raids in Europe and Africa, and the final group was conventional fighting in the Battle of the Bulge. These are classic conventional combat examples and look a lot more like the colonial West African engagements than the Sandinistas' engagements.

The post–World War II group statistics do not seem radically different from the World War II data, which is surprising considering their nature. Of the forty-seven cases, six are from a conventional war (three from the Korean War and three from the 1956 Arab-Israeli War). The rest are from various insurgencies, interventions, commando raids, and actions that would now be called irregular warfare. This means this data set should be different in nature from the conventional warfare data. That it is not is either because it uses small, highly variable data sets (which can be easily corrected with more cases) or because there is really not a significant difference in company-level combat between insurgencies and conventional warfare. Perhaps a company-level combat is a combat is a combat, and there is no need for further differentiation. We are not sure that this is the case, but for this analysis, due to the small number of cases, we cannot prove that it is not the case. Therefore we have simply put all the engagements into the same hopper for analysis. This includes the five engagements coded as recent (1981 to present), for with only five cases, there was no basis for keeping them separate from the other post–World War II cases.

Engagements by Unit Size

Having made the decision to look at the entire population of ninety-eight cases as one whole uniform data set, we have 196 data points for analysis (both defender and attacker). We do have statistics on strength and losses for a dozen other relevant but not completed cases that we included in the database. By definition, some of these are not company-level actions, but they do provide useful examples because of their theater, time, and nature. So we added the four conventional engagements from the Battle of the Bulge, six engagements from the Falkland Islands, and two engagements from the Invasion of Grenada. This nominally gives us thirteen recent engagements and provides a little more balance to the data set. We now have a total of 220 data points for analysis.

These data are displayed in the simple scattergram in figure 12.2, first by attacker, then by defender, and then for all data points. In this case we simply looked at percentage of losses based on unit size.

The two lines in the graph are the Microsoft Excel trend line and the logarithmic line. The correlation coefficient is −.05769. This graph shows almost

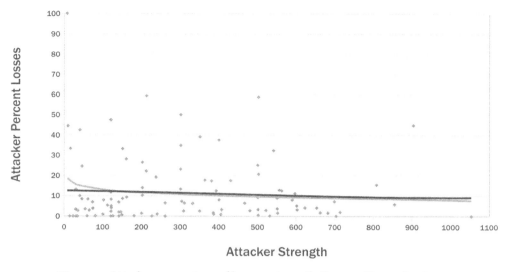

Fig. 12.2. Attacker percentage of loss vs. strength. Source: Dupuy Institute.

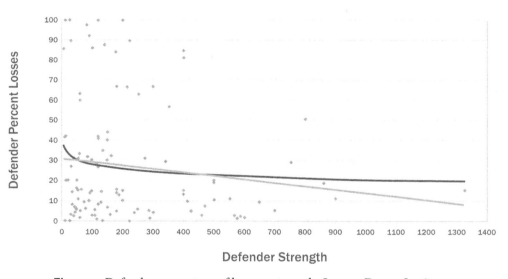

Fig. 12.3. Defender percentage of loss vs. strength. Source: Dupuy Institute.

a straight line except for cases where the unit strength is less than fifty. This would suggest the casualty multiplier for force size ranging from 500 to 1,000 (a value of 8) should be extended down to cover 51 to 1,000.

For the defenders, there is clearly more of a relationship between unit size and loss rates (fig. 12.3). The trend line clearly shows such a relationship, and the correlation coefficient is −.13405. The Microsoft Excel logarithmic line shows much less change as the units get larger, except for units under 300 and especially for units of 100 or fewer. This would argue for some change in value below 501 and another, higher value for attrition below 101.

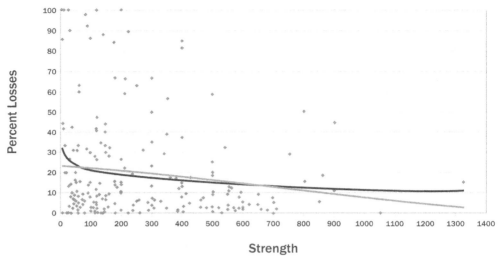

Fig. 12.4. Attacker and defender percentages of loss vs. strength. Source: Dupuy Institute.

Ignoring posture (attacker vs. defender), all 220 data points are graphed in figure 12.4. In this case the trend line shows a relationship, and there is a correlation coefficient of −0.07375. The logarithmic line shows much less change over size except for units with fewer than 200 troops.

These three graphs all support the point that a casualty multiplier of 20 for fewer than 500 troops may be too large in relation to the multiplier of 8 for forces of 500 to 1,000.

The aggregate statistics for these 110 cases are presented in table 12.9.

Table 12.9. Statistics for 110 Combat-Level Actions

	All 110 Cases
Number of cases	110
Average attacker strength	303
Average defender strength	220
Weighted force ratio	1.38
Duration (hours)	8.86
Front (km.)	0.65 (22 cases where we have data)
Attacker density (men per km.)	763.78 (22 cases where we have data)
Average attacker casualties	33
Average defender casualties	51
Weighted percentage of losses for attacker	10.95
Weighted percentage of losses for defender	23.04
Distance advanced (in km.)	1.21
Attacker wins	69

Table 12.10. Loss Rates Compared to Strength Increments of
Fifty (Percentage of Averages)

Category	Attacker Cases	Percentage of Casualties	Defender Cases	Percentage of Casualties
1–50	16	12.90	21	32.10
51–100	9	3.90	20	63.51
101–150	16	8.66	21	62.44
151–200	10	9.16	12	62.94
201–250	5	19.59	5	50.30
251–300	6	22.21	6	43.36
301–350	6	11.03	1	29.41
351–400	7	13.60	5	54.53
401–450	3	7.34	2	22.43
451–500	9	14.29	5	16.50
501–550	6	8.31	0	—
551–600	6	8.67	5	17.16
601–650	2	4.25	1	9.23
651–700	4	2.85	1	5.29
701–750	1	1.97	0	—
751–800	0	—	2	44.40
801–850	2	10.63	0	
851–900	1	44.78	2	18.07
1,050	1	0.19	—	—
1,324	—	—	1	15.11

Breaking these out by strength increments of fifty is illustrative (table 12.10). Note that these numbers were based on what we called "weighted averages"; that is, they are calculated based on the averages for each category (percentage of averages) as opposed to being an average of the averages (average of percentages). We take the average losses of all the engagements in that category and divide by the average strength of all the engagements in that category. It is not an average of the percentage of losses; we have one percentage value for each engagement and then take an average of them (table 12.11).

Table 12.11. Loss Rates Compared to Strength Increments of
Fifty (Average of Percentages)

Category	Attacker Cases	Percentage of Casualties	Defender Cases	Percentage of Casualties
1–50	16	**17.89**	21	28.42
51–100	9	3.90	20	**31.92**
101–150	16	8.67	21	**25.39**

151–200	10	9.45	12	**30.72**
201–250	5	20.37	5	**33.24**
251–300	6	21.37	6	**28.56**
301–350	6	10.64	1	29.41
351–400	7	13.55	5	50.23
401–450	3	7.14	2	**7.31**
451–500	9	14.18	5	**11.89**
501–550	6	8.28	0	—
551–600	6	8.76	5	**3.85**
601–650	2	4.25	1	9.23
651–700	4	2.84	1	5.29
701–750	1	1.97	0	—
751–800	0	—	2	39.78
801–850	2	10.76	0	—
851–900	1	44.78	2	14.86
1,050	1	0.19	—	—
1,324	—	—	1	15.11

The numbers in bold are those values that are significantly different from the weighted averages. For the attackers, this occurs in only one case. For the defenders it occurs often and in significant areas. We tend to use weighted averages because of the highly disparate data we are working with. For example, losing 8 out of 10 people is not the same as losing 8 out of 990; the average of those two numbers is 40.40 percent, while the weighted average is 1.60 percent. This is a big difference.

In this case, though, we are averaging in categories of fifty, and therefore there is not a strong reason to use the weighted averages, as each engagement in each category is of similar size. Still, we know of no rules or convention specifying whether—when looking at percentage of losses—one should use weighted averages or simply use an average of the percentage of losses.

As the original construct we are testing had a casualty multiplier of 8 for forces from 500 to 1,000 and a casualty multiplier of 20 for forces fewer than 500, we compared those forces in those two categories to see if one category is producing casualties 2.5 times larger than the other. The results appear in table 12.12.

Table 12.12. Weighted Averages

Percentage of Averages					
Category	Casualty Multiplier	Attacker Cases	Percentage of Casualties	Defender Cases	Percentage of Casualties
1–500	20	87	12.85	98	47.26
501–1,000	8	22	26.25	11	22.77
Average of Percentages					
Category	Casualty Multiplier	Attacker Cases	Percentage of Casualties	Defender Cases	Percentage of Casualties
1–500	20	87	12.55	98	28.87
501–1,000	8	22	8.65	11	13.00

Table 12.13 presents these numbers as a ratio between the 501–1,000 category and the 1–500 category. For example, if the value of the 501–1,000 category is 8, then the value of the 1–500 category should be around 16 rather than 20 or 21.

Table 12.13. Ratio between the Two Strength Categories

Casualty Multiplier	Attacker Average Weighted	Percentage	Defender Average Weighted	Percentage
2.5 to 1	.049 to 1	1.45 to 1	2.08 to 1	2.22 to 1

The question then becomes: Should there be any further subdivision in the 1–500 category? If we break the category into bands of 100 (table 12.14), we still do not see any real pattern, which was also the case for bands of 50 (see tables 12.10 and 12.11).

Table 12.14. Weighted Averages

Percentage of Averages				
Category	Attacker Cases	Percentage of Casualties	Defender Cases	Percentage of Casualties
1–100	25	7.60	41	54.21
101–200	26	8.90	33	62.67
201–300	11	21.17	11	46.16
301–400	13	12.53	6	51.24
401–500	12	12.78	7	18.02

	Average of Percentages			
Category	Attacker Cases	Percentage of Casualties	Defender Cases	Percentage of Casualties
1–100	25	12.85	41	30.13
101–200	26	8.97	33	27.33
201–300	11	20.91	11	30.69
301–400	13	12.20	6	46.76
401–500	12	12.42	7	10.59

There is not much argument here for differentiation by category. The attacker data indicate that casualty rates are constant across the spectrum of values. The defender data indicate that the rate may be lower from 401 to 500, but this is based on only seven data points. Therefore we conclude that the attrition multiplier is a constant from 1 to 500.

Still, there was a higher start point in the 1–50 range when we used the logarithm graphs, although that is the nature of a logarithmic line. We could test for 1–50 compared to the rest of the data (51–500), as shown in table 12.15.

Table 12.15. Weighted Averages

	Percentage of Averages			
Category	Attacker Cases	Percentage of Casualties	Defender Cases	Percentage of Casualties
1–50	16	12.90	21	32.10
51–500	71	12.85	77	47.90

	Average of Percentages			
Category	Attacker Cases	Percentage of Casualties	Defender Cases	Percentage of Casualties
1–50	16	17.89	21	28.42
51–500	71	11.35	77	28.99

None of this argues for a higher value for 1–50 as opposed to 51–500. In fact it seems to establish that the logarithmic line does not fit and to argue for some form of step-wise line, with the breakpoint somewhere between 400 to 600.

As there is a reason to believe that 401–500 is at a different value than 1–400, and may be at different values than 501–1,000, we decided to test this. The results are in table 12.16.

Table 12.16. Weighted Averages

Percentage of Averages				
Category	Attacker Cases	Percentage of Casualties	Defender Cases	Percentage of Casualties
1–400	75	12.89	91	55.15
401–500	12	12.78	7	18.02
501–600	12	8.49	5	17.16
601–1,000	10	9.97	6	26.24
Average of Percentages				
Category	Attacker Cases	Percentage of Casualties	Defender Cases	Percentage of Casualties
1–400	75	12.58	91	30.28
401–500	12	12.42	7	10.59
501–600	12	8.52	5	3.85
601–1,000	10	8.81	6	20.63

Once again we are not producing a result that disagrees with the original concept by Dupuy, that there was one value for 1–500 and another value for 501–1,000. For the attackers, there is clearly no such argument. For the defenders, the data are fuzzier and do argue for a breakpoint at 400. As the number of cases in the 401–500 category is very low (only seven), there is no reason to make any changes based on this.

Conclusion

This test is interesting for a number of reasons. First, Dupuy's construct, which was also coded into his QJM and TNDM models, found that the unit loss rates were higher for smaller units. He specifically provided values or multipliers that were applied to the percentage of loss of the unit. It appears from these data that his first assumption was correct. It also appears that the use of multipliers and their values are reasonable. As shown by the data in this chapter, if the value of the casualty multiplier for a force ranging from 501 to 1,000 is 8 (battalion-level combat), then the value of the casualty multiplier for a force ranging from 1 to 500 should be more like 16. Dupuy estimated that value to be 20. It does appear that the categorization, including the step-wise categories, all fit nicely with the new data we used.

This is a completely independent look at the elements of Dupuy's constructs using newly researched data, including a significant proportion of post–World

War II data (55 percent of the data set). The results ended up coming close to what Dupuy had originally postulated based on World War II data.

One of the concerns with Dupuy's modeling work was that the same model and values were used for all levels of combat, except for the casualty rates. One could input data from an army-level engagement of hundreds of thousands of men over several days, or a company-level engagement of a couple of hundred people over a couple of hours. The model would provide a result regardless of the size of the unit. The model did have a table that converted the casualties based on unit size, but that was the only change based on unit size. As can be seen here, that table appears to be close to correct. Furthermore, as can be seen here, there are no other elements of the data from company-level actions that differentiate them from the division-level data provided in previous chapters. The data are similar for a range of issues: force ratios, linear density, advance rates, and so forth. The primary difference appears to be loss rates.[11] These seem to be tied to unit size fairly consistently, even though the company-level data span almost a hundred years.

Loss rates appear to be surprisingly consistent over time. This is hard to comprehend given how much weapons have improved over the past hundred years. Obviously many other things have changed over time to compensate for this. We will explore these subjects in the next chapter.

13. The Effects of Dispersion on Combat

Firepower kills, disrupts, suppresses, and causes dispersion.

—TREVOR N. DUPUY, *Understanding War*

From the 1600s through the 1800s groups of men with muzzle-loading harque-busiers and muskets faced each other thousands of times across the field of bat-tle.[1] At the end of the day, often as many as 20 or 30 percent of those engaged would be casualties. Almost four hundred years later, in the battles of World War II and the Arab-Israeli wars, division-size forces faced each other in battle, and rarely did either side suffer more than 3 percent losses in a day; often they suffered less than 1 percent. Guns were rifled, powerful artillery was used, and there were tanks, planes, and all kinds of modern communication devices. The effectiveness and lethality of weapons have continued to increase over the past four hundred years, yet the loss rates among forces in combat have declined.

This effect was identified by Dupuy in his various writings, starting with *Evo-lution of Weapons and Warfare*. A graph of the battle casualty trends over time is reproduced here from *Understanding War* (see fig. 13.1). He postulated that forces continued to disperse over time to compensate for the increased lethality of weapons. Warfare has gone from men in brightly colored uniforms stand-ing shoulder to shoulder as they marched into the fight, to forces spread out widely across the battlefield. A battle in the 1600s–1800s often put ten thou-sand to twenty thousand or more men in an area measuring a couple of square

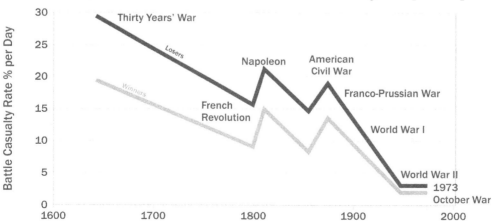

Fig. 13.1. Average daily battle casualty rates, 1600–1973. Source: Dupuy, *Understanding War*. Redrawn by Jay Karamales.

kilometers. Now divisions of ten thousand to twenty thousand are operating on fronts 10 to 20 kilometers wide and with considerably more depth. Over time units have continued to spread and scatter and find ways to reduce the effects of the increased lethality of weapons; this is dispersion.

As dispersion has changed dramatically over time one would expect that casualties would also change. I therefore used the Land Warfare Data Base (LWDB) of 605 engagements from 1600 to 1973 to look at dispersion and casualties over time.[2]

To be able to group these data into meaningful categories, I split the wars into fourteen chronologically based categories. Measuring the results by years scattered the data; measuring the results by centuries assembled the data in too gross a manner; and measuring the results by war left a confusing picture due to the number of small wars in the database with only two or three battles in them. I needed a categorization system that put the battles into usable chronological categories. These categories are shown in table 13.1.

Table 13.1. Chronological Categories of Wars

Category	Years	Number of Examples	Number of Listed Battles[1]
Thirty Years War	1618–1648	18	20
English Civil War	1642–1652	9	15
Other wars	1650–1699*	21	12+
Other wars	1700–1755	15	46+
Seven Years War	1756–1763	18	48
Revolutionary War	1775–1783	14	43
French Revolutionary Wars	1792–1802	23	51
Napoleonic Wars	1803–1815	33	140
Other wars	1816–1859	19	63+
American Civil War	1881–1865	49	143
Other wars	1860–1905	30	123+
World War I	1912–1920**	131	68++
World War II	1937–1945***	172	92+++
Arab-Israeli wars	1967, 1968, 1973	53	0++
Other post–World War II wars	****	—	44+

1. From Clodfelter, *Warfare and Armed Conflicts*.

*Includes one battle before 1650.

**Includes Balkan Wars and Russo-Polish War.

***Includes one Spanish Civil War battle and several Russo-Japanese engagements.

****The only post–World War II battles that this version of the LWDB looks at is the Arab-Israeli wars from 1967 to 1973. It thus leaves out the Korean War, the Vietnam War, and anything after 1973. This was corrected in later versions of the database.

To give some idea of how representative the battles listed in the LWDB were for covering the period, I have included a count of the number of battles listed in Micheal Clodfelter's two-volume work *Warfare and Armed Conflicts, 1618–1991*. In the case of World War I, World War II, and later, battles tend to be defined as a division-level engagement, of which there were tens of thousands in those wars.

I then tested the data based on the fourteen periods. These tests included the following:

1. Average strength by war (fig. 13.2)

2. Average losses by war (fig. 13.3)

3. Percentage of losses per day by war (fig. 13.4)

4. Average number of people per kilometer by war (fig. 13.5)

5. Losses per kilometer of front by war (fig. 13.7)

6. Strength and losses per kilometer of front by war (fig. 13.8)

7. Ratio of strength and losses per kilometer of front by war (fig. 13.9)

8. Ratio of strength and losses per kilometer of front by century (fig. 13.10)

A review of average strengths over time by century and by war showed no surprises (see fig. 13.2). Up through around 1900, battles were easy to define: they were one- to three-day affairs between clearly defined forces at a single locale. The forces had a clear left flank and right flank that were not bounded by other friendly forces. After 1900 (and in a few cases before), warfare was fought on continuous fronts, and a battle was often a large multicorps operation. It is no longer clear what is meant by a battle, as the forces, area covered, and duration can vary widely. For the LWDB, each battle was defined as the analyst wished. In the case of World War I, there were a lot of very large battles, which drove up the average force size. In the case of World War II, there were a lot of division-level battles, which brought down the average force size. In the case of the Arab-Israeli wars, there are nothing but division- and brigade-level battles, which brought down the average force size.

The interesting point to note about figure 13.2 is that the average attacker strength in the sixteenth and seventeenth century is lower than the average defender strength. Later it is higher. This may be due to anomalies in data selection.

Average losses by war (fig. 13.3) suffers from the same battle definition problem.

Percentage of losses per day (fig. 13.4) is a useful comparison. Note the definite downward patterns from the Napoleonic through the Arab-Israeli wars,

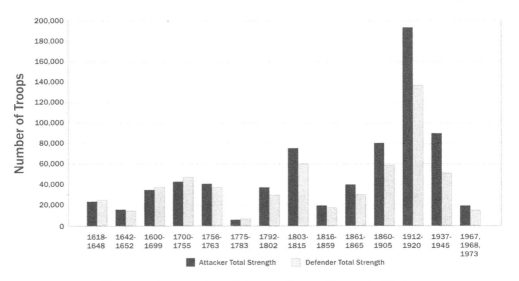

Fig. 13.2. Average strength by war. Source: Dupuy Institute.

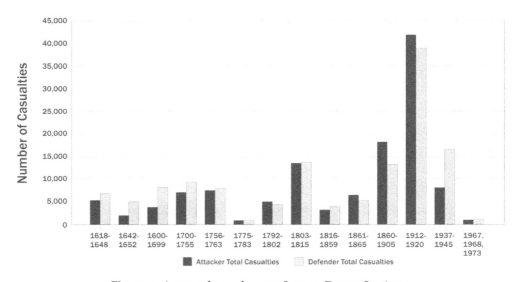

Fig. 13.3. Average losses by war. Source: Dupuy Institute.

a very clear indication of the effects of dispersion. It would appear that from the 1600s to the 1800s the pattern was effectively constant and level, and then it declined in a very systematic way. This partially contradicts Dupuy's writing and graphs (fig. 13.1). It also appears that after this period of decline the percentage of losses per day were being set at a new, much lower plateau.

Looking at the actual subject of dispersion, the dispersion of people (measured in people per kilometer of front) remained relatively constant from 1600 through the American Civil War (see fig. 13.5). Dupuy defined dispersion as

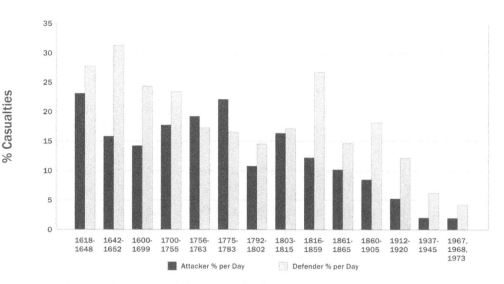

Fig. 13.4. Percentage of losses per day by war. Source: Dupuy Institute.

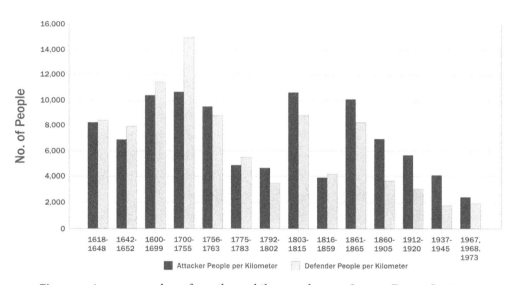

Fig. 13.5. Average number of people per kilometer by war. Source: Dupuy Institute.

the number of people in a box-like area. Unfortunately it is hard to consistently measure the depth of a battle formation. The left and right flanks of a unit are relatively easy to identify, but it is more difficult to know how deep the unit is deployed. Furthermore the density of occupation of this box is far from uniform and usually has a very forward bias. By the same token, fire delivered into this box is not uniform and has the same very forward bias. Therefore I am quite comfortable measuring dispersion based on unit frontage, more so than by front multiplied by depth.

Note that when comparing the Napoleonic Wars to the American Civil War, dispersion remains about the same. Yet according to the average casualties (fig. 13.3) and the average percentage of casualties per day (fig. 13.4), the rate of casualty accumulation is lower in the American Civil War. (This too partially contradicts Dupuy's writings.) There is no question that with the advent of the Minié ball, allowing for rapid-fire rifled muskets, the ability to deliver accurate firepower had increased.

The average number of people per linear kilometer between World War I and World War II differs by a factor of a little over 1.5 to 1. Yet the actual difference in casualties (see fig. 13.4) is much greater. While one can postulate that the difference is the change in dispersion squared (basically Dupuy's approach), this does not seem to explain the complete difference, especially in light of the difference between the Napoleonic Wars and the American Civil War.

Instead of discussing dispersion, we should be discussing "casualty reduction efforts," which consist of three elements:

1. Dispersion

2. Increased engagement ranges

3. More individual use of cover and concealment

These three factors together result in the reduced chance to hit. They are also partially interrelated, as one cannot make more individual use of cover and concealment unless one is allowed to disperse. Therefore the need for cover and concealment increases the desire to disperse, and the process of dispersing allows one to use more cover and concealment.

Command and control are integrated into this construct, allowing dispersion, and conversely dispersion creates the need for better command and control. Therefore improved command and control in this construct does not just operate as a force modifier but also enables a force to disperse.

Intelligence becomes more necessary as the opposing forces use cover and concealment and the ranges of engagement increase. By the same token, improved intelligence allows you to increase the range of engagement and forces the enemy to use better concealment. This whole construct could be represented by the diagram in figure 13.6.

I may have stated the obvious here, but this construct is probably provable in each individual element, and the overall outcome is measurable. Each connection between the boxes in figure 13.6 may also be measurable. Therefore, to measure the effects of a reduced chance to hit, one would need to complete the following formulae (assuming these formulae are close to being correct):

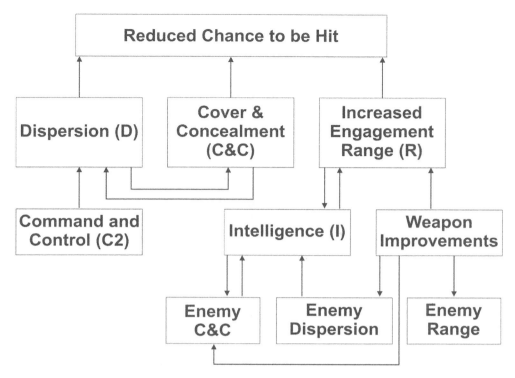

Fig. 13.6. Reduced chance to be hit. Source: Dupuy Institute.

$(K * \Delta D) + (K * \Delta C\&C) + (K * \Delta R) = H$

$(K * \Delta c_2) = \Delta D$

$(K * \Delta D) = \Delta C\&C$

$(K * \Delta W) + (K * \Delta I) = \Delta R$

   K = a constant

   Δ = the change in . . . ("Delta")

   D = dispersion

   $C\&C$ = cover and concealment

   R = engagement range

   W = weapon's characteristics

   H = the chance to hit

   c_2 = command and control

   I = intelligence, or ability to observe

Certain actions lead to a desire for certain technological and system improvements. This includes the effect of increased dispersion, leading to a need for better command and control, and increased range, leading to a need for bet-

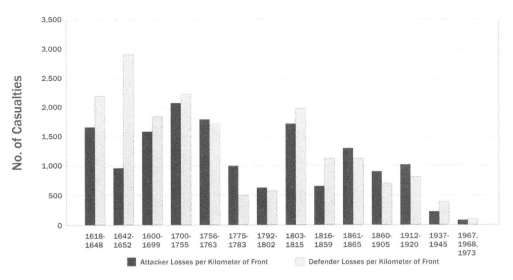

Fig. 13.7. Losses per kilometer of front by war. Source: Dupuy Institute.

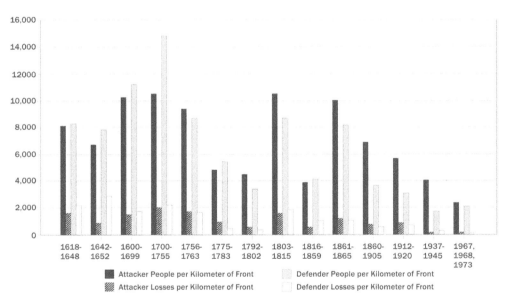

Fig. 13.8. Strength and losses per kilometer of front by war. Source: Dupuy Institute.

ter intelligence. I am not sure these are measurable. Figure 13.6 also shows how the enemy impacts this. And there is an interrelated mirror image of this construct for the other side.

I focus on measuring these changes because I hope to find some means of measuring the effects of a "revolution in warfare." The past four hundred years of history have given us more revolutionary inventions impacting war than we can reasonably expect to see in the next one hundred years. An understanding of how warfare changed in response to technological developments in the past can serve as a basis for estimating what the impact of new changes will be. In particular I would like to measure the impact of increased weapon accuracy, improved intelligence, and improved command and control on combat.

For the purposes of combat modeling, I would very specifically like to work out an attrition multiplier for battles before World War II (and theoretically after World War II) based on reduced chance to be hit ("dispersion"). For example, in a battalion-level model validation effort at the Dupuy Institute, we used an increased attrition multiplier to model the World War I engagements based on Dupuy's work.[3]

Figure 13.7 reports average losses per kilometer of front by war and is followed by figure 13.8, which shows strengths and losses per kilometer. As the graphs are a little difficult to read, the data in these graphs are included in table 13.2 along with some other comparative statistics.

Table 13.2. Strength and Losses per Kilometer of Front

Category	Strength per Kilometer of Front	Losses per Kilometer of Front	Strength Divided by Losses[1]	Strength per Kilometer Relative to World War II Data[2]	Losses per Kilometer Relative to World War II Data[3]
1618 Attacker	8,148	1,649	4.9	2.8	6.4
1618 Defender	8,329	2,193	3.8	2.8	6.4
1642 Attacker	6,765	942	7.2	2.5	6.4
1642 Defender	7,902	2,903	2.7	2.5	6.4
1699 Attacker	10,324	1,573	6.6	3.6	5.7
1699 Defender	11,341	1,830	6.2	3.6	5.7
1755 Attacker	10,629	2,063	5.2	4.3	7.1
1755 Defender	14,866	2,222	6.7	4.3	7.1
1765 Attacker	9,511	1,785	5.3	3.1	5.8
1765 Defender	8,747	1,702	5.1	3.1	5.8
1775 Attacker	4,851	977	5.0	1.7	2.4
1755 Defender	5,506	487	11.3	1.7	2.4

1792 Attacker	4,630	605	7.7	1.4	1.9
1792 Defender	3,471	563	6.2	1.4	1.9
1803 Attacker	10,644	1,683	6.3	3.2	6.1
1803 Defender	8,798	1,959	4.5	3.2	6.1
1859 Attacker	3,965	637	6.2	1.4	2.9
1859 Defender	4,223	1,111	3.8	1.4	2.9
1861 Attacker	10,135	1,282	7.9	3.1	4.0
1861 Defender	8,266	1,111	7.4	3.1	4.0
1905 Attacker	6,991	885	7.9	1.8	2.6
1905 Defender	3,755	689	5.4	1.8	2.6
1912 Attacker	5,784	1,009	5.7	1.5	3.0
1912 Defender	3,165	814	3.9	1.5	3.0
1937 Attacker	4,169	214	19.5	1.0	1.0
1937 Defender	1,814	386	4.7	1.0	1.0
1967 Attacker	2,533	67	37.8	0.76	0.26
1967 Defender	2,019	89	22.7	0.76	0.26

1. The inverse of this is percentage of losses.

2. This number is calculated by taking the total of the strength per kilometer of front for both the attacker and the defender and dividing it by the same for the World War II data (5,983).

3. This number is calculated by taking the total of the losses per kilometer of front for both the attacker and the defender and dividing it by the same for the World War II data (600).

In his combat modeling Dupuy used a World War II dispersion factor of 3,000 (which I gather translates into 333 men per square kilometer).[4] The data in table 13.2 show a linear dispersion per kilometer of 2,992 men, so, assuming a depth of 10 kilometers for a deployed World War II division, this number parallels Dupuy's.[5]

One final chart I have included depicts the ratio of strength and losses per kilometer of front by war (see fig. 13.9). Each line on the bar graph measures the average ratio of strength over casualties for either the attacker or defender.

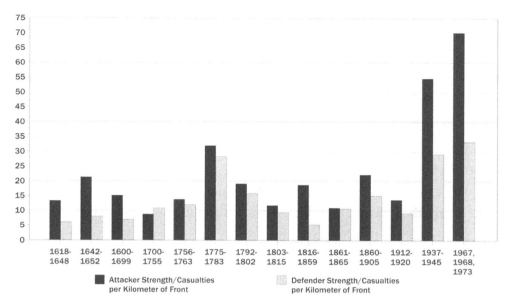

Fig. 13.9. Ratio of strength and losses per kilometer of front by war. Source: Dupuy Institute.

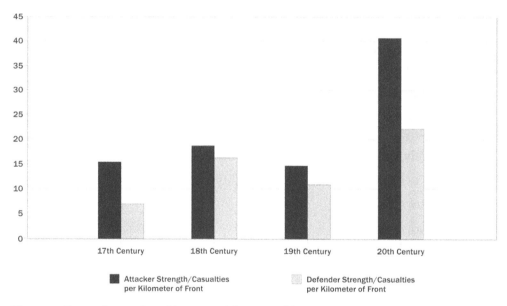

Fig. 13.10. Ratio of strength and losses per kilometer of front by century. Source: Dupuy Institute.

Being a ratio, unusual outcomes resulted in some unusually high ratios. I took the liberty of removing six data points because they appeared lopsided. Three of these points are from the English Civil War and were far out of line with everything else. These points represented three Scottish battles in which a small group of mostly sword-armed troops defeated a "modern" army. Also removed were Walcount (1689), Front Royal (1862), and Calbritto (1943). Figure 13.10 is the same chart except by century.

Again one sees a consistency in results for over three hundred years of war, in this case going all the way through World War I, then an entirely different pattern with World War II and the Arab-Israeli wars.

All this points to a very tentative set of conclusions:

1. Dispersion has been relatively constant between 1600 and 1815 and was driven by factors other than firepower.

2. Since the Napoleonic Wars units have increasingly dispersed (found ways to reduce their chance to be hit) in response to increased lethality of weapons.

3. As a result of this increased dispersion, casualties in a given space have declined.

4. The ratio of this decline in casualties over area has been roughly proportional to the strength over an area from 1600 through World War I. Starting with World War II, the number of people has dispersed faster than the rate of increase in weapon lethality, and this trend has continued.

5. In effect, the number of people dispersed in direct relation to increased firepower from 1815 through 1920 and after that time dispersed faster than the increase in lethality.

6. In the period after World War II, the number of people has gone back to dispersing (reducing their chance to be hit) at the same rate that firepower is increasing.

7. Effectively, there are four patterns of casualties in modern war:

Period 1 (1600–1815): Period of Stability

 a. Short battles.

 b. Short frontages.

 c. High attrition per day.

 d. Constant dispersion.

 e. Dispersion decreasing slightly after late 1700s.

 f. Attrition decreasing slightly after mid-1700s.

Period 2 (1816–1905): Period of Adjustment[6]

 a. Longer battles.

 b. Longer frontages.

 c. Lower attrition per day.

 d. Increasing dispersion.

e. Dispersion increasing slightly faster than lethality.

Period 3 (1912–1920): Period of Transition

    a. Long battles.

    b. Continuous fronts.

    c. Lower attrition per day.

    d. Increasing dispersion.

    e. Relative lethality per kilometer similar to past, but lower.

    f. Dispersion increasing slightly faster than lethality.

Period 4 (1937–present): Modern Warfare

    a. Long battles.

    b. Continuous fronts.

    c. Low attrition per day.

    d. High dispersion (perhaps constant over time?).

    e. Relative lethality per kilometer much lower than in the past.

    f. Dispersion increased much faster than lethality going into the period.

    g. Dispersion increased at the same rate as lethality within the period.

Note that by "dispersion" above, I often mean "reduced chance to be hit," which consists of dispersion, increased engagements ranges, and use of cover and concealment.

So the question is: Will the warfare of the next fifty years see a new period of adjustment, where the rate of dispersion (and other factors) adjusts in direct proportion to increased lethality, or will there be a significant change in the nature of war?

One of the reasons I wandered into this subject is that we were using our combat models to predict combat before World War II. We therefore were focused on trying to find some correlation between dispersion and casualties but could not get any type of fit. And we could not find anyone who had calculated a correlation between dispersion and casualties.[7]

It became clear to me that if there is any such correlation, it is buried so deep in the data that it cannot be found by a casual search. I suspect that I could find a mathematical connection between weapon lethality, reduced chance to hit (including dispersion), and casualties. This would require some improvement to the data, some systematic measure of weapons lethality, and possibly some clever mathematics. Certainly a subject worth pursuing at another time.

14. Advance Rates

> There is no direct relationship between
> advance rates and force strength ratios.
>
> —TREVOR N. DUPUY, *Understanding War*

The Dupuy Institute has done very little additional work on opposed advance rates.[1] This is not because there is nothing to be done; it is simply because no one has contracted us to do any work in this area. The issue of rates of advance and how to calculate them is an example of significant combat methodologies within a wide range of models that have not been adequately studied. Most models still base their rates of advance on force ratios. The source of these constructs is not known but was most likely first drawn from the 1958 edition of the U.S. Army *Field Manual 105-5: Maneuver Control*. We have seen no documentation establishing that such a construct exists.

The first extensive study on advance rates that we are aware of was yet another HERO study done in 1972.[2] This study was created in the early stages of campaign model building but not before several large campaign models had already been created, including ATLAS and the Concepts Evaluation Model (CEM).[3] Modeling preceded data gathering, although the data and analysis were not that far behind. With only six cases to draw from, the study authors concluded that the analysis could not be completed without a larger database. They nevertheless confirmed the feasibility of determining historical rates of advance for large forces in combat and identifying the operational and environmental factors influencing those rates. Based on this limited sample, they also tentatively concluded that force ratios, however calculated, do not influence rates of advance.[4] This study was not followed up by any other work for almost twenty years. In 1990 Robert Helmbold of the Center for Army Analysis conducted a study that once again found no correlation between force ratios and advance rates. The study then established an advance rate structure tied to force ratios for use in the CEM model run by CAA.[5]

This was it! In over sixty years of analysis and combat modeling only two major studies were done relating force ratios to advance rates, and both studies were inconclusive. But virtually every model in existence has to have some method of calculating advance rates, and as such a wide variety of ad hoc methodologies have developed, most connecting force ratios to advance rates, many

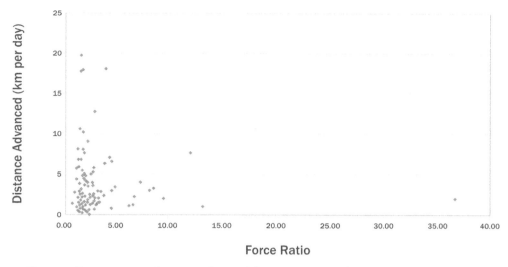

Fig. 14.1. Force ratio vs. distance advanced (outcomes IV–VI). Source: Dupuy Institute.

of them in a direct or even linear relationship. However, a simple comparison of force ratios to advance rates shows no clear relationship.[6]

Just to make it a little harder to fathom, the use of firepower scoring systems has fallen out of favor in the army modeling community. Nevertheless models like CEM still needed a force ratio to calculate advance rates. In the case of CEM the designers used a simple count of the number of men (effectively a firepower score of one per man) to calculate a force ratio, regardless if the men were armed with tanks or spears. This is odd, for the modeling structure spends considerable time conducting attrition calculations using detailed runs from the Combat Sample Generator (COSAGE) and the Attrition Calibration (ATCAL) using single shot probability of kill (SSPK) data carefully developed from data provided by the Army Material Systems Analysis Activity (AMSAA), yet it uses a very gross methodology for advance rates, a subject of similar significance.

Again, this is not an uncommon problem with many models in that they expend considerable effort modeling one part of the phenomenon of combat while glossing over other very significant elements (like human factors). In many cases this prioritization appears to be driven by whatever data were conveniently available, and little effort has been expended to correct these data shortfalls.

In our Capture Rate Study we did test force ratios against advance rates. As expected, there was no direct correlation, which the work of Dupuy and Helmbold had already shown. These tests were performed for outcome IV and also

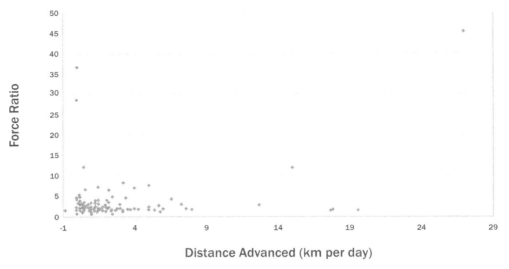

Fig. 14.2. Distance advanced vs. force ratio. Source: Dupuy Institute.

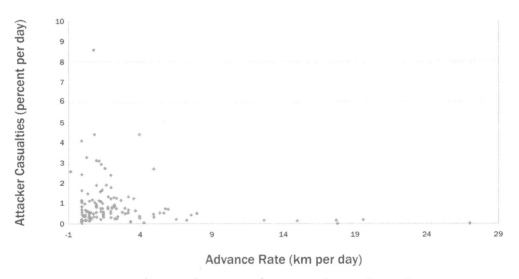

Fig. 14.3. Attacker casualty rate vs. advance rate. Source: Dupuy Institute.

for outcomes IV–VI. As can be seen in figure 14.1, which shows the results of the second test, in all but one case in which there was an advance of 5 kilometers or more per day, the force ratio was less than 5 to 1, and in many cases it was less than 2 to 1.

This noise is typical of any test of force ratios to advance rates, regardless of the data set used.[7] We tested the subject again during our urban warfare studies. In that case we compared force ratios to advance rates for nominally 137 cases of combat (46 urban and conurban and 91 nonurban; see fig. 14.2).[8] These are the same engagements used in the analysis of the ETO urban and nonurban engagements discussed in chapter 16. We did no further analysis of this beyond the ETO data as it clearly was not a trend influencing the results of our analysis of urban warfare.

We also compared force ratio to attacker loss rate. Figure 14.3 uses the same ETO data but was never included in our reports, although we used it in our briefings. It clearly shows attacker casualties declining to below 1 percent per day as the advance rate rises above 5 kilometers per day.

We concluded that advance rate is tied to outcome. This first showed up in our *Capture Rate Study, Phases I and II*, where we found a relationship between average distance opposed advanced (in kilometers per day) compared to outcome, as shown in table 14.1. The table demonstrates a similar relationship between advance rates and outcome regardless of theater, although the advance rates at Kursk tend to be higher. This table was based on seventy-six Italian Campaign engagements, seventy-seven engagements mostly from the Ardennes Campaign (Battle of the Bulge), and forty-nine Kursk engagements.[9]

Table 14.1. Advance Rate Compared to Outcome

	I	II	III	IV	V	VI
Italian Campaign	—	—	0.74	1.76	2.52	—
Ardennes	0	0.36	0.45	3.71	5.00	1.90
Kursk	0.08	1.31	-0.58	5.18	11.43	5.77

We produced similar tables in our urban warfare study. For example, table 14.2 is based on forty-three urban engagements and eighty-seven nonurban engagements from the ETO in 1944–45.

Table 14.2. Average Daily Advance Rate by Outcome, in Kilometers (Urban and Nonurban)

	I	II	III	IV	V	VI	VII
Urban cases	3	3	0	31	2	0	4
Advance rate	9*	0.73	-	0.96	7.80	-	0.13
Nonurban cases	1	7	17	44	16	1	1
Advance rate	0	0.36	1.06	3.02	5.37	1.50	0

*Includes one case with a 27-kilometer-per-day advance rate.

We did a similar comparison for ninety-seven engagements from the Battle of Kursk and in and around Kharkov in 1943 (table 14.3).

Table 14.3. Average Daily Advance Rate by Outcome, in Kilometers (Kursk and Kharkov)

	I	II	III	IV	V	VI
Germans attacking, Kharkov	0	0	—	6.20	18.00	—
Germans attacking, Kursk	0	2.53	1.35	5.08	9.99	5.77
Soviets attacking, Kharkov	—	0.33	0.56	10.00	11.00	—
Soviets attacking, Kursk	—	0	-0.43	5.50	—	—

The pattern is clear. Usually there is no advance for outcome I (limited action). The advance rate for outcome II (limited attack) is usually limited to less than a kilometer. Outcome III (failed attack) is also usually limited to a kilometer or so. For outcome IV (attack advances) the advance is often 3 to 10 kilometers a day, while for outcome V (defender penetrated) it is often from 5 to 20 kilometers a day. Note that the advance rates for the Eastern Front cases are higher than for the Western Front. For outcome VI (defender enveloped) the advance rate is low, which is not surprising as these often become mop-up operations. The data in tables 14.2 and 14.3 are the average advance rates per day for the category given. They are discussed in more detail in chapter 16.

This is all we have done on advance rates. Certainly more could be done to account for a range of factors, including terrain, force type, and weather, but to date we have not looked specifically at advance rates other than as they relate to other issues we were examining. The work Dupuy did on advance rates therefore remains the most extensive and detailed on the subject.

We did compare advance rates to mission effectiveness scores. These scores are, of course, analyst determined, so they are a precise number imprecisely determined. But they are useful for comparisons. A graph from that same Capture Rate Study (fig. 14.4) uses the "net mission effectiveness" score, in which the defender's score is subtracted from the attacker's score. The higher the score, the higher the degree of adjudged attacker success. Scores below zero indicate defender success, with the lower score (higher absolute value) indicating more defender success. We used 202 data points for this test. As can be seen, mission success scores below −2 had almost no advance. Otherwise advance rates and adjudged mission effectiveness scores were not closely related. This indicates that advance rates should be used with caution as a measurement of mission success.

Beyond that, there is not much new on advance rates. One curious feature of opposed advance rates is that they have not changed much over time. In our

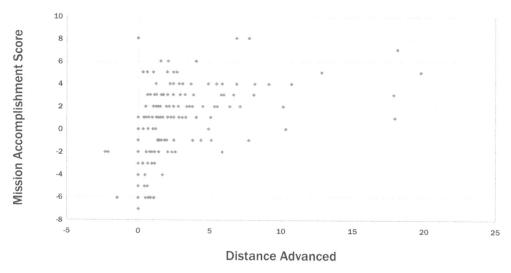

Fig. 14.4. Distance advanced vs. mission accomplishment score. Source: Dupuy Institute.

database of 243 engagements from 1600 to 1900, the average advance rate is 1.05 kilometers per day, the highest being 13 kilometers from a U.S. Civil War battle (Opequon Creek in 1864). Of our 29 division-level engagements from 1904 to 1918 the average advance rate is 2.27 kilometers per day, the highest being 35 kilometers (Megiddo in 1918). If that engagement is left out, the average is only 1.06 kilometers per day. Of our 657 engagements from 1938 to 1945 our average advance rate is 2.87 kilometers per day, the highest being 75 kilometers (1st Cavalry Division in the Philippines in 1945). There are still only two examples in our World War II cases of advance rates above 30 kilometers a day. Only with our post–World War II engagements do we see a significant change. In those 66 division-level engagements, we end up with an average advance rate of 11.12 kilometers per day. But there are a number of very high advance rate cases among the Gulf War engagements. If the Gulf War engagements are separated from the Arab-Israeli cases, the average advance rates for the 51 Arab-Israeli cases from 1956 to 1973 is 6.34 kilometers, and the average for the 15 Gulf War engagements of 1991 is 27.36 kilometers per day.

These higher advance rates are primarily because these are armored actions in desert or open terrain against opponents less capable than the attacker (Israelis against the Egyptians or Syrians in 1973; Americans against the Iraqis in 1991). It is hard to say that anything had fundamentally changed. It appears the differences were mostly caused by one side being armored, operating in open terrain, and facing less capable opponents.

Just for comparison, in the U.S. Army advance on Baghdad in 2003, the Third Infantry Division (Mechanized) advanced over 300 miles from the Kuwait border to the outskirts of Bagdad in fifteen days (19 March–2 April 2003). This is over 30 kilometers a day. While this was an opposed advance, the opposition was extremely limited and primarily left for the follow-up forces to clean up. This rate was not dissimilar to Allenby's during the Battle of Megiddo in 1918, where he advanced 167 kilometers over three days, except he was using a cavalry force with almost no mechanization. Starting on 3 April 2003, the Third Infantry Division (Mechanized) encountered organized Iraqi resistance outside of Baghdad, and for the next seven days the advance rate was reduced to a couple of miles a day.

Obviously, opposed advance rates are primarily driven by the conditions of combat; they have not been radically changed by all the technological developments over the past four hundred years. This is despite the fact that vehicle speeds have increased substantially, formations have become faster and more agile, and unopposed movement has sped up during this time.

15. Casualties

> The killed-to-wounded distribution of personnel casualties in twentieth-century warfare is consistent.
>
> —TREVOR N. DUPUY, *Understanding War*

Historically, wounded-to-killed ratios for units in combat have tended to range between two wounded for every person killed to more than four wounded for every person killed.[1] For example, the esteemed historian Theodore A. Dodge estimated that the wounded-to-killed ratio in ancient battles ranged from 2.1 to 2.2 to 1 for the attacker.[2] An effort in 1952 determined that the ratio for battles from 1704 to 1871 was 4.4 to 1.[3] It is unknown whether the killed included those who died of their wounds (DOW). This is significant. For example, in the U.S. Civil War, 14 percent of the wounded in the U.S. Army died from their wounds. The wounded-to-killed ratio was 4.55 to 1 if DOW is not counted among the killed, but it is 2.38 to 1 if DOW is counted.[4] For most purposes the ratios I discuss will be based on that later calculation, which is the total wounded who lived (meaning not including those who died of wounds) divided by the sum of those killed and those who died of wounds.

Dupuy claims, "About 20% of battle casualties are killed immediately. This corresponds to a wounded-to-killed ratio of 4:1. About 65% of battle casualties survive their wounds, even with minimal care. This leaves about 15% of those hit who are seriously wounded and not likely to live without medical care. The proportion of seriously wounded who survived had increased over the past century and a half from less than 5% of those hit to more than 12% due to improvements in medical evacuations and treatment."[5] He published table 15.1 in his book *Attrition*.

Table 15.1. U.S. Army Wounded-to-Killed Ratios in U.S. Wars

	Ratio of Wounded to Killed	Ratio of Surviving Wounded to Battles Deaths and Died of Wounds
Mexican War (1846–48)	3.72	2.18
Civil War (1861–65)	4.55	2.38
Spanish-American War (1898)	5.88	3.94
Philippine Insurrection (1899–1902)	3.81	2.72
World War I (1917–18)	5.96	4.10

WITHOUT GAS	4.20	2.88
World War II (1941–45)	3.57	2.41
WITHOUT USAAF*	4.25	2.77
Korean War (1950–53)	4.02	3.56
Vietnam War (1957–73)	4.45	4.16

Source: Dupuy, *Attrition* (1995), 49. I added the dates.

*U.S. Army Air Forces

The pattern for wounded-to-killed ratios was to remain around four wounded for every killed for the better part of two hundred years. This was the case for the Mexican War and the U.S. Civil War (3.72 and 4.55, respectively), through World War I and World War II (4.20 without gas for World War I and 4.25 not counting the air force for World War II), and into the modern era (4.02 in the Korean War and 4.45 in the Vietnam War). The U.S. Army in the Gulf War (1991) suffered 98 killed in battle and 354 wounded, for a wounded-to-killed ratio of 3.61 to 1.[6] In contrast, the United States has fought two wars over the past decade, in Iraq and Afghanistan, which are producing wounded-to-killed ratios of around 9 to 1. This is a very significant difference.

U.S. losses in Iraq from March 2003 through 2012 were 4,486 killed and 32,223 wounded. U.S. losses in Afghanistan as of 31 December 2013 were 2,301 killed and 17,674 wounded (reported only through September 2012). Of the 4,486 killed in and around Iraq, 3,545 were hostile and 941 were nonhostile, while of the 2,301 killed in and around Afghanistan, 1,825 were hostile and 476 nonhostile. This produced a wounded-to-killed ratio of 9.09 to 1 for Iraq and 9.68 to 1 for Afghanistan. For the U.S. Army alone the wounded-to-killed ratio for Iraq is 8.68 to 1 and for Afghanistan is 9.53 to 1. The Marine Corps' ratio is even higher.[7]

Is this change a result of improved medical care over the past couple of decades? Certainly care has improved, but can it alone account for such an impressive change? Some of the difference may be due to changes in lethality of weapons, a different mix of causative agents, the widespread use of body armor, quicker evacuation times, or better access to first aid. What has changed to shift the 4 to 1 wounded-to-killed ratio to nearly 10 to 1? If one hundred people were casualties in a fight, at a 4 to 1 ratio, twenty of those people would be dead. At 9 to 1, only ten would be dead. This is a big difference (especially to those ten who get to live). In effect, we have cut the mortality rate in half.

Just to clarify terminology, a casualty is anyone who is killed, wounded, or missing. The wounded include the subgroup "died of wounds"; these are people who were wounded and still living when they got to the hospital, but subsequently died while under medical care. Units often report them separately from those "killed in action" (those who died before getting to a hospital). As such, rapid evacuation can increase the number of DOW cases, converting some who would otherwise be categorized as KIA.

The data from past American wars show that during the Mexican War and U.S. Civil War, 13 to 14 percent of the wounded died of their wounds. By 1898 this rate declined to fewer than 7 percent and remained between 6 and 10 percent until 1973, except during the Korean War. This trend demonstrates the effect of proper medical care and medical facilities, which effectively cut in half the number of DOW. In Iraq and Afghanistan, however, the change in the wounded-to-killed ratio is much greater than can be attributed to just reducing the number of DOW.

Lethality of Weapons

Probably a major cause of this change is the mix of causative agents from war to war, especially when comparing the losses in a conventional war to those in a guerrilla war. Not all weapons have the same lethality. A person who has been shot with .22 caliber rifle does not have the same chance of mortality as a person hit by an AK-47. Although .22 caliber guns are usually not found on the battlefield, there are many types of weapons there that wound significantly more than they kill. One causative agent that unbalanced the statistics for World War I was gas warfare, which created scenarios in which fifty men were wounded for every one killed.[8] Because the use of gas in warfare was banned shortly after World War I, this example was excluded from table 15.1. Artillery on the battlefield also tends to wound more than kill, as do mortars, mines, and a host of other weapons. Some sample lethality statistics from the *Textbook of Military Medicine* are shown in table 15.2.

Table 15.2. American Casualties in the Bougainville Campaign:
Casualty Generation and Lethality by Weapon

Weapon	Total Casualties	Living	Dead	Lethality of Weapon
Mortar	693	611 (43%)	82 (22%)	0.12
Rifle	445	302 (21%)	143 (38%)	0.32
Grenade	224	210 (15%)	14 (4%)	0.06
Artillery	193	172 (12%)	21 (6%)	0.11
Machine gun	152	64 (4%)	88 (24%)	0.58
Mine	34	21 (2%)	13 (3%)	0.38
Miscellaneous*	47	35 (3%)	12 (3%)	0.26
Totals	1,788**	1,415	373	
				Average Lethality: 0.21

Source: U.S. Department of the Army, Office of the Surgeon General, *Textbook of Military Medicine*, 59.

*Aerial bombs, pistols, bayonets, and similar weapons.

**The original source gave a value of 1,799, which appears to be incorrect.

The Bougainville Campaign was an amphibious invasion and conventional fight in jungle terrain conducted by the U.S. Marine Corps, the U.S. Army, and the Australian Army against the Japanese during World War II from November 1943 to August 1945. The average lethality comes to a little less than four wounded for every one killed (1,415/373 = 3.79). As can be seen in the table above, direct fire weapons like rifles have a wounded-to-killed ratio of 2.13 to 1, while artillery and mortars have a ratio of 8.19 or 7.45 to 1. The two extremes in the data are grenades (15 to 1) and machine guns (0.73 to 1).

The army's *Textbook of Military Medicine* cites a number of lethality figures, summarized in tables 15.3–7. Table 15.3 is a German Army survey, which was not fully documented. The data includes German casualties on the Eastern Front from 1941 to 1944. The size of the population, the sampling method, the data collection, and other aspects of the study are not known.[9] It is possible too that the Germans reported wounded differently than the Americans; this is discussed in greater depth below.

Table 15.3. German Casualties on the Eastern Front

Wounding Weapon	Killed in Action (%)	Seriously Wounded (%)	Lightly Wounded (%)	Calculated Lethality*
Infantry projectiles**	30	31	39	0.30
Land mine	22	40	38	0.22
Aircraft bomb	20	37	43	0.20

Weapon			
Artillery shell	19	29	52	0.19
Hand grenade	17	18	65	0.17
Mortar shell	8	31	61	0.08
Armor-piercing and antitank shells	69	22	9	0.69
Bayonet	64	14	22	0.64
Blow from rifle butt	62	31	7	0.62
Run over by tank	34	33	33	0.34

Source: U.S. Department of the Army, Office of the Surgeon General, *Textbook of Military Medicine*, 58–61.

*I calculated this column from the data provided, which is reported by percentage killed in action, percentage seriously wounded, and percentage slightly wounded.

**Includes rifles, machine guns, submachine guns, and pistols.

Other World War II lethality data included a survey of British casualties in the Normandy Invasion and a large collection of data from U.S. operations in Europe. These are fully detailed in the *Textbook of Military Medicine,* so I will only summarize them in tables 15.4–15.7.[10]

Table 15.4. British Casualties in the Normandy Invasion (June–July 1944)

Weapon	Percentage of Total Casualties	Calculated Lethality
Mine	4	0.19
Bomb	4	0.24
Shell	39	0.27
Mortar	21	0.18
Grenade	1	0.14
Gunshot	31	0.39
Bayonet	—	0.31
Multiple	—	—

Table 15.5. Estimated Lethality of Weapons Used against the U.S. Army during World War II

Wounding Weapon	Lethality Killed	Killed and Died
Small arms	0.34	0.38
Explosive projectile shells	0.22	0.26
Rockets and bombs	0.22	0.26
Grenades	0.05	0.08
Mines	0.18	0.22

Table 15.6. Estimated Lethality of Weapons in Korea

Wounding Weapon	Lethality: Killed in Action	Total Killed in Action and Died of Wounds
Small arms	0.23	0.26
Explosive projectile	0.20	0.22
Shells, rockets, and bombs	0.17	0.34
Grenades	0.03	0.04
Land mines	0.22	0.25
Other fragmentation munitions	0.50	0.54

Table 15.7. U.S. Army Casualties in Vietnam: Outcome by Type of Weapon

WOUNDING WEAPON	Lethality Assumptions	
	A*	B**
Small arms	0.49	0.30
Fragmentation munitions	0.14	0.07
Mines and booby traps	0.15	0.08

*Assumption A: excluding those carded for record only, 23 percent were fatally wounded.

**Assumption B: including those carded for record only, 12 percent were fatally wounded.

All these tables demonstrate the same result, which is that small arms are more lethal and should produce a wounded-to-killed ratio of 1.56 to 2.33.[11] Fragmentation munitions are less lethal and should produce a ratio of 2.70 to 13.29.[12] Thus the choice of wounding agent, which is determined by the nature of the operation, has a potentially large impact on the wounded-to-killed ratio.

Recent Lethality Data

Since Vietnam there have been a number of additional calculations of lethality, all from operations with considerably fewer data points than those in World War I and II, Korea, and Vietnam. Examples are provided in tables 15.8–15.10.

Table 15.8. British Casualties in Northern Ireland

Wounding Weapon	Lethality
Low-velocity bullets	0.08
High-velocity bullets	0.37
Fragmentation munitions	0.13
Homemade bombs	0.06

High-explosive devices	0.22	
Hand-thrown missiles	—	

Source: U.S. Department of the Army, Office of the Surgeon General. *Textbook of Military Medicine*, 67. Based on 1,754 cases. This table has been abbreviated from the original.

Table 15.9. Weapons Effects in the 1982 Israeli-Lebanon War

Wounding Weapon	Percentage of Total Wounded	Lethality
Shells (mortars, cannons, rockets)	77	0.11
Bullets	23	0.31

Source: U.S. Department of the Army, Office of the Surgeon General. *Textbook of Military Medicine*, 68. Based on 1,174 cases. This table has been abbreviated from the original.

Table 15.10. Weapons Effects in the 1982 Israeli-Lebanon War

Wounding Weapon	Calculated Lethality
Artillery	0.21
Small arms	0.28
Bombs	0.22
Rockets	0.24
Grenades	0.14
Mines	0.12

Source: U.S. Department of the Army, Office of the Surgeon General. *Textbook of Military Medicine*, 68. Based on 947 cases. This table has been abbreviated from the original.

Nothing in these tables changes the bigger picture provided by the earlier and larger U.S. data sets. It does not appear that lethality of weapons are increasing, or, more to the point, lethality is not increasing faster than the improvement of medical care.

Mix of Causative Agents

Wounded-to-killed ratios are definitely influenced by the causative agent. Direct-fire weapons, such as rifles and machine guns, tend to kill more than 25 percent of the people they wound (although some of these are multiple hits). In contrast, fragmentation weapons, such as artillery rounds, mortars, and other high-explosive rounds, tend to kill around 10 percent of the people they wound. Booby traps and mines also tend to wound significantly more people than they kill.

The mix of causative agents has changed over time, and these changes have a major impact on the wounded-to-killed ratios. For example, table 5.11 lists the percentages of U.S. casualties inflicted by different agents.

Table 15.11. Casualties by Causative Agent in Three Wars

Agent	KIA World War II	KIA Korea	KIA Vietnam	WIA World War II	WIA Korea	WIA Vietnam
Small arms	32	33	51	20	27	16
Frags (fragmentation)	53	59	36	62	61	65
Mines	3	4	11	4	4	15
Punji stakes	—	—	—	—	—	2
Other (bayonets, etc.)	12	4	2	14	8	2

Source: Clodfelter, *Vietnam in Military Statistics*, 241.

The mix of causative agents changes depending on the nature of the war. As the author and veteran Micheal Clodfelter writes:

> Because it remained a small-unit, infantryman's war, U.S. casualties in Vietnam were inflicted more by infantry weapons that by the big guns or aircraft of the enemy, as in the world wars and Korea. The fragmentation wounds that the U.S. troops did suffer in Southeast Asia were characteristically more from the explosion of grenades or small mortar rounds than from the big projectiles of heavy artillery or aerial bombs that are usually the predominant executioners in modern warfare (and were the prime killers of the North Vietnamese and Viet Cong battle dead). Thus, while the percentage of frag wounds was higher among U.S. troops in Vietnam than it was in WWII or Korea, the ratio was lower for frag wounds that proved fatal.[13]

Two more tables in Dupuy's *Attrition* show artillery being the causative agent more in conventional warfare, and certainly more in positional warfare (World War I and parts of the Korean War). Vietnam had a higher percentage of injuries due to small arms, which have a lower wounded-to-kill ratio, but Vietnam also had a higher percentage of casualties due to mines and booby traps (tables 15.12 and 15.13).[14]

Table 15.12. Causes of Wounded in Action in Twentieth-Century Wars (U.S. only)

	Percentage of wounds caused by				
	Small Arms	Shell Fragments	Mines and Booby Traps	Toxic Gas	Other
World War I	19	46	—	32	3
World War II (without gas)	28	68	—	—	4
World War II	32	53	3	—	12
Korean War	33	59	4	—	4
Vietnam War	51	36	11	—	2

Table 15.13. Percentage of Battle Casualties Caused by
Artillery or Mortar Shell Fragments

World War I	71
World War II	55
Korean War	60
Vietnam War	43

But it does not take much of a difference to change the wounded-to-killed ratio. For example, we looked at the daily action reports of the units in I Corps in Vietnam from July 1968 to June 1969 (the year after the Tet offensive) and counted the losses from each case of engagement. In the case of the 1st Marine Division 32.4 percent of its losses were caused by mines, and at least 14.5 percent were caused by mortars. This division had a wounded-to-killed ratio of 8.68 to 1. At the same time, to the north, the 3rd Marine Division had only 12 percent of its losses caused by mines, although it similarly had 15 percent caused by mortars. The 3rd Division clearly had a larger percentage of losses caused by firefights and more lethal weapons, and it was involved in more conventional fighting. As a result its wounded to killed ratio was 7.10.

Posture

Wounded-to-killed ratios may also vary by posture. We have tested this extensively in our conventional warfare databases but have not established that this is conclusive. The problem is that the wounded-to-killed ratio is influenced by the number of missing, a number that usually increases for the side that is the defender. Tables 15.14 and 15.15 demonstrate this with some data from the Ardennes Campaign Simulation Data Base and the Kursk Data Base.[15]

Table 15.14. Wounded-to-Killed Ratios in the Ardennes Campaign

	U.S. Army	UK Army	German Army*
Ardennes, 16–23 December	4.85 to 1	1.67 to 1	3.25 to 1
Ardennes, 24 December–1 January	5.65 to 1	2.89 to 1	3.08 to 1
Ardennes, 2–16 January	5.12 to 1	4.59 to 1	2.99 to 1

*This includes all German ground forces, including ss and Paratroop units, which for administrative purposes did not report to the German Army. The data apply only to divisions and independent brigades; they do not include independent attached battalions and other smaller units, headquarters, or other nondivisional units. Data from Dupuy et al., *Hitler's Last Gamble*, 464–77.

Table 15.15. Wounded-to-Killed Ratios at the Battle of Kursk

	German Army*	Soviet Army**
Kursk, 4–11 July	5.11 to 1	2.29 to 1
Kursk, 12–18 July	4.54 to 1	2.68 to 1

Source: Kursk Data Base, Dupuy Institute.

*For the first period (4–11 July) German casualties were 3,773 killed and 12,273 wounded. For the second period (12–18 July) German casualties were 1,839 killed and 8,354 wounded.

**For the first period (4–11 July) Soviet casualties were 14,191 killed and 32,446 wounded. For the second period (12–18 July) Soviet casualties were 12,855 killed and 34,515 wounded.

In the Ardennes the Germans were on the strategic offensive through 23 December 1944. From 24 December through 1 January 1945, the Germans were on the offense in some areas, while the Allies were counterattacking in other areas of the front. After 1 January 1945 the Allies were on the offense. Half of their losses in this campaign were suffered in this last period. As can be seen, the wounded-to-killed ratio in the first period, when the Allies were on the defense, is lower than in the later periods, when the Allies were on the offense. The same is true for the Germans: their ratio is higher during the first period, when they were on the attack, and lower later. Still, the differences here are not very large.[16]

In the Battle of Kursk the Germans were on the strategic offensive through 15 July 1943. But on 12 July the Soviets launched a massive front-wide counterattack. Subsequent days were mixed in offensive and defensive actions, until the Soviets took the offensive again on 18 July. Again the same pattern appears: the Germans had a higher wounded-to-killed ratio during the first period, when on the offense, while the Soviets' higher ratio was in the second period, when they were on the offense.

These are very large and comprehensive data collections, so the results should be considered significant.[17] The Ardennes database consists of sixty-eight Allied and German divisions and German brigades fighting over thirty-two days, while the Kursk database consists of sixty-four German and Soviet divisions and Soviet armored corps fighting over fifteen days. Although there is clearly a difference in the results, this may not be caused by differences in posture. For example, the differences may be entirely caused by a higher number of missing in action on the defense if the missing in action has a higher wounded-to-killed ratio than the population that was not missing in action.

We retested the data in situations where we knew the number of missing, which was the case with our Kursk data. The concern with the Kursk data is the large number of missing, especially on the Soviet side of the engagements.

For the Germans 3.53 percent of their battle casualties were missing when they were the attacker and 2.76 percent when they were the defender. Rarely did the Germans lose more than 10 percent of their casualties as missing. This happens in only 9 out of 192 cases, 8 when on the offense and 1 on the defense. Two of these cases were due to low losses, as was true for the time they were on the defense, but five cases come from the Corp Raus infantry fight on 5–8 July.[18] As German data were relatively consistent in size and scale, we did no further analysis there.

In contrast, 20 percent or more of Soviet casualties are often missing in action. We divided the Soviet data into three categories: those cases where fewer than 10 percent of the casualties were missing in action, those cases where 10 to 25 percent were missing in action, and those cases where more than 25 percent were missing in action. The resulting data produced the comparison in table 15.16.

Table 15.16. Wounded-to-Killed Ratio with Three Categories of Missing

	Number of Cases	German Wounded-to-Killed Ratio	Soviet Wounded-to-Killed Ratio
WHEN GERMANS ATTACKED	124	4.99	2.28
Soviets missing <10%	38	4.84	2.70
Soviets missing 10–25%	37	5.54	2.29
Soviets missing >25%	49	4.78	2.11
WHEN SOVIETS ATTACKED	68	4.66	2.85
Soviets missing <10%	37	4.77	3.28
Soviets missing 10–25%	18	4.61	2.41
Soviets missing >25%	13	4.46	2.82

The Soviets' wounded-to-killed ratio is higher when they are attacking rather than defending, and this is true for each of the three categories of missing. Even when over 25 percent of the Soviet casualties were missing, their wounded-to-killed ratio was higher when attacking (2.82) than when they were defending (2.11).

The reason for this difference was probably best summarized by Dr. Fyodor Sverdlov (Col., USSR), who explained that if you are wounded in the attack, you just drop out of the attack, but if you are wounded in the defense, you are still on the battlefield and can be wounded again.[19] If the defender is seriously wounded, it is harder to remove him from an existing fight. In addition the defender sometimes is overrun, further complicating the situation. As such, it is natural to expect the wounded-to-killed ratio for the attacker to be higher than for the defender.

The loss scenarios in nonconventional operations are often similar to those of the offense in conventional combat, in that in most cases wounded personnel can drop out of combat and seek medical care. One would therefore expect the wounded-to-killed ratios for counterinsurgent forces to be close to the ratios for offensive conventional combat. That is indeed the case. The wounded-to-killed ratio of the U.S. Army on the offensive in the Ardennes Campaign was 5.12 to 1. The average ratio of the U.S. Army in I Corps in Vietnam from July 1968 to June 1969 was around 6 to 1.[20]

A survey of U.S. Army casualties by posture was conducted for Vietnam. The analysts looked at "search and destroy" missions from 1966 and determined that 42 percent of the wounded were as a result of bullets, while 50 percent were due to fragments. A "search and destroy" mission is essentially an offensive mission. In contrast, bullets accounted for 16 percent of the wounded in "base defense" missions in 1970, and fragments accounted for 80 percent. Thus these "base defense" missions would be expected to have a higher wounded-to-killed ratio, as long as the base was not overrun (a very rare occurrence for Americans in Vietnam). This again shows that posture can influence wounded-to-killed ratios, in this case in favor of the defense.[21]

These results make the argument that there was not a significant difference in combat care or evacuation in the U.S. Army in 1944 compared to 1968. This is an interesting and surprising point. One would expect that the wounded-to-killed ratio in Vietnam would be higher than in World War II because of better casualty care, quicker evacuation (especially with helicopters), and a higher percentage of casualties from mortar and mine attacks. Yet this does not appear to be the case.

Let us look back at the formulation where twenty out of one hundred casualties were killed using traditional combat statistics, while ten out of one hundred casualties were killed in Iraq and Afghanistan. In Vietnam the wounded-to-killed ratio of 6 to 1 equates to fourteen out of one hundred casualties being killed. From Vietnam to the present, improvements in medical care and evacuation, the development of body armor, changes in lethality of weapons, and the differing operations on the battlefield have resulted in an improvement in life-saving medical care of less than 50 percent (ten vs. fourteen dead). Improvements in medical care and evacuation are part of that difference, but certainly not all of it.

The Situation in Iraq and Afghanistan

As the wars in both Iraq and Afghanistan developed, the primary cause of wounded, responsible for over half of American deaths, became IEDs (improvised explosive devices).[22] Some IEDs are mines wired to explode on command; others are actual artillery shells wired to explode on command. Many are specifically constructed for this use.

We do not know the lethality of an IED, although the U.S. Army certainly has the means to calculate this. Most likely their lethality is more akin to a mortar or an artillery shell or even a grenade than the higher lethality of rifle fire. Using the Bougainville figures, this could be a lethality ranging from 0.05 to 0.12. This by itself would explain a significant amount of the difference in wounded-to-killed ratios in Iraq and Afghanistan compared to previous wars.

In the case of Afghanistan over 50 percent of the killed are from IEDs. We don't know how many are wounded by IEDs, but the number is likely even higher than 50 percent. It may be that the mix of weapons in Iraq and Afghanistan is such that the lethality is lower than it was in Vietnam. This would help explain some of the difference in the wounded-to-killed ratios.

Wounded-to-Killed Ratios by Service

The wounded-to-killed ratio varies by service. In the air forces, where the nature of combat tends to result in either a fatal crash or almost no casualties, ratios are expected to be lower than for ground forces. The same applies to the navy up through World War II, where ships that sank produced considerable fatalities and ships that did not sink usually produced few casualties. Since World War II, the U.S. Navy has not lost any major ships in combat, so its wounded-to-killed ratios are more similar to ground combat, as the primary target is now shore-deployed naval personnel or those acting as corpsmen for the Marine Corps.

Table 15.17. U.S. Wounded-to-Killed Ratios by Service in Four Modern Wars

	World War I	World War II	Korea	Vietnam
Army	3.83	2.41	2.80	3.14
WITHOUT USAAF	—	2.97	N/A	N/A
Marines	3.87	3.41	5.56	3.94
Navy	1.90	1.02	3.44	2.63
Coast Guard	—	—	—	—
Army Air Corps/U.S. Air Force	—	0.37	0.31	1.91

For example, table 15.17 compiles the data by service from World War I, World War II, Korea, and Vietnam.[23] Of interest is the fact that since World War I the U.S. Marine Corps' ratios are almost always higher the U.S. Army's. As both are ground forces with very similar organization, equipment, training, and doctrine, we would expect the ratios to be about the same. Table 15.18 looks at these two services in more detail.

Table 15.18. U.S. Army and U.S. Marine Corps Wounded-to-Killed Ratios

	U.S. Army	U.S. Marines
World War I	3.83	3.87
World War II	2.41	3.41
PACIFIC THEATER	2.62	3.41
ALL COMBAT DIVISIONS	3.44	—
ALL PACIFIC THEATER COMBAT DIVISIONS	3.22	—
Korean War	2.80	5.56
Vietnam War	3.14	3.94
Other operations (1965–94)	6.46	0.89
LESS TRUCK BOMBING IN 1983	6.62	2.25
Gulf War (1991)	3.65	3.58
Iraq (2003–11)	8.68	10.16
Afghanistan (2001–present)	9.98	13.13

The wounded-to-killed ratio in World War I did not differ significantly between the two services. In World War I the Marine Corps formed the second brigade of the U.S. 2nd Infantry Division, and the 1st Brigade was a U.S. Army formation. This created a laboratory-like situation where the two services' brigades were fighting side by side against the same enemy in the same environment. Furthermore they had the same medical system, as the field hospital was a division-level asset. The results are as expected (table 15.19).

Table 15.19. U.S. Army and U.S. Marine Corps Wounded-to-Killed Ratios (World War I, 2nd Infantry Division)

	U.S. Army	U.S. Marines	U.S. Navy
Total for 2nd Division in World War I	3.38	3.62	6.83
Belleau Woods, 6 June–1 July 1918	5.13	3.88	—

We see some differences in the wounded-to-killed ratios in World War II, even for the same theater (table 15.20).

Table 15.20. U.S. Army and U.S. Marine Corps Wounded-to-Killed Ratios (World War II)

	U.S. Army	U.S. Marines
WORLD WAR II	2.41	3.41
PACIFIC THEATER*	2.62	3.41

ALL COMBAT DIVISIONS		3.44		—	
ALL PACIFIC THEATER COMBAT DIVISIONS		3.22		—	

Source: Clodfelter, *Warfare and Armed Conflicts*, 958.

A more direct comparison of U.S. Army to Marine Corps losses looks at the losses by division. The U.S. Army published this information in 1946, and it shows that among the ninety infantry, cavalry, and armored divisions for which they collected data, the U.S. Army had 117,891 killed, 482,416 wounded, and 20,371 died of wounds. This comes to a wounded-to-killed ratio of 3.49 to 1, with 4.05 percent dying of wounds. The data are very consistent, with the ratio dropping below 3 to 1 in only nine of the ninety cases.[24]

Of the ninety U.S. Army divisions, twenty-two were committed primarily to the Pacific Theater, where 18,651 individuals were killed, 74,990 were wounded, and 4,551 later died of wounds. The result is a wounded-to-killed ratio of 3.23 to 1, with 5.72 percent dying of wounds.

A comparison to losses in the six U.S. Marine Corps divisions would be ideal, but we have found marine losses recorded only by campaign, not by division. Still, the nature of these operations is such that a direct comparison to the army data is in order. These data show that for ground actions from Guadalcanal to Okinawa, 15,023 marines were killed, 63,442 were wounded, and 3,372 later died of wounds. This results in a wounded-to-killed ratio of 3.45 to 1, with 5.05 percent dying of wounds.

There were a number of Pacific Theater campaigns where the U.S. Army and the U.S. Marine Corps fought side by side. We examined them all and in most cases found no clear pattern in their wounded-to-killed ratios.[25]

But the large extended island fight on Okinawa (1 April–22 June 1945) did produce the casualty comparison illustrated in table 15.21.[26] It is this Okinawa comparison that first brought attention to the differences in wounded-to-killed ratios between the U.S. Marine Corps and the U.S. Army.[27]

Table 15.21. U.S. Army and U.S. Marine Corps Wounded-to-Killed Ratios (Okinawa)

Unit	KIA	WIA	MIA	Nonhostile	Ratio
XXIV CORPS	4,412	17,435	81	12,554	3.95
DIVISIONS					
7TH INFANTRY	1,122	4,689	3	4,825	4.18
27TH INFANTRY	711	2,520	24	1,969	3.54
77TH INFANTRY	1,018	3,968	40	2,100	3.89

96TH INFANTRY	1,506	5,912	12	2,817	3.93
Corps Troops	55	346	2	843	6.29
III MARINE AMP. CORPS	2,779	13,609	119	10,217	4.90
DIVISIONS					
1ST MARINE	1,115	6,745	41	5,101	6.05
2ND MARINE	7	26	61	1	3.71
6TH MARINE	1,622	6,689	15	4,489	4.12
Corps Troops	35	149	2	626	4.26

In the overall aggregate statistics from World War II, the Marine Corps clearly had a better wounded-to-killed ratio. This appears to be driven by the specifics of their combat. If the U.S. Army divisions in the Pacific Theater are compared to the Marine Corps, the difference is much less, 3.41 versus 3.22. When the Marine Corps and the U.S. Army operated side by side, the differences are not clear and a pattern cannot be discerned, except for Okinawa. Still, it would appear that there were some real differences in the wounded-to-killed ratios between the U.S. Army and the Marine Corps in World War II. There was no such difference in World War I. A comparison over time shows the trends depicted in table 15.22.

Table 15.22. U.S. Army and U.S. Marine Corps Wounded-to-Killed Ratios over Time

	U.S. Army	U.S. Marines	Notes*
World War I	3.38 to 1	3.62 to 1	From U.S. 2nd Infantry Division
World War II	3.49 to 1	3.45 to 1	Division-level data
PACIFIC THEATER ONLY	3.23 to 1	3.45 to 1	
Korea	3.66 to 1	6.11 to 1	
Vietnam	3.13 to 1	3.93 to 1	

*The data for Vietnam are from the *1994 Defense Almanac*. The World War I data are from Clodfelter, *Warfare and Armed Conflicts*, 789. The World War II data are from appendix IV and V of Lawrence, "Background Paper on Wounded-to-Killed Ratios." The Korea War data for the U.S. Army are from Reister, *Battle Casualties and Medical Statistics*, 4, 16. The Marine Corps data are from its official history, Meid and Yingling, *U.S. Marine Operations in Korea 1950–53*, 5:575.

In Korea the U.S. Army's wounded-to-killed ratio was about the same as in World War II: the total number of casualties reported by the Surgeon General was 18,769 killed in action, 77,788 wounded in action and admitted to medical treatment facilities, and 14,575 slightly wounded in action and carded for record only.[28] The Surgeon General's counts of DOW are the best figures to relate to wounded admissions to medical treatment facilities. Among the 77,788 wounded admitted to medical treatment facilities in Korea, 1,957 died of wounds, representing a fatality rate of 2.5 percent, markedly lower than the 4.5 percent recorded for all of World War II.[29] These figures produced a wounded-to-killed ratio of 3.66 to 1, including DOW among the killed, and a ratio of 4.36 to 1 if the slightly wounded are included.

The Marine Corps in Korea lost 4,262 killed in action (including DOW; captured and died; and missing in action, presumed dead) and 26,038 wounded in action.[30] Even when including captured and died in the KIA count, this provides a wounded-to-killed ratio of 6.11 to 1. This ratio is particularly high, considering that in the past (World War I and World War II) U.S. Army and U.S. Marine Corps ratios had been close. The nature of operations for the U.S. Marine Corps and the U.S. Army in Korea were very similar, and in most cases they fought side by side. So one would expect similar ratios. Even with the slightly wounded in action counted, the army ratio is considerably lower, 4.36 to 1.

The U.S. Marine Corps having a higher wounded-to-killed ratio is a trend that starts with the Korean War and continues to the present day. The situation was similar in Vietnam, as shown in table 15.23.

Table 15.23. U.S. Army and U.S. Marine Corps Wounded-to-Killed Ratios (Vietnam)

	U.S. Army	U.S. Marines	
Hospital care required	3.35 to 1	4.10 to 1	(Does not include died while missing)
Hospital care not required	6.98 to 1	7.06 to 1	(Does not include died while missing)
Percentage died of wound	3.5	2.8	(Of those who required hospital care)

Source: U.S. Department of Defense, Office of the Assistant Secretary of Defense (Comptroller), Directorate for Information, Operations and Control, 15 January 1976, Table 1051.

Vietnam, which was nearly ideal when it came to modern medical support and evacuation times, also shows no increase in the wounded-to-killed ratios in its data. The aggregate data for the U.S. Army are 30,905 battle deaths and 96,802 wounded, a wounded-to-killed ratio of 3.13 to 1. Data for the Marine Corps are 13,082 battle deaths and 51,392 wounded, for a ratio of 3.93 to 1. Of the 153,303 who were wounded in Vietnam, there were another 150,375 who were wounded but did not require hospitalization.[31]

The phenomenon has been examined in some detail in the case of Vietnam.[32] In I Corps in Vietnam from the middle of 1968 to the middle of 1969, the Marine Corps and U.S. Army fought side by side, deployed in an almost checkerboard fashion. Near the Demilitarized Zone (or DMZ) was the 1st Brigade, 5th Infantry Division (Mechanized), and the 3rd Marine Division. South of the 3rd Marine Division was the 1st Cavalry Division and the 101st Airmobile Division, both airmobile units. South of them was the 1st Marine Division, operating in an environment very different from the more conventional warfare-like battle space of the 3rd Marine Division. South of the 1st Marine Division was the U.S. Army Americal Division (23rd Infantry Division). A comparison of wounded-to-killed ratios from these six units is provided in table 15.24, from north to south.

Table 15.24. Unit Comparison from Division Reports, July 1968–June 1969

Unit	Ratio
1st Brigade, 5th Infantry Division	5.51 to 1
3rd Marine Division	7.10 to 1
1st Cavalry Division	6.57 to 1
101st Airborne Division	6.12 to 1
1st Marine Division	8.68 to 1
23rd Infantry Division	6.32 to 1

What stands out in table 15.24 is that the wounded-to-killed ratio is higher for the U.S. Marines than for the U.S. Army, despite their having similar operating environments and similar medical evacuation support. The ratio is higher compared to those of units the marines are operating next to. All the forces had some of the better medical treatment of the time. The difference in wounded-to-killed ratios between the 3rd Marine Division and the 1st Marine Division is probably related to the combat environment, as the 3rd Marine Division was engaged in a more conventional warfare setting with more firefights and direct-fire engagements. The 1st Marine Division was involved in more guerrilla warfare–type operations with a higher frequency of booby traps and mines.

Iraq and Afghanistan

More recent research has produced the wounded-to-killed ratios for Iraq (2003–11) and Afghanistan (2001–present) presented in tables 15.25 and 15.26.[33]

Table 15.25. U.S. Wounded-to-Killed Ratios in Iraq (2002–2011)

	Ratio	Number Killed
U.S. Army	8.68	2,594
U.S. Marines	10.16	849
U.S. Navy	9.95	64
U.S. Air Force	14.93	30
U.S. servicemen	9.09	3,537

Table 15.26. U.S. Wounded-to-Killed Ratios in Afghanistan (2001–February 2012)

	Ratio	Number Killed
U.S. Army	9.98	1,039
U.S. Marines	13.13	324
U.S. Navy	4.14	72
U.S. Air Force	5.33	63
U.S. servicemen	10.00	1,532

This difference in wounded-to-killed ratios continues with the two most recent wars in Iraq and Afghanistan, as shown in table 15.27.

Table 15.27. U.S. Army and U.S. Marine Corps Wounded-to-Killed Ratios (Iraq and Afghanistan)

	U.S. Army	U.S. Marines
Iraq (2003–11)	8.68	10.16
Afghanistan (2001–February 2012)	9.98	13.13

A snapshot of the fighting in Fallujah in November 2004, where the army and the marines fought side by side, shows the same pattern (table 15.28). The wounded-to-killed ratio from the four marine battalions is 7.91 to 1, while it is only 6 to 1 for the two U.S. Army battalions. Complete calculations are shown in table 15.29.

Table 15.28. U.S. Wounded-to-Killed Ratios in Fallujah, November 2004

FALLUJAH ASSAULT FORCE

Unit	Killed in Action	Wounded in Action	Returned to Duty	Non-Battle Deaths	Non-Battle Injuries
Headquarters Regimental Combat Team-1	—	5	5	—	—
3rd Battalion/1st Marines	22	206	123	—	8
3rd Battalion/5th Marines	8	56	39	—	4
3rd Light Armored Reconnaissance Battalion	1	36	11	—	5
Headquarters Regimental Combat Team-7	—	15	14	—	1

1st Battalion/8th Marines	16	102	51	—	16
1st Battalion/3rd Marines	10	79	45	—	11
ARMY UNITS					
2nd Battalion/2nd Infantry	5	24	16	—	1
2nd Squadron/7th Cavalry	1	12	5	1	—
REST OF AL-ANBAR PROVINCE					
2nd Brigade/2nd Infantry	—	9	6	—	1
2nd Battalion/11th Marines	—	1		—	1
31st Marine Expeditionary Unit	—	2		—	1
2nd Light Armored Reconnaissance Battalion	—	7	5	—	—
2nd Reconnaissance Battalion	1	—	—	—	—
2nd Tank Battalion	—	3	5	—	2
2nd Assault Amphibious Battalion	1	12	7	—	3
Total	65	582	339	1	54

Source: Estes, U.S. Marines in Iraq.

Table 15.29. U.S. Wounded-to-Killed Ratios for Units in Fallujah

Unit	Ratio
3rd Battalion/1st Marines	9.36 to 1
3rd Battalion/5th Marines	7.00 to 1
1st Battalion/8th Marines	6.375 to 1
1st Battalion/3rd Marines	7.9 to 1
Weighted average for 4 marine battalions	7.91 to1
Rest of marines (Headquarters Regimental Combat Team-1, Headquarters Regimental Combat Team-7, and 3rd Light Armored Reconnaissance Battalion)	56.00 to 1
Army	6.00 to 1
Marines in rest of al-Anbar Province	17.00 to 1
U.S. Army and U.S. Marine Corps combined	8.95 to 1

All this clearly demonstrates that there is a consistent difference in wounded-to-killed ratios between the U.S. Army and the U.S. Marines. In the case of World War II, there is reason to argue that there was little or no difference between the two services based on a comparison of their side-by-side operations. However, it may be that the U.S. Marines reported 6 to 41 percent more wounded in that war.[34] In the case of Vietnam, it appears that the U.S. Marines reported 12 to 37 percent more wounded.[35] And in Iraq and Afghanistan it appears that the U.S. Marines reported 17 to 32 percent more wounded.[36]

The primary reason for this difference appears to be different reporting requirements and casualty definitions and is probably not due to differences in medical care because both services had a robust, well-supported care system. Neither is it likely due to evacuation regimes. For example, in Vietnam both services made extensive use of helicopters for quick evacuation, and the U.S. Army usually had more helicopters available. Finally, it is not likely due to operational environment; as can be seen in Vietnam, where units operated side by side against the same or similar enemy and in similar environments, the differences are still there. It is probably not due to the marines being tougher to kill than soldiers. Instead it would appear that the Marine Corps is simply counting 20 to 30 percent more people wounded, regardless of the other factors. This was the conclusion of our study on this subject.[37]

The U.S. Army Casualty Reporting System

The U.S. Army's definition of *wounded* has mostly been the same since World War I: a soldier is wounded when he spends the night in the hospital or is excused for duty for as much as one day for medical care.[38] This is a fairly standard definition, used by most armed forces of the world.[39] It excludes the 20 to 30 percent of casualties who are lightly wounded and require no significant medical care. The army records them as "carded for record only."

For example, in World War II the U.S. Army had 599,724 wounded admissions and 123,836 carded for record only.[40] In Korea the numbers were 77,788 wounded in action and admitted to medical treatment facilities and 14,575 lightly wounded in action and carded for record only.[41] In Vietnam the numbers were 96,811 wounded and 104,725 carded for record only.[42]

The current Department of Defense definition of *wounded in action* does not provide clear direction on who is counted and who is not. In contrast, the army's *Field Manual 8-55* dated September 1994 specifically states, "A battle casualty who requires admission to an MTF [medical treatment facility] or who dies of wounds after reaching an MTF is reported as WIA. Subsequent reporting as died of wounds (DOW) may be required. The WIA category includes the DOW received in action, but excludes the KIA."[43]

The U.S. Marine Corps Casualty Reporting System

It is harder to determine exactly who the Marine Corps counts as wounded and who it does not. The Marine Corps' recording of wounded in World War I is assumed to be the same as the army's, as they were part of the 2nd Infantry Division and were processed through an army hospital.

The definition the marines used in World War II appears to be the same as or similar to the army's, although the differences in the wounded-to-killed ratios in Okinawa point to the possibility that the Marine Corps may have started counting everyone wounded at that time.

After World War II they clearly counted lightly wounded soldiers as wounded and counted more people wounded than the U.S. Army did. This difference shows up in the statistics from Korea and Vietnam and is codified in the 1969 Marine Corps *Casualty Procedures Manual* promulgated by USMC Order P3040.4, dated 9 June 1969. It states, "Minor injuries or wounded neither requiring admission to a medical facility nor involving loss of personnel are also considered battle casualties for reporting purposes."[44]

We have not been able to locate a definition after 1969 that specifies who the Marine Corps is counting as wounded. Even in the most recently revised *Casualty Procedures Manual*, promulgated by USMC Order P3040.4D, dated 15 April 1996, there is nothing that specifically indicates how they define *wounded*.

Reporting of Wounded by Other Nations

The fact that different armies report their wounded differently, and that this could affect the results of analysis, was first brought to my attention by Dr. Hugh Cole back in 1989, before we looked at the differences between the U.S. Army and the U.S. Marine Corps.[45] His comments led me to look into the issue using the Ardennes Campaign Simulation Data Base (data from 16 December 1944 to 16 January 1945) and the Kursk Data Base (data from 4 to 18 July 1943). These data are presented in tables 15.30 and 15.31.[46]

Table 15.30. Ardennes (Battle of the Bulge), 16 December 1944–16 January 1945

	U.S. Army	UK Army	German Army
Killed	6,328	222	11,048
Wounded	32,712	977	34,168
Missing	23,399	263	29,243
Total	62,439	1,462	74,459
Wounded-to-Killed Ratio	5.17 to 1	4.40 to 1	3.09 to 1

Table 15.31. Kursk, Belgorod Offensive, 4–18 July 1943

	German Army	Soviet Army
Killed	5,612	27,046
Wounded	27,627	66,961
Missing	1,142	32,801
Disease and Non-Battle Injury	2,380	1,116
Total	36,761	127,924
Wounded-to-Killed Ratio	4.92 to 1	2.48 to 1

As can be seen, there are notable differences in the wounded-to-killed ratios of opposing forces. The differences are large enough that they are probably not driven by operational considerations (although this certainly influenced the figures). They are probably driven by different reporting habits and standards, and in the case of the Soviet Army, the poor state of their medical facilities. Soviet evacuation of casualties was also sometimes haphazard. For example, in the Soviet advance in early 1943, they left their rear-echelon hospitals well to the rear, resulting in a gap of hundreds of miles between the forward army and army group (front) hospitals and the rear-area medical treatment facilities.

The difference in the wounded-to-killed ratios for the Germans at Kursk in 1943 (4.92 to 1) compared to eighteen months later in the Ardennes (3.09 to 1) is probably driven by the large number of missing (and mostly surrendered) in Ardennes and the fact that the Germans were primarily on the offensive at Kursk and on the defensive for over half the time during the Battle of the Bulge. The German evacuation and medical system was probably also working better at Kursk compared to the Ardennes.

The Impact of Wounded-to-Killed Ratios on Combat Modeling and Casualty Estimation

Most combat models and casualty estimation methodologies I am aware of track casualties in one of two ways: either they record the count of personnel who are casualties (whether killed, wounded, or missing) or they track equipment losses and then convert those into personnel losses.

In the first case the model usually provides an overall casualty figure; there is no procedure within the casualty determination process to distinguish between killed, wounded, and missing. The disposition of the casualty is usually determined after the modeling run by assigning a certain percentage as killed, a higher percentage as wounded, and a certain percentage as missing (if this last statistic is even considered). Usually the sources for this assignment are historical data, and in many cases they are the same works that are referenced in this chapter.

In the second case the model calculates the number of personnel losses based on equipment losses. A number of sources are used; one is a HERO survey of World War II data on the number of equipment losses per one thousand people lost in combat.[47] The data in that study were simply reversed to provide a ratio of personnel to equipment losses. The categories killed, wounded, and missing were determined after the model run by assignment, if needed. Again, this is usually done from historical data.

In the end almost every model I am aware of ends up assigning the number of killed, wounded, and missing based on historical data, based on a figure of total casualties created by the model.[48]

Each of the four issues concerning the wounded-to-killed ratios that I have addressed in this chapter—the change in the ratio over time, the difference by service and nation, the difference by causative agent, and the difference by posture—has a unique impact on various modeling efforts.

The differences in the ratio over time indicate that modeling efforts that break out casualties by killed, wounded, and missing need to use recent breakdowns for killed and wounded. The change in ratios from 3 or 4 to 1 in World War II to the current 9 to 1 indicates that some adjustments need to be made to address the improvements in casualty care, evacuation, and body armor.

The differences in the ratios by service and nation are a little more complex. For example, if a model's output is a casualty report, is the count based on a U.S. Army definition of a casualty (a wounded person) the U.S. Marine Corps definition, or some other definition? If a combat model designed by the U.S. Army is used for analysis by the Marine Corps (and most combat models the Marine Corps uses come from the U.S. Army or are jointly developed with them), does that mean the casualties must be increased by 20 or 30 percent to match the USMC definition of who is counted as wounded? How does this affect operations with other nations, which have their own definition of a casualty? This problem potentially exists with any analysis related to a joint or a combined operation (operation with other nations).

According to my observations, most casualty outputs from combat models and casualty estimation procedures are based on the U.S. Army's definition of wounded and therefore do not include the lightly wounded that would be carded for record only. This is the case with some of the models that base casualties on equipment losses, as the data for this conversion originally came from a survey of U.S. Army losses in World War II.

The differences in the ratios by causative agent need be addressed, especially in the current combat environment, where most casualties are caused by IEDs and suicide bombers. The lethality of these weapons is lower compared to the mix of weapons that units faced in more conventional combat.

Some models track each soldier, and the weapon that wounded him or her can be identified (for example, Combat XXI). By assigning a lethality rate or other similar manipulation to each casualty, it is possible to assemble a list of wounded and killed that addresses differences in causative agent. However, the accuracy of such a process will still be suspect without some rigorous research and proper validation.

On the other hand, if the breakdown of casualties is developed from a total casualty count, then such a breakdown needs to be adjusted depending on mix of weapons faced. This might be as simple as having one list for conventional combat, one list for guerrilla warfare, and perhaps a different list for small unit actions. It does depend on the model and what it is being used for, and again, the accuracy of such a process will be suspect without some rigorous research.

The differences in the ratio by posture are a less significant point than the other three but should probably be addressed also. I have observed that many combat model and casualty estimation procedures do not properly or realistically address missing in action.[49] If the primary cause of difference in wounded-to-killed ratios by posture is due to the number of missing in action, this would indicate that missing in action does need to be addressed. Clearly it influences the medical loads for the friendly force.

Most likely the ratios are different (especially if missing in action is considered) whether you are the attacker or the defender, and the number of captured or missing in action definitely varies by posture and the outcome of the battle.[50] As such, any breakdown of casualties by killed, wounded, and missing needs to consider the posture and possibly other conditions of combat. Also, guerrilla wars usually have different relationships than conventional combat, so adjustments by posture and nature of combat would be useful.

Overall the problem is that the differences in wounded-to-killed ratios have not been seriously considered in modeling efforts. It is clear that these vary over time, by service and nation, by causative agent, by posture, by body armor use, and other factors. Any future modeling effort needs to address these minor but present differences. This is especially true if the models are being used to determine medical requirements. The issue of adjustment by service needs to be addressed for any casualty estimation effort or analytical modeling effort that addresses both the U.S. Army and U.S. Marine Corps.

16. Urban Legends

A single urban area can become a "resource magnet" that demands seemingly more than its fair share of manpower and other assets.

—RUSSELL W. GLENN, *Heavy Matter* (RAND Corporation, 2000)

The U.S. Defense Department is very trendy, but not in the typical sense of the word. Some trends are responses to perceived threats from a potential enemy, such as the obsession with developing longer range weapons to engage Soviet second-echelon forces. Some trends are responses to attempts to apply new technology, like the Davy Crockett mortar companies that were supposed to deliver nuclear mortar rounds in the middle of a tactical fight, or the army's oddly designed Pentomic division that was supposed to survive on such a nuclear battlefield. Yet other trends are a response to an intellectual force or idea that catches people's imagination, whether this is the latest business theory book or a buzz phrase pushed as an idea. The fear of the effects of fighting in cities, or urban warfare, was one of these recent trends. I'm not sure where this trend got started, but it was certainly promulgated by RAND, whose reputation is such that even their bad ideas are given credence.

In the late 1990s a series of reports postulated that urban combat would be more common and more intense than regular conventional combat. These reports were coming from some very distinguished outfits, including RAND.[1] The reports painted a scenario in which urban warfare was unavoidable and would become common. Such warfare would also require a significant amount of forces, much higher densities, much higher casualties, much higher levels of stress, and so on. Cities were going to suck armies in with their increasing densities and losses.[2] Urban warfare was going to be much more difficult and much more intensive than anything seen before in conventional warfare.

As a result the Dupuy Institute was contracted in 2001 to do a three-part study focused primarily on how to represent such urban operations in current combat models. We looked at what the casualty rates and advance rates would be in an urban compared to a nonurban environment. This was a pretty straightforward effort.

Because we had never specifically studied urban warfare before, we went into this effort with an open mind, conducted a brief literature search to see what everyone was currently saying about urban warfare, and laid out a simple experimental plan. We decided to do a laboratory-like side-by-side comparison of urban and nonurban combat. To do so we needed many cases of urban combat and compatible or similar cases of nonurban combat. We decided to start where the data were easy to obtain and could easily be worked with, which meant the operations of the U.S. Army and its allies in France and Germany in 1944–45.

After the landing in Normandy in June 1944, the U.S. Army pushed up the Normandy peninsula to take the city of Cherbourg (the U.S. VII Corps attack on 21–30 June 1944). The Allies broke out of the beachhead at Normandy in late July and, spearheaded by Patton's Third Army, rolled across France all the way to the border of Germany by September. This led to the next major urban fight in the theater: the attack on Aachen by the U.S. 30th and 1st Infantry Divisions starting on 2 October and continuing to 21 October. Paris had been declared an open city, and there was little other urban fighting in the march across France. But there was one urban fight for Paris, the U.S. V Corps' liberation of Paris on 25 August 1944. For their part, the Germans were determined to hold on to the enveloped coastal cities opposite the English Channel, which resulted in the Allies isolating them and taking them in September 1944. This generated battles at Boulogne, Calais, Dieppe, Le Havre, and Brest.[3]

The European Theater of Operations offered more accessible and better records for the opposing sides than did most other theaters in World War II (although not nearly as good as the Italian Campaign). All the armies involved (American, British, Canadian, and German) had doctrines similar to the modern U.S. Army, and the performance differences between the various forces were not as significant as in some other theaters of the war, like the Eastern Front (Germany vs. the Soviet Union in World War II).

The Phase 1 Effort

We determined that at least forty-six division-level engagements occurring in an urban environment could be created from the ETO data. While many of the engagements were not urban, most did occur in built-up terrain near the cities or in large villages and so were useful for analysis. We labeled this terrain *conurban* from the word *conurbation*. The completed ETO engagements are listed in table 16.1.

Table 16.1. Engagements around Urban Areas

	Urban	Conurban	Nonurban
Aachen	9	12	2
Boulogne	3	2	2

Calais	1	2	3
Dieppe	1	—	—
Le Havre	2	1	—
Cherbourg	2	1	4
Brest	5	5	2
Paris	1	—	—
Total	24	22	14

This gave us only forty-six examples of urban engagements to compare to fourteen nonurban, but from our past work and other databases we had another seventy-seven examples of nonurban engagements from Normandy, the Pursuit across France, Westwall and Lorraine, and the Ardennes (Battle of the Bulge). Most of these (fifty-seven cases) were from the Battle of the Bulge. So we ended up comparing forty-six urban and conurban engagements to ninety-one nonurban engagements from the same theater and same year of the war.

First we did a series of simple comparisons of the data in aggregate. We compared the twenty-five urban engagements from the Channel Ports, Brest, and Paris to the twenty-one nonurban engagements from Normandy and the Breakout and Pursuit period. There are clear differences between these urban and nonurban engagements, but these were almost certainly driven by the higher force ratios in the urban engagements, where the average force ratio was twice that of the nonurban engagements. This was probably driving the rest of the differences in statistics for these two data sets. Still, the attacker loss rates for urban terrain were much lower than for nonurban terrain.

We also compared the twenty-one urban engagements from Aachen to the rather large data set of seventy nonurban engagements from Westwall, Lorraine, and Ardennes. This data set firmly established the pattern that attacker loss rates and the advance rates in urban terrain were lower than in nonurban terrain. This is in direct contradiction to the claims of some urban warfare theorists.

We also compared urban and conurban engagements to each other, to make sure we were not incorrectly mixing and combining different terrain types. We were not. The statistics from the urban and the conurban engagements were similar, and therefore we were comfortable lumping these two data sets together. We also compared the mix of terrain types in the nonurban data. All of these comparisons are provided in detail in our first urban warfare report.[4]

At least for the ETO, the data showed that urban engagements resulted in lower casualties and lower advance rates than nonurban engagements. So, having examined the data, we then analyzed the 137 cases of urban and nonurban combat in the ETO in some depth in an attempt to determine the impact of urban terrain on (1) mission success (outcome), (2) casualties and casualty rates, (3) advance rates, (4) force density (linear), (5) armor loss rates, (6) force ratios, and (7) duration of combat (time).

The Effect of Urban Terrain on Outcome

We had determined in previous work that the outcome of an engagement influences casualties. In this case the outcomes were defined as six types, ranging from no attack (which usually had very low casualties for both sides) to a defender being enveloped (which usually had very high casualties for the defender). The breakdown of outcomes among the data sets (table 16.2) needed to be examined.

Table 16.2. Engagement Outcomes

	Channel Ports, Brest, and Paris	Normandy and Breakout and Pursuit
I. Limited action	3	—
II. Limited attack	—	—
III. Failed attack	—	6
IV. Attack advances	14	11
V. Defender penetrated	4	3
VI. Defender enveloped	—	—
VII. Other	4	1

	Aachen	Westwall, Lorraine, and Ardennes
I. Limited action	—	1
II. Limited attack	3	7
III. Failed attack	—	11
IV. Attack advances	17	37
V. Defender penetrated	—	13
VI. Defender enveloped	—	1
VII. Other	1	—

We had learned from our capture rate studies (discussed in chapter 8) that the outcome of the engagement is the primary determiner of casualty rates. Therefore we compared engagements of similar outcomes and force ratios. Table 16.3 summarizes the outcomes "attack failed," "attack advances," and "defender penetrated" (outcome categories III–V) when compared to force ratio.[5]

Table 16.3. Force Ratios Compared to Outcome

Force Ratio	Cases	Terrain	Result
0.55 to 1.01 to 1	5	Nonurban	Attack failed
1.23 to 1.38	3	Nonurban	Attack failed
1.15 to 1.48	9	Nonurban	Attack advances
1.18 to 1.29	4	Nonurban	Defender penetrated
1.53 to 1.88	7	Nonurban	Attack failed
1.50 to 1.87	19	Nonurban	Attack advances
1.51 to 1.64	3	Nonurban	Defender penetrated
1.72 to 1.95	4	Urban	Attack advances
2.20 to 2.56	2	Nonurban	Attack failed
2.01 to 2.87	11	Nonurban	Attack advances
2.01 to 2.99	15	Urban	Attack advances
2.01 to 2.64	2	Nonurban	Defender penetrated
3.02 to 4.62	10	Nonurban	Attack advances
3.23 to 5.26	10	Urban	Attack advances
3.03 to 4.28	2	Nonurban	Defender penetrated
4.16 to 4.78	2	Urban	Defender penetrated
6.43 to 7.56	2	Nonurban	Attack advances
7.12 to 12.11	2	Urban	Attack advances
6.98 to 8.20	2	Nonurban	Defender penetrated
6.46 to 11.96 to 1	2	Urban	Defender penetrated

From this comparison, it is clear that the force ratios have a major impact on the outcomes. The lack of any failed urban attacks is due to the favorable force ratios. The lowest force ratio of an urban attack is 1.72 to 1, and only four attacks are less than 2.00 to 1. Of the nine nonurban attacks between 1.71 and 2.00 to 1, only three failed. No attacks, urban or nonurban, executed with a ratio above 2.56 to 1 failed. There were a total of ten urban attacks made between 2.00 to 1 and 2.56 to 1 and nine nonurban attacks made in the same range. Two of the nonurban attacks in these cases failed.

Thus it appears that force ratios are a major factor in determining outcome. It does not appear that the difference between urban and nonurban terrain significantly influenced this result, nor can a difference be seen between rugged terrain and nonrugged terrain.[6] Also the difference between rolling and mixed, rugged and mixed, or rugged and wooded terrain does not seem to have significantly influenced the outcomes. If a difference in the effect between rolling terrain and rugged terrain cannot be demonstrated, then the difference in effect between urban and nonurban terrain is also likely to be of the same order of effect, or less. However, the difference in terrain could affect combat power, and the difference caused by this effect could be 20 to 30 percent without its showing up in this analysis. Such small differences cannot be conclusively demonstrated given the small number of cases and the considerable variation found in these data. However, it is possible to create some specific rules relating force ratios to outcomes.

Table 16.4. Summation of Force Ratios Compared to Outcomes, ETO

Force Ratio	Result
0.55 to 1.01 to 1.00	Attack fails
1.15 to 2.56 to 1.00	Attack may succeed
2.71 to 1.00 and higher	Attack advances

It is in the "attack may succeed" area where we may detect some differences caused by terrain effects. In the range of 1.15 to 2.56 to 1.00 we also found the statistics in table 16.5. For the urban versus nonurban cases, we found the statistics in table 16.6.

Table 16.5. Outcomes for Attacks from 1.15 to 2.56 to 1.00

Cases	Attack Fails	Attack Advances	Defender Penetrated
55	12 (21.82%)	35 (63.64%)	8 (14.55%)

Table 16.6. Outcomes Based upon Terrain

	Cases	Attack Fails	Attack Advances	Defender Penetrated
Urban	14	0	14	0
Rolling	25	6 (24.00%)	17	2
Rugged	30	6 (20.00%)	18	6

Little can be concluded from these data, which appear to support a null hypothesis. That is, the terrain (be it urban vs. nonurban or rolling vs. rugged) has no significantly measurable influence on the outcome of battle.

The Effect of Urban Terrain on Casualties

As I said earlier, and as discussed in our capture rate studies and in chapter 8 of this book, the outcome of a battle, rather than the force ratio, is the primary determiner of the loss rate. A simple comparison of average losses by outcome (listed as outcomes I through VII) demonstrates this (table 16.7).

Table 16.7. Average Losses by Outcome, ETO

CHANNEL PORTS, BREST, AND PARIS	I	II	III	IV	V	VI	VII
Number of cases	3	—	—	14	4	—	4
Average percentage of attacker losses/day	0.40	—	—	0.53	.031	—	.037
Average percentage of defender losses/day	40.25	—	—	20.74	61.35	—	100
NORMANDY AND PURSUIT							
Number of cases	—	—	6	11	3	—	1
Average percentage of attacker losses/day	—	—	3.34	0.87	0.54	—	0.04
Average percentage of defender losses/day	—	—	5.59	5.22	3.71	—	100
AACHEN							
Number of cases	—	3	—	17	—	—	1
Average percentage of attacker losses/day	—	0.70	—	0.57	—	—	0.18
Average percentage of defender losses/day	—	3.69	—	4.92	—	—	22.47
WESTWALL, LORRAINE, AND ARDENNES							
Number of cases	1	7	11	37	13	1	—
Average percentage of attacker losses/day	0.03	0.86	1.85	0.90	0.59	0.39	—
Average percentage of defender losses/day	0.45	1.21	4.15	3.19	6.54	21.30	—

The percentages used were simple straight averages. The result would change slightly if a weighted average was used, or if outliers were deleted, but the overall relationship within the data would not change. The data show two trends (if one compares similar outcomes in the urban data sets with similar outcomes in the nonurban data sets). First, the attacker casualties are lower in the urban than in the nonurban data. Second, the defender casualties are higher than the attacker casualties and, more significant, the ratio of attacker to defender casualties is more favorable to the attacker in urban warfare. These tendencies may have been driven by the selection of the urban engagements and to a lesser extent the selection of the nonurban engagements.

The selection of the nonurban engagements is not unbiased. The Normandy Campaign and Breakout and Pursuit data sets' primary problem is that they contain too few cases. Another twenty or so examples were needed. The large amount of Ardennes data is more robust but still has some problems. A number of the German offensive engagements come from the early part of the campaign, when they suffered a number of sharp repulses inflicted by some very determined U.S. units fighting in terrain that was unsuited to the armor-heavy formations the Germans deployed. A number of the cases are from the U.S. Third Army counterattack in late December, which was particularly successful against what appears to have been a somewhat demoralized opponent. As a result the database contains an excess of particularly stubborn and successful defenses and a series of particularly successful attacks. This probably skews the casualty figures slightly.

Yet although having more data would provide a more refined and accurate analysis, it likely would not change the overall results. Any way the data are sectioned, there are fewer attacker casualties in the urban engagements than in the nonurban engagements, and the casualty exchange ratio favors the attacker as well. Because of the selection of the data there is some question whether these observations can be extended beyond these data, but there is not much support for the notion that urban combat is a more casualty-intense environment than nonurban combat.

The Effect of Urban Terrain on Advance Rates

Opposed advance rates may be influenced by urban terrain. The DuWar databases record advance rates in kilometers per day. Table 16.8 provides a simple summary of this relationship.

Table 16.8. Advance Rates in the ETO

	Number of Cases	Average Advance Rate (in km.)	Five Highest Advance Rates (in km.)
Channel Ports	22	2.49	27, 15, 2.5, 1.7, 1.5
Normandy and Pursuit	17	2.59	12.7, 7.3, 6, 4, 3.6
Aachen	21	0.96	3, 2.25, 2.1, 1.8, 1.5
Ardennes	70	2.81	19.6, 17.8, 17.7, 8, 7.6

The average advance rates are very much driven by the high advance rates, for example the 27-kilometer one-day advance for one of the Channel Port engagements. If 10 kilometers were used as a maximum advance rate (meaning that 10 kilometers was substituted for any figure greater than that), the averages in table 16.9 would result.

Table 16.9. Modified Advanced Rates in the ETO

	Number of Cases	Average Advance Rate (in km.)	Average Force Ratio	Weighted Force Ratio
Channel Ports	22	1.49	8.01	4.33
Normandy and Pursuit	17	2.43	3.55	2.02
Aachen	21	0.96	2.43	2.29
Ardennes	70	2.45	2.13	1.69

This does not result in a great difference in the nonurban engagement data sets but does show them to have a nearly identical average rate (2.43 and 2.45), while both urban data sets show a much lower average (1.49 and 0.96). As the average combat ratio of the Channel Ports engagements is noticeably higher than that of the Aachen engagements, it is not surprising that they have a higher average advance rate as well.

The urban data set is characterized by a large number of limited or minor advances. Categorizing the advance rates by the number of cases for each distance advanced can best show this (table 16.10).

Table 16.10. Distance Advanced by Case, ETO

Advance	Channel	Normandy	Aachen	Ardennes
Negative or zero	5	3	0	13
Up to 1 km./day	9	5	15	10
Up to 2 km./day	5	3	3	17
Up to 3 km./day	1	1	3	10
Up to 4 km./day	0	2	0	7
Up to 5 km./day	0	0	0	4
5–10 km./day	0	2	0	6

In 67.44 percent of the urban cases, the advance was less than 1 kilometer per day, compared to 35.63 percent in the nonurban cases. Advance rates of less than 3 kilometers per day accounted for 95.35 percent of the urban cases but only 71.26 percent of the nonurban cases. These differences are despite the higher force ratios and more favorable outcomes that characterize the urban engagement data set. Therefore one of the primary results of urban terrain is that it slows opposed advance rates. It may be possible to produce a more precise estimate based on outcome, as presented in table 16.11.

Table 16.11. Average Daily Advance Rate in Kilometers by Outcome, ETO

	I	II	III	IV	V	VI	VII
URBAN							
Cases	3	3	0	31	2	0	4
Advance rate	9*	0.73	—	0.96	7.80	—	0.13
NONURBAN							
Cases	1	7	17	44	16	1	1
Advance rate	0	0.36	1.06	3.02	5.37	1.50	0

*Includes one case with a 27-kilometer-per-day advance rate.

Looking further into the outcome IV (attack advances) engagements, since this is the only place where we have a statistically significant number of engagements for both sides, we find the results in table 16.12.

Table 16.12. Distance Advanced in Outcome IV Engagements

Advance	Urban	Nonurban
Negative or zero	1	1
Up to 1 km./day	19	8
Up to 2 km./day	7	17
Up to 3 km./day	4	5
Up to 4 km./day	0	4
Up to 5 km./day	0	4
5–10 km./day	0	3
greater than 10 km/day	0	2

There is no question that the averages are heavily influenced by the number of nonurban advance rates greater than 3 kilometers a day. However, if those are deleted we still have an average of 0.96 kilometers per day for urban engagements compared to an average of 1.41 for nonurban engagements, both based on thirty-one total cases. If the two highest advances for the nonurban engagements are excluded (19.6 and 17.8 kilometers per day), leaving the highest advance rate at 7.6, then the average is 2.27 kilometers per day based on forty-two cases. Overall, the data are very consistent, with urban advance rates being one-half to one-third of nonurban advance rates. Table 16.13 provides a summary.

Table 16.13. Urban vs. Nonurban Advance Rates

	Cases	Urban	Nonurban	Ratio
Channel Ports (urban) vs. Normandy (nonurban) engagements	22 vs. 17	2.49	2.59	0.96
Aachen (urban) vs. Ardennes (nonurban) engagements	21 vs. 70	0.96	2.81	0.34
Channel vs. Normandy engagements, modified	22 vs. 17	1.49	2.43	0.61
Aachen vs. Ardennes engagements, modified	21 vs. 70	0.96	2.45	0.39
Outcome IV engagements	31 vs. 44	0.96	3.02	0.32
Outcome IV engagements, low force ratio attacks	14 vs. 12	1.23	2.59	0.47

Outcome IV engagements, medium force ratio attacks	12 vs. 7	0.66	1.76	0.38
Outcome IV engagements, high force ratio attacks	5 vs. 3	0.94	3.55	0.26

The Effect of Urban Terrain on Force Density

The linear density of the attacker, which is the number of attacker personnel per kilometer of front, was the primary measurement used for this analysis. We chose this factor rather than a measure of area density since it is often not known where the rear boundary of a unit was, as the boundary was often applied inconsistently, and since it would include many personnel of service and service support units rather than combat and combat support units.[7] The attacker density was chosen because it was larger than the defender density except for the seven cases where the defender outnumbered the attacker. We utilized the attacker density throughout the analysis for consistency. The average density for each data set is specified in table 16.14. These obviously contain a few outliers. The five lowest and highest cases in each set are listed in table 16.15.

Table 16.14. Average Attacker Linear Density, ETO

	Number of Cases	Average Linear Density	Weighted Average Linear Density
Channel Ports	20	4,614.17	3,331.89
Normandy	17	2,072.20	1,869.96
Aachen	21	2,089.17	1,773.26
Ardennes	70	2,068.95	1,355.58

Table 16.15. Lowest and Highest Densities, ETO

	Five Lowest Cases	Five Highest Cases
Channel Ports	1,299.78	19,332.08
	2,331.08	16,300.00
	2,331.08	11,816.40
	2,331.08	5,774.25
	2,331.08	4,365.19
Normandy	709.67	4,075.00
	721.15	3,446.40
	902.64	3,129.20
	1,103.40	2,833.33

	1,464.78	2,833.00
Aachen	1,188.67	7,718.80
	1,344.96	3,401.86
	1,464.00	2,924.82
	1,575.80	2,823.13
	1,580.00	1,784.33
Ardennes	264.57	12,800.00
	268.32	10,932.78
	272.07	4,394.00
	564.96	4,228.89
	580.96	4,000.00

As can be seen, the linear densities above ten thousand are outside of the norm, as are those below three hundred. Table 16.16 removes the two highest and the two lowest densities from the Ardennes set and the three highest and three lowest from the Channel Ports set.

Table 16.16. Modified Average Attacker Linear Density, ETO

	Number of Cases	Average Linear Density
Channel	14	2,777.35
Normandy	17	2,072.20
Aachen	21	2,089.17
Ardennes	66	1,826.68

Now the Channel Ports have the highest density of all data sets, while the Ardennes has the lowest. This is not surprising as the Channel engagements were mostly sieges with narrowly defined frontages and the Ardennes was mostly heavily wooded terrain with a much more limited road net. It does not appear that the urban nature of the terrain is what is making the difference. The difference in linear density between the urban and nonurban cases is summarized in table 16.17.

Table 16.17. Urban vs. Nonurban Linear Density

	Number of Cases	Ratio of Linear Densities, Urban vs. Nonurban
CHANNEL VS. NORMANDY	20 vs. 17	
Average		2.23
Weighted average		1.78
Adjusted average		1.34
AACHEN VS. ARDENNES	21 vs. 70	
Average		1.01
Weighted average		1.31
Adjusted average		1.14

In light of the similarity of the Aachen data to the Ardennes data, and of the Aachen data to the Normandy data (which are nearly identical), one is left with the conclusion that the higher (by a factor of 2) density in the Channel Ports cases is mostly because they were akin to sieges rather than field battles. While there is some difference between the Aachen and Ardennes cases, it is probably due to the restricted nature of the terrain in the Ardennes more so than the urban terrain of Aachen. There is thus little evidence that operations in urban terrain result in a higher linear density of troops, although the data do seem to trend in that direction.

The Effect of Urban Terrain on Armor

Much of the current discussion and analysis of the effects of urban warfare point to the heavy armor losses suffered by the attacking Israelis in the city of Suez in October 1973 and by the Russians at Grozny in January 1995. However, in our analysis of forty-six cases of urban combat, we found no such heavy armor loss. In fact armor losses were fairly low in most of the urban operations examined, although we did not have loss data for all the engagements.[8] Table 16.18 shows our armor loss data.

Table 16.18. Armor Strength and Losses in ETO Engagements

	Number of Cases	Average MBT* Strength	Number of Cases	Average Daily Tank Losses	Average Percentage of Tank Losses	Weighted Percentage of Tank Losses
CHANNEL PORTS						
Attacker	25	170.68	15	0.74	0.49	0.37
Defender	11	8.36	2	6.94	100.00	64.19

NORMANDY						
Attacker	21	185.24	16	7.83	4.48	3.57
Defender	12	43.25	4	2.77	1.94	4.54
AACHEN						
Attacker	21	150.90	16	7.00	2.74	3.33
Defender	21	37.10	19	4.47	14.86	12.67
ARDENNES						
Attacker	70	99.89	51	7.00	6.23	5.66
Defender	70	42.50	44	6.63	10.11	13.55

*MBT stands for main battle tank, a post–World War II term used here to refer to medium and heavy tanks (but not light tanks), including tank-like vehicles armed with 75mm guns or larger that are not self-propelled artillery.

The aggregated figures in table 16.18 provide a pretty clear picture, even though the loss data are incomplete. All of these operations, whether urban or nonurban, tended to have "tank-heavy" attackers. The defenders had some armor, except in the Channel Ports cases, where they were limited to a small company-size contingent of open-top, lightly armored tank destroyers. The average daily tank losses for the attacker in the Aachen, Normandy, and Ardennes cases were almost identical. The daily percentage of loss for the attacker shows that the armor losses in urban terrain were lower than in nonurban terrain. The results in the Channel Ports engagements are skewed by the very one-sided armor forces engaged, and as a result Allied armor losses were very low. Defender armor losses were not always well recorded.

As seen in table 16.19, the total number of tanks recorded lost is fairly small (although, again, not all engagements had losses recorded).

Table 16.19. Total Tank Losses, ETO Engagements

	Attacker Total Tanks Lost	Defender Total Tanks Lost
Channel	12	15
Normandy	316	28
Aachen	112	90
Ardennes	607	496

In the Channel Ports engagements, the worst case was four tanks lost in a single day by the attacker. For the defender it was thirteen lost in one day, when the city of Brest surrendered. However, the Brest case is anomalous as it is not known on which particular day of the twenty-four-day battle any of the armored vehicles were lost, so we assigned all the armor losses to the last day.

The Aachen cases generated some substantial armor losses. However, it appears that few of them were due to urban fighting or that they were incurred within the city. The five days of heaviest armor loss for the attacker (thirty, twenty-five, twelve, nine, and eight tanks lost) were part of the 30th Infantry Division attack between 3 and 8 October 1944, fought in a mixture of rolling-mixed and conurban terrain. This attack also accounted for three of the six highest tank losses by the defender. These six days of battle (six cases) accounted for eighty-seven tanks lost by the attacker (78 percent) and thirty-six tanks lost by the defender (40 percent). Armor losses declined after the battle transitioned into what is coded as conurban terrain. Outside of these cases, both attacker and defender never lost more than seven tanks in a day, except for one case where the defender lost fourteen. It does not appear that armor losses from fighting in the urban and conurban terrain around Aachen were higher than those in the nonurban terrain; in fact they appear lower.

Overall it appears that armor losses in urban terrain are the same as or lower than armor losses in nonurban terrain and in some cases are significantly lower in urban terrain.

The Effect of Urban Terrain on Force Ratios

We utilized force ratios as part of the analyses to section the database. Here the question is whether force ratio is a dependent variable; that is, does the presence of urban terrain lead an attacker to fight with a higher force ratio or a lower one? Table 16.20 shows the average force ratio for the various engagements in the ETO.

Table 16.20. Average Force Ratios in ETO Engagements

	Number of Cases	Average Force Ratio	Weighted Force Ratio
Channel Ports	25	8.01	4.33
Normandy	21	3.55	2.02
ALLIED ATTACKS ONLY	17	4.00	2.12
Aachen	21	2.43	2.29
Ardennes	70	2.13	1.69
U.S. ATTACKS ONLY	47	1.96	1.78

Although the force ratio for the Channel Ports engagements is clearly higher than for the Normandy engagements, this is probably driven entirely by the nature of the operations. The nonurban battles were a mixture of engagements that were not always carefully organized and include four German counterattacks. These German attacks were executed at a low force ratio and are excluded from the results for "Normandy: Allied attacks only" in table 16.20.

The Aachen urban data are much closer in general to the nonurban data, although they are still higher than the Ardennes nonurban data. The Ardennes data include twenty-three German attacks, with an extreme mixture of both low and high force ratio attacks. However, the data set does not change much if those twenty-three are removed so that only American attacks are shown.

The Channel Ports and Aachen urban engagements were effectively set-piece engagements. The attacker had time to mass forces and make detailed, thoroughly planned and rehearsed preparations for an offensive. The higher force ratio probably reflects that fact more than any intrinsic effect of the terrain, especially in the case of the Channel Ports and Brest, where the defender was isolated and incapable of reinforcement.

The Effect of Urban Terrain on the Duration of Combat

Due to the nature of the data collected, little concrete information could be determined concerning the effect of cities on the duration of combat. In the DuWar DLEDB the determination of the length of an engagement is based on one of two different criteria.

One criterion is event-based; that is, an engagement is considered to last only until an easily determined milestone is reached. That milestone could be a breakpoint or another decision point in the engagement (e.g., the achievement of assigned objectives, the arrival of significant reinforcements, the descent of night). This criterion is also utilized when the records available do not support the analysis of an engagement by discrete time segments as finite as a day. Most of the engagements in the original HERO Land Warfare Database were of this type.

The other criterion is based solely on time and is normally a single day. As such, the average length of the engagement has nothing to do with the time required to complete the engagement. Most of the engagements added to the original LWDB as part of the DuWar DLEDB are of this type.

As a result, little regarding time requirements can be concluded from a direct analysis of the database. This issue is addressed further in the case studies that look more closely at the battles of Brest and Aachen and is discussed in chapter 17.

Phase 1 Conclusions

The overall conclusions that may be derived from an analysis of the data looked at in Phase 1 of this effort are:

1. Urban combat did not significantly influence the mission accomplishment (outcome) of the engagements.

2. Urban combat may have influenced the casualty rate. If so, it appears that urban warfare resulted in a reduction of the attacker casualty rate and a more favorable casualty exchange ratio compared to nonurban warfare. Whether or not these differences are caused by the data selection or by the terrain differences is difficult to say, but regardless, there appears to be no basis to the claim that urban combat is significantly more intense with regard to casualties than is nonurban warfare.

3. The average advance rate in urban combat should be one-half to one-third that of nonurban combat.

4. There is little evidence that urban terrain results in a higher linear density of troops, although the data do seem to trend in that direction.

5. The loss of armor in urban terrain is the same as or lower than that found in nonurban terrain, and in some cases is significantly lower.

6. Urban combat does not significantly influence the force ratio required to achieve success or effectively conduct combat operations.

7. Nothing could be determined from an analysis of the data regarding the duration of combat (time) in urban versus nonurban terrain.

The Second Phase: The Dupuy Institute Heads East

The second phase of this effort was completed more than a year later. Our Phase 1 conclusions were based on too few data, and the data were specifically defined to cover only one area of World War II. Adding the Eastern Front data provided us with more data points and a much broader coverage. Because of the data limitations, we were forced to reach conclusions in the first phase that had not been firmly established. So we used the second phase to test those conclusions with another data set.

We again chose engagements so as to minimize cost by building on existing work and to allow us to compare the results not only in aggregate but also by region, time, and opponent. Thus we created Kharkov engagements to compare to the existing Kursk engagements that the Dupuy Institute had previously assembled.

The three battles for Kharkov in February, March, and August 1943 are certainly not as famous as the Eastern Front urban fighting in Stalingrad during the fall of 1942. However, we chose Kharkov over Stalingrad for a number of reasons. First, we had already collected relevant nonurban engagements that we could compare them to. They were not only closely linked temporally and geographically but involved many of the same units and commanders. Second, Kharkov was the largest city fought over on the Eastern Front prior to

1945. It was the fourth largest city in the Soviet Union and larger than Stalingrad (as measured by prewar population). Third, it was fought over three times in one year, giving a range of differing operational conditions. Fourth, in two of the cases the Soviets were the attackers, and in the other case the Germans were the attackers. Fifth, no one else had analyzed these operations in depth.

This does not mean that the Dupuy Institute felt that examining Kharkov was more important or a better choice than examining Stalingrad. In fact as a result of our examination of Kharkov we came to the conclusion that a detailed examination and analysis of Stalingrad would be extremely useful, especially in light of the low level of losses suffered during the fighting in and around Kharkov. We recommended that Stalingrad be examined if there was going to be a fourth phase of this contract.

For the second phase, the Soviet research effort was finished and complete engagements were created covering almost all the fighting in, near, and around Kharkov in 1943. This included the Soviet offensive in February, the German counteroffensive in March, and the next Soviet offensive in August. The breakdown of engagements is presented in table 16.21.[9]

Table 16.21. Kharkov Engagements

	February 1943	March 1943	August 1943
Urban	2	5	7
Conurban	9	23	5
Nonurban	0	0	0

These fifty-one urban engagements were then compared to sixty-five nonurban Kursk engagements created as part of other work we were doing and a book on Kursk I was working on.[10]

We did have some problems with the research, which showed the weaknesses and limitations of secondary sources. To determine what units were involved in the engagements, the Dupuy Institute originally relied on detailed maps from a reputable secondary source showing division locations for most days in the fighting around Kharkov. Since this was the only secondary source that recorded Soviet division locations in the Kharkov fighting, there was no way to crosscheck it until after our archival research was well under way. However, it became clear as our research in the Soviet records progressed that many of these locations were incorrect. It appears that many were derived from German intelligence documents rather than Soviet sources. There were division-size units involved in the fighting that were not marked on these maps, and there were units shown involved in the area that were not there in reality. In some cases the maps in question had over half of the divisions incorrectly located. As a result, after having completed our initial round of research in the Soviet records, we were forced to send our Russian researcher back to the archives to do additional work. Thus the Soviet research evolved into an iterative process, which was certainly not time efficient and required more than one return to the archives. In the end we had our researcher go back through the army maps and assembled a master map showing where all the Soviet units were on each day of February and March. This allowed us to finally conclude with confidence that we had assembled all the necessary materials from all units involved. All this additional work did not allow us time to complete all the engagements that we had intended to.[11]

We also had some problems with the German material. The German records did not have the same level of detail that we had seen in the Kursk records for July 1943. To begin with, we were not regularly getting daily casualty reports, and the German casualty reporting for March was particularly poor. We found ourselves making far more use of interpolation and estimation of German losses than we had expected or desired. However, as the German casualties throughout these battles remained fairly low, no gross errors were made as a result. Still, in a number of cases we did not know what the German losses were for a particular division for a specific day, although we did know what they were over a period of time or across an entire corps.

German air data were very sparse, and we were missing the daily sortie counts that we had for the Kursk data. We estimated German air activity by examining the unit reports of both sides and noting what they claimed attacked them and what their counts were of enemy sorties. There is still more data that could be gathered on this from the Soviet side. While this methodology has some weaknesses, we know from our experience with the Kursk data that actual counts of enemy sorties per day tend to be plus or minus 50 percent of the actual number of sorties known. Therefore we are comfortable that the sortie counts from the ground units give us a count within the correct order of magnitude.

As an outgrowth of the Kursk project, we compared German kill claims (both air and armor) to actual Soviet losses and vice versa. We found that the German kill claims were often of the same order of magnitude as the Soviet losses. In contrast, we discovered that at Kursk the Soviet claims of German losses (both air and armor) were regularly off by a factor of 5 or 10. For that reason we did not make use of any Soviet claims for German losses. Where we had German claims of Soviet losses (air and armor), we did make use of these figures if we did not have data available from the Soviet records. Regardless, the count of Soviet plane and tank losses drawn from the German reports is small, usually one or two vehicles per engagement.

Otherwise all data used for the Kharkov and Kursk engagements are drawn from primary sources, the original unit records. Those for the German forces are from the Captured German Records at the U.S. National Archives. Those for the Soviet forces are from the Russian Military Archives at Podolsk.

Again we started with a series of simple comparisons of the aggregate data. We compared the fifty-one urban engagements from Kharkov to the sixty-five nonurban engagements from Kursk. But this was not a meaningful comparison as there is a clear performance difference between the German and the Soviet forces. We statistically examine this difference in depth in our *Capture Rate Study, Phases I & II* and also address it in chapter 8 of this book. The comparison was further complicated by the number of engagements in rough and rugged terrain in the Kursk data. We needed to separate the German offensive engagements from the Soviet ones and remove the engagements in rugged terrain from the data set.[12]

Instead we compared the twenty-eight cases of the Germans attacking in urban terrain (urban and conurban) to the thirty-one cases of the Germans attacking in rolling terrain in Kursk. We also compared the twenty-three cases of the Soviets attacking in urban terrain to the fifteen cases of the Soviets attacking in rolling terrain. We noted that, compared to the nonurban operations, these urban operations had higher success rates, lower attacker casualties, lower defender casualties, higher advance rates, and lower linear densities. We do not believe this properly represents the differences between urban and nonurban terrain, nor does it provide much support for some of the claims that have been made about the nature of urban warfare.

Using Eastern Front data we then attempted to answer the same question we had asked using the 137 cases of urban and nonurban combat in the European Theater of Operations: What was the impact of urban terrain on (1) mission success (outcome), (2) casualties and casualty rates, (3) advance rates, (4) force density (linear), (5) armor loss rates, (6) force ratios, and (7) duration of combat (time)?

Because of the importance in shaping the data played by the operational conditions and the performance differences between the opposing forces, we did not get the clear and satisfactory answers we obtained in the first phase. So while these data do provide some confirmation of the results of the first phase of the study, they also further muddy the water, though they do not contradict the results of the first phase.

The Effect of Urban Terrain on Outcome

As the outcome of an engagement clearly influences casualties, the breakdown of outcomes among the data sets needs to be examined. Both sets of data in table 16.22 show a tendency for the urban engagements to have more successes than the nonurban engagements. As was discussed in depth in the capture rate studies, the outcome of the engagement appears to be the primary determiner of casualty rates. Therefore, for our analysis, we compared engagements of similar outcomes and force ratios. Tables 16.23 and 16.24 summarize the results for outcomes III (attack fails), IV (attacker advances), and V (defender penetrated).[13]

Table 16.22. Outcomes of Selected Eastern Front Engagements

	Germans Attacking Kharkov	Kursk
I. Limited action	2	4
II. Limited attack	1	6
III. Attack fails	—	2
IV. Attacker advances	21	9
V. Defender penetrated	4	7
VI. Defender enveloped	—	3
VII. Other	—	—
	Germans Attacking Kharkov	Kursk
I. Limited action	—	—
II. Limited attack	3	5
III. Attack fails	9	7
IV. Attacker advances	10	3
V. Defender penetrated	1	—
VI. Defender enveloped	—	—
VII. Other	—	—

Table 16.23. German Attacker

Force Ratio	Cases	Terrain	Result
0.63	1	Nonurban	Attack fails
0.63	1	Nonurban	Attacker advances
1.01	1	Nonurban	Attacker advances
1.01–1.38	6	Urban	Attacker advances
1.18	1	Nonurban	Defender penetrated
1.23–1.32	2	Nonurban	Attacker advances

1.35	1	Nonurban	Defender penetrated
1.39	1	Urban	Defender penetrated
1.40–1.59	6	Urban	Attacker advances
1.42	1	Nonurban	Attacker advances
1.87	1	Nonurban	Attack fails
1.91	1	Nonurban	Attacker advances
2.07	1	Nonurban	Defender penetrated
2.10–2.11	2	Nonurban	Attacker advances
2.65–2.67	2	Urban	Defender penetrated
2.69–2.98	2	Nonurban	Defender penetrated
3.19	1	Urban	Attacker advances
3.60	1	Nonurban	Attacker advances
3.79–5.79	2	Nonurban	Defender penetrated
4.31–6.47	7	Urban	Attacker advances
6.63	1	Urban	Defender penetrated
9.42	1	Urban	Attacker advances

Table 16.24. Soviet Attacker

Force Ratio	Cases	Terrain	Result
0.40–0.42	2	Urban	Attacker advances
0.43–0.57	3	Urban	Attack fails
0.51	1	Nonurban	Attack fails
0.67	1	Urban	Attacker advances
0.85–1.20	4	Nonurban	Attack fails
1.20–1.23	3	Urban	Attack fails
1.20–1.29	3	Urban	Attacker advances
1.34	1	Nonurban	Defender penetrated
1.40	1	Urban	Attack fails
1.53	1	Urban	Attacker advances
1.65	1	Nonurban	Attacker advances
1.91–2.24	3	Urban	Attacker advances
2.08–2.12	2	Urban	Attack fails
2.31	1	Urban	Defender penetrated
2.54	1	Nonurban	Defender penetrated
2.87–2.89	2	Nonurban	Attack fails

The ETO data showed that force ratios had a major impact on the outcome; there were no failed urban attacks due to unfavorable force ratios, the lowest force ratio in an urban attack was 1.72 to 1, and only four attacks were made at less than 2.00 to 1. In the Kharkov data we had no failed German attacks, and the attacks were conducted at odds as low at 1.01 to 1. We have attacks for the Soviets in urban terrain at odds as low as 0.40 to 1, and seven failed attacks at odds from 0.43 to 2.12 to 1.

These data too show a relationship between force ratios and outcome, but it differs between the Germans and the Soviets. In the case of the Germans, attacks up to a ratio of 1.87 to 1 failed, but there were only two of them. The Germans did have successful attacks at ratios as low as 0.63 to 1. In the case of the Soviets, attacks of up to 2.89 to 1 failed, and there were sixteen failed attacks. The Soviets did have three successful attacks at very low odds (0.40, 0.42, and 0.67 to 1), but these were urban engagements at Kharkov, where the German Grossdeutschland Division was withdrawing anyway (12, 13, and 20 February). The lowest odds in a successful straightforward attack were 1.2 to 1 (in both an urban and a nonurban case).

We established force ratio guidelines as a result of the ETO data, presented in table 16.25. Revising that table to include percentages based on all data results in table 16.26.

Table 16.25. Force Ratios Compared to Outcomes, ETO

Force Ratio	Result
0.55 to 1.01 to 1.00	Attack fails
1.15 to 2.56 to 1.00	Attack may succeed
2.71 to 1.00 and higher	Attacker advances

Table 16.26. Force Ratios Compared to Chance of Success, ETO and Eastern Front

ETO

Force Ratio	Result	Percentage of Failure	Number of cases
0.55 to 1.01 to 1.00	Attack fails	100	5
1.15 to 1.88 to 1.00	Attack usually succeeds	21	48
1.95 to 2.56 to 1.00	Attack usually succeeds	10	21
2.71 to 1.00 and higher	Attacker advances	0	42

GERMANS ATTACKING SOVIETS

Force Ratio	Result	Percentage of Failure	Number of cases
0.63 to 1.06 to 1.00	Attack usually succeeds	20	5
1.18 to 1.87 to 1.00	Attack usually succeeds	6	17

| 1.91 to 1.00 and higher | Attacker advances | 0 | 21 |

Force Ratio	Result	Percentage of Failure	Number of cases
0.40 to 1.05 to 1	Attack usually fails	70	10
1.20 to 1.65 to 1.00	Attack often fails	50	11
1.91 to 2.89 to 1.00	Attack sometimes fails	44	9

It appears that force ratios are a major factor in determining outcome. It does not appear that the difference between urban and nonurban terrain significantly influenced this result. We cannot see a difference between results in urban terrain and nonurban terrain. This is similar to what we saw from the ETO data. As noted in the first phase of this study, the difference in terrain could affect combat power, but differences as small as 20 to 30 percent cannot be conclusively demonstrated given the small number of cases and the considerable variation found in the data.

We did look further into the effects of terrain only in those engagements where the attack may have succeeded. We found that the German failures occurred only in nonurban terrain and that Soviet failures were split nine to seven between urban and nonurban terrain. We were not left with any clear evidence of the influence of terrain on the outcome of battles.

The Effect of Urban Terrain on Casualties

As discussed in chapters 8 and 9, the outcome of a battle rather than the force ratio is the primary determiner of the loss rate. A simple comparison of average losses by outcome demonstrates this (table 16.27).

Table 16.27. Average Losses by Outcome, Eastern Front

Germans Attacking, Kharkov	I	II	III	IV	V	VI
Number of cases	2	1	0	21	4	—
Average percentage of attacker losses/day	0.06	0.44	0.54	0.46	—	—
Average percentage of defender losses/day	1.04	4.02	4.67	13.31	—	—
Germans Attacking, Kursk						
Number of cases	4	6	2	9	7	3
Average percentage of attacker losses/day	0.23	0.56	0.68	1.30	1.22	0.75
Average percentage of defender losses/day	0.16	0.70	1.33	5.34	7.92	38.32
Soviets Attacking, Kharkov						
Number of cases	—	3	9	10	1	—

	—					—
Average percentage of attacker losses/day	—	1.81	2.11	1.76	2.88	—
Average percentage of defender losses/day	—	0.51	0.51	0.78	0.53	—
Soviets Attacking, Kursk	I	II	III	IV	V	VI
Number of cases	—	5	7	3	—	—
Average percentage of attacker losses/day	—	0.78	3.37	3.54	—	—
Average percentage of defender losses/day	—	0.30	0.86	1.03	—	—

The percentages we used were simple straight averages. The result would change slightly if a weighted average was used, or if outliers were deleted, but the overall relationship within the data would not change. The data show two trends (if one compares similar outcomes in the urban data sets with similar outcomes in the nonurban data sets). First, as was true with the Phase 1 data, the attacker casualties were lower in urban than in nonurban warfare.

Second, in Phase 1 the defender casualties were higher and, more significant, the ratio of attacker casualties to defender casualties was more favorable to the attacker in urban warfare. These tendencies may have been driven by the selection of the urban engagements and, to a lesser extent, the selection of the nonurban engagements. For Phase 2, the same trend is noted in the outcome III and IV engagements, where most of the data are clustered. The data are not as clear outside of those outcomes, but these do make up a smaller number of cases.

Still, it would appear that there are fewer attacker casualties in the urban engagements than in the nonurban engagements, and the casualty exchange ratio favors the attacker as well. These data again do not provide much support for the notion that urban combat is a more casualty-intense environment than nonurban combat.

The Effect of Urban Terrain on Advance Rates

Opposed advance rates may be influenced by urban terrain. The Kursk and Kharkov data demonstrate this in table 16.28. (Recall that the DuWar databases record advance rates in kilometers per day.)

Table 16.28. Advance Rates in the Eastern Front

	Number of Cases	Average Advance Rate (in km.)	Five Highest Advance Rates (in km.)
Germans attacking, Kharkov	28	7.22	22, 20, 20, 16, 14
Germans attacking, Kursk	31	4.86	18, 10.7, 10.6, 10, 9
Soviets attacking, Kharkov	23	5.09	22, 17, 16, 15, 11
Soviets attacking, Kursk	15	0.90	10.2, 3.6, 2.7, 0.8, 0

As in Phase 1, these averages are driven by a few cases with high advance rates. When we limited the advance rates to 10 kilometers in Phase 1, we were able to see a consistent pattern between urban and nonurban advance rates. However, when we limited the rates in Phase 2, no pattern appeared. For example, the average advance rate (modified) became 5.47 versus 4.56 and 3.70 versus 0.89. We simply got higher advance rates in the urban areas in the Phase 2 data than in the nonurban areas. This is almost certainly being driven by the conditions of combat. Table 16.29 compares the data to the force ratio.

Table 16.29. Advance Rates Compared to Force in the Eastern Front

	Number of Cases	Average Advance Rate	Average Force Ratio	Weighted Force Ratio
Germans attacking, Kharkov	28	7.22	2.97	2.20
Germans attacking, Kursk	31	4.86	2.42	1.64
Soviets attacking, Kharkov	23	5.09	1.26	1.15
Soviets attacking, Kursk	15	0.90	1.59	1.49

In Phase 1 the urban data set was characterized by a large number of limited or minor advances. This was not the case for the Phase 2 data, as demonstrated in table 16.30. (Table 16.31 repeats the Phase 1 results for comparison.)

Table 16.30. Distance Advanced by Case, Eastern Front

Advance	German Kharkov	German Kursk	Soviet Kharkov	Soviet Kursk
Negative or zero	4	6	6	11
Up to 1 km./day	0	2	6	1
Up to 2 km./day	6	2	2	0
Up to 3 km./day	1	2	1	1
Up to 4 km./day	1	3	1	1
Up to 5 km./day	2	1	0	0
5–10 km./day	7	12	1	0
Greater than 10 km./day	7	3	6	1

This is a very different data set from the one we got from Phase 1 (see table 16.10).

The Phase 1 urban data set is characterized by a large number of limited or minor advances. The Phase 2 set has no clear pattern. From the Phase 1 data it would appear that one of the primary results of urban terrain is that it slowed opposed advance rates. Phase 1 even provided a more precise estimate of this, concluding that the average advance rate in urban combat should be one-half to one-third that of nonurban combat.

We believe that these conclusions are still true and will explore this in more depth when we examine the specifics of the Kharkov operations. For reference, the advance rates based on outcome in the Phase 2 data are presented in table 16.31.

Table 16.31. Average Daily Advance Rate in Kilometers by Outcome, Eastern Front

	I	II	III	IV	V	VI
Germans attacking, Kharkov	0	0	—	6.20	18.00	—
Germans attacking, Kursk	0	2.53	1.35	5.08	9.99	5.77
Soviets attacking, Kharkov	—	0.33	0.56	10.00	11.00	—
Soviets attacking, Kursk	—	0	-0 .43	5.50	—	—

The Effect of Urban Terrain on Force Density

Contrary to previous studies of urban combat, in Phase 1 we saw little evidence that operations in urban terrain resulted in a higher linear density of troops, although the data did seem to trend in that direction. A simple look at the Kursk and Kharkov data in table 16.32 offers little indication that urban terrain resulted in higher densities.

Table 16.32. Average Attacker Linear Density, Eastern Front

	Number of Cases	Average Linear Density	Weighted Average Linear Density
Germans attacking, Kharkov	28	1,801.07	1,477.87
Germans attacking, Kursk	31	2,553.51	2,109.69
Soviets attacking, Kharkov	23	1,278.32	1,005.22
Soviets attacking, Kursk	15	1,753.52	1,613.56

The dominant pattern here is that the Kursk operations occurred in a higher density than the Kharkov operations did. But this probably has nothing to do with terrain and a lot to do with the operational conditions. The Germans also had a higher linear density than the Soviets, partly as a result of their tendency to attack at higher odds.

A look at the outliers does not indicate that the data sets are influenced much by them, and tends to show that the data can achieve the same unit densities and the same low densities regardless of terrain. None of this adds support to the idea that there are higher densities in urban terrain operations. The high and low linear densities are listed in table 16.33.

Table 16.33. List of Lowest and Highest Densities, Eastern Front

	Five Lowest Cases	Five Highest Cases
Germans attacking, Kharkov	280.00	3,649.13
	544.25	3,365.38
	753.04	2,865.14
	805.91	2,846.57
	913.50	2,744.06
Germans attacking, Kursk	338.28	5,207.44
	504.43	5,205.90
	758.58	4,378.63
	1,576.44	3,762.97
	1,609.90	3,753.24
Soviets attacking, Kharkov	203.65	3,457.80
	238.00	2,623.60
	416.00	2,106.44
	475.86	2,061.78
	548.71	1,848.56
Soviets attacking, Kursk	392.20	2,990.50
	676.76	2,989.26
	769.12	2,906.38
	875.26	2,886.34
	1,030.41	2,399.50

As all the data sets have similar highs and lows, there seems to be no argument for making any further adjustments to the data. The data set of Germans attacking at Kharkov includes three engagements that were in purely urban terrain. These engagements, while having a higher linear density than the other Kharkov engagements, do not have a higher linear density than the typically higher density Kursk engagements.

The Effect of Urban Terrain on Armor

As stated earlier, much of the current discussion and analysis of the effects of urban warfare focus on the heavy armor losses of the Israelis at Suez and the Russians at Grozny. However, in our analysis of forty-six cases of urban combat in Phase 1, we found no such heavy armor loss. In fact armor losses were fairly low in most of the urban operations examined, although we did not have loss data for all the engagements.[14] For Phase 2 we conducted a similar analysis and again found few examples of heavy armor losses (table 16.34). This time we had a complete set of data points for armor strengths and losses. Again the data do not indicate that armor losses are higher in urban terrain than non-urban, but they do show that the Kursk operations tended to be more armor heavy, leading to higher losses.

Table 16.34. Armor Strength and Losses, Eastern Front

	Number of Cases	Average MBT Strength	Average Daily Tank Losses	Average Percentage of Tank Losses	Weighted Percentage of Tank Losses
GERMANS ATTACKING, KHARKOV					
Attacker	28	45.61	2.79	5.05	5.00
Defender	28	5.57	1.29	8.28	16.90
GERMANS ATTACKING, KURSK					
Attacker	31	148.16	19.03	7.83	9.70
Defender	31	67.81	20.16	12.31	17.69
SOVIETS ATTACKING, KHARKOV					
Attacker	23	10.00	1.61	5.44	11.71
Defender	23	25.70	1.57	3.53	5.82
SOVIETS ATTACKING, KURSK					
Attacker	15	55.80	5.80	4.29	4.79
Defender	15	59.13	5.73	6.44	7.44

The losses in tanks for these engagements were not large, except for the German attacks at Kursk, although the Kursk armor figures would be somewhat different if we included all the engagements from the German offensive in the south. The total losses for the engagements used are provided in table 16.35.

Table 16.35. Total Tank Losses, Eastern Front

	Attacker Total Tanks Lost	Defender Total Tanks Lost
Germans attacking, Kharkov	78	36
Germans attacking, Kursk	590	625
Soviets attacking, Kharkov	37	36
Soviets attacking, Kursk	87	86

In the ETO battles the largest number of tanks lost in a single urban engagement was fourteen. For the Eastern Front engagements, we did not find even that level of activity. There the worst single-day loss in an urban engagement was nineteen tanks, the second-worst case was eighteen, and the third-worst was eight. Furthermore there is no indication that the losses took place in urban terrain. The actual losses in the three purely urban engagements were never more than six tanks in a day.

In Phase 1 we concluded that armor losses in urban terrain were the same as or lower than armor losses in nonurban terrain. And in some cases armor losses are significantly lower in urban terrain. The Phase 2 data seem to confirm this (at least as measured on a daily basis, but also apparently for the entire urban fight).

The Effect of Urban Terrain on Force Ratios

In Phase 1 we concluded that urban combat did not significantly influence the force ratio required to achieve success or effectively conduct combat operations. After analyzing the data in table 16.36, we arrived at the same conclusion in Phase 2.

Table 16.36. Average Force Ratios, Eastern Front

	Number of Cases	Average Force Ratio	Weighted Force Ratio
German attacks, Kharkov	28	2.97	2.20
German attacks, Kursk	31	2.42	1.64
Soviet attacks, Kharkov	23	1.26	1.15
Soviet attacks, Kursk	15	1.59	1.49

The Effect of Urban Terrain on the Duration of Combat

Again, due to the nature of the data collected, little concrete information could be determined concerning the effect of cities on the duration of the combat.

Phase 2 Conclusions

The Phase 2 conclusions repeated and were supportive of those derived from the ETO data in Phase 1.

1. The conclusion that urban combat did not significantly influence mission accomplishment (outcome) was further supported. The data do show a tendency for urban engagements not to generate penetrations.

2. The conclusion that urban combat may have influenced the casualty rate was further supported. In fact it appears that urban combat resulted in a reduction of the attacker casualty rate and a more favorable casualty exchange ratio compared to nonurban warfare. There still appears to be no basis for

the claim that urban combat is significantly more intense than nonurban warfare with regard to casualties.

3. There was no strong evidence of a reduction in the advance rates in urban terrain in the Eastern Front data. The Dupuy Institute still stands by its original conclusion that the average advance rate in urban combat should be one-half to one-third that of nonurban combat.

4. Again there is little evidence that the presence of urban terrain results in a higher linear density of troops, but unlike the ETO data, the Phase 2 data did not show a tendency to trend in that direction.

5. Phase 2 further supported the conclusion that the loss of armor in urban terrain is the same as or less than that found in nonurban terrain, and in some cases is significantly lower.

6. Again urban combat did not significantly influence the force ratio required to achieve success or effectively conduct combat operations.

7. Again nothing could be determined from an analysis of the data regarding the duration of combat (time) in urban versus nonurban terrain.

The Third Phase: The Dupuy Institute Heads Even Farther East

The next follow-on phase of the study continued to round out the cases and look at more modern cases, including post–World War II engagements. Although it did not materially affect our earlier conclusions, Phase 3 did extend this work even further, making the picture clearer and more definitive. The objective was to examine a series of engagements in urban terrain beginning in World War II and extending over time to the latest urban fighting in Iraq. To do so we examined the effects of urban terrain as it occurred during the Battle of Manila in World War II, the Inchon-Seoul Campaign in the Korean War, the Tet Offensive in the Vietnam War, and fighting in Panama, Mogadishu, Baghdad, and other minor conflicts since World War II.

However, to achieve this we were forced to accept the fact that complete two-sided data for these engagements, normally one of our methodological requirements, are unobtainable in most of the cases. Only in the case of the Battle of Manila were we comfortable with enemy strength data and the estimation methodology used to derive enemy losses.[15] As a result, with a few exceptions, the other engagements are necessarily one-sided and reflected the effects of urban warfare on the only "Blue" side (normally also the attacking side). For that reason, except in the case of Manila, we focused our attention on casualties incurred by the attacking forces in urban operations.

Between the three phases of this effort we had assembled enough urban engagements to have a fairly representative selection of the total population of urban engagements. Early in this effort we had developed a list of 117 urban (and village) battles since 1900 for possible study. While not exhaustive, this list was the most extensive we were aware of. There are surprisingly few examples of large-scale urban combat. With the completion of Phase 3 we had examined 22 (18.8 percent) of these cases in depth. Of the 38 major urban battles on that list (division level or larger), we had examined 17 (44.7 percent). This had generated 153 two-sided engagements and 151 one-sided engagements. We were comfortable that, at this stage, we had conducted a thorough and representative look at urban engagements.

Only 3 of the remaining 21 major urban battles are known to have good data for both sides. The biggest remaining untapped source of data is the Battle of Stalingrad, which could yield over 100 division-level engagements. This was to be the focus of our future work.

The Engagements

Since we decided we could forgo the need for two-sided data in this phase of the study, the collection of engagements was relatively easy and allowed us to create a very robust data set totaling 207 urban and 163 nonurban engagements. The data were used to make the same comparisons we did before, using the one-sided data only for analysis of casualty rates and duration. We used the two-sided data (Manila) just as we did the ETO and Kharkov data.

The 370 engagements of this data set included 94 from the Pacific Theater of Operations, specifically the Battle of Manila in February and March 1945. These broke down further into 53 urban and 41 nonurban engagements. No conurban engagements were mixed in with this data set. This made up our collection of two-sided data that could be compared directly with the ETO and Kharkov data.

Our data collection also included 10 Korean War urban engagements that occurred during the Inchon-Seoul Campaign of September 1950. We had 65 division-level urban engagements from the Vietnam War's Tet Offensive in 1968 and 57 parallel nonurban engagements to go with them. Also in that data set were 56 battalion-level urban engagements. From the Middle East wars and other engagements we had 14 division-level urban engagements and 65 nonurban engagements to compare them to. We also had 9 modern battalion-level urban engagements. These were drawn from operations in Beirut, Lebanon, in 1982–84; Panama in 1989; Khafji, Saudi Arabia, in 1991; Mogadishu, Somalia, in 1992–93; and Baghdad, Iraq, in 2003. This was a significant collection of 142 division-level urban engagements to be compared to 163 nonurban engagements. We also had 74 battalion-level urban engagements.[16]

Table 16.37 contains a list comparing the attackers in all the division-level urban engagements to the attackers in all the relevant nonurban engagements. It is a summary of all the data presented to date.[17]

Table 16.37. Attackers in Division-Level Engagements, All Periods

URBAN

	PTO	Korea	Tet	Other*	ETO	EF** (German Attacks)	EF (Soviet Attacks)
Average strength	12,099	28,304	6,294	10,903	34,601	17,080	17,001
Average casualties	78	30	94	254	178	86	371
Average casualties/day	78	30	39	59	169	86	371
Average percentage loss/day	0.63	0.71	0.78	0.56	0.50	0.49	1.95
Weighted percentage loss/day	0.65	0.71	0.62	0.54	0.49	0.50	2.18

NONURBAN

	PTO	Tet	Other	ETO	EF (German Attacks)	EF (Soviet Attacks)
Average strength	17,445	13,232	18,991	21,060	27,083	27,044
Average casualties	663	44	377	469	276	761
Average casualties/day	221	22	191	237	206	653
Average percentage loss/day	0.83	0.19	1.56	1.09	1.00	2.39
Weighted percentage loss/day	1.27	0.17	1.01	1.13	0.76	2.41

*Includes Middle East wars.

**Eastern Front

While this summary is not the end point of our analysis, it is very interesting to compare the urban and nonurban engagements. A simple glance at the numbers establishes that there are many contradictions with some of the current assumptions made about urban operations.[18] In particular the urban operations have lower attacker casualties than the nonurban, except in the case of the Tet Offensive.[19] The following conclusions are based on this insight.

The Effect of Urban Terrain on Outcome

There were no failed urban attacks in the PTO urban data, so no failures could be attributed to unfavorable force ratios. However, the lowest force ratio of an urban attack was 1.40 to 1, and only fifteen of the fifty-three urban attacks were less than 2.54 to 1.

The data did show a relationship between force ratios and outcome, but it differs by nation. In the case of the Germans on the Eastern Front, one nonurban attack as high as 1.87 to 1 failed. The Germans did have a successful nonurban attack as low as 0.63 to 1, but a second nonurban attack at the same odds failed. Overall just two of fifty-nine urban and nonurban German attacks resulted in failure (3.39 percent). In the case of the Soviets, attacks of up to 2.89 to 1 failed, and there were a total of sixteen failed attacks out of thirty-eight urban and nonurban cases (42.10 percent). The Soviets did have three successful attacks at very low odds (0.40, 0.42, and 0.67 to 1), but these were urban engagements in which the Germans were already withdrawing. The lowest odds in a successful Soviet straightforward attack were 1.20 to 1 (in both an urban and a nonurban case). American forces in the PTO failed in the attack in nonurban terrain in one case, at 7.08 to 1, but had only four failures in total out of ninety cases (0.04 percent), all of them in nonurban terrain (four of thirty-seven cases, or 10.81 percent; see table 16.38).

Table 16.38. PTO Data, U.S. attacking Japanese

Force Ratio	Result	Chance of Failure (%)	Number of cases
1.40 to 2.89 to 1.00	Attack succeeds	0	20
2.92 to 3.89 to 1.00	Attack usually succeeds	21	14
4.35 to 1.00 and higher	Attack usually succeeds	4	26

The Effect of Urban Terrain on Casualties

As discussed in our capture rate studies and Phase 1 and 2 of the urban warfare studies, the outcome of a battle, rather than the force ratio, is the primary determinant of loss rates. The simple comparison of average losses by outcome in table 16.39 demonstrates this.

Table 16.39. Average Losses by Outcome, PTO

PTO Urban	I	II	III	IV	V	VI	VII
Number of cases	0	21	0	21	3	8	0
Average percentage of attacker losses/day	—	0.50	—	0.87	0.48	0.42	—
Average percentage of defender losses/day	—	24.17	—	6.71	42.05	41.03	—
PTO Nonurban	I	II	III	IV	V	VI	VII
Number of cases	0	1	4	18	14	0	0
Average percentage of attacker losses/day	—	0.06	0.77	1.06	0.58	—	—
Average percentage of defender losses/day	—	5.64	13.12	18.94	9.62	—	—

Once again the percentages used were simple straight averages. Once again, the result would change slightly if a weighted average was used or outliers were deleted, but the overall relationship within the data would not change. And once again the data show two trends if one compares similar outcomes in the urban data sets with similar outcomes in the nonurban data sets. First, attacker casualties are lower in urban than in nonurban warfare (except in the case of outcome II, where the nonurban data are skewed because there is only a single case for comparison). This was also true in Phases 1 and 2.

Second, as in Phases 1 and 2, the Phase 3 PTO data suggest that casualty rates and casualty exchange ratios favor the attacker in urban terrain. As noted, in the data from Phase 1, defender casualties were higher and the ratio of attacker casualties to defender casualties was more favorable to the attacker in urban warfare and these tendencies may have been driven by the selection of the engagements. For Phase 2 the same trend was noted in the outcome III and IV engagements, where most of the data are clustered. The data were not as clear outside of those outcomes, but these do make up a smaller number of cases. In the Phase 3 PTO data the trend again is not as clear: for outcome IV the ratio is more favorable for the nonurban cases, while for outcome V the ratio is more favorable for urban cases. However, on the whole the exchange ratios in the PTO are much higher than for the other cases. But it is hard to place much reliance on data with such lopsided exchange ratios.

Still, it would appear that attacker casualties in the urban engagements are lower than in the nonurban engagements, and the casualty exchange ratio may favor the attacker as well. These data do not provide much support for the notion that urban combat is a more casualty-intensive environment than nonurban combat.

The Effect of Urban Terrain on Advance Rates

Table 16.40 examines advance rates in the PTO urban and nonurban data.

Table 16.40. Advance Rates in the PTO

	Number of Cases	Average Advance Rate (in km.)	Five Highest Daily Advances (in km.)
PTO urban	53	0.32	4, 2, 2, 2, 2
PTO nonurban	37	4.69	75, 20, 20, 12, 11

As in Phases 1 and 2, these averages are driven by a few cases with high advance rates. When these advance rates were limited to 10 kilometers, we found a consistent pattern between the urban and nonurban advance rates in Phase 1 but not in Phase 2. In the Phase 3 PTO data the average advance rate (modified) would be 0.32 for the urban cases and 2.31 for the nonurban cases. Table 16.41 compares the advance rate to the force ratio.

Table 16.41. Advance Rates Compared to Force in the PTO

	Number of Cases	Average Advance Rate	Average Force Ratio	Weighted Force Ratio
PTO urban	53	0.32	20.09	3.99
PTO nonurban	37	4.69	4.07	4.25

In Phase 3 the PTO urban data set was characterized by a large number of limited or minor advances as shown in table 16.42. This was also the case in the Phase 1 ETO data, but it was not the case for the Phase 2 Eastern Front data.

Table 16.42. Distance Advanced by Case, PTO

Advance	PTO Urban	PTO Nonurban
Negative or zero	29	3
0–1 km./day	18	24
1–2 km./day	5	1
2–3 km./day	0	1
3–4 km./day	1	1
4–5 km./day	0	0
5–10 km./day	0	2
Greater than 10 km./day	0	5

From the Phase 1 data it appeared that one of the primary characteristics of urban terrain is that it slows opposed advance rates. Phase 1 even provided a fairly precise estimate of this effect: the average advance rate in urban combat should be one-half to one-third that of nonurban combat. The PTO data are even more extreme than that, with urban advance rates decreasing to about one-tenth of those found in the nonurban engagements. However, given that this represents just the single case of Manila, it is difficult to conclude anything other than that this may represent an extreme case.

The Effect of Urban Terrain on Force Density

As mentioned, we have seen little evidence that operations in urban terrain resulted in a higher linear density of troops, although the data seemed to trend in that direction in the Phase 1 ETO cases. An examination of the Phase 2 Eastern Front data also provided little indication that higher troop densities result from urban terrain. In the case of Phase 2 it appears that the weighted average urban densities were in fact lower—by about 17.39 percent—than the nonurban densities. However, both the urban and the nonurban densities in the Phase 3 Pacific Theater data (table 16.43) were much higher than those found in either the European Theater (table 16.44) or the Eastern Front (table 16.45).

Table 16.43. Average Attacker Linear Density, PTO

	Number of Cases	Average Linear Density	Weighted Average Linear Density
PTO urban	53	3,706.13	3,112.81
PTO nonurban	37	6,751.05	3,768.08

Table 16.44. Average Attacker Linear Density, ETO

	Number of Cases	Average Linear Density	Weighted Average Linear Density
ETO urban	46	3,461.45	2,620.45
ETO nonurban	91	2,069.70	1,480.51

Table 16.45. Average Attacker Linear Density, Eastern Front

	Number of Cases	Average Linear Density	Weighted Average Linear Density
EF Germans attacking, urban	28	1,801.07	1,477.87
EF Soviets attacking, urban	23	1,278.32	1,005.22
EF Germans attacking, nonurban	47	2,355.21	1,601.94
EF Soviets attacking, nonurban	18	1,540.94	1,522.22

The outliers found in Phase 1 and 2 did not have much influence on the data sets; they tended to show that the same unit densities and the same low linear densities occurred regardless of terrain. Since all the data sets have similar highs and lows, there seems to be no argument for making any further adjustments to the data. The set of German attacks on the Eastern Front in urban terrain did include three engagements that occurred in purely urban terrain. These engagements, while having a higher linear density than that of the other Eastern Front urban engagements, did not have a higher linear density than the typical Eastern Front nonurban engagements. None of this reinforces the idea that there are noticeably higher densities found in urban terrain operations. The trend appears to be that urban linear density may be somewhat lower than nonurban linear density.

The Effect of Urban Terrain on Armor

Recall that in our analysis of forty-six cases of urban combat in Phase 1, we did not find the heavy armor loss predicted by the Israeli and Russian cases. In fact armor losses were fairly low in most of the urban operations examined, although we did not have loss data for all the engagements. We conducted a similar analysis in Phase 2 and again found few examples of heavy armor losses in urban terrain. These data again showed no clear indication that armor losses were higher in urban than in nonurban terrain. However, the Eastern Front nonurban operations tended to be more armor heavy, which led to losses being higher (simply by virtue of the fact that more armor was present). In the PTO engagements armor losses in the urban cases averaged 0.51 percent per day, while in the nonurban cases they were 0.67 percent per day.

Overall the loss in tanks in the Eastern Front engagements was not large except for the German attacks at Kursk, although the Kursk armor figures would be somewhat different and probably even higher if they included all the engagements from the German offensive in the south. Compare the Kharkov and Kursk data in table 16.35 to the ETO data in table 16.46.

Table 16.46. Total Tank Losses in the ETO Engagements

	Attacker Total Tanks Lost	Defender Total Tanks Lost
Urban	124	105
Nonurban	923	524

The largest number of tanks lost in a single urban engagement in the ETO was fourteen. In the Eastern Front it appears to have been never more than six, and in the PTO it was five. As in Phases 1 and 2, we conclude from the Phase

3 data that armor losses in urban terrain are the same as or lower than armor losses in nonurban terrain, in some cases significantly lower.

The Effect of Urban Terrain on Force Ratios

As we did in Phases 1 and 2, in Phase 3 we asked whether urban terrain leads an attacker to fight with a higher or a lower force ratio. Table 16.47 presents the data.

Table 16.47. Average Force Ratios: PTO, Eastern Front, and ETO

	Number of Cases	Average Force Ratio	Weighted Force Ratio
PTO			
Urban	53	20.09	3.99
Nonurban	37	4.07	4.25
EF			
Germans attacking, urban	28	2.97	2.20
Germans attacking, nonurban	31	2.42	1.64
Soviets attacking, urban	23	1.26	1.15
Soviets attacking, nonurban	15	1.59	1.49
ETO			
Urban	46	5.46	3.42
Nonurban	91	2.46	1.80
ALLIED ATTACKS ONLY	17	4.00	2.12
U.S. ATTACKS ONLY	47	1.96	1.78

In Phases 1 and 2 we concluded that urban combat did not significantly influence the force ratio required to achieve success or effectively conduct combat operations. The PTO data in Phase 3 contain the highest force ratios found in any of the engagements but apparently only reflect the specific circumstances that occurred at Manila. There the force ratios were driven by the fact that the Japanese defense was initially fragmented and partly defeated in detail (in part due to the rapid American advance on the city). The Japanese forces were also isolated from reinforcements and steadily declined in strength over the course of the battle.

The Effect of Urban Terrain on the Duration of Combat

As in Phases 1 and 2, and for the same reasons, little regarding time requirements can be concluded from a direct analysis of the Phase 3 database.

1. Phase 1: Urban combat did not significantly influence the mission accomplishment (outcome) of the engagements.

Phase 2: This conclusion was further supported. The data do show a tendency for urban engagements not to generate penetrations.

Phase 3: This conclusion was further supported.

2. Phase 1: Urban combat may have influenced the casualty rate, resulting in a reduction of the attacker casualty rate and a more favorable casualty exchange ratio compared to nonurban warfare.

Phase 2: This conclusion was further supported.

Phase 3: This conclusion was further supported.

3. Phase 1: The average advance rate in urban combat should be one-half to one-third that of nonurban combat.

Phase 2: There was no strong evidence of a reduction in the advance rates in urban terrain in the Eastern Front data.

Phase 3: There was strong evidence of a reduction in the advance rates in urban terrain in the PTO data.

4. Phase 1: There is little evidence that the presence of urban terrain results in a higher linear density of troops, although the data do seem to trend in that direction.

Phase 2: This conclusion is supported, except the data did not show a tendency to trend in that direction.

Phase 3: The PTO data show the highest densities found in the data sets for all three phases. However, it does not appear that the urban density in the PTO was significantly higher than the nonurban density. So it remains difficult to tell whether or not the higher density was a result of the urban terrain or was simply a consequence of the doctrine adopted to meet the requirements found in the Pacific Theater.

5. Phase 1: The loss of armor in urban terrain is the same as or lower than that found in nonurban terrain and in some cases is significantly lower.

Phase 2: This conclusion was further supported.

Phase 3: This conclusion was further supported.

6. Phase 1: Urban combat did not significantly influence the force ratio required to achieve success or effectively conduct combat operations.

Phase 2: This conclusion was further supported.

Phase 3: This conclusion was further supported.

7. Phase 1–3: Nothing could be determined from an analysis of the data regarding the duration of combat (time) in urban versus nonurban terrain.

Attacker Casualty Trends in Modern Urban and Nonurban Combat

To recapitulate, in the three phases of this study we assembled a set of urban and nonurban combat engagements that occurred between July 1943 and April 2003, a span of nearly sixty years. Unfortunately, with some minor exceptions, developing consistent and reliable data for both sides in the engagements of the wars since World War II has been either very difficult or impossible. However, we have been able to create a consistent set of data that includes duration of the engagement and the strength and casualties of the attacker, calculated as average casualties, average casualties per day, average percentage of loss per day, and weighted percentage of loss per day. Table 16.48 places them in rough chronological order (the category of Other/Middle East wars actually spans from 1944 to 2003, so it overlaps in part the Korean- and Vietnam-era engagements).

Table 16.48. Overview of all Urban and Nonurban Engagements

EASTERN FRONT ENGAGEMENT OVERVIEW

	Urban and Conurban, Germans Attacking	Nonurban, Germans Attacking
Number of engagements	28	47
Average attacker strength	17,080	27,083
Average battle length (days)	1	1
Average attacker casualties	86	276
Average attacker casualties per day	86	206
Average attacker percentage of loss per day	0.49	1.00
Weighted attacker percentage of loss per day	0.50	0.76

	Urban and Conurban, Soviets Attacking	Nonurban, Soviets Attacking
Number of engagements	23	18
Average attacker strength	17,001	27,044
Average battle length (days)	1	1
Average attacker casualties	371	761
Average attacker casualties per day	371	653
Average attacker percentage of loss per day	1.95	2.39
Weighted attacker percentage of loss per day	2.18	2.41

EUROPEAN THEATER OF OPERATIONS ENGAGEMENT OVERVIEW

	Urban and Conurban	Nonurban
Number of engagements	46	91
Average attacker strength	34,601	21,060

	Urban	Nonurban
Average battle length (days)	1	2
Average attacker casualties	178	469
Average attacker casualties per day	169	237
Average attacker percentage of loss per day	0.50	1.09
Weighted attacker percentage of loss per day	0.49	1.13

PACIFIC THEATER OF OPERATIONS ENGAGEMENT OVERVIEW*

	Urban	Nonurban
Number of engagements	53	37
Average attacker strength	12,099	17,445
Average battle length (days)	1	3
Average attacker casualties	78	663
Average attacker casualties per day	78	221
Average attacker percentage of loss per day	0.63	0.83
Weighted attacker percentage of loss per day	0.65	1.27

KOREAN WAR ENGAGEMENT OVERVIEW

	Urban	Nonurban
Number of engagements	10	—
Average attacker strength	18,304	—
Average battle length (days)	1	—
Average attacker casualties	130	—
Average attacker casualties per day	130	—
Average attacker percentage of loss per day	0.71	—
Weighted attacker percentage of loss per day	0.71	—

VIETNAM WAR TET OFFENSIVE ENGAGEMENT OVERVIEW

	Urban	Nonurban
Number of engagements	65	57
Average attacker strength	6,294	13,232
Average battle length (days)	2	2
Average attacker casualties	94	44
Average attacker casualties per day	39	22
Average attacker percentage of loss per day	0.78	0.19
Weighted attacker percentage of loss per day	0.62	0.17

OTHER/MIDDLE EAST WARS ENGAGEMENT OVERVIEW

	Urban	Nonurban
Number of engagements	14	65

Average attacker strength	10,903	18,991
Average battle length (days)	4	2
Average attacker casualties	254	377
Average attacker casualties per day	59	191
Average attacker percentage of loss per day	0.56	1.56
Weighted attacker percentage of loss per day	0.54	1.01

*Less two cases of Japanese nonurban attacks.

Attacker strength is based on the engagements selected. This has a direct influence on the number of casualties incurred. However, the daily percentage loss does not appear to be dependent on the size of the force, so long as the data set consistently is kept within the size limits of the echelon in question, in this case division level. So I will not examine the relationship between the average and weighted-average percentage of loss per day in the different sets, with the sets arranged according to "time" order (earliest to latest).

Table 16.49. Comparison of Attacker Urban Casualty Data, All Data Sets

Urban	PTO	Korea	Tet	Other	ETO	EF (German Attacks)	EF (Soviet Attacks)
Average percentage of loss/day	0.63	0.71	0.78	0.56	0.50	0.49	1.95
Weighted percentage of loss/day	0.65	0.71	0.62	0.54	0.49	0.50	2.18

It is readily apparent in table 16.49 that the data set for the Eastern Front (Soviet Attacks) constitutes an outlier with respect to the other data sets. Our understanding of why such outliers exist has been fully explained in the Phase 2 report and in other reports prepared by the Dupuy Institute over the years.[20] Suffice it to say that we believe such outliers are dependent on human factors rather than on variables between urban and nonurban terrain.

Excluding the Eastern Front (Soviet Attacks) outlier, the weighted-average percentage per day loss for the attackers in the six data sets is 0.58. The lowest value found, in the ETO, is within 18.37 percent of that, while the highest, in Korea, is within 22.41 percent of that. None approaches the 1.05 weighted-average nonurban rate found for the total data set in this study (excluding the anomalous Eastern Front [Soviet Attacks] and Tet Offensive; see below) or the 1.00 percent per day division-level casualty rate expected from data derived from U.S. experience in World War II.[21] So it now appears that we may answer the original question posed at the outset of this study with some confidence.

Have Casualties or Casualty Rates Incurred in Urban Operations Changed over Time?

There is nothing in these data sets that would support the notion that urban warfare has become more deadly or intense over the course of the past sixty years. Nor does there appear to be any solid evidence for the notion that urban combat in the "third world" differs in any way from urban combat in other areas.

The slightly higher loss rates found in the Pacific Theater of Operations as opposed to the other two data sets derived from World War II are likely a consequence of the fanatically suicidal resistance put up by the Japanese in the defense of Manila. That could be considered analogous to the fanatical and suicidal terrorist forces currently being encountered by Western forces in the third world. However, it appears unlikely that in the foreseeable future Western forces will encounter eighteen thousand such suicidal terrorists, a large proportion of them trained and equipped to the standards of conventional military forces, defending their cities. Even among Muslim fanatics that kind of suicidal fanaticism is expressed through more individualistic, personal offensive actions rather than coordinated defensive actions. We have seen little evidence in the various wars of the Middle East of such fanaticism carrying over to organized conventional defensive warfare.[22]

Furthermore it appears that another culprit responsible for the slightly higher rates in Manila could be the construction of the city itself. Since the city was in a known earthquake zone much of it was built in the 1920s and 1930s to be earthquake-proof, which at that time meant many buildings were constructed of heavily reinforced concrete and steel. The result was that many buildings, and especially large governmental buildings, were readily converted to bunkers and pillboxes that were impervious to all but the heaviest direct-fire weapons.[23] This construction was much sturdier than that found currently in most parts of the third world—and even most of those in the first world.

Table 16.50. Comparison of Attacker Urban versus Nonurban Casualty Data, All Data Sets

Urban	PTO	Korea	Tet	Other	ETO	EF (German Attacks)	EF (Soviet Attacks)
Average percentage of loss/day	0.63	0.71	0.78	0.56	0.50	0.49	1.95
Weighted percentage of loss/day	0.65	0.71	0.62	0.54	0.49	0.50	2.18

Nonurban	PTO	Tet	Other	ETO	EF (German Attacks)	EF (Soviet Attacks)
Average percentage of loss/day	0.83	0.19	1.56	1.09	1.00	2.39
Weighted percentage of loss/day	1.27	0.17	1.01	1.13	0.76	2.41

In addition to the Soviets, we find a second outlier: the nonurban data from the Tet Offensive in the Vietnam War (table 16.50). Comparing these to the urban losses during Tet we find they were nearly four times the nonurban rate and were quite simply a reflection of the unique character of that operation. In essence, during Tet virtually all of the offensive capability of the NVA/VC was directed at the cities and towns of South Vietnam to the near total exclusion of operations outside those urban areas. This is the sole example we have found where large-scale nonurban operations resulted in a lower casualty rate than contemporaneous urban operations.

However, if we exclude these two outliers, we find that the weighted average of 1.05 percent per day in the other five data sets is not far from the 1.00 percent per day division-level casualty rate that was expected from U.S. experience in World War II. The lowest case, Eastern Front (German Attacks), is 24 percent lower, while the highest case, the Pacific Theater of Operations, is just 27 percent higher.

Battalion-Level Urban Engagements

In the course of developing the data sets for Phase 3, a number of urban warfare engagements were found that were at a much smaller level than the division-level engagements normally used for our analyses. These are included here (table 16.51) for reference only. However, as for the division-level urban cases assembled in the three phases of this project, the weighted percentage of loss per day in the battalion-level urban cases is much lower than otherwise expected for brigade- or battalion-level operations.[24] Given that future U.S. military operations could involve engagements in cities with forces much smaller than division level, it may be desirable to expand and refine this data set. Their aggregate statistics are provided for reference.

Table 16.51. Battalion-Level Urban Engagements

	Tet	Other
Number of engagements	56	9
Average battle length (days)	2	7
Average strength	1,912	1,290
Average casualties	71	38
Average casualties per day	37	5
Average percentage of loss per day	1.01	3.85
Weighted percentage of loss per day	1.94	0.39

The Impact of Urban Terrain on Operations

The primary result of urban terrain, according to the data derived from the analysis, is to reduce advance rates significantly, reduce casualties to some extent, and so to extend the duration of combat. Fundamentally combat in urban terrain will take longer than in nonurban terrain.

For the effects of urban terrain on operations, two scenarios need to be considered: when the urban terrain can be bypassed and when it cannot. Those cases where the urban terrain can be bypassed are the most common. To create a situation where it cannot be bypassed means that the city would have to stretch indefinitely to the left and right, or that the flanks of the city would be solidly anchored on otherwise impassable terrain. These conditions, even with increased urbanization in the world, are hard to come by and usually occur only on islands or peninsulas.

Therefore the vast majority of urban terrain encountered will be flanked by nonurban terrain. Operations in these nonurban flanks will potentially advance at a pace two to four times that of the urban operations (assuming forces are distributed evenly across the battlefield). Under normal circumstances the urban area will be bypassed on one or both flanks and will be threatened with envelopment within a few days of an operation beginning.[25] Furthermore, as the attacker is usually aware that faster progress can be made outside the urban terrain, the tendency is to weigh one or both flanks and not bother to attack the city until it is enveloped. This will, of course, result in either the defender withdrawing from the urban terrain, which is what traditionally has occurred, or an assault and eventual mop-up operation by the attacker of the enveloped defenders. This has been the consistent pattern in the past and will likely continue to be so in the future for those cases where urban terrain, regardless of its increased size or density, has nonurban flanks.

This is in fact what occurred in all three cases at Kharkov. In February Soviet forces pushed around the western side of the city, while another Soviet group actually penetrated along the seam between the Das Reich ss and LSSAH Divisions and enveloped the city from the south. The defender was left with no choice but to withdraw.

There was a similar scenario in March. The Germans moved a powerful force west of the city, breaking through the Soviet position and circling around north of the city. Over the course of three days the Germans managed to continue the drive around to the eastern side of the city, while other German elements began pushing south of the city. This operation produced a three-day battle for the city, but it was a battle created primarily as a result of errors on both sides. There was no good reason for the Germans to commit the better part of two divisions to drive into the developing encirclement, and there was no good reason for the Soviets to concentrate their forces and remain in the encirclement. The Soviet forces quickly abandoned Kharkov, as was their only practical option, resulting in a city fight that was not particularly intense.

The August battle was conducted by many of the same forces and commanders that had been involved in the first two battles. It was quickly resolved by two Soviet drives—again west of and south of the city—resulting in a potential envelopment that caused the Germans to withdraw. In the August battle the fighting in front of the city, other than the one poorly planned Soviet attack, was at best limited and desultory. For comparison the average daily losses from the February engagements were 575.82 (German and Soviet losses added together); in March they were 493.18, and in August they were 363.17. It is tempting to draw the conclusion that a learning curve was in effect and that the forces involved in August focused primarily on enveloping the city and did not waste time defending it or fighting for it. There is no question that the most important lesson learned from the three battles of Kharkov is that one should just bypass cities rather than attack them.

The attacker is usually aware that faster progress can be made outside the urban terrain and that the tendency is to weigh one or both flanks and not bother to attack the city until it is enveloped. This is indeed what happened in two of the three cases at Kharkov and was also the order given by the Fourth Panzer Army, which was violated by the ss Panzer Corps in March.

On the other hand, it is possible that one could encounter a situation where the urban terrain cannot be bypassed or securely enveloped. The most notable example of such a scenario is in South Korea, where Seoul, anchored to the west (left flank) by the sea, extends for some 25 kilometers inland and is then flanked to the east (right) by a substantial mountain range. While this is an important case for U.S. defense planning purposes, it is one of the few hot spots in the world where this situation is found. An examination of an atlas shows few other cities in the world that cannot be bypassed or enveloped.

This apparently is the primary reason there are so few examples of urban combat to be found. Examining our list of 117 urban operations, only two such cases come to mind. The first is Shanghai in 1932, where the Japanese made an amphibious landing onto the Chinese mainland and then had to fight their way into the city. The second is Stalingrad in 1942, where the city paralleled a broad river that the Germans were not well positioned or prepared to cross. Still, Stalingrad was not an objective the Germans were forced to take, and the operation there became very much influenced by a political desire to take the city, a desire that vastly exceeded its military and economic value.

Many of the other urban battles on the list tend to be cases where the city became partially or completely enveloped before being taken (including Kharkov, Hue, and the second Russian occupation of Grozny). This has been the norm in the past and will probably remain the norm in the future.

Finally, there are two cases on that list where the attacker suffered serious armor losses in taking cities: the first battle of Grozny in 1995 and the Battle for Suez City in 1973. As I've mentioned these two examples are often cited to support assumptions that armor losses in cities are high, when in fact our data show the opposite to be true. These are the only two major examples we have of excessive armor losses in taking a city (although there are certainly some others). In both of these cases the reason for making a quick armor strike was fundamentally political. In the case of Suez City it was a strike attempting to seize the city by coup-de-main after a cease-fire had already been agreed upon. This was for the sake of strengthening the Israeli postwar negotiating position and was not done for firm military reasons, as the war had effectively ended![26]

The first attack on Grozny was also politically motivated, as the Russian Army was under considerable political pressure to resolve the Chechen issue quickly. Unlike the Suez City battle, which was over in a few hours, the Grozny operation lasted several days. It was an incompetent waste of armor and soldiers' lives in an attempt to fulfill a politically driven timetable.

While these two examples provide a firm warning against sending armor into cities without proper reconnaissance and infantry support, the same can be said of sending armor into any difficult terrain without support. These two examples (and Stalingrad) may be better used to quantify the impact of political agendas on casualties than to quantify the effects of urban areas on casualties.

One must also note that since this study was done, the United States invaded Iraq and conducted operations in some major urban areas, albeit against somewhat desultory and ineffective opposition. In the southern part of Iraq the two major port cities of Umm Qasar and Basra were first enveloped before any forces were sent in to clear them. Baghdad could have been enveloped if sufficient forces were available. As it turned out, it was not seriously defended. The recent operations in Iraq again confirm the observations made in this study. The later two battles of Fallujah also confirm our findings concerning loss and advance rates.

Changes in Technology and Possible Impact on Urban Warfare

Since the data used for this analysis are from combat that occurred over fifty years ago, one needs to consider what changes have occurred in the world that may change the results of such an analysis. There are at least three changes that may be easily identified. First are changes in technology that make weapons more accurate, more lethal, faster, better protected, or more flexible. Second are changes in the environment, which may make cities larger, taller, or denser. Third are changes resulting in a revolution or evolution in warfare created by the synergistic effects of changes in technology, particularly within information and communications systems.

CHANGES IN WEAPONS TECHNOLOGY

While weapon technologies have improved, it is difficult to think of a single technological development that has changed the nature of urban combat. If one assumes rough technological parity between opposing forces, which was true in our World War II cases, then urban fighting between forces with rough technological equality does not appear to be significantly different, outside of a possible revolution in military affairs (discussed below).

Still, there is an overall tendency in modern combat to disperse, engage at greater ranges, and make greater use of cover and concealment and mobility. While the urban environment provides considerable cover and concealment, it also brings opposing forces into what are sometimes very close ranges. The modern capability to deliver devastating and accurate firepower to an area affects the urban environment. The larger bomb loads, larger bombs, fuel-air explosives, multiple-launch rocket systems, and other weapon systems that can deliver sudden and accurate devastation will still force armies to remain dispersed, concentrating only briefly when needing to execute an operation. The modern battlefield is expected to be somewhat more fluid and dispersed than that of World War II, and as such, we may discover that the urban fight will often transition into and from urban terrain with greater frequency. The use of conurban terrain to establish a series of strong points may also be more limited, since these strong points are more vulnerable. With more fluid operations and increased dispersion, it is difficult to say whether armed forces in the future will spend more or less time holding, defending, and fighting in urban terrain.

Nearly all the combat operations involving the U.S. military in the past fifty-five years have been against opponents that were technologically inferior, and in some cases noticeably so. Our World War II data do not examine combat between forces with a radical technological difference. The application of widely disparate technology has not been analyzed in this effort.

CHANGES IN THE NATURE OF CITIES

First and foremost, cities are much larger on average than they were in the mid-twentieth century. However, while size may have an effect at the operational level, the data analyzed in this study are division-level, effectively tactical combat. For this analysis a larger city would simply imply a larger engagement without changing the nature of the engagement. So this does not affect the results of the analysis.

The average density of cities may also have changed, but we have not measured this. Densities of building per square meter might have some effect on the analysis, but it is uncertain to what extent. The increasing density of cities caused by the increasing height and area of buildings is fairly insignificant. Most urban combat appears to occur at, or very near, ground level. It is unlikely that a thirty-story building would be defended by ten times as many troops as a three-story building, and it is just as unlikely that ten times the number of troops would be required to attack it. The fact that the linear density of troops did not change noticeably between the different World War II nonurban, conurban, and urban terrain cases in the database does not support the idea that an increase in the density of urban terrain will result in a significant increase in the linear density of troops.

The urban environments measured in this study were well-established French and German towns and cities. The buildings tended to be well constructed, with considerable use of masonry, brick, stone, and other durable and resistant materials. There is little reason to believe that modern urban constructions are more solidly or strongly built, and it appears that the opposite may in fact be true.[27] Therefore we do not feel that changes in size, density, building height, or construction techniques in modern cities obviate or significantly modify this analysis.

In the past fifty years the size, extent, and number of "shantytowns" in many third world cities have changed. These tend to contain insubstantial structures and are often of relatively low density compared to more developed areas of cities. They also tend to consist mostly of low-lying structures. None of our combat examples occurred in urban terrain that is comparable. Still, since these shantytowns are of lower density, lower height, and often of insubstantial construction compared to the examples analyzed, there is little reason to believe that differences between fighting in them and fighting in other urban areas are any more significant than the differences already measured between nonurban and urban terrain. In fact the differences may be less significant than the differences between nonurban and urban terrain that we measured, although the degree is uncertain. Therefore I am comfortable stating that the changes in urban terrain over time have not had a significant impact on the results found in this study.

CHANGES IN WARFARE: REVOLUTION OR EVOLUTION?

Many have postulated that there has been, or that we are on the verge of, a revolution in warfare created by the synergistic effects of increased weapons accuracy, improved intelligence (including targeting information), and improved and widespread communications. Recent U.S. conventional operations have increased this perception due to our opponents being technologically inferior, not particularly well trained, or simply incompetent, while the United States has enjoyed air supremacy and the luxury of outgunning our opponents. The data used in this study are for forces that are relatively similar in technology and competency. There are no real-world examples in the past twenty-five years of combat between conventional armed forces with similar levels of advanced technology and military competence.[28]

Nevertheless there certainly have been changes in these areas, and this may have some impact on or may even obviate the data presented in this study. However, to date this revolution has been one-sided: only the United States has fully explored and developed the systems, training, and management required for execution of this revolutionary new style of warfare.[29] Therefore it is difficult to determine how much of the effect of the revolution seen is the result of fighting technologically inferior foes and how much is due to revolutionary effects of new technologies. The enemy forces the United States has engaged with these new systems have had little countermeasure capability and have mostly resorted to dispersal and hiding to protect themselves. Eventually we may encounter a competent opponent with equivalent technology, but this does not appear to be something that the United States will have to face anytime in the next two to three decades. Quite simply, as the only superpower, and with the third through sixth richest nations of the world as strong allies, the United States will not face an opposing force with the economic power to develop a modern technologically advanced army capable of fighting on equal terms. Thus any discussion of the revolution in military affairs fundamentally refers to a one-sided revolution.

The question remains: How will these changes affect the urban fight? First, increased weapon accuracy by itself will not revolutionize fighting in urban terrain. What will make the difference is the ability to observe, target, and communicate enemy locations. This is an area where urban terrain has a potentially significant degrading effect. It is more difficult to observe and identify targets in urban terrain, and as a result conducting precision strikes against them is more difficult. Added to that, built-up areas also give targets easily accessible hard cover.

This may make urban terrain a preferred battleground area, especially for the lower technology force. But while this can have a significant operational impact on combat, this study does not address that issue. Instead this study has focused on the effects of urban terrain, as compared to nonurban terrain, in seven major areas of interest:

Force ratios: There is no reason to assume that the force ratios in urban warfare engagements will change as a result of a revolution in military affairs. They are driven almost invariably by the result of the operations and the conditions of combat and are fundamentally not terrain-specific.

Mission success (outcome): There is no reason to assume that the outcome in urban warfare engagements will change as a result of a revolution in military affairs. The results are driven almost invariably by the conditions of combat and are fundamentally not terrain-specific.

Casualty rates: These may also decline relative to casualty rates in nonurban terrain due to the relatively better cover and concealment found in urban as opposed to nonurban terrain.

Armor loss rates: These may not change as much due to urban terrain. As the key for protection is cover and concealment, this may be better obtained in wooded areas with substantial usable overhead cover than in the more exposed streets of a city, especially something like a shantytown.

Duration of combat (time): Duration of combat may change to the extent that advance rates change, but they may change even more, becoming relatively slower than advance rates in nonurban terrain. This is because it may be easier for targets in urban terrain to find cover and concealment relative to nonurban terrain. With potentially more time required to identify and target the enemy, the differences in duration of combat in urban terrain as opposed to nonurban terrain may become more marked.

Advance rates: These may change, but there is no reason to believe that they will change more quickly than those in nonurban terrain. Since these are "opposed advance rates," they are relatively unaffected by changes in technology and are mostly affected by the conditions of combat.

Linear density: This may be affected for the same reasons as the duration of combat. Fundamentally, as weapons accuracy and effectiveness increase, so does dispersal. As forces in urban terrain may be better protected against enemy systems, we may see a greater disparity between linear density of forces in urban versus nonurban terrain.

All these changes are relative to changes in nonurban terrain. One would expect to see even more reduced casualty rates, increased linear density, and more extended duration of combat in urban terrain. This may conspire to make the urban environment the terrain of choice for the lower-technology defender (or the lower-technology attacker, for that matter), especially for infantry forces.

This still begs the question of how to maintain operational control of the areas outside the city and keep the urban area from being isolated, as has usually been the case. If anything, a revolution in military affairs points to the ability to even more effectively and quickly isolate a city. This leaves most urban warfare scenarios as mop-up operations, where the defenders are isolated and where the technologically advanced attackers conduct operations at a pace of their own choosing. While these mop-up operations can be particularly difficult and painful for the individual soldier, militarily they are operations that will invariably be resolved in the favor of the attacker.

It does not appear that the actual effects of a revolution in military affairs, if one truly exists, will change significantly the intensity or nature of urban combat, except in those cases where the city cannot be isolated. As I pointed out, because of geography this is a very rare occurrence.

Insofar as casualties are concerned, we have in fact been unable to find any clear-cut increase in lethality associated with the urban environment from World War II to the present day. Nor for that matter have we found a clear-cut increase in lethality in general from World War II to the present day. We have found that—with the sole exception of the Tet Offensive cases—lethality in urban operations is less than that found in related nonurban operations. Table 16.52 recapitulates the average percentage losses over time in the periods that we investigated in the three completed phases of this study.

Table 16.52. Comparison of Attacker Division-Level Urban vs. Nonurban Casualty Data, All Data Sets

Urban	1943	1943	1944	1945	1950	1968	1944–2003
	EF (GERMAN ATTACKS)	EF (SOVIET ATTACKS)	ETO	PTO	KOREA	TET	OTHER
Average percentage of loss/day	0.49	1.95	0.50	0.63	0.71	0.78	0.56
Weighted percentage of loss/day	0.50	2.18	0.49	0.65	0.71	0.62	0.54
Number of cases	28	23	46	53	10	65	14

Nonurban	1943	1943	1944	1945	1968	1944–2003	
	EF (GERMAN ATTACKS)	EF (SOVIET ATTACKS)	ETO	PTO	TET	OTHER	
Average percentage of loss/day	1.00	2.39	1.09	0.83	0.19	1.56	—
Weighted percentage of loss/day	0.76	2.41	1.13	1.27	0.17	1.01	—
Number of cases	47	18	91	37	57	65	—

Over time the average weighted percentage of loss per day in urban operations from 1943 to 2003—a sixty-year time span—ranges from 0.50 to 0.71 if Soviet attacks are excluded. In contrast, the average weighted percentage of loss per day in nonurban terrain ranges from 0.76 to 1.27 if the Soviet attacks and Tet are excluded.

These data can be plotted over time by simply inserting the various percentages of loss per day for each of the engagements under the appropriate year (fig. 16.1). To do so we have eliminated the Eastern Front Soviet attacks (urban and nonurban) and Tet Offensive nonurban outliers and have normalized the intervening years where there are no data points. The result is interesting and clearly establishes that over the past sixty years urban warfare has remained less intense than nonurban warfare (at least at the division level and as measured as a percentage of loss per day).

The sole point at which the two lines intersect—during the 1973 Arab-Israeli War—may shed some light on why the belief exists that urban warfare is more costly and/or intense than warfare in other types of terrain. Quite simply, the urban case in the 1973 war, the Battle of Suez City, is one unique engagement fought during that entire war and is just one of thirty-two engagements from that war that was fought in urban terrain. And it is one of the few cases that

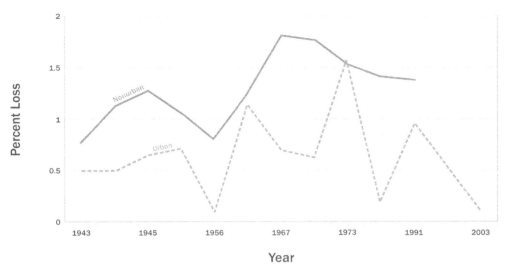

Fig. 16.1. Percentage of loss per day, 1943–2003: Urban vs. nonurban terrain.
Source: Dupuy Institute.

we have found where division-level urban combat was as intense as the average nonurban combat during the same campaign. In just seven of the thirty-one nonurban engagements in the 1973 war was the attacker percentage per day loss higher than the 1.57 percent found at Suez City, and in only two of those were the attackers Israeli. Nor were the Israeli armor losses extraordinary at Suez City; they amounted to only about eleven tanks, for a loss rate of just 4.6 percent per day. This may be contrasted to the 11.43 percent per day armor loss that the Israelis averaged in the nine nonurban attacks they made against the Egyptians in the 1973 war.[30]

That Suez City stands out as unique should hardly be surprising. What is surprising is that it—and the few other possible outliers we have found—has become identified as the typical urban battle rather than as a unique case. In that respect Suez City and the other outliers may provide copious lessons to be learned for future battles in urban terrain, but they should not be accepted as the norm. On that note, however, it is somewhat depressing to see that many lessons of urban warfare apparently learned by the different combatants in World War II were forcibly relearned in later wars. That the mistakes made in earlier urban battles are repeated over and over again in later wars—such as avoiding sending unsupported armor into built-up areas—is more than somewhat perplexing. Worse, we have been unable to find any example in World War II of the misemployment of armor in an urban environment that mirrors the foolishness exhibited by the attackers at Suez City or Grozny. Thus it could be supposed that any benefit of a technological evolution in warfare over time might be counterbalanced in part by the simple failure to draw adequate lessons from the past.

Future Development

The three phases of the urban warfare study provided data for 239 urban and conurban cases compared to 300 nonurban division-level cases. In addition we gathered data on another 65 battalion-level urban cases. This is certainly the most extensive and detailed analysis of the impact of urban terrain on division-level engagements that has ever been done. We also did an analysis of urban combat at the army level based on fifty operations, of which a half-dozen included significant urban terrain. This work confirmed that the effects of urban areas on army-level operations were similar to what we have already identified.

The one remaining piece of work was to assemble a set of division-level engagements from the Battle of Stalingrad. The fundamental problem with the Kharkov urban engagements is that they simply lacked the intensity and set-piece environment of the Kursk nonurban engagements. So even though the Kharkov and Kursk engagements were similar in terms of unit size, area, and time, the nature of the operations was actually very different, with Kursk being more intense, denser, slower, and bloodier. This makes it difficult to reconcile the results of any direct comparison between the two.

In contrast the Battle of Stalingrad between August and November 1942 was the most intense and famous urban fight in history. Engagements developed from these battles compared to the existing Kursk engagements could show us if there really was a difference in densities, intensities, or advance rates between the Eastern Front urban and nonurban battles. At Stalingrad there were three separate phases of the urban fighting. Beginning on 23 August 1942 the XIV Panzer Corps of the German Sixth Army, led by the 16th Panzer Division, penetrated into the northern suburbs and to the Volga River. The Germans held the Volga position against Soviet counterattacks for several weeks. A dozen or more urban and conurban engagements could be generated from this phase. The main German assault by the entire Sixth Army constituted the next phase. This began with an advance by eleven German divisions from positions just outside the city on 13 September. The Germans continued to systematically reduce the defenses through 20 November, when they were ordered to halt the attack in the aftermath of the Soviet counteroffensive known as Or ation Uranus that began on 19 November. By 23 November the Sov had completely surrounded the Sixth Army inside the city. The ments from 13 September to 20 November could generate ov division-days of action. The final phase consisted of elements

German divisions holding the city and slowly starving to death while fixed in place by Soviet forces.[31] The overwhelmed German forces surrendered on 2 February 1943. Theoretically the final phase could generate as many as fourteen hundred division-days of combat, but few of those would have occurred inside the city. Perhaps as many as five hundred more division-days of urban engagements could be found.

The Dupuy Institute recommended assembling engagements from the urban fighting beginning on 23 August and immediately thereafter, including much of the urban fighting in September and, if need be, October. There is not much to be learned from the encirclement and isolation of the German forces in late November. We had checked the availability of records for this period and determined that they exist and in sufficient detail to create many engagements.

We were about to be awarded a contract to do such work, but in August 2005 Hurricane Katrina hit Louisiana and the U.S. Gulf Coast and all Department of Defense funds not committed to important work were shifted to covering expenses for the rescue and clean-up efforts. The urban warfare study ended before we examined Stalingrad.

A second area to explore is an expanded study of battalion-level engagements in both urban and nonurban terrain. We had taken a small step in beginning to collect such data, but the number of engagements needs to be greatly expanded and a large number of nonurban engagements need to be added as well. This is the level at which many U.S. operations are currently being conducted, making the need for an in-depth study that much more important (although the recent war in Iraq did include division-level operations). A battalion-level study would also address some of the problems we found when using division-level data. First, we have found few engagements that were purely urban; many of them were fought in a mixture of nonurban and urban or conurban terrain, or in purely conurban terrain. This is because division-level engagements are usually fought on frontages of 10 to 20 kilometers or more. By studying battalion-level engagements we will find operations conducted over much smaller frontages, so most of the engagements should be more purely urban. Second, the differentiation between urban and conurban terrain should disappear to some extent because the built-up area of a town or village is often not significantly different from those in a city. The biggest problem with assembling a battalion-level database will be actually finding sufficient two-sided battalion-level data. As such, the Dupuy Institute recommended a study of division-level engagements in Stalingrad first before taking on the task of assembling battalion-level engagements.

Endnote: Definition of Urban Terrain

One of the first issues encountered in this study was defining what exactly constitutes *urban* terrain. Urban terrain may vary from suburban sprawl and large villages to Manhattan-like urban development. We subcategorized the urban terrain engagements into four types:

1. Urban terrain: a well-developed built-up area with a number of buildings taller than two stories, that is, cities, including warehouses, industrial parks, rail yards, and regular parks.

2. Suburban terrain: the suburban areas that typically surround American and other cities, primarily consisting of housing and small business buildings and typified by some degree of continuous development and settlement.

3. Conurbation: "an aggregation of continuous networks of urban communities" or a "city surrounded by large numbers of urban districts." The Dupuy Institute specifically uses this term to describe the pattern of settlement commonly seen in Europe, where large numbers of small and medium villages or built-up areas exist around cities, with large tracts of undeveloped land between them. A division-level operation would be expected to encompass one or more of these villages, and they would serve as significant strongpoints in any defensive scheme.

4. Shantytowns: the rather extensive collection of low-lying and fairly insubstantial temporary structures that often make up significant sections of major cities in third world countries.

Operations before, during, and after the City Fighting

Another issue encountered was the possible necessity of characterizing and analyzing the operations that occur before, during, and after the city fighting. They may be defined as:

1. Approach operations: the engagements that occur when approaching an urban area and just before entering it. There may be some difference in these operations when they are compared to operations in other nonurban terrain.

2. Proximity operations: the engagements that occur in the nonurban terrain around a city or built-up area during fighting in those areas. These may differ from other nonurban operations in that their purpose and pacing may be driven by what occurs in the adjacent urban areas. Also, since they occur at the same time and in the same area, and often with the same units as those fighting in the city, these are particularly useful for comparison to the related urban operations.

3. Exit operations: the engagements fought after the urban area has been penetrated and when the engagement transitions back to nonurban terrain. It is unknown if there is any difference between exit operations and other operations in nonurban terrain, but it appears worth exploring further.

4. Mop-up operations: the engagements—often fought by smaller units—to clear or secure a city. This often includes combat—usually at a much lower level of intensity—and can sometimes consume considerable time and resources. As such, these operations need to be studied further.

17. The Use of Case Studies

In addition, the requisite force concentrations and the higher tempo of operations mean that foodstuffs, water, and ammunition are consumed more rapidly than they would be elsewhere.

—RUSSELL W. GLENN, *Heavy Matter* (RAND Corporation, 2000)

The venerable case study is the traditional primary analytical tool of the historian. Unfortunately there are limitations to case studies, primarily, if you pick the right cases, you can prove any point you wish. History is such a massive and complex subject that you can always find something in the past that will support whatever point you wish to make, regardless of how bizarre or out of step it is with the greater reality. In fact I believe this is where RAND and some of the other organizations and people discussing the perils of urban warfare went astray. By focusing on three exceptions—Stalingrad, Suez, and Grozny—they lost track of the norm. Instead of analyzing the 120 or more urban engagements since 1900, they picked the three worst cases and then made rules based on them. This was not an analytical understanding, in the sense that they did not parse the various engagements at Stalingrad into their component parts and then compare them to nonurban engagements. It was more impressionistic, as though, having read books and stories, they concluded that the combat was really nasty and confusing and stressful.

Unfortunately, military history is often the study of exceptions. In their writings, military historians tend to focus on the high points of the battles, the exciting fights, and the interesting fights. After all, they are trying to write a good, readable book, not just present data. What often gets lost is the norm, or what is typical. A typical engagement is not nearly as interesting as the unusual or extreme fights. As such, a casual reading of history will often give the impression of higher losses and more dynamic outcomes than what occurred in most units on most days.

Some perspectives on urban warfare appear to have grown out of reviewing other studies and accounts, interviewing participants, and observing training exercises.[1] These are all somewhat subjective approaches. Using training exercises as a data source is fraught with problems. First, they are not real combat: nobody dies. This point makes all the difference in the world about how people behave. Training exercises are notorious for producing losses and casualty rates wildly higher than numbers in the real world, by a factor of 10 or 20.[2] Therefore any lessons learned from a training exercise need to be tempered with the understanding that they run very hot, meaning at a much higher pace and with much higher losses than would be expected in reality.

Armed with a selection of case studies and observations, RAND and others decided to draw conclusions and trend lines that applied to warfare in general. One conclusion was "the requisite force concentrations and the higher tempo of operations mean that foodstuffs, water, and ammunition are consumed more rapidly than they would be elsewhere."[3]

We at the Dupuy Institute are not averse to using cases studies; we simply prefer not to use them as our only analytical tool. We prefer to have a solid base of normative data to back up what we are doing. We look for the norms and the typical situation and use case studies only as part of a further examination of the subject.

Over the course of numerous studies, we have discovered that a byproduct of research into one subject is an accumulation of data that are usable for analysis beyond what was originally contracted. As has become our habit, as time and budget have allowed, we have examined other facets of the problem and looked at the issues in ways different from what was originally proposed. The urban warfare project included a number of unplanned analytical efforts.

First, some of the data can shed light on other issues, such as the relationship between force ratios and casualty ratios, force ratios and distance advanced, unit size and casualty rates, and so on. Second, we collected data not only on the fighting in cities but also on the fighting that occurred while getting to the city, the fighting that went on around the city, the fighting during the exit from the city, and related mopping-up actions in the city. This led us to look at issues such as advance rates and casualties involving the same forces that advanced on the city, fought in the city, and conducted the pursuit after exiting the city. We also discovered some interesting documents on battle fatigue, written by the division psychiatrist of the U.S. 29th Infantry Division, which participated in the Battle for Brest. This led us to a generalized examination of nonbattle casualties and the relationship they may have had to urban combat. We also explored some of the available data relating to the expenditure of ammunition and other consumables in urban versus nonurban combat. Finally, we conducted a brief overview of the tempo, tactical lessons learned, supporting weapons used, and armored vehicle losses suffered in urban combat. These were discussed in our reports as a series of case studies covering the Battle of Aachen, the Battle for Brest, and the Channel Port battles.

Of course this tendency to discover new data, new ways of seeing the data, and new lines of inquiry during the research process is part of the reason we also believe that the research and analytical efforts need to be integrated and be performed by members of the same team. We believe it is a mistake to have separate researchers and analysts; they should be the same people, or at least on the same team, to be able to fully understand and utilize the data. We do not believe that you can be a good analyst without expertise in the subject you are analyzing, and the best way to gain that expertise is to do the research yourself.

In the original Phase 1 of the effort, as Richard Anderson was collecting material on casualties for the fighting in the channel ports, he noticed that he had regular reports of battle fatigue from some of the units involved and that they reported before, during, and after the fighting in the city. We therefore decided to conduct a little case study as part of this effort, even though this was not in our contract.

Case Study: Urban Combat Operations and Battle Casualties

Some writers have postulated that urban combat operations incur large numbers of casualties by the opponents, and particularly by the attacker. Some have postulated that these casualties and associated casualty rates tend to be much higher than those found in operations in other types of terrain. In one recent study of urban warfare the following statement was made: "The cost to the attacker was considered high in the majority of the cases. Attacker cost was deemed high in casualties, time, and resources, respectively, in 68, 55, and 59 percent of the cases studied. ('High cost' is, of course, relative to the percentage of total resources and time expended and the results achieved. A high cost does not necessarily imply that the results were not worth the price.)"[4]

In another recent study, done for the U.S. Marine Corps, a casualty estimate for combat in urban terrain was developed.[5] The Dupuy Institute summarized the predictions of that study as follows:

For offensive operations in urban terrain, a rate of 30 to 50 casualties per 1,000 troops per day (3.0 to 5.0 percent-per-day) should be expected, with a battalion (evidently considered to be about 500 strong) suffering 25 casualties per day and a brigade (about 5,000 strong) suffering 250 casualties per day.

For transitional operations in urban terrain a rate of 15 to 30 casualties per 1,000 troops per day (1.5 to 3.0 percent-per-day) should be expected. A battalion would suffer fewer than 15 and a brigade fewer than 150 casualties.

For defensive operations in urban terrain a rate of 10 to 15 casualties per 1,000 troops per day (1.0 to 1.5 percent-per-day) should be expected. A battalion will suffer fewer than 20 and a brigade fewer than 50 casualties.

An extrapolation of these rates would imply that division-level offensive operations in urban terrain should result in a 9.0 to 15.0 percent-per-day casualty rate, that in transitional operations the divisional rate would be 4.5 to 9.0 percent-per-day, and that in defensive operations the divisional rate would be 3.0 to 4.5 percent-per-day. However, these rates are actually three to fifteen times higher than the average percent-per-day casualty rate experienced by U.S. Army divisions in engagements during World War II![6] They are also much higher than the actual attrition rates experienced in urban combat in the case studies found in our work. These figures from the U.S. Marine Corps study are outside of any norms we have found.

The 2nd U.S. Infantry Division Casualty Experience in the Battle for Brest

For the U.S. 2nd Infantry Division in the Battle for Brest, it is possible to derive very accurate daily divisional battle casualty data. On 1–18 September the division suffered a total of 111 KIA, 952 WIA, and 29 MIA, for a total of 1,092 battle casualties.[7] The average daily divisional battle casualty rate for the period was 0.384 percent, approximately one-eighth the rate estimated in the study done for the Marine Corps.

The Battle for Brest can be separated into three distinct phases. In the first phase (25 August–9 September) U.S. forces were engaged in open terrain, fighting through a fortified belt surrounding the city, in an effort to close up on the outskirts of the city itself. It was not until the evening of 8 September that house-to-house fighting began, and the division was not fully engaged in the city proper until early on 10 September.[8] During this phase the 2nd Division suffered its peak level of attrition for the month on 2 September, when 136 battle casualties (a rate of 0.983 percent-per-day) were lost. The overall average attrition rate for the period 1–9 September during the first phase was 0.446 percent-per-day.

In the second phase (10–14 September) the division battled through the outskirts of the city, reaching the city wall (part of the fortifications built to protect the city and naval base in the seventeenth and eighteenth centuries) at the end of the period. The fighting was characterized as house-to-house and was considered very intense. The peak was on 10 September, when ninety-two casualties (a rate of 0.639 percent) were incurred. Nevertheless, the average casualty rate decreased to 0.427 percent-per-day.[9] The daily casualty rates also decreased as the division drove into the urban area, from 0.639 on 10 September, to 0.497 on 11 September, to a similar 0.507 on 12 September, to 0.226 on 13 September, and 0.265 on 14 September.

In the third phase (15–18 September) the division initially paused to regroup, mop up, and contemplate the problem presented by the formidable city wall.[10] On 15 and 16 September division and corps artillery pounded the area inside the old city wall as the division mopped up the area outside it. Direct and indirect artillery fire and careful probing for weak points eventually developed a few weak points in the barrier, and the assault into the heart of the city began on 17 September. An initial, small penetration was made at 1830 hours but was repulsed. A later attack, at 2000 hours, penetrated south along the course of the Enfold River. A minor German counterattack failed, and with their defenses compromised, the garrison surrendered at 1530 hours on 18 September.

The average casualty rate for this period was 0.203 percent-per-day, with, as would be expected, a peak of 0.244 percent-per-day on 17 September. During the lull of 15 and 16 September, when artillery hammered the city and mopping up of the suburbs was completed, the rate fell to 0.215 and 0.143 percent, respectively. During the opening attack on the wall on 17 September the rate climbed to 0.244 percent, falling to 0.209 percent on the last day of fighting. Even if only the last two days of fighting in the heart of the built-up area of the city were considered, the average loss rate would have been only 0.226 percent-per-day.

The 1st U.S. Infantry Division Casualty Experience in the Battle for Aachen

The losses of the 1st Division at Aachen follow a pattern similar to that experienced by the 2nd Division at Brest. In the two-week-long battle the division suffered a total of 1,096 battle casualties for an average loss rate of 0.593 percent-per-day.[11]

On the first day of the battle, 8 October, the division suffered 150 battle casualties, for a loss rate of 1.066 percent. This relatively high level of attrition was maintained on 9 October, when casualties totaled 104 for a loss rate of 0.733 percent. On both of these days the division was attacking to the north from positions well east of the city in an effort to isolate the city from the main German defensive line. No fighting occurred in the built-up area of the city, and the initial attack seized the only major conurban area in the zone of the first two days of fighting—the town of Verlautenheide—before the Germans could develop a defense of it.

On the following day, 10 October, the first mention of house-to-house fighting in the division zone was made, when elements of the 18th Infantry successfully attacked the village of Haaren.[12] The 26th Infantry, which was tasked to assault the city itself, made a limited attack to seize positions overlooking the city and sent a surrender demand under flag of truce into the city. The division loss this day was 69, for a rate of 0.494 percent, half that of the first day and about two-thirds that of the previous day. Fighting on the outskirts of the city at Verlautenheide and Haaren continued for the next two days as the Germans attempted numerous counterattacks. Division losses were 0.448 percent on 11 October and 0.518 percent on 12 October. The 26th Infantry continued to clear the factory areas on the outskirts of the city and met with only moderate resistance.

On 13 October the 26th Infantry completed clearing out the factory areas and the 18th Infantry consolidated its positions at Haaren and Verlautenheide. The division losses were only 54 for a rate of 0.379 percent. On 14 October the drive into the city continued, with little other activity reported in the division zone. Losses totaled 71 for a rate of 0.429 percent.

The following day saw the beginning of a major counterattack by German forces seeking to reestablish contact with the city garrison. The 18th Infantry at Haaren and Verlautenheide easily repulsed the attack, but on their right the 16th Infantry had more difficulty. Despite this threat, the 26th Infantry continued the methodical clearing of the city without interruption. The intense German counterattacks continued through 16 October. Unsurprisingly the losses of the 1st Division increased during this period. On 15 October the loss was 76 for a rate of 0.542 percent, increasing to 112 and 0.789 percent on 16 October. By 17 October the first major German counterattack was defeated. On that day the 1st Division losses decreased to 58 and a rate of 0.408 percent. The 26th Infantry continued to make slow progress into the city.

On 18 October the Germans made a second attempt to relieve the city. The heaviest weight of the German counterattack fell on the 18th Infantry defending Haaren and Verlautenheide, while the 26th Infantry continued to advance in the city, seizing the city center (made up of a complex of buildings in a park-like setting, the Palace Hotel, and the Kurhaus on Observatory Hill). Losses were 103 for a rate of 0.660 percent. The German counterattack continued on 19 October, strongly supported by artillery, which inflicted heavy casualties on the 18th Infantry. The 26th Infantry continued to methodically clear the city block by block. Losses were the heaviest since the beginning of the offensive on 8 October, a total of 112 for a rate of 0.864 percent.

Casualties on 20 October continued to be high; there were a total of 100 for a rate of 0.710 percent. Resistance in the city remained strong, but the counterattacks to relieve the city petered out. However, German artillery support continued to be strong and inflicted numerous casualties. A reflection of this may be seen in the ratio of KIA to WIA in the 1st Division during the battle. Overall the ratio from 8 to 21 October was 1 to 5.67 (151 KIA to 856 WIA), higher than the 1-to-4 or 1-to-5 range that would normally be expected. In the final four days of the battle, as German artillery support increased, the ratio too increased, to 1 to 8.26 (27 KIA to 111 WIA).[13]

On 21 October the defenders of the city capitulated, ending the battle. Losses declined to a total of 36 for a rate of 0.261 percent.

The effects of the fighting in the city of Aachen on the casualties of the 2nd Division are difficult to assess. Unlike at Brest, it is less clear when the fighting at Aachen transitions from countryside to conurban and then urban terrain. Furthermore only two of the eight battalions of the division were actively engaged in the battle fought in the city, and only two or three more were engaged in the conurban village complex outside the city. The peak loss rates incurred during the period when urban combat was going on (16 and 18–20 October) are closely associated with a period of strong German counterattacks to relieve the city and a strong increase in German artillery support. It may also be significant that what was evidently one of the most difficult objectives in the city, the spa hotel complex on Observatory Hill, consisted of several large buildings surrounded by park land.

It may be that additional insights could be gained by an examination of the regimental and battalion-level loss rates in this battle. However, such an examination was outside the scope of the current phase of this study, and—in the interests of time and budgetary constraints—was not researched.

Casualty Rates versus Advance Rates in Urban Combat

We did graph seven examples from the channel ports, comparing these advances up to and into the city as far as daily casualty experience and advance rate of the attacker. We found an inverse relationship between the two. That is, lower advance rates appear to be associated with higher casualty rates, and vice versa. Figures 17.1–17.4 demonstrate this relationship.

Summary

The assumption that combat in an urban environment produces higher numbers of battle casualties and/or loss rates is unsupported. In fact indications are that the opposite may be true, that combat in an urban environment produces lower numbers of casualties and/or loss rates.

Case Study: Urban Combat Operations and Combat Stress

Combat is a stressful environment by any measure. *Battle fatigue, shell shock, combat exhaustion*, and *posttraumatic stress syndrome* are just a few of the terms that have been applied to the effects of combat on the human psyche. Anecdotally it would appear that the loss of situation awareness, limited communica-

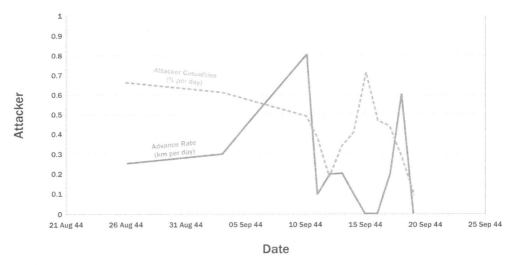

Fig. 17.1. Casualty rate vs. advance rate: Attack on Brest. Source: Dupuy Institute.

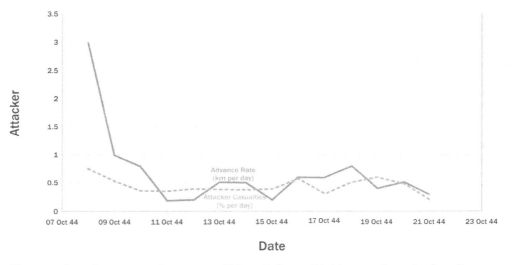

Fig. 17.2. Casualty rate vs. advance rate: U.S. 1st Infantry Division attack on Aachen. Source: Dupuy Institute.

tions, and close proximity of the enemy found in urban combat increases the stresses felt by soldiers in that environment. However, just as for battle casualties, no evidence can be found for the effects of increased stress in urban combat.

The 29th U.S. Infantry Division Combat Exhaustion Study

One very interesting document relating to combat stress was prepared by Maj. David L. Weintrob, the division psychiatrist of the 29th Division in the European Theater of Operations on 2 October 1944.[14] Division psychiatrist was a

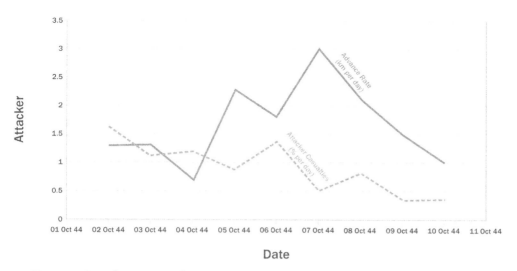

Fig. 17.3. Casualty rate vs. advance rate: U.S. 30th Infantry Division attack on Aachen. Source: Dupuy Institute.

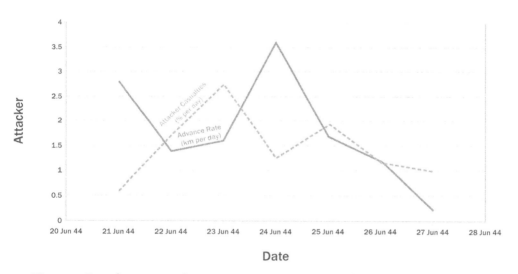

Fig. 17.4. Casualty rate vs. advance rate: U.S. VII Corps attack on Cherbourg. Source: Dupuy Institute.

position authorized by the War Department Table of Organization on 12 January 1944, just five months prior to D-Day and over two years after the first major commitment of U.S. Army ground forces in North Africa. Officially the division psychiatrist was attached to the division staff as an advisor to the division surgeon.[15]

Luckily, prior to D-Day it was decided to provide the psychiatrist with a staff of five enlisted medical personnel, a ward tent, and twenty cots as part of the clearing company of the division's 104th Medical Battalion. By 18 June, twelve days after the division entered combat, the Combat Exhaustion Section had doubled in size and was attempting to treat 50 patients. From 21 June to 10 July admissions averaged 8 to 12 per day. Then on 11 July the division began its major push to seize the road junction at Saint-Lô. Over the following eight days 501 combat exhaustion cases were admitted. By 14 July the division commander realized that drastic steps had to be taken to handle the sudden influx of patients and authorized another expansion of the Combat Exhaustion Section, to a medical staff of fifteen, a kitchen staff, and accommodations for 250 patients. By the time the 29th Division was committed to operations at Brest it had had considerable experience in handling and treating combat exhaustion.

However, most revealing for the purposes of this study of urban combat is the statistical analysis of combat exhaustion prepared by Major Weintrob as an appendix to his report on combat exhaustion. He divided his survey into a four-week period (from the invasion on 6 June to 9 July) and five two-week periods, ending on 17 September (effectively the end of division operations in the city of Brest).

During the entire period 1,822 combat exhaustion cases and 14,503 other nonfatal battle casualty cases (wounded in action) were admitted, for a total of 16,325 nonfatal battle casualties over fourteen weeks. A total of 1,033 combat exhaustion cases were returned to duty, of which 291 were later readmitted for combat exhaustion.[16] Thus combat exhaustion represented 11.16 percent of the total nonfatal casualties (wounded and exhaustion) for the entire period of the Normandy and Brittany campaigns.

However, during the Battle for Brest the incidence of combat exhaustion cases (and battle casualty cases) was dramatically lower than during any other period of the campaign. From 4 to 17 September—a period that encompasses the brutal fighting for the fortified line outside Brest, the fighting in the suburbs, and the fighting in the central city itself—there were only 75 cases of combat exhaustion admitted in the division and 1,582 cases of other nonfatal battle casualties. Thus combat exhaustion made up only 4.53 percent of the nonfatal battle casualties during the Battle for Brest, about 40 percent of the average for the entire campaign.

In fact the peak incidence of combat exhaustion actually occurred some weeks prior to the Battle for Brest. During the period 23 July–6 August there were 552 combat exhaustion cases admitted, constituting 15.53 percent of the total nonfatal battle casualties admitted.[17] In his analysis Major Weintrob made no association with (or mention of) urban combat operations and combat exhaustion. Rather he quite convincingly found a direct correlation between the number of poorly trained and prepared replacements assigned to the division and the incidence of combat exhaustion. During the entire period he found that 694 of the combat exhaustion cases admitted (38.09 percent) were replacements.

Nonbattle Casualty Experience in Other Divisions in Urban Combat

Although less precise, an analysis of the casualty experience of the other divisions involved in the urban engagements in this study tends to reinforce the view that urban combat is not necessarily a more stressful form of combat. In these cases daily or periodic data for combat exhaustion admissions could not be found. However, the daily sick reports of the divisions are available and reinforce the impression gained from the 29th Division combat exhaustion study.[18]

During the Battle for Brest (1–18 September) the U.S. 2nd Infantry Division, which was most closely involved in the battle in the urban areas of the city, reported a total of 980 battle casualties (KIA, WIA, and MIA). That was an average of 54.44 battle casualties per day. There were also 608 sick casualties reported, for an average of 33.78 per day, with a peak of 54 reported on 5 September. For the period when the division was battling through the fortified outskirts of the city (1–9 September) the number of sick per day averaged 41. For the period of fighting in the built-up area outside the city wall (10–14 September) the number of sick per day averaged 28.4, with a peak of 40 reported on 12 September. For the final fighting in the city center (15–18 September) the number of sick per day averaged 24.25, with a peak of 29 on 17 September.

The daily divisional sick rate (number of sick divided by divisional strength) reveals the same pattern. Overall the rate averaged 0.239 percent-per-day, with a peak of 0.376 on 5 September. For the period 1–9 September the average was 0.289 percent-per-day; for 10–14 September it was 0.200 percent-per-day, with a peak of 0.282 on 12 September; and for 15–18 September it was 0.174 percent-per-day, with a peak of 0.208 on 17 September.

The U.S. 1st Infantry Division experience at Aachen (8–21 October 1944) shows somewhat more variation. The division suffered a total of 1,180 battle casualties during the two-week period and 625 casualties from sickness, an average of 44.6 per day and an average rate of 0.344 percent-per-day. On 16 October, during the fighting in the city center, the peak number of sick casualties was reported as 66, or 0.465 percent. During the fighting to encircle the city, in the conurban areas to the east and northeast (8–12 October), the average number of daily sick was 43.6 or 0.312 percent-per-day. During the following nine days (13–21 October) the average number of daily sick was 51.2 or 0.362 percent-per-day.

It could be assumed that the increased number of sick during the nine-day battle in the city of Aachen was at least partly a consequence of an increase in the incidence of combat exhaustion. However, if so there is no mention of such in the divisional G-1 or medical reports. In fact the monthly G-1 summaries of the 1st Division for September, October, and November all make note of an increased sick rate during the month. For September, when the number of daily sick averaged 29.2, it was reported that "near the end of the month there was an increase noted in the sick rate. This was attributed to the fact that the leading elements of the Division were in foxholes close to a determined enemy, and the weather was very cold and rainy." For October, when the number of daily sick averaged 42.1, it was reported that "there was an increase in the sick rate due to the weather which was unfavorable with rain and cold wind for the greater part of the month." For November, when the number of daily sick averaged 71.3, it was noted that "weather was highly unfavorable, and despite the early issuance of overcoats and overshoes, the sick rate showed a marked increase."[19]

Unfortunately no comparable daily sick data have been found for the Canadian and British units engaged at the Channel ports in September 1944, and only fragmentary and aggregate sick data appear to be available for the German and Soviet units engaged at Kharkov in 1943.

Summary

There appears to be little justification for the assumption that combat in an urban environment is any more stressful than in any other environment. The evidence from the experience of the 2nd and 29th Divisions is that the incidence of sickness and combat exhaustion may actually decrease in an urban environment. The contradictory evidence from the 1st Division experience appears likely to have been a result of the extremely poor weather conditions found in the fall of 1944.

The assumption that combat in an urban environment is more stressful than in other environments is at best unsupported and may in fact be contradicted.

Case Study: Logistical Expenditures in Urban Operations

As far as the logistical burden of urban operations is concerned, Glenn asserts that "the requisite force concentrations and the higher tempo of operations mean that foodstuffs, water, and ammunition are consumed more rapidly than they would be elsewhere."[20] Like most of the assertions regarding urban warfare in Glenn's and many other papers referenced in this study, this declaration of fact is unsupported by any of the data we have been able to find on actual urban operations. An analysis of actual expenditures—when they are known—in the urban engagements examined shows little evidence that they are higher than those experienced in combat outside an urban environment.

Ammunition Expenditure in the Battle for Brest

The amount of ammunition planned for and actually expended in the Battle for Brest was laid out in the extensive after-action reports of the VIII Corps artillery.[21] The initial fire plan called for a reserve of three units of fire in the corps ammunition supply point before the operation began. This request was denied by corps headquarters, which required an estimate based on a set, ten-day plan of operations. Corps artillery then forecast a need for 345,200 rounds of artillery ammunition based on "knowledge of the difficulties of supply for an operation so far removed from the sources of supply and on the lack of communication facilities to supply agencies."[22]

When the operation began, initial stocks of ammunition were limited to at most 1.5 units of fire, and only for a few calibers. The scale of the limitations imposed by the logistical constraints may be better understood by considering that if every artillery piece concerned had had 1.5 units of fire available at the start, only 45,162 rounds would have been available.[23] Nevertheless the corps artillery successfully prosecuted the attack, expending in the end a total of 421,763 rounds from 22 August to 19 September, an average of 14,544 rounds per day.

That expenditure, although it appears large, was actually unremarkable. During the course of the entire European Campaign in World War II the average number of rounds expended by the two most common artillery pieces, the 105mm M2 and 155mm M1 Howitzer, for units in an attack posture, were 241.6 rounds-per-gun-per-day and 160.6 rounds-per-gun-per-day, respectively.[24] The actual expenditure in the VIII Corps attack on Brest averaged 78 and 43 rounds-per-gun-per-day, respectively, about one-third to one-quarter the normal experience and not dissimilar from the average expenditure found for all postures (attack, movement, and static) during the European Campaign, which was 86.6 and 38.6 rounds-per-gun-per-day, respectively.

The experience of the 1st Division artillery in the Battle for Aachen was also similar to the average found for all postures in Love's study.[25] The average daily expenditure for the division's sixty-six howitzers was:

8 October	77.65
9 October	65.39
10 October	55.36
11 October	102.70
12 October	66.62

13 October   35.65

14 October   35.20

15 October   133.06

16 October   40.47

17 October   39.18

18 October   60.44

19 October   79.79

20 October   34.05

21 October   (report missing)

Average   63.50

The two peak days, 11 and 15 October, warrant some additional investigation. On 11 October the VII Corps historical report noted that the 1st Division artillery "worked in close support with fighter-bomber groups of the IX TAC [Tactical Air Command] throughout the period to give Aachen a heavy pounding . . . and the Div Arty fired 63 missions on the city. A heavy concentration [apparently 10 missions] was fired on an enemy counter-attack against the 3rd [evidently meant to be 1st] Bn, 18th Inf . . . other missions fired were 60 [or 50; the number was overtyped in the original] harassing, 33 vehicle, 18 tank, 7 mortar and machine gun, and 20 miscellaneous."[26]

This account indicates that somewhere between 191 and 211 missions were fired in support of the 1st Division, of which only about one-third were fired into the city. All of the missions fired into the city were preparatory or destructive in nature, since no attacks were made on that day into the city.

On 15 October the situation was somewhat more ambiguous. The VII Corps report noted: "1st Division: Division artillery was extremely active during the period due to the several enemy counter-attacks. Fired 255 missions as follows: 95 counter-attack, 60 tank, 37 personnel, 14 mortar and machine gun, 7 vehicle, 4 counter-battery, and 7 miscellaneous." The strongest German counterattack on 15 October was directed against the 16th Infantry, which was entirely engaged in the open countryside east of the city. However, it was stated that the 3rd Battalion, 26th Infantry fighting in the city received "a counter-attack . . . [which] caused the loss of several houses east of OBSERVATORY HILL."[27]

It is evident that the expenditure of artillery ammunition in urban operations was no more than that in other operations. In the two cases where extensive data are available, Brest and Aachen, the expenditure was actually less than the average expenditure rates for all postures and was about one-third to one-quarter the average expenditure rates expected for an attack posture.

Expenditure Rates for Other Types of Ammunition

It is possible to compare the expenditure rates for other types of ammunition (small arms, mortar, and antitank guns), as well as artillery ammunition, between a division engaged in urban operations and a division engaged in nonurban operations. I will compare the experience of the U.S. 2nd Infantry Division during the Battle of Brest with that of the U.S. 90th Infantry Division during the Normandy Campaign.

The average daily expenditures for the 2nd Division for the period 24 August–20 September 1944 (twenty-eight days) and for the 90th Division for the period 1–31 July 1944 (thirty-one days) are enumerated in table 17.1.

Table 17.1. Daily Ammunition Expenditures, 2nd and 90th Infantry Divisions

SMALL ARMS	2nd Division	90th Division
Cal. 30 Carbine	1,441.07	7,251.52
Cal. 30 Ball, 5 clip*	1,553.57	9,855.23
Cal. 30 Ball, 8 clip**	22,050.29	27,885.90
Cal. 30 Ball, MG	16,491.07	30,382.90
Cal. 45 Ball***	3,578.57	2,611.39
Cal. 50 MG	12,620.71	2,627.39
Rocket, AT HE****	41.68	42.71
Grenade, Hand, frag.*****	423.29	512.06
Adapter, Grenade Projector******	77.93	17.19
Grenade, Rifle, Smoke, W.P.	16.29	74.52
MORTARS		
60mm	826.71	511.77
81mm	1,367.04	2,209.55
AT GUN		
57mm	65.07	65.48
ARTILLERY		
105mm Howitzer, M3	408.25	450.77
105mm Howitzer, M2	1,896.84	2,577.81
155mm Howitzer, M1	471.82	346.81

*For the Browning automatic rifle, the standard squad light automatic weapon.

**For the M1 rifle, the standard rifle issued to infantrymen.

***For the M1911 pistol and the M1 and M3 submachine guns.

****For the 2.35-inch "Bazooka" antitank rocket launcher.

*****The 2nd Division also reported the expenditure of 449 offensive (concussion-type) grenades (16.04 per day) and 1,053 smoke and colored-smoke grenades (37.61 per day). The 90th Division did not record expenditures for these types.

******This adapter allowed standard hand grenades to be launched from the standard M1 rifle. In addition the 2nd Division reported expending 2,508 antitank rifle-grenades (89.57 per day). The 90th Division did not record expenditures for this type.

A few comments are warranted. The consumption pattern for small arms is interesting. It is generally assumed (and on occasion remarked upon in the after-action and "lessons learned" reports) that carbines and submachine guns are preferred weapons for urban combat.[28] However, although the consumption of Cal. 45 ammunition by the 2nd Division at Brest was 1.37 times higher than that of the 90th Division, the consumption of Cal. 30 Carbine ammunition was 5.03 times lower than that of the 90th Division! But it should be remembered that the carbine at this time was a substitute for the pistol and that the submachine gun was not a priority item of issue in the infantry regiment Table of Equipment.[29] It appears likely that the difference in expenditures may be more a factor of different numbers of weapons being available in the two divisions.

The consumption of machine-gun ammunition also appears perfectly explicable. The greater range and penetrative capability of the Cal. 50 round over the Cal. 30 round likely made it more desirable as a weapon to interdict the streets of Brest.[30] However, in nonurban operations the excessive weight of the Cal. 50 machine gun itself made it less desirable, especially in mobile operations, a situation that did not pertain to the essentially static fighting at Brest. Note that the overall consumption of machine-gun rounds is about the same in both cases.

The consumption pattern for grenades does not appear to be radically different in the two cases either, except possibly in the case of rifle grenades. However, again it appears that the availability of a particular type of weapon or ammunition may have been just as significant as the tactical advantage one type had over another in the urban environment.[31]

The consumption of mortar ammunition is also perfectly reasonable. There appears to be little difference between the urban and nonurban case. The higher consumption of 60mm mortar ammunition was likely from their noted use as an extemporaneous rifle grenade by wiring the shell to the M1 grenade projector adapter.[32]

Nothing else of significance may be deduced from this comparison, although it further reinforces the assumption that artillery ammunition expenditure rates are not excessive in urban warfare. I conclude that ammunition expenditure in an urban environment varies somewhat from that in a nonurban environment, but the variation is a matter of type and degree rather than quantity.

Other notable expenditures recorded by the 2nd Division but unfortunately not by the 90th Division were the following:

5,050 pounds of TNT

1,331 pounds of demolition blocks

600 pounds of cratering explosive

5,770 feet of prima-cord

2,600 feet of time fuse

600 fuse lighters

2,530 electric blasting caps

350 non-electric blasting caps

50 Bangalore torpedoes

Although significant in number, the total weight of these items was probably considerably less than 5 tons, a fraction of the 3,735 tons of ammunition reported expended by the 90th Division during July.

Consumption of Food and Water

The assumption that fighting in an urban environment somehow increases the consumption of basic items like food and water is somewhat mystifying, to say the least.[33] Unfortunately we found no exact measure of food and water consumption in the urban combat cases examined. However, there was no explicit mention of problems with food or water supply in the narratives of any of the urban engagements, nor was there any mention of specific problems with food or water supply in any of the extensive "lessons learned" reports associated with these engagements. In this case the absence of any specific information is taken as a refutation of the assumption.

Conclusions from Phase 1

The Effect of Urban Terrain on Stress in Combat

Urban terrain was no more stressful a combat environment during actual combat operations than nonurban terrain.

The Effect of Urban Terrain on Logistics

The expenditure of artillery ammunition in urban operations was not greater than that in nonurban operations. In the two cases where exact comparisons could be made, the average expenditure rates were about one-third to one-quarter the average expenditure rates expected for an attack posture in the European Theater of Operations as a whole.

The evidence regarding the expenditure of other types of ammunition is less conclusive, but again expenditures in urban terrain do not appear to be significantly greater than the expenditures in nonurban terrain. Expenditures of specialized ordnance may have been higher in urban terrain, but the total weight expended was a minor fraction of that for all of the ammunition expended.

There is no evidence that the expenditure of other consumable items (rations, water, or POL (petroleum, oil, and lubricants) was significantly different in urban as opposed to nonurban combat.

Case Study: Ammunition Expenditure in the Battle for Manila

In Phase 1 we were able to draw some conclusions as to the possible impact of urban warfare on ammunition expenditure based on a study of the battles of Brest and Aachen and on other data on ammunition expenditure in the European Theater of Operations (Love's report).[34] Less complete data were available for the urban and nonurban operations in Phase 2, but nevertheless they appeared to support the conclusions that were reached in Phase 1. For Phase 3 some data were available for artillery ammunition expenditure by the U.S. XIV Corps during the campaign. Those expenditures were expressed as both totals and daily averages and were given in rounds, units of fire, cubic feet, tons, and truck loads.[35] The periods were:

> 9 January to 3 March: including the initial landings at Lingayen Gulf, the advance to Manila, the beginning of the urban battle on 4 February, and the course of the urban battle until 3 March, when the city was secured. Thus during about half this period the XIV Corps was engaged in nonurban operations (9 January–4 February), and during the other half it was engaged in urban operations (5 February–3 March). This phase would be equivalent to that referred to in Love's report as "all postures" (attack, movement, and static).

> 22 February to 3 March: including the assault on the Intramuros (in which extensive use of artillery was made to demolish parts of the old city wall) and the final assaults to mop up the last pockets of Japanese resistance. During this phase all but minor elements of XIV Corps were engaged in urban operations. This phase would be equivalent to Love's "attack posture."

> 3 March to 1 June: including the corps operations on Luzon after the Battle of Manila. During this phase XIV Corps was engaged in nonurban operations. This phase would be equivalent to Love's "all postures."

The average daily number of rounds of artillery ammunition XIV Corps expended by type during each period are presented in table 17.2.

Table 17.2. Average Daily Artillery Ammunition Rounds Expended, XIV Corps

	75mm Howitzer	105mm Howitzer	155mm Howitzer	155mm Gun
9 Jan–3 Mar	637	4,074	935	102
22 Feb–3 Mar	1,040	4,934	1,235	104
3 Mar–1 Jun	1,069	1,254	328	None

Rounds-per-gun on a daily average are computed in table 17.3.

Table 17.3. Daily Average by Rounds per Gun

	75mm Howitzer	105mm Howitzer	155mm Howitzer	155mm Gun
9 Jan–3 Mar	39.81	30.42	17.41	8.50
22 Feb–3 Mar	43.33	27.41	20.18	8.67
3 Mar–1 Jun	44.54	16.99	9.48	None

We were unable to develop any rates for the 75mm Howitzer in Phase 1. During the Manila Campaign it was part of the 11th Airborne Division as part of the divisional "light" artillery. So if we combine those types we should have something fairly akin to the 105mm "light" artillery in the ETO (table 17.4).

Table 17.4. Daily Average by Rounds per Gun (revised)

	"Light" Artillery	155mm Howitzer	155mm Gun
9 Jan–3 Mar	31.43	17.41	8.50
22 Feb–3 Mar	29.28	20.18	8.67
3 Mar–1 Jun	23.95	9.48	None

The expenditure rates for our ETO cases in Phase 1 are presented in table 17.5.

Table 17.5. Ammunition Expenditures Rates, ETO

	105mm Howitzer	155mm Howitzer	Both
Battle of Brest	78.00	43.00	—
Battle of Aachen	N/A	N/A	63.00
ETO (all postures)	86.60	38.60	77.87
ETO (attack)	241.60	160.60	226.87
2nd Infantry Division (urban)	75.37	39.32	—
90th Infantry Division (nonurban)	96.65	28.90	—

The rates for the Manila Campaign are dramatically lower than in any of the other cases. Even when we combine the 75mm and 105mm howitzers as "light" divisional artillery, they have half to one-eighth the rate found for the 105mm in the ETO. The difference in rates for the 155mm howitzer is similar, with the expenditure in Manila again being about half to one-eighth that of the ETO.

However, the nonurban 3 March–1 June phase during the Manila Campaign exhibits even lower rates than the earlier urban and combined urban and non-urban phases. Thus, although it is logical that the restrictions on artillery fire that were in place at Manila would have had an effect on the rates, that evidently was not a significant factor. Rather the rates in the campaign as a whole were simply much lower than in the ETO, whether or not the fighting was in urban or nonurban terrain. Nonetheless there appears to be no basis for arguing that ammunition expenditure rates were typically higher in the urban fighting in Manila than in the nonurban cases.

18. Modeling Warfare

Can we rely upon computer combat simulations?

—Trevor N. Dupuy, "Can We Rely upon Computer Combat Simulations?"

Much of the work the Dupuy Institute has done over the years has been related to and in support of the U.S. Army and Department of Defense combat modeling and operations research community. As such, we have been focused on not only finding truths (defense is the stronger form of combat) but also in measuring what their values are. This has led to our sometimes unique and esoteric quantitative analysis of history.

The underlying problem with the world of casualty estimation and combat modeling is that the empirical data needed to create credible constructs have not been sufficiently collected nor analyzed. A combat model is by its very nature a theory of combat (or at least a hypothesis). The starting point in understanding any combat model or casualty estimation methodology is to understand the underlying data that was used to develop it. So what data have been used to develop these constructs?

Early Casualty Estimation

The earliest casualty estimation methodology used by the United States was the one-sided look-up table, exemplified by the U.S. Army's *Field Manual 101-10-1/2*. The earliest version of such a table that we were able to locate is the 1932 edition of the U.S. War Department's *Staff Officer's Field Manual*, which was developed from World War I data. This use of World War I data continued in subsequent editions, even throughout World War II. In August 1945 the manual still used World War I data, but it had shaved off the references to World War I and to any original sources. The draft version of the September 1947 manual was based on World War II data. Some Korean War (1950–53) data were added in February 1959. Other than changes in the enemy prisoner-of-war capture rates, civilian internees, and patient admission rates, the data used in the U.S. Army's *Field Manual* casualty estimation tables have remained unchanged since 1959.[1]

The process of this change is very poorly documented. At this stage, there is probably no one left on this planet who can tell anyone exactly where each of the figures in those tables came from or exactly from what data they were developed. We also do not know specifically who developed these figures. This is not atypical. Another alarming example of how tables for movement and advance rates in combat were developed has been told by Wilbur Payne (former deputy undersecretary of the army for operations research) at the International Society of Military Operational Researchers in 1988.[2]

The figures now used in these look-up tables are a mixture of World War II and Korean War data; the data are undocumented and untraceable, and it is unknown if they are being used as originally intended. It is also unknown which parts of these tables are based on actual data as opposed to analyst conjecture. It is impossible to reconstruct the process that led to these figures. We are left to accept the data as an article of faith. This is hardly scientific. This use of seemingly hard data for casualty estimation and modeling that is otherwise not documented is a theme repeated over the decades.

The data are also one-sided; that is, they determine casualty rates depending only on friendly strength and conditions of combat (usually posture). It is irrelevant whether a force is facing one enemy soldier or one million. It is possible to create two-sided look-up tables, but to date this has been done only once.[3] The primary reason two-sided data have not been developed is cost.[4] As limited as development and documentation of the data were in the *Staff Officer's Field Manual*, the same data were also used for elements in certain combat models.[5]

More sophisticated and better-documented one-sided look-up tables have been created. Among these are the casualty estimation process in *Chairman of the Joint Chiefs of Staff Guide 3161*, which clearly identifies the source of the data, and FORECAS, which is also fairly transparent about where its data came from.[6] Still, these efforts are relatively simple and somewhat gross. More sophisticated attempts at modeling combat, and therefore casualty estimation, have been attempted. This leads us into the world of combat modeling.

Combat Modeling

The U.S. Army began combat modeling with its war-gaming rules for conducting training exercises. These quantified war-gaming procedures for field maneuvers date back to at least the 1932 rules manual, with the creation of "power factors" for artillery pieces. The 1941 version, drafted under the supervision of Brig. Gen. Lesley McNair, incorporated firepower scores over range for individual weapons, using the summed scores to create force ratios, which were then used to determine whether or not a unit advanced. It also provided a casualty rate assessment procedure that accounted for some of the conditions of combat. These were all to be modified or adjusted by umpire decision, as required to best reflect type of fire, posture, and so on. There was significant input from the umpires, making this partly "free kriegspiel." These were documented in the FM 105-5 *Umpire Manual*. The 10 March 1944 version was only twenty-six pages in length, but the manual would grow much larger with time.

The 1958 version added a construct connecting force ratios to both rates of advance and casualty exchange ratios. We do not know what the basis for this was. In the 1964 edition of FM 105-5 (now titled *Maneuver Control*), a new breakpoints methodology ("breakpoints" being shorthand for forced changes to posture) arbitrarily set the attacker's breakpoint at around 20 percent casualties and the defender's breakpoint at around 40 percent at the battalion-level. By 1964 most of the constructs used in the early combat models existed in the *Maneuver Control* manual. These included losses related to force ratios; force ratios modified by terrain, posture, and a range of other factors; advance rates based on force ratios; and a nonlinear degradation of combat value due to percentage of losses (effectively creating a breakpoint). There were tables of armor losses based on force ratios and specific rules for the effects of artillery and air on ground units. There were also rules for a corps quick game that set different values for formations based on unit strength and posture. This was all supposed to be tempered by umpire judgment, but the rules were sufficiently well developed that this was not often needed. "Firepower" was relabeled "combat power" in 1967.

These rules, like the army's look-up tables, were not sourced and were clearly not rigorously developed. They were a limited evolution of the earlier 1944 manual, with the 4.2-inch Mortar having a firepower score of 15 in 1944 and a combat power score of 15 in 1973. Some changes had been made over time; for example, the 81mm Mortar was reduced from 15 to 12 in 1973.[7] The basis and reason for these changes are not known.

The early theater-level and operational-level combat models relied heavily on these traditional army gaming elements for their inputs. In the case of army combat model TACSPIEL, they were a primary input, although the functions in that model were adjusted by analyst judgment based on a few simple comparisons.[8] They were also used for the various "quick games" efforts. For many other models elements were borrowed freely. The *Maneuver Control* manuals were the starting point for many war-gaming concepts, which were based on traditions developed from army training and experience, not from any rigorous analytical work done by the operations research community. They include three questionable traditions—breakpoints, advance rate versus force ratios, and casualties related to force ratios—that have been challenged and fundamentally proven invalid as represented. The issue of advance rates versus force ratios is covered in chapter 14 of this book, and the issue of casualties as related to force ratios is covered in chapters 8 and 9. I will discuss breakpoints briefly below.

As with the look-up tables, the source for each part of these rules is impossible to discern. They are a series of rules of thumb and judgment calls that are not documented and almost certainly not supported by hard data. As such, while they were indeed a very well-developed methodology for resolving combat issues during a maneuver, they were not based on any identifiable solid data. Still, they were instrumental in the development of combat modeling; many of their constructs, including firepower scores, casualties based on force ratios, and advance rates based on force ratios, made their way into combat modeling without serious testing or analysis.

The operations research community's own ground combat modeling effort began in 1953, with the development of CARMONETTE at ORO.[9] By 1965 ORO and RAC had created the first hierarchy of combat models, covering combat at the tactical, operational, and strategic levels.[10] What did the operations research community know and understand about ground combat at that point?

The community had assembled a body of work from UK Operations Research Group 2 and others based on observations of combat in Northwest Europe in 1944 and 1945. It had done a series of observations and reports on the fighting in Korea, mostly related to armor, close air support operations, infantry operations and weapon usage, combat communications, body armor, and certain human factors. It had done some preliminary studies on a few combat phenomena, such as breakpoints. In most cases these were only initial or preliminary studies based on limited data. There was, of course, a large body of nonquantitative writing on the phenomenon of combat by various historians and theorists, but this material was of limited use to the operations research community without further research and quantification.

The original breakpoints study was done in 1954 by Dorothy Clark of ORO.[11] Clark examined forty-three battalion-level engagements where the units "broke," including measuring the percentage of losses at the time of the break. Clark correctly determined that casualties were probably not the primary cause of the breakpoint and also declared the need to look at more data. Obviously forty-three cases of highly variable social science–type data with a large number of variables influencing them are not enough for any form of definitive study. Furthermore she divided the breakpoints into three categories, resulting in one category based on only nine observations. Also, as should have been obvious, these data would apply only to battalion-level combat. Clark concluded, "The statement that a unit can be considered no longer combat effective when it has suffered a specific casualty percentage is a gross oversimplification not supported by combat data." She also stated, "Because of wide variations in data, average loss percentages alone have limited meaning."[12]

Yet even with her clear rejection of a percentage of loss formulation for breakpoints, the 20 to 40 percent casualty breakpoint figures remained in use by the training and combat modeling community. Charts in the 1964 *Maneuver Control* field manual showed a curve with the probability of unit break based on percentage of combat casualties.[13] Once a defending unit reached around 40 percent casualties, the chance of breaking approached 100 percent. Once an attacking unit reached around 20 percent casualties, the chance of its halting (type I break) approached 100 percent, and the chance of its breaking (type II break) reached 40 percent. These data were for battalion-level combat. Because they were also applied to combat models, many models established a breakpoint of around 30 or 40 percent of casualties for units of any size (and often applied to division-sized units).

To date we have absolutely no idea where these rule-of-thumb formulations came from and despair of ever discovering their source. These formulations persist despite the fact that in fifteen (35 percent) of the cases in Clark's study, the battalions had suffered more than 40 percent casualties before they broke. Furthermore at the division level in World War II, only two U.S. Army divisions (and there were ninety-one committed to combat) ever suffered more than 30 percent of casualties in a week![14] Yet there were many forced changes in combat posture by these divisions well below that casualty threshold.

The next breakpoints study occurred in 1988.[15] There was absolutely nothing of any significance (providing any form of quantitative measurement) in the intervening thirty-five years, yet there were dozens of models in use that offered a breakpoint methodology. The 1988 study was inconclusive, and since then nothing further has been done.[16]

This seemingly extreme case is a fairly typical example. A specific combat phenomenon was studied only twice in the past fifty years, both times with inconclusive results, yet this phenomenon is incorporated in most combat models. Sadly, similar examples can be pulled for virtually each and every phenomena of combat being modeled. This failure to adequately examine basic combat phenomena is a problem independent of actual combat modeling methodology.

Over the past fifty years more than 150 ground combat models and ground combat casualty estimation methodologies have been developed by the DOD and related organizations.[17] For a population of over 150 cases, the number of actual categories we felt were needed to describe the attrition methodology was surprisingly small. After over fifty years of development, there are only a handful of approaches to modeling ground combat.

We did create a populated taxonomy of combat models for a report on casualty estimation methodologies.[18] This taxonomy ended up coding the combat models into fifteen categories, but for all practical purposes, we ended up with only five commonly used categories: (1) historically based one-sided look-up tables, (2) Monte Carlo simulations, (3) force ratio/firepower score models, (4) Lanchester-type models, and (5) the hierarchy of models systems. These five categories accounted for eighty-three of the ninety-nine models and methodologies we examined, or almost 84 percent. Each of the remaining eleven categories had only a couple of examples and, with the exception of the Marine Corps model CASEST, are not extensively used inside the industry today. It is difficult to explain why we have not seen more extensive use of methodologies like regression analysis models and historically based two-sided look-up tables.[19]

The hierarchy of models approach invariably starts with a Monte Carlo simulation, while the use of Lanchester equations for ground combat models has been pretty much discredited and has fallen out of favor.[20] Therefore the entire casualty estimation industry is fundamentally wedded to one of three approaches: (1) look-up tables based on one-sided historical data, (2) playing individual combat systems using a probability-of-kill calculation (Monte Carlo simulation), or (3) aggregate scoring of weapons by a firepower or combat score. While there is some variation within those three approaches, the variations are refinements and are not fundamentally different.

Look-up tables were originally a set of tables commanders could consult to get an idea of the magnitude of casualties their units might incur during various types of operations. They are usually developed from historical data. They are still used today for some casualty estimation efforts. The Monte Carlo simulations are the primary combat models used by the U.S. Army today. Broadly speaking, these are stochastic models that are run many times, and the results are statistically processed to produce a normal distribution around a mean value. They usually are based on the firing capabilities of individual weapons and tend to be tactical ground combat models. They are often based on a calculated single shot probability of kill for a specific weapon system against a specific target, and the individual weapons fight each other on a computerized battlefield.

The alternative to this often labor-intensive modeling effort is the force ratio/firepower score model. In this approach, each weapon system is assigned a ranked value (or perhaps several values, depending on target type). The values for all the weapons on a side are totaled and compared to the total for the opposing side to form a ratio. This ratio is used to determine attrition rates, movement of the forward edge of battle area (FEBA, or the front line), breakpoints, or other phenomena. The Dupuy Institute's TNDM is one of these models.

The hierarchy of models approach was developed in the late 1960s. It postulates a low-level, high-resolution model that calculates the lethality of a given weapon system against another given weapon system. This produces a series of lethality tables that are passed up to a larger scope model, usually of battalion, division, or corps size. This intermediate model in turn feeds into a campaign or theater model. This arrangement is perceived to produce trustworthy results since the entire spectrum of engagement size is modeled at one level or other; in reality, however, no one has validated an entire hierarchy of models system (although a top-level, or results, validation has been performed at least once). The real advantage of such a system is that it allows the army to measure the impact of technical and equipment changes on the overall campaign. RAND is unusual in having a hierarchical model, the Joint Integrated Contingency Model (JICM), that uses both approaches, a force ratio/firepower score model based on their "situational force scoring" and a set of tables from a Monte Carlo simulation run.

Lanchester-type models for modeling ground combat are slowly disappearing inside the industry. In these models the attrition engine is based on the differential equations developed by Frederick Lanchester in the early twentieth century, or variations thereof. In general, Lanchester posits that attrition rates can be calculated by calculating the size of the force on each side times the rate at which it inflicts casualties and applying attrition-rate multipliers (determination of which is an art unto itself). While the equations themselves are logical, elegant, and internally consistent, no one has ever been able to demonstrate that the attrition rates in Lanchester models have any connection to historical data.

Most of these approaches were developed early in the history of combat modeling. As I mentioned earlier, the oldest approach is the one-sided historical look-up tables, used by U.S. Army as early as 1932.[21] The U.S. Army also developed the force ratio/firepower score methodology, with "power factors" first appearing in the 1932 *Manual for Umpires of Field Maneuvers* and the force ratios and firepower scores appearing in the 1941 version of the *Umpire Manual* drafted by Brig. Gen. McNair and his staff. Monte Carlo simulations of tactical combat were first developed by ORO in 1953, and the hierarchy of models approach was developed by ORO in 1965 (and refined by Clark in 1969). Lanchester-type equations, which were first proposed in 1902, were first used in a ground combat model in 1969.[22] There have been no major new approaches or new categories of methodologies created in the past thirty years, except for the two-sided historically based look-up tables first developed by the Dupuy Institute in 2000 for its Capture Rate Study and the USMC's one-sided look-up tables based on two-sided model runs in CASRATE and CASEST in 1991.[23]

This focus on analysis was to model warfare, and invariably to model weapons. Many of the models were built on the assumption (at least implicitly) that warfare is a duel between weapon systems, not a fight between people or formations. What has been left out in almost all cases was an attempt to model humans, or address human factors. As I showed in chapters 4 through 7, not only are human factors important, they can be a force multiplier of at least 3.

Human Factors

The overwhelming missing element in almost all these modeling methods is human factors. A historically based look-up table does represent human factors, as they are an integral part of the historical data the table is derived from. But the Monte Carlo simulations, Lanchester-type models, and hierarchy of model efforts almost exclusively do not explicitly or implicitly model human factors. In some cases, the models are designed to address human factors in the most basic form (for example, JICM), but these functions are rarely used in analysis.

Human factors clearly are extremely important in combat. Yet in the analytical world, most of the combat models simply assume parity between forces and go about measuring the performance of weapons systems.[24] But it is necessary to account for these differences to draw valid conclusions from the historical record. This can be done by using only data that minimize opponent's differences, by developing a method to adjust the data to account for these differences, or by using a side-by-side analysis that compares only data from the same opponents. Of course the first two of these methods requires some means of measuring human factors.

The Use of Combat Models

Combat models are used for a wide range of purposes. The modeling community developed during the height of the Cold War with the Soviet Union. The major and central threat for the analysis of ground action during this period of several decades was a Soviet invasion of central Europe or all of Europe with a heavily armored force. As such, the community had a single overriding scenario to analyze and this simplified and influenced model design. This led the community to focus on modeling armor and examining division-level combat. The models developed a degree of permanence, as the basic scenario remained unchanged for decades, and they became integrated into the planning, including logistics planning, of U.S. forces. For example, model runs were used to determine ammunition expenditure rates. These forecasted expenditure rates were used to help determine the stockage levels needed for the prepositioned munitions for the U.S. Army in Europe. The models eventually became part of the annual DOD planning cycle and were used to determine whether the United States could hold in Europe with its current force as well as determine needed supply levels, needed force structure, what changes in structures would improve the U.S. situation in Europe, and a host of other questions.[25] The war in Europe was played out thousands of times on computers in the United States, and U.S. forces were continually refined, supplies adjusted, and new plans made based on the results of those model runs. The Soviet Union did not have this capability.[26]

Luckily the accuracy of these models was never tested by the Soviet Union. They were, however, tested by Iraq. In 1990 the Iraqi Army, under direction of Saddam Hussein, invaded and occupied the neighboring nation of Kuwait. President George H. W. Bush decided to commit the U.S. Army to removing the Iraqis from Kuwait. Now the models developed to analyze how to stop a heavily armored Soviet-style force with a defending U.S. Army were being used to measure the heavily armored U.S. force against the defending Iraqis. If the models were well designed, they should have produced accurate casualty estimates and accurate logistics estimates. But when both were tested, the results were mixed (and in many cases classified). The biggest shortfall was the models' inability to model an army as poor as the Iraqis'. The war was over quicker, with considerably fewer casualties and less logistics usage than some of the models predicted. There was a massive buildup of supplies; the docks were stacked to the limit with ammunition and other materiel, materiel that had to be shipped back or destroyed.

The Criticism

Obviously this state of affairs has not passed unnoticed. The first major paper examining the development of models, simulations, and games and providing considerable criticism of the models and the processes used to create them was published in 1972, nineteen years into the combat modeling process. It was a RAND report by Martin Shubik and Garry D. Brewer and was the first of three major papers over the decades produced by RAND on this subject.[27] Shubik and Brewer surveyed 132 models, including some of the major ground combat casualty estimation models in use at that time.[28] Their conclusions addressed the purposes of simulations and their production, operation, use, and costs. Among their points were these:

Notwithstanding the emergent professionalism, the tenuousness of much of the data being used, the immature extent and level of validation, and the relative neglect of such important scientific and operational procedures as sensitivity analysis and scrutiny of the appropriateness of work for specific operations environments and scenarios, make it easy to infer that advocacy rather than scientific preferences prevails. . . .

Basic research and knowledge is lacking. The majority of the MSGs [models, simulations, and games] sampled are living off a very slender intellectual investment in fundamental knowledge. . . . In the "softer" subjects that bear directly on applied MSGs there is a need for studies of panic behavior (the "breaking point" hypothesis, for example), threat and confrontation, and especially human factors and motivation. . . . The need for basic research is so critical that if no other funding were available we would favor a plan to reduce by a significant proportion all current expenditures for MSGs and to use the savings for basic research.[29]

The paper also addressed poor documentation, the problems with large models, validation, and a host of other concerns.

In 1975 John Stockfisch of RAND published *Models, Data, and War: A Critique of the Study of Conventional Forces*, examining the basis of firepower scores and other attempts to model weapons effects (such as lethal area and SSPKs) in some depth and demonstrating the weaknesses in research that underlie them. Dr. Stockfisch made the point that "the need for better and more empirical work, including operational testing, is of such a magnitude that a major reallocating of talent from model building to fundamental empirical work is called for."[30] This, of course, repeats Shubik and Brewer's criticism. Yet there was a boom in ground combat model designs after 1972 that was certainly not supported by a similar growth in "fundamental empirical work."

Stockfisch made a broader point, which parallels the points I am making, about the use of the scientific method within DOD:

The conditions described result from an imbalance between empirical and theoretical endeavor in DOD analysis and study. The image of scientific activity—depicting theories and models independently tested by experiment or by experience, with the empirical work in turn providing new insight that contributes to theoretical advance—does not seem to prevail in the military establishment. Unverified findings of modeling conducted by one organization can be taken as "fact" by another organization and used as inputs for the latter's model. Sets of numbers that constitute "data" can be admixtures of subtle concepts, subjective evaluations, and limited but hard evidence based on actual physical testing. The particular testing, however, may have been undertaken for purposes remote from the use that another study makes of the data. The lethal area concept and estimates of killing a tank given a hit . . . illustrate this point.[31]

Various observers, including the Dupuy Institute's own Trevor N. Dupuy, periodically posted further critiques.[32] While some adjustments were made in response to these criticisms, the criticisms were not always well received by the defense establishment. For example, in 1987 the deputy undersecretary of the army for operations research wrote in response to Dupuy's article "Can We Rely upon Computer Combat Simulations?," "I would like to give my answer to Col. Dupuy's question about reliance on combat simulations. I believe that, by and large, we can rely on them for analyzing combat and helping to design forces. I say that because most of the simulations Col. Dupuy is concerned about represent a consensus of significant parts of the analytic and military community, and because their results are widely reviewed and checked in various ways against real-world experience."[33]

In 1986 the Office of the DUSA (OR) reviewed the U.S. Army Concepts Analysis Agency's Casualty Estimation Process.[34] This process used a hierarchy of models, including COSAGE and CEM, to provide casualty estimates for personnel replacement and training base requirement planning. Due to concerns over large year-to-year variations in the estimates and questions about "certain inputs of dubious validity," DUSA (OR) convened a subcommittee of the Casualty Estimation Steering Committee to assess the process. The subsequent report stated that "the overall perception of the committee about the Process was of a 'band-aid and bailing wire' system containing internal inconsistencies and many arbitrary or poorly understood inputs. Some parts of it appear not to be well understood by those who use it; there has apparently been little effort to understand it better through controlled sensitivity analysis; and it has not been validated in almost any sense." On the constituent models the committee observed: "COSAGE was one of the weaker links in the Process, primarily because of the lack of verification and validation when results appear to justify serious concern. With regard to the other models of the Process, the committee recommended investigation of the problems identified in the study according to their respective remaining lifetimes."[35]

The committee also examined the inputs related to casualty estimation used in COSAGE and CEM. Of twenty-four inputs used by COSAGE, four were drawn from empirical testing data, seven were based on analyst judgment, and thirteen were of unknown derivation or based on unknown data. CEM used thirty-six casualty-related inputs, of which two were from empirical test data, eleven were based on analyst judgment, twenty were of unknown derivation or based on unknown data, and three were taken from the U.S. Army's *Field Manual 101-10* tables.[36]

Despite both broad-based and detailed criticism of both the concepts and actual execution of the models, the problems across the industry were not corrected, and by and large most combat models were without a solid foundation in real-world data. Paul K. Davis and Donald Blumenthal emphasized this in their 1991 RAND report, *The Base of Sand Problem: A White Paper on the State of Military Combat Modeling*: "In contrast to this interest in model-related *technology*, there has been far too little interest in the *substance* of the models and the validity of the lessons learned from using them. In our view, the DOD does not appreciate that in many cases the models are built on a base of sand."

While it was refreshing that the combat modeling community was still able to conduct public self-criticism, in fact there was little difference in the state of affairs that produced Shubik and Brewer's critique in 1972, Stockfisch's in 1975, and Davis and Blumenthal's in 1991. Another nineteen years were lost in which the data underlying the model structures were still not being corrected across the spectrum.

The related issue of validation was also used to address the scientific foundation of model construction. We were involved in one validation effort, assembling a large campaign database on the Battle of the Bulge in the late 1980s that could be used for model validation. It was then used for a validation test on CEM in the early 1990s and is the only case we are aware of using a large historical database to validate a combat model.[37] In 1997 the scientific advisor at TRADOC wrote a memorandum that primarily referenced material I had provided him, raising the issue of model validation (effectively testing the model to real-world data). He pointed out that "validation of models is not being done, regardless of what the regulations say."[38] There was effectively no response from the community; modeling continued as before, with no major validation efforts I am aware of. The claim made in that memorandum still stands today.

It was as if, when Pons and Fleischmann announced that they had created cold fusion in 1989, everyone had just accepted them at their word and ignored all those pesky critics.[39] This was the case with the combat modeling community, where the criticisms of the methodologies were simply ignored and business continued as usual. The combat modeling community thus remains mired in a series of theories (combat models) it developed with insufficient data. It has not bothered to collect the data to test these theories but willingly produces estimates that are used for real-world applications. Not only are the individual functions and models not tested, but even testing the overall model to the real world (validation) is rarely done.

This is not the case for all models and all parts of the community, but no corner of the community has been pure, in the sense that it has tested the hypothetical basis of the model construction to real-world data to see if it is a valid approach, then constructed the model based on a series of constructs and elements that have been rigorously tested, and then had the entire model rigorously tested to real-world data to see if it is valid. Needless to say, independent validation has almost never been done (as was done by other scientists testing Pons and Fleischmann's cold fusion experiment). We cannot think of an example.[40]

Elements of this process have been performed, and as always, there are ongoing improvement programs that are addressing some of these problems. One can argue that it is merely a perception problem, seeing the glass as half-empty when in fact it is half-full and things are improving. But combat modeling has existed for sixty years, since the original promise shown by CARMON-ETTE, and U.S. Army casualty estimation methodologies have existed for at least eighty-two years. Considering the number of people and the amount of money the U.S. Army has spent on operations research and combat modeling over the years, and the amount of time that the community has had to study these issues, this glass is filling very, very slowly.[41] For that reason I will adamantly maintain that indeed the glass remains half-empty, for it is being filled at an unacceptably slow rate.

In the end the primary reason for these problems is that the community has not spent the money and time to do the basic research necessary to create a solid data underpinning for its combat models.

Developments since the Gulf War

The Gulf War was the first time we were able to compare the actual model to the results, although some historical validations had also been done in an attempt to address the same issues. The results were uneven and, as in many cases, were classified.

In 2003 the United States participated in another conventional campaign. For the 1991 Gulf War it spent six months building up an impressive force of over a half-million troops, along with a quarter-million allies. This was a force intended to remove the Iraqis from Kuwait, an advance of around 100 miles. For the 2003 invasion of Iraq the United States initially planned for a force of 250,000, but then scaled back to 75,000. This force advanced over 500 miles and conquered the whole of Iraq. Some casualty estimates were done at the time, but the Dupuy Institute was not involved in estimates for the conventional war in Iraq.[42] Apparently the defense community was now implicitly accounting for human factors, for unlike the Gulf War, the community did not see the need for overwhelming force to invade Iraq in 2003, nor was there as much concern over high casualties.[43] The United States suffered 850 casualties in the Gulf War in 1991; in 2003 U.S. casualties totaled 691 from 19 March to 1 May.[44] The United States was then involved for the next decade with two major insurgencies in Iraq and Afghanistan that together have cost over 6,000 American lives and resulted in total deaths of over 200,000.[45]

Modeling and casualty estimates for insurgencies were almost totally unaddressed during the four decades of the Cold War and in the decade afterward. Only now, after another decade of fighting, are people beginning to look at this issue. In many respects the defense modeling community has been in stasis since the end of the Cold War, and even over the past two decades there have been only limited developments and improvements. The emphasis in modeling has shifted to training systems.

The Way Forward

We at the Dupuy Institute do believe in a more "pure science" view of how the casualty estimation process and combat modeling should be developed. We do believe that any such methodology needs to be based on real-world data and clearly documented. In light of over sixty years of efforts required to fill this half-empty glass, we do believe that there is a strong argument for a more rigorous, data-intensive approach to casualty estimation methodologies. We recommend adopting a scientific approach, as we do not feel that anything that approaches the scientific method has been systematically applied in the past. We do feel that our comments only reinforce the basic idea stated in Morse and Kimball's *Methods of Operation Research*, "Operations research is a scientific method of providing executive departments with a quantitative basis for decisions regarding the operations under their control."[46]

19. Validation of the TNDM

The QJM is both a model and a theory of combat.

—TREVOR N. DUPUY, *Understanding War*

A combat model is a theory of combat (or at least a hypothesis). The Dupuy Institute has its own combat model, a force ratio/firepower score model that has existed in various forms for over forty years. The Tactical Numerical Deterministic Model was developed by Dupuy in the early 1990s as the successor to the Quantified Judgment Model of the 1970s. It was designed to be a mathematical representation of ground combat (including tactical air support), derived empirically from detailed examination of a large number of actual engagements during World War II and the 1967 and 1973 Middle East wars.

The TNDM was an evolution of Dupuy's Quantified Judgment Method of Analysis (QJMA), as presented in his two books, *Numbers, Predictions, and War* (1977) and *Understanding War: History and Theory of Combat* (1987). The QJMA has two elements: (1) determination of quantified combat outcome trends based on modern historical combat experience in more than two hundred examples of twentieth-century combat, mostly World War II and the 1967 and 1973 Arab-Israeli wars; and (2) extrapolation of historical trends to contemporary and future combat on the basis of developments and changes in firepower and mobility technology.

The original version of the TNDM, the QJM, was developed in 1968–69 by analyzing sixty engagements in Italy in 1943–44. An iterative process was used to establish numerical relationships that explained "reasonably well," in Dupuy's words, the rules (i.e., values of sundry variables) that applied during these particular engagements. This engagements model matched the historical results from which they were developed with an accuracy of about 92 percent.[1] Over the years the model was refined by testing against various other databases of historical combat.

As I noted, the QJMA was published in book form in 1979, along with the QJM database that was used to develop it. In the years since, various aspects of the model and its validation efforts have been examined or debated in print numerous times. One of the most notable debates was sparked by comments made by John Sloan Brown in his 1986 book, *Draftee Division: The 88th Infantry Division in World War II*. Brown's arguments were refuted, also in print, by Niklas Zetterling and me in Zetterling's 2000 book, *Normandy 1944: German Military Organization, Combat Power and Organizational Effectiveness.*

Since the QJM is the only combat model that has ever been fully explained in a commercial book, it has by default become both one of the most widely known and one of the most widely criticized models. Some of the criticisms have also been commercially published, as have rebuttals to them. No other combat model has had such a public airing.[2]

The primary strength of the QJM/TNDM is that it has been extensively tested and validated against actual historical data; indeed it was developed in part through an exhaustive analysis of historical combat data. The initial validation of the TNDM was secondhand, in the sense that the closely related previous model, the QJM, was validated in the 1970s to two hundred World War II and 1967 and 1973 Arab-Israeli battles. The data used for the validations, and parts of the results of the validation, were published, but no formal validation report was issued. The validation was conducted in house by Dupuy's organization HERO. The data used were mostly from division-level engagements, although they included some corps- and brigade-level actions.

The TNDM is, in the most basic sense, simply a determining mechanism for a battle. As such, it adjudicates winner and loser, assesses personnel losses and equipment losses, and determines the rate of advance. It does not have a methodology for determining movement or how an engagement develops. These must be handled either with another model (as South Africans did with their use of the TNDM) or with the traditional grease pencil, overlay, and map approach (as Dupuy did). The TNDM does not have any graphical output; it is entirely text-based.

The TNDM does not model air beyond the tactical air support level, and it does not have a naval component. It does address amphibious operations and naval gunfire support but is concerned with only how naval and air support influence the ground battle, not how they affect each other. There is no logistics model in the TNDM; therefore, supply is not addressed, and, more important, neither is ammunition expenditure.

After its initial development using a sixty-engagement World War II database, the QJM was tested in 1973 by application of its relationships and factors to a validation database of twenty-one World War II engagements in Northwest Europe in 1944 and 1945. The original model proved to be 95 percent accurate in explaining the outcomes of these additional engagements. Overall accuracy in predicting the results of the eighty-one engagements in the developmental and validation databases was 93 percent.[3]

During the same period, the QJM was converted from a static model that predicted only success or failure to one capable of also predicting attrition and movement. This was accomplished by adding variables and modifying factor values. The original QJM structure was not changed in this process. The addition of movement and attrition as outputs allowed the model to be used dynamically in successive "snapshot" iterations of the same engagement.

From 1973 to 1979 the QJM's formulae, procedures, and variable factor values were tested against the results of all of the fifty-two significant engagements of the 1967 and 1973 Arab-Israeli wars (nineteen from the former, thirty-three from the latter). The TNDM was able to replicate all of those engagements with an accuracy of more than 90 percent.[4]

In 1979 the improved QJM was revalidated by application to sixty-six engagements. These included thirty-five from the original eighty-one engagements (the development database) and thirty-one new engagements, which included five from World War II and twenty-six from the 1973 Middle East war. This new validation test considered four outputs: success/failure, movement rates, personnel casualties, and tank losses. The TNDM predicted success/failure correctly for about 85 percent of the engagements. It predicted movement rates with an error of 15 percent and personnel attrition with an error of 40 percent or less. While the error rate for tank losses was about 80 percent, it was discovered that the model consistently underestimated tank losses because input data included all kinds of armored vehicles, but output data losses included only numbers of tanks.[5]

In 1990 Dupuy, with the collaborative assistance of Dr. James G. Taylor (author of *Lanchester Models of Warfare*), introduced a significant modification in the model: the representation of the passage of time. Instead of resorting to successive snapshots, the introduction of Taylor's differential equation technique permitted the representation of time as a continuous flow. While this new approach required substantial changes to the software, the relationship of the model to historical experience was unchanged.[6] This revision of the model also included the substitution of formulae for some of its tables so that there was a continuous flow of values across the individual points in the tables. It included some adjustment to the values and tables in the QJM. Finally, it incorporated a revised operational lethality index (OLI) calculation methodology for modern armor (mobile fighting vehicles) to take into account all the factors that influence modern tank warfare.[7] The model was reprogrammed in Turbo PASCAL (the original had been written in BASIC). The new model was called the Tactical Numerical Deterministic Model.

Building on its foundation of historical validation and proven attrition methodology, in December 1990 HERO used the TNDM to predict the outcome of and losses from the impending Operation Desert Storm (1991 Gulf War).[8] It was the most accurate (and lowest) public estimate of U.S. war casualties provided before the war, differing from most other public estimates by an order of magnitude.

Also in 1990 Dupuy published an abbreviated form of the TNDM in his book *Attrition: Forecasting Battle Casualties and Equipment Losses in Modern War*. A brief validation exercise using twelve battles from 1805 to 1973 was published in this book.[9] This version was used for creation of M-COAT and was also separately tested by a student (Lt. Ramazan Gözel) at the Naval Postgraduate School in 2000.[10] This version did not have the firepower scoring system; neither M-COAT, Gözel's test, nor Dupuy's twelve-battle validation included the OLI methodology that is in the primary version of the TNDM.

The Gulf War Predictions

On 13 December 1990 Dupuy testified to the U.S. House of Representatives on the U.S. losses if UN forces intervened to expel Iraqi forces from Kuwait. This estimate was privately developed by Trevor N. Dupuy & Associates (TNDA) using the TNDM. TNDA estimated that U.S. casualties would probably not exceed 2,000, with fewer than 500 dead assuming a successful air campaign (e.g., Iraq withdraws from Kuwait). TNDA created multiple estimates to allow for different contingencies. Its highest estimate was 3,000 dead and 20,000 total casualties; the lowest was 300 dead and 1,800 total casualties. Assuming that a ground campaign was going to be necessary to expel Iraqi forces from Kuwait TNDA estimated 1,280 battle deaths and 8,000 total casualties.[11]

TNDA also suggested that ground combat would likely not exceed ten days (it lasted a mere one hundred hours), and would certainly last less than forty, even if U.S. forces went to Baghdad. (Incidentally, when U.S. forces drove to Baghdad in 2003 it took approximately twenty days from the start of the operations on 20 March to the formal occupation of Baghdad on 9 April.)[12]

Dupuy then expanded TNDA's estimate into a book, *If War Comes: How to Defeat Saddam Hussein*, which mapped out multiple operational and strategic options and provided casualty estimates and a final estimate roughly in line with his House testimony. Dupuy revised and expanded on the estimates provided in his House testimony, suggesting a low of 190 dead and 380 total casualties for a nine-day air campaign to a high of 2,149 dead and 11,700 total casualties (allowing for 50 percent underestimation). *If War Comes* was published on 13 January 1991, four days before the Gulf War air campaign began.

Throughout the period of deployment called Operation Desert Storm (7

August 1990 to 17 January 1991) Dupuy had the lowest public estimate of U.S. casualties. The accuracy of the TNDM prediction has been noted in a number of sources.[13] Many public and private sources estimated between 10,000 and 30,000 U.S. killed. Gen. Norman Schwarzkopf's prewar estimates ranged from 10,000 to 20,000 casualties.[14] Prior to the Gulf War, the U.S. military had shipped more than 20,000 body bags to the Persian Gulf.[15] Senator Sam Nunn, chairman of the Senate Armed Services Committee, claims the potential cost and length of the war influenced him to oppose the war and push for sanctions.[16]

In reality the war consisted of a thirty-eight-day air campaign followed by a four-day ground campaign. In the days before the ground campaign, Dupuy stated on a national news program that the number of casualties was going to be much lower than his estimate.[17] Actual U.S. casualties in the Gulf War were 382 killed from all causes, with 511 non-U.S. coalition killed from all causes.[18] Total U.S. battle deaths were 147.[19]

Three Independent Validation Efforts

Starting in 1996 the TNDM underwent three independent validation efforts, one for corps-level operations, one for division-level operations, and one for battalion-level operations. The battalion-level validation was done in 1996, while the other two were conducted in 2006. They were done by the staff of the Dupuy Institute under my direction.

The Dupuy Institute had a contract from Boeing in 2006 to test some modern weapons systems using the TNDM. This was an effort to look at the efficacy of the Future Combat System (FCS) using the TNDM. As part of that test we decided to baseline our model runs to historical data and used the data from the Battle of Kursk.

The TNDM was also given a limited independent validation test back to its original World War II data around 1997 by Niklas Zetterling of the Swedish War College, who retested the model to about fifteen or so Italian Campaign engagements. This effort included a complete review of the historical data used for the validation back to their primary sources; details were published in the *International TNDM Newsletter*.[20]

There has been one other effort to correlate outputs from QJM/TNDM-inspired formulae to historical data using the Ardennes and Kursk campaign-level (i.e., division-level) databases.[21] This effort did not use the complete model, only selective pieces of it, and achieved various degrees of "goodness of fit." While the model is hypothetically designed for use from squad level to army group level, to date no validation has been attempted below battalion level or above corps level.

The data from the Battle of Kursk came from the Division-Level Engagement Data Base Kursk engagements, created by the Dupuy Institute. The DLEDB is a database of 752 division-level engagements from 1904 through 1991. They are mostly a single day in length but can range from a fraction of a day to five days, depending on the battle and the records.[22] This powerful database has been used for a range of studies, including the capture rate studies, the situational awareness study, and our three urban warfare studies.[23] The Kursk engagements in our database came from the updated version of the Kursk Data Base and from my book *Kursk: The Battle of Prokhorovka*. Most of the data were derived from the unit records of both sides.

As part of our contracted work, we first baselined (or validated) the model to two divisions. One was the Leibstandarte ss Adolf Hitler Panzer Grenadier Division. This ss division was developed from Hitler's bodyguard and was part of the ss Panzer Corps at Kursk. We recommended to our customer that he do a second, similar, but non-ss division, just to be balanced and avoid criticism. This expanded the test to include the Gross Deutschland Panzer Grenadier Division from the neighboring XLVIII Panzer Corps at Kursk. We then tested each of these divisions using the TNDM for the twelve days they were on the offensive (4–15 July 1943). The Gross Deutschland Division had two separate engagements on 6 July caused by its penetration of the first Soviet defensive lines and its lateral movement before attacking the next Soviet defensive position.

After a review of that work, our customer asked us to go back and repeat the comparison, this time using corps. We stayed in the same area and timeframe and did the validation using the XLVIII Panzer Corps and its neighboring ss Panzer Corps. This was done for each day of the battle for each corps. In both cases the opposing Soviet forces were identified as those that primarily opposed them on that day and their data assembled for that day. This effort effectively generated two separate validations: one of twenty-four days of combat at corps level and one of twenty-five cases (twenty-three of them for one day) of combat at the division level.

We believe that all validations should be independent, but we were not able to achieve this primarily because we were the only ones intimately familiar with the data and the model. Therefore we separated the work: I provided the orders of battle for each engagement including the air support, Richard Anderson set up and ran the engagements, and Dr. Victoria Plamadeala-Johnson analyzed

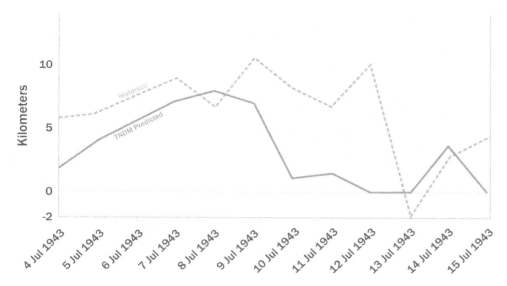

Fig. 19.1. Predicted vs. historical advance rates: XLVIII Panzer Corps. Source: Dupuy Institute.

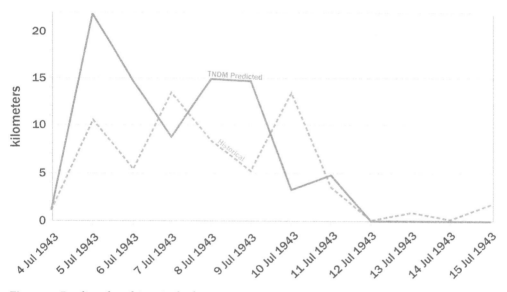

Fig. 19.2. Predicted vs. historical advance rates: II ss-Panzer Corps. Source: Dupuy Institute.

the results of the engagements. This was done in part to make sure that no systematic or personal bias was introduced into the validation.

We assigned the Germans a combat effectiveness value of 3 for these engagements, based in part on our work for the Army Medical Department, in which we used a CEV of 2.5.[24] Needless to say, the results would have been very different if we gave both sides equal combat capabilities, but as this was not the case, there was no reason to test it.

Having assembled the data (which was a pretty painstaking process), run the engagements (which was not nearly as labor-intensive), and analyzed the results, we decided to measure the TNDM's performance in six areas.

1. Win/Lose

In predicting the winner and the loser, the TNDM predicted the correct outcome in twenty-one of twenty-four cases. The DLEDB contains a field that determines the winner of engagement; I filled in this field before the analysis began, in many cases (over half the cases in the division-level engagements) years before we had this contract. The results could be "attacker win," "draw," or "defender win." The TNDM predicted draws for the SS Panzer Corps on 13 and 15 July, when they were in fact marginal wins. The model predicted draws for the XLVIII Panzer Corps for 15 July, when it was a marginal win (the Soviets withdrew during the night). In all reality, considering the nature of the engagements on 13 and 15 July, one could argue whether they were a draw or a German win. The model never declared that one side won when the other side did, so overall it was a stellar performance by the TNDM.

2. Advance Rates

We tracked opposed advance rates for each day in our engagements. Therefore it was a simple matter to compare the historical advance rates with what the combat model generated. Comparisons for each of the German corps are illustrated in figures 19.1 and 19.2.

As can be seen, the model did a fairly good job of matching the historical rates. In the case of SS Panzer Corps it was close overall, with several days being under- or overestimated by a factor of 2. I doubt that there are any combat models out there that would do better. The model for XLVIII Panzer Corps does well through 9 July, but from 10 through 12 July the model did much worse.

This discrepancy was probably caused in part because on the afternoon of 9 July the XLVIII Panzer Corps turned two of its armored divisions to the west and exploited the gaps in the Soviet defenses there. So the corps was advancing to the west, perpendicular to its original line of advance. The historical advance rate shows this push to the west, while the push to the north historically came to a halt.

3. German Casualty Rates

Again it was a simple comparison by day for each corps of the number of historical German combat losses (killed, wounded, and missing) compared to the model prediction. For most of the time we had good daily reports of

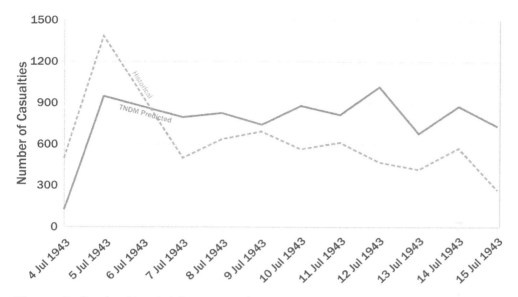

Fig. 19.3. Predicted vs. historical German casualties: XLVIII Panzer Corps. Source: Dupuy Institute.

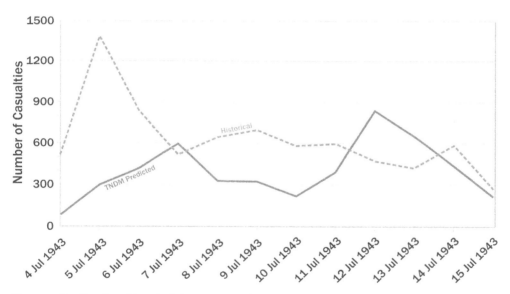

Fig. 19.4. Predicted vs. historical German casualties: II ss-Panzer Corps. Source: Dupuy Institute.

losses by each German division in each corps, so the daily historical data are pretty accurate in this case. Comparisons for each of the German corps are illustrated in figures 19.3 and 19.4.

The model for the XLVIII Panzer Corps' predicted losses couldn't have been much more on target, but the ss Panzer Corps' historical losses were in many cases much higher than the model predicted. This is hard to explain

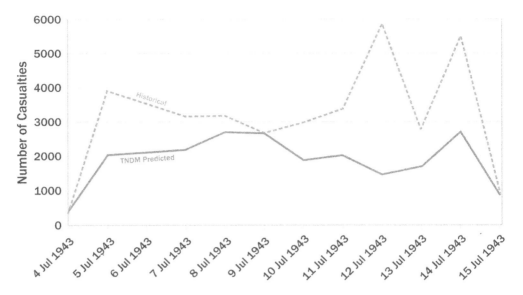

Fig. 19.5. Predicted vs. historical Soviet casualties against XLVIII Panzer Corps. Source: Dupuy Institute.

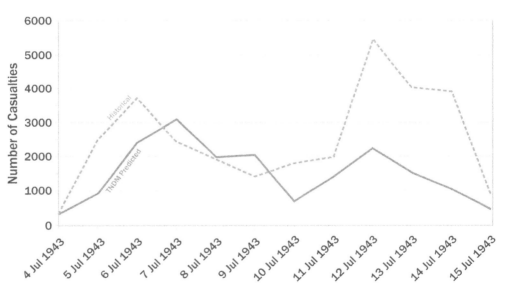

Fig. 19.6. Predicted vs. historical Soviet casualties against II ss-Panzer Corps. Source: Dupuy Institute.

without speculating as to the nature of how the ss fought or their competency relative to the regular German Army (the Wehrmacht).

4. Soviet Casualty Rates

Here again we did a simple comparison by day for each corps of the number of Soviet combat losses (killed, wounded, and missing). These are the losses from the Soviet units that faced the German corps in question. Often these were units from several corps or even more than one army. Data on the Soviet losses came from Soviet unit records, but they did not always provide us with a daily loss report. So in some cases Soviet losses were derived from a periodic report. Therefore the daily historical data are not perfect, but in aggregate they are accurate. Comparisons for Soviet forces facing each of the German corps are illustrated in figures 19.5 and 19.6

It was hard for the model to do as badly as the Soviets actually did. We had noted this tendency in previous validations and discussed the problem to some extent in our battalion-level validations. The Soviet forces consistently lost more people than the model predicted. On 12 July, the date of the famous Battle of Prokhorovka, the Soviets attacked across a broad front with very limited success. This certainly drove up their losses.

5. German Armor Loss Rates

We did a simple comparison between the historical number of tanks lost each day (damaged, destroyed, or abandoned; most were damaged) and the number of armored vehicles the model predicted would be lost. This case was complicated because our loss figures included tanks that broke down. This was due to the nature of the historical data: we usually have daily ready-for-action reports for each type of tank, but no systematic loss reports. Therefore we can only determine how many fewer tanks were not available the following day, and we do not know how many of the missing tanks were broken down versus damaged, nor how many repaired tanks showed up with the unit that day. Still, the figures are close to accurate and are the best that can be obtained. Comparisons for each of the German corps are illustrated in figures 19.7 and 19.8.

The model underpredicted the Germans' armored losses for 5 and 6 July but was otherwise accurate. There are two reasons for this underprediction. First, the Germans were fighting through an extensive minefield and field fortifications. While the model does address these, the nature and extent of the ones used at Kursk were unique. Second, the German historical data include broken-down tanks. The XLVIII Panzer Corps was assigned a unit

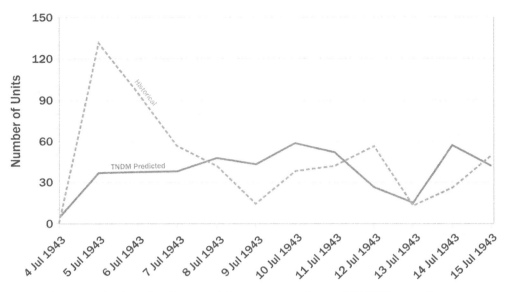

Fig. 19.7. Predicted vs. historical German armor losses: XLVIII Panzer Corps.
Source: Dupuy Institute.

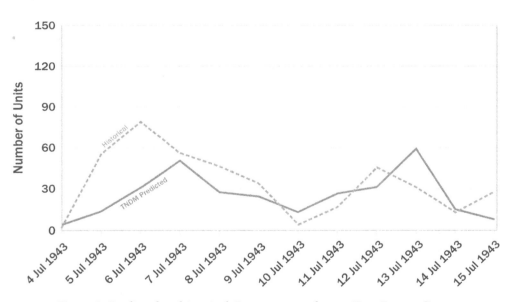

Fig. 19.8. Predicted vs. historical German armor losses: II ss-Panzer Corps.
Source: Dupuy Institute.

of 200 new Panther tanks that had not been properly tested before being released for use. This caused a considerable number of breakdowns in the first couple of days, an estimated 120 tanks! The German historical figures reflect this. If these are removed, historical losses are very much in line with the TNDM predicted losses. Overall the model did a good job here.

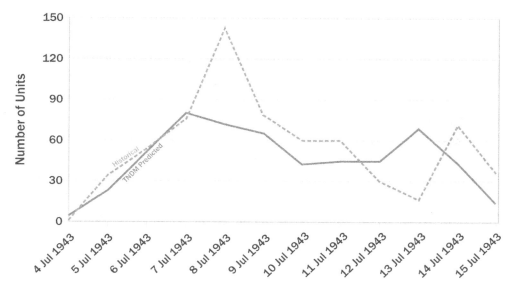

Fig. 19.9. Predicted vs. historical Soviet armor losses against XLVIII Panzer Corps. Source: Dupuy Institute.

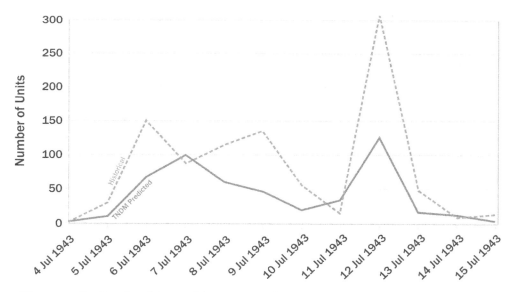

Fig. 19.10. Predicted vs. historical Soviet armor losses against II ss-Panzer Corps. Source: Dupuy Institute.

6. Soviet Armor Loss Rates

The model had problems predicting opposing Soviet armor losses because, again, we did not know how many vehicles were damaged versus broken down. (The Soviets had a much higher percentage of destroyed tanks compared to their total number of tanks lost compared to the Germans.) We do not think that the Soviets repaired as many tanks during the battle as the Germans did. We also had a problem similar to the problem with their casualty reports, in that we had armor losses only for some units in aggregate reports covering several days. Still, the data we had were a reasonable representation of the real situation and in aggregate are correct. Comparisons for Soviet forces facing each of the German corps are illustrated in figures 19.9 and 19.10.

Note, though, that the model's predictions of Soviet armor losses facing the XLVIII Panzer Corps are pretty much dead-on except for two days. The model had more difficulty with the ss Panzer Corps, especially when it came to the Battle of Prokhorovka (12 July), but still the predicted results were way off for only three days. In general the predictions of the Soviet armor losses were pretty good and better than for the Soviet casualties.

Summation: Historical Result versus Model Run

Overall I am comfortable asserting that the TNDM was a good predictor of the outcome, advance rates, German casualty rates, German armor loss rates, and Soviet armor loss rates for both corps tested. It tended to underpredict Soviet casualty rates.

Table 19.1 shows the statistics in aggregate. (The historical figure is listed first, followed by the predicted result.)

Table 19.1. Historical Results vs. Model Results for Corps Engagements

	24 Corps Engagements
1. Win/Lose	21 correct (88%)
2. Advance rates (in km.)	
WEHRMACHT	80.5 vs. 38.0 (47%)
SS	63.3 vs. 83.3 (132%)
3. German casualty rates	
WEHRMACHT	7,491 vs. 9,607 (128%)
SS	7,899 vs. 4,812 (61%)
4. Soviet casualty rates	
VS. WEHRMACHT	35,702 vs. 22,504 (63%)
VS. SS	29,311 vs. 17,602 (60%)
5. German armor loss rates	
WEHRMACHT	470 vs. 463 (99%)*
SS	403 vs. 305 (76%)
6. Soviet armor loss rates	
VS. WEHRMACHT	621 vs. 544 (78%)
VS. SS	964 vs. 507 (53%)

*Less the 120 Panthers that broke down

We also looked specifically at one division in each corps, the Gross Deutschland and the Leibstandarte ss Adolf Hitler (lssah) Panzer Grenadier divisions at Kursk, from 4 to 15 July 1943. These engagements were run in the tndm for each day, and for the two engagements of the Gross Deutschland Division on 6 July. This provided a validation test of twenty-five division-level engagements.

The two divisions were very similar in structure, as ss Panzer Grenadier divisions were patterned on the Gross Deutschland Division. There were minor differences in the mix and number of armor vehicles and the mix and number of guns, but otherwise they were parallel organizations of similar structure and size. They were larger than the standard German panzer division. The main difference between these two units was that the Gross Deutschland Division had attached to it the 39th Panzer Regiment, which had around 200 Panther tanks. These were extremely unreliable; it is estimated that within a few days about 120 of these had broken down, in addition to about 40 being lost in combat. The remaining Panthers were effectively integrated into the Gross Deutschland's Panzer Regiment on 6 July, and thereafter the division was effectively the same as the ss divisions in structure.[25]

1. Win/Lose

For the division-level engagements, the tndm correctly predicted the outcome in twenty-four of twenty-five cases. In the Gross Deutschland attack on 15 July, the attacker won, but the model predicted the defender would win. This error is understandable since the main defending unit, the V Guards Tank Corps, had withdrawn from Tolstoye Woods during the night of 14 and 15 July. The Germans were then able to successfully clear the woods in the morning but made no attempt to carry the attack into the V Guards Tank Corps' new position. As a result the Germans were able to successfully attack and advance a substantial distance without significant casualties being incurred by either themselves or the Soviets, a situation that is difficult to model. Overall we consider this to be a very good performance by the model, being able to correctly predict the winner in 96 percent of the cases. This is in line with the corps-level predictions but better.

2. Advance Rates

As with the corps-level validation, we compared the historical advance rates with what the combat model generated. Figures 19.11 and 19.12 chart this comparison for each of the German divisions.

In general, this is a very good performance by the model. There are about

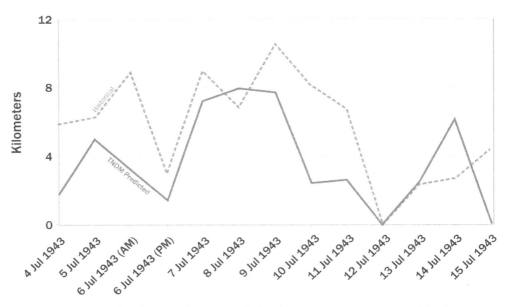

Fig. 19.11. Predicted vs. historical German daily advance rates: Gross Deutschland Panzer-grenadier Division. Source: Dupuy Institute.

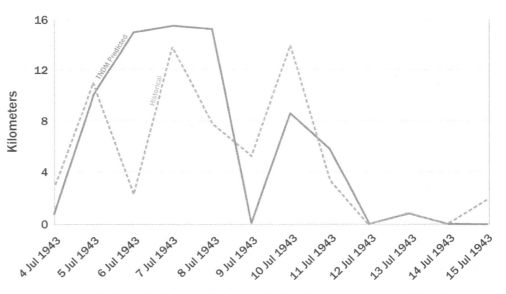

Fig. 19.12. Predicted vs. historical German daily advance rates: LSSAH Division. Source: Dupuy Institute.

four days across both cases where it is really off, but the TNDM predictions otherwise track closely with the historical data. The three cases that are really off are those for the Gross Deutschland Division for 6 July a.m., 10 July, and 11 July. In all three of those cases, the Gross Deutschland was making a lat-

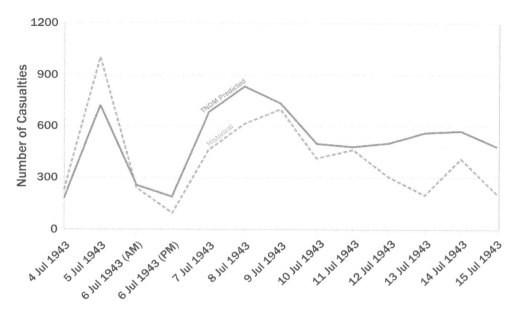

Fig. 19.13. Predicted vs. historical German casualties: Gross Deutschland Panzergrenadier Division. Source: Dupuy Institute.

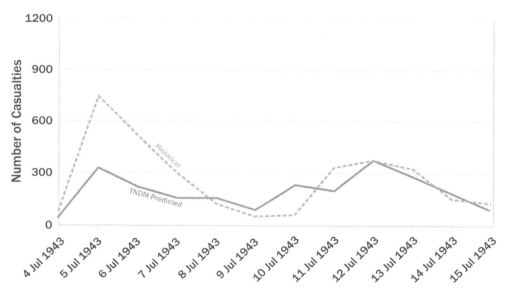

Fig. 19.14. Predicted vs. historical German casualties: LSSAH Division. Source: Dupuy Institute.

eral move across the battlefield against an out-of-position opponent. The historical advance rates for these divisions were determined years before we ever started this analysis and are part of the Kursk Data Base.

3. German Casualty Rates

Again, it was a simple comparison by day for each division of the number of historical German combat losses (killed, wounded, and missing) compared to the model prediction. For most of the time we had good daily reports of losses by each German division; in the case of the Gross Deutschland Division, we had revised and corrected daily loss figures assembled several months after the battle. So the historical data were very accurate. Comparisons for each of the German divisions are illustrated in figures 19.13 and 19.14.

If I ever wanted to use a single chart to show the power of the TNDM, the Gross Deutschland Division's casualty chart is the one I would use. Casualty prediction doesn't get much better than this. We know the daily casualty data we have from Gross Deutschland are accurate; they are revised data assembled well after the battle.

For the LSSAH Division, we have a couple of days where the predicted casualties are low (5 and 6 July), but otherwise the TNDM did a good job of predicting German division-level losses.

4. Soviet Casualty Rates

We did a simple comparison by day for each division of the number of historical Soviet combat losses (killed, wounded, and missing) compared to the model's prediction. These are the losses from the Soviet units that faced the German divisions in question. In many cases these were units from several divisions or even more than one corps. Data on the Soviet losses came from Soviet unit records, but these did not always provide us with a daily loss report. So in some cases Soviet losses are derived from a periodic report. This left us with imperfect daily historical data, but in aggregate they are accurate. Comparisons for Soviet forces facing each of the German divisions are illustrated in figures 19.15 and 19.16.

Facing the Gross Deutschland, predictions of the Soviet losses are noticeably off on only one day, 12 July, the day of the infamous bloody Soviet counterattack. Predictions for the LSSAH Division zone were also very good. The TNDM did a much better job of predicting the Soviet casualties for forces facing these two German divisions than it did for the Soviet forces facing the two German corps.

5. German Armor Loss Rates

We compared the number of tanks lost each day (damaged, destroyed, or abandoned; most were damaged) with the number predicted by the model. We encountered the same problems with the armor loss counts as with the

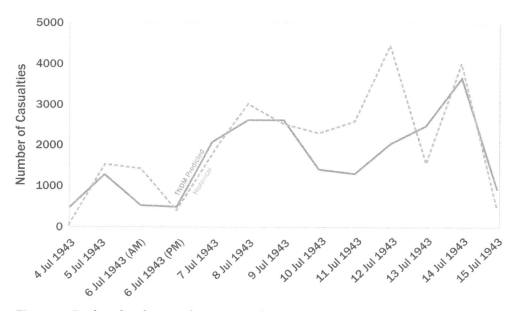

Fig. 19.15. Predicted vs. historical Soviet casualties against Gross Deutschland Panzergrenadier Division. Source: Dupuy Institute.

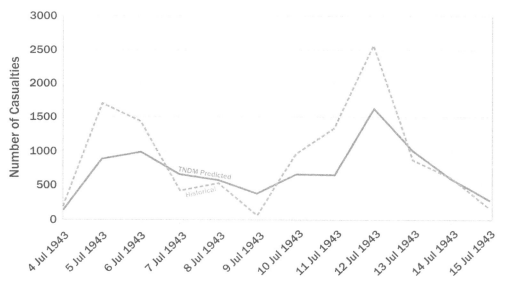

Fig. 19.16. Predicted vs. historical Soviet casualties against LSSAH Division.
Source: Dupuy Institute.

corps-level validation. Comparisons for each of the German divisions are
illustrated in figures 19.17 and 19.18.

Of course the Gross Deutschland figures are heavily influenced by the
large number of Panthers that broke down during the first couple of days

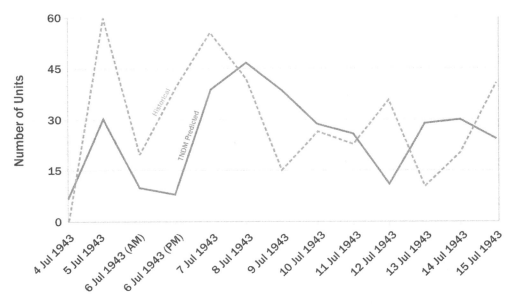

Fig. 19.17. Predicted vs. historical German armor losses: Gross Deutschland Panzergrenadier Division. Source: Dupuy Institute.

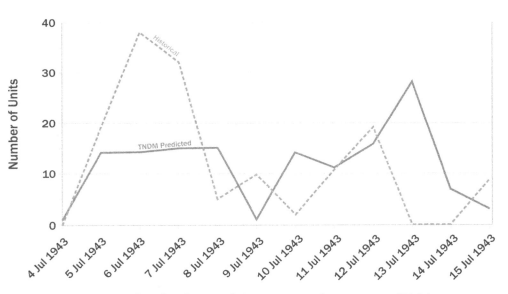

Fig. 19.18. Predicted vs. historical German armor losses: LSSAH Division. Source: Dupuy Institute.

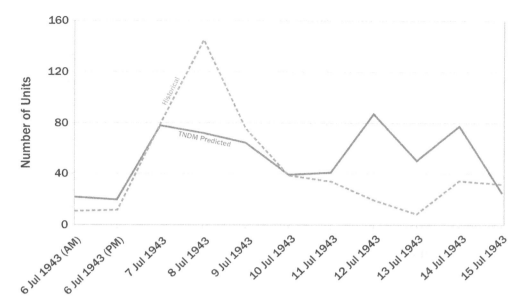

Fig. 19.19. Predicted vs. historical Soviet armor losses against Gross Deutschland Panzer-grenadier Division. Source: Dupuy Institute.

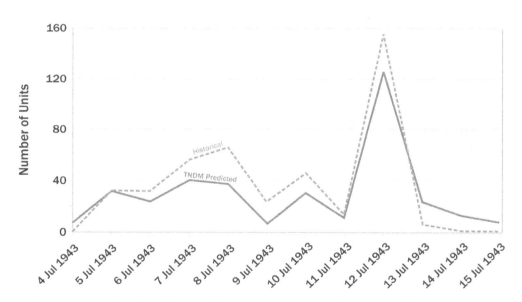

Fig. 19.20. Predicted vs. historical Soviet armor losses against LSSAH Division. Source: Dupuy Institute.

of the offensive (probably around 120). After that the predicted line does a fairly good job of following historical armor losses, except on 12 and 13 July.

The TNDM predictions for the LSSAH Division losses went astray for 6 and 7 July, and we have no explanation for this. On 13 July the division did not attack, so the high predicted losses there may be indicative of the way we chose to run that engagement.

6. Soviet Armor Loss Rates

We encountered the same problems with the Soviet armor loss counts as we did with the corps-level validation. Comparisons for Soviet forces facing each of the German divisions are illustrated in figures 19.19 and 19.20.

The Soviet armor losses against the Gross Deutschland Division were not always well predicted. There were no Soviet armor losses recorded against this division for 4 or 5 July. (There was little armor in the area.) The model underpredicted for 8 July and overpredicted for 12–14 July. Considering how complex the fighting was on those days, this is not all that surprising. (The division was restoring a position that had been penetrated by Soviet armor.)

Like the Gross Deutschland Division's casualty chart, the chart of the LSSAH Division's Soviet armor loss shows the power of the TNDM.

Summation: Historical Result versus Model Run

The TNDM was a good predictor of the outcome, advance rates, German casualty rates, Soviet casualty rates, German armor loss rates, and Soviet armor loss rates for both divisions tested. Table 19.2 reprints the statistics for the corps-level validation to compare with the division-level statistics. (The historical figure is listed first, followed by the predicted result.)

Table 19.2. Historical Results vs. Model Results for Corps and Division Engagements

	24 Corps Engagements	25 Division Engagements
1. Win/Lose	21 correct (88%)	24 correct (96%)
2. Advance rates (in km.)		
WEHRMACHT	80.5 vs. 37.99 (47%)	74.9 vs. 48.3 (64%)
SS	63.3 vs. 83.3 (132%)	62.4 vs. 70.4 (113%)
3. German casualty rates		
WEHRMACHT	7,491 vs. 9,607 (128%)	5,386 vs. 6,718 (125%)
SS	7,899 vs. 4,812 (61%)	3,204 vs. 2,318 (72%)
4. Soviet casualty rates		
VS. WEHRMACHT	35,702 vs. 22,504 (63%)	26,348 vs. 21,890 (83%)
VS. SS	29,311 vs. 17,602 (60%)	10,705 vs. 8,365 (78%)

5. German armor loss rates		
WEHRMACHT	470 vs. 463 (99%)*	390 vs. 328 (84%)*
SS	403 vs. 305 (76%)	146 vs. 139 (95%)
6. Soviet armor loss rates		
VS. WEHRMACHT	621 vs. 544 (78%)	488 vs. 571 (117%)
VS. SS	964 vs. 507 (53%)	430 vs. 357 (83%)

*Less the 120 Panthers that broke down.

I believe these two validations clearly establish the model as a good predictor of corps- and division-level combat. Furthermore, as the use of the CEV was essential in getting the results that we did, it demonstrated the importance of considering human factors when analyzing warfare between different armed forces.

The Battalion-Level Validation of the TNDM

Under my guidance the Dupuy Institute undertook a battalion-level validation of the TNDM in late 1996. This effort tested the model against seventy-six engagements from World War I, World War II, and the post-1945 world including the Vietnam War, the Arab-Israeli wars, the Falklands War, Angola, and Nicaragua. This effort was thoroughly documented in the TNDM *Newsletter*.[26] The validation was not fully independent, as the model tested was a commercial product of the Dupuy Institute and the person conducting the test was an employee of the Institute. On the other hand, it was one of the more independent and better-documented validations of a casualty estimation methodology, for the following reasons:

- The data were independently assembled (for other purposes before the validation) by a number of different historians.
- There were no calibration runs or adjustments made to the model before the test.
- The data included a wide range of material from different conflicts and times (from 1918 to 1983).
- The validation runs were conducted independently. (Susan Sims conducted the validation runs; I evaluated them.)
- All the results of the validation were published.
- The people conducting the validation were independent.
  - (a) There was no contract, management, or agency requesting the validation.
  - (b) None of the validators had previously been involved in designing the model and had only very limited experience in using it.
  - (c) The original model designer did not oversee or influence the validation.[27]

The validation tested seventy-six battalion-level engagements: twenty-three from World War I (April–November 1918) using data drawn from the Land Warfare Data Base, twenty-three from World War II (December 1941–February 1945) using data drawn from either the LWDB or research by David L. Bongard, and thirty from post–World War II engagements (1951–89) using data drawn from either the LWDB, a HERO report on Vietnam engagements, or research by Bongard.

The entire validation effort was documented in a series of articles in the *International TNDM Newsletter*, available online at the Dupuy Institute website.[28] The results of winner predictions, presented in table 19.3, were published in volume 1, number 4, and the model was run with and without CEV.

Table 19.3. Winner Predictions in the TNDM Battalion-Level Validation (1997)

		Without CEV		With CEV	
	CASES	PERCENTAGE CORRECT	PERCENTAGE DEAD WRONG	PERCENTAGE CORRECT	PERCENTAGE DEAD WRONG
World War I	23	57	22	78	17
World War II	23	74	17	74	4
Modern	30	73	17	97	3
Battalion-level	76	68	18	84	8

The outcome of an engagement is either "attacker wins," "draw," or "defender wins." So when we say the TNDM predicted the outcome correctly in 84 percent of the cases, that means it achieved exactly the correct result (i.e. "attacker win" prediction when the attacker actually won). When the prediction was "dead wrong," the model predicted something like "attacker win" when in fact it was a defender win.

The results of the casualty estimates were printed in volume 1, number 4 and appear here in table 19.4. The TNDM tended to underpredict losses by a factor of 2 in the battalion-level test, with high variability in the results.

Table 19.4. Predicted vs. Actual Casualty Rates in TNDM Battalion-Level Validation (1997)

	Attacker			Defender		
	AVERAGE PERCENTAGE OF LOSSES	PREDICTED WITHOUT CEV	PREDICTED WITH CEV	AVERAGE PERCENTAGE OF LOSSES	PREDICTED WITHOUT CEV	PREDICTED WITH CEV
World War I	8.05	6.93	7.45	26.29	25.88	29.41
Standard deviation		7.21	5.42		29.25	27.74

World War II	7.36	5.11	5.62	26.58	11.16	14.25
Standard deviation		8.91	8.49		32.20	29.38
Modern	12.26	4.01	4.55	26.84	8.63	11.94
Standard deviation		16.14	14.63		27.66	25.75
Total	9.50	5.22	5.75	26.59	14.62	17.93
Standard deviation		11.94	10.73		29.57	27.49

The TNDM was revised as a result of this validation. First, a fanaticism factor was added to the model, so that if one side faced a "casualty-insensitive" opponent, both sides' losses were multiplied by 2.5. Second, a time factor was introduced that made all engagements of less than four hours count as four hours for the casualty estimation effort. The results of these two changes, or "special considerations," modified the results of thirty-one of the seventy-six engagements. Of those, seven of the World War I engagements were modified due to the time factor, seven of the World War II engagements were modified due to "casualty-insensitive" systems (engagements included the Japanese Army), and seventeen of the post–World War II engagements were modified, two due to the time factor and fifteen due to "casualty-insensitive" systems (engagements included Viet Mihn, Viet Cong, North Vietnamese, and Indonesian armies). The breakdown is in table 19.5.

Table 19.5. Revised Predicted vs. Actual Casualty Rates in TNDM Battalion-Level Validation (1997)

	Attacker		Defender	
	AVERAGE PERCENTAGE OF LOSSES	PREDICTED WITH CEV	AVERAGE PERCENTAGE OF LOSSES	PREDICTED WITH CEV
World War I	8.05	7.92	26.29	36.52
Standard deviation		4.87		23.44
World War II	7.36	7.93	26.58	22.41
Standard deviation		7.56		27.81
Modern	12.26	11.77	26.84	22.49
Standard deviation		12.30		21.45
Total	9.50	9.44	26.59	26.71
Standard deviation		9.18		24.12

These two modifications definitely produced a better fit while addressing factors that do not usually occur in most combat scenarios. An examination of the forty-five engagements that were not modified found that they had reasonably good fits. While we considered this to be a valid adjustment, as opposed to a curve-fitting exercise, the Dupuy Institute prepared a second validation database of 112 engagements against which to test the revised model. This second validation test was never completed due to time and budget constraints. The TNDM is currently configured to include these two "special considerations," but they rarely come into play and did not at all for the division- or corps-level validation.

The battalion-level test also included advance rates, armor losses, and artillery losses, but we never completed the analysis and write-up of these, again due to time and budget constraints.

This was the only update or change to the TNDM made since Trevor Dupuy passed away in 1995. As such, all three of these validations were against the model as Dupuy designed it. The TNDM is the only model tested to corps-level, division-level, and battalion-level data, giving some confidence in its scalability. The results of all the validations have been published.[29]

20. Conclusions

Military history is the laboratory of the soldier.

—TREVOR N. DUPUY, *Understanding War*

Trevor Dupuy wrote *Understanding War* in an attempt to develop a theory of combat.[1] The purpose of this book was to expand and expound upon that theory. I chose not to do so directly, point by point, as my analysis came about through a series of unrelated studies. Instead I chose simply to present the data I had and leave it to the reader to compare it to the writings of Dupuy, or Clausewitz, or whatever theoretical work or modeling construct the reader desires.

Dupuy created thirteen "timeless verities of combat," which are presented in appendix 1 of this book. He also developed fifteen combat advance rate verities and twenty-eight combat attrition verities, which are in appendixes 2 and 3. Certainly it is worth the reader's time to examine and read through them. Of the fifty-six verities, the work of the Dupuy Institute verified and validated five: (1) "Defensive strength is greater than offensive strength"; (2) "Surprise substantially enhances combat power"; (3) "There is no direct relationship between advance rates and force strength ratios"; (4) "Casualty rates of small forces are higher than those of large forces"; and (5) "There is no direct relationship between force ratios and casualty rates."[2]

Of the other fifty-one verities, our work tangentially provided support for eleven: "Superior combat power always wins," "Advance against opposition requires local combat power preponderance," and nine of the combat attrition verities.[3] Because much of our work over time has been focused on measuring casualty rates and doing casualty estimation, we were able to verify or support eleven of the twenty-eight combat attrition verities, but only two of the fifteen combat advance rate verities and only three of the thirteen timeless verities of combat.

We were able to establish some data values for several verities. This was certainly the case for surprise and unit size. We also clearly established what force ratios were needed to achieve victory with both forces roughly matched in ability and with forces very much not matched in ability. We also established the impact of human factors on combat, addressed in Dupuy's discussions of "superior combat power."

There are forty verities that our work does not directly address.[4] They may indeed be fully supported with more analysis, but to date we have not done that work, though we have no doubt that some of them, like "Advance rates are reduced by difficult terrain," are certainly correct.

Working independently for over a decade, the Dupuy Institute has not found any data or work that contradicts or proves false any of the 56 verities. We were not trying to do so in any case. Perhaps if we looked further and harder, we would find something, but on the whole, Dupuy's body of work has stood up well to our repeated testing.

Dupuy always considered his QJMA and the models that resulted from it (the QJM and TNDM) to be a major part of his life's work. In chapter 19 I briefly reviewed the model and then reviewed the validation efforts made of the model. Most important, the Dupuy Institute independently conducted a validation of the model at corps, division, and battalion levels; TNDM did well, predicting outcome correctly in well over 90 percent of the cases, and did a good job of predicting advance rates, casualties, and armor losses. Our efforts certainly helped to further validate the model and reinforce its value as an analytical tool. No other combat model has undergone such extensive validation.[5]

This book did bypass some of the work the Dupuy Institute has done over the past decade. I did not tap the work on medium-weight armor nor the rather extensive work on the value of mines in warfare. The study of medium-weight armor looked at its use in a range of historical combat scenarios, and the landmine studies were a series of seven reports examining the possible effects on the U.S. military of a ban on landmines. This work did not conveniently tie directly back to Trevor Dupuy's work, so it was left out of this book. Also not addressed was our extensive work on insurgencies, peacekeeping, and small-scale contingency operations, which are discussed in depth in my book *America's Modern Wars: Understanding Iraq, Afghanistan and Vietnam.*[6]

Included in this book are those parts of our work that can be tied to a general discussion of the nature of warfare. For example, our capture rate studies developed an extensive set of charts and tables to be used to estimate captures of enemy prisoners of war based on engagement outcomes. Obviously these have little interest for the general reader, while the work we did on engagement outcomes has a broader applicability. I did, however, extensively present two of our studies, above and beyond what was needed to address Dupuy's verities: our study on the value of situational awareness and our three studies on urban warfare. They make up chapters 10, 11, 16, and 17. Hopefully there was enough new and unique material there to make it worth the reader's while.

The overarching conclusion of this book is that there is considerable value in Dupuy's original work for understanding warfare, for analysis of warfare, and for modeling of warfare. All the work presented here was conducted after Dupuy had passed away and was not done to prove, test, or disprove what he had done. But as we pulled up new collections of data and tested them back to something Dupuy had already examined, we often found they matched surprisingly well. It was this repeated unintentional validation that led us to decide to go back and actually match what we had independently done to what Dupuy had done. As can be seen, his work has pretty much survived our challenge (although we admit that it was a friendly challenge).

It is the nature of the scientific process that hypotheses and theories need to be tested and challenged. In a sense the Dupuy Institute is attempting to add that rigor to a field that often does not operate with much rigor. In a profession where errors in judgment can result in the loss of lives, a thorough understanding of warfare is vital. I hope I have shown here a little bit of how that can be achieved.

Much more work remains to be done. Conventional warfare is far from passé. The models of conventional combat developed during the bad old days of the Cold War need to be updated to properly address human factors, a subject that some in the analytical community barely even acknowledge. In most conflicts we will be engaging in the future, human factors will be an issue. The irregular militias that many nations and groups host as an army are not as capable at conventional combat as our highly trained all-volunteer forces. This mismatch in capability is part of our defense planning, even if it is not part of our combat models. For example, we invaded Iraq in 2003 with 75,000 troops; the Iraqi Army at that time had a strength of 350,000 troops.[7] Our plans were based on an understanding that there was a performance, morale, and motivation difference between the two armies. This is going to be the case far more often than not. Methodologies must be put in place to address these disparities if combat models and the analytical community are going to have any valuable contribution to make in the future.

Methodologies also need to be able to better address lower levels of combat. By nature of the Cold War threat faced for more than thirty years, models tended to be designed to address division-level combat and larger campaigns. Many combat actions in the future will (hopefully) involve only company- and maybe battalion-level actions. We need to better understand how this combat works and how it differs from the division-level and higher combat that we have spent so much time studying.

We also need to integrate the new weapons and technologies into the modeling and analytical structures. For a few years it looked like we were fighting wars using only drones making very selected and targeted airstrikes. But as the rise of ISIL has shown, there are limits to what can be done with this approach. Conventional armies can take and hold ground; aircraft, drones, and the latest pieces of technology cannot.

The post–Cold War world appears to be a world of many small conflicts. We are no longer facing mutual assured destruction (whose acronym, appropriately, is MAD), although both the United States and Russia maintain that capability. There is no longer fear that civilization will be exterminated in a massive nuclear World War III. The worst-case apocalyptic scenarios seem very remote now. That said, the terrorist attacks on 11 September 2001 proved that the United States is not immune to attack and that we do have to remain engaged with the rest of the world to some degree. Certainly U.S. armed forces will be part of that engagement, and they will be called upon to fight a range of wars, from drone strikes and special operations to full-scale guerrilla wars and conventional campaigns. All must be addressed and planned for.

Appendix 1

Dupuy's Timeless Verities of Combat

1. *Offensive action is essential to positive combat results.* This is like saying, "A team can't score in football unless it has the ball." Although subsequent verities stress the strength, value, and importance of defense, this should not obscure the essentiality of offensive action to ultimate combat success. Even in instances where a defensive strategy might conceivably assure a favorable war outcome—as was the case of the British against Napoleon, and as the Confederacy attempted in the American Civil War—selective employment of offensive tactics and operations is required if the strategic defender is to have any chance of final victory.

2. *Defensive strength is greater than offensive strength.* Clausewitz said that "Defense is the stronger form of combat." It is possible to demonstrate by the qualitative comparison of many battles that Clausewitz is right, and that posture has a multiplier effect on the combat power of a defending military force that takes advantage of terrain and fortifications, whether hasty and rudimentary or intricate and carefully prepared. There are many well-known examples of an attacker's need for a preponderance of strength in order to carry the day against a well-placed and fortified defender. One only has to recall Thermopylae, the Alamo, Fredericksburg, Petersburg, Verdun, and Tobruk to realize the advantage employed by a defender with smaller forces well-placed and well-protected.

3. *Defensive posture is necessary when successful offense is impossible.* Even though offensive action is essential to ultimate combat success, a combat commander opposed by a more powerful enemy has no choice but to assume a defensive posture. Since defensive posture automatically increases the combat power of his force, the defending commander at least partially redresses the imbalance of forces. At a minimum he is able to slow down the advance of the attacking enemy, and he might even beat him. In this way, through negative combat results, the defender may ultimately hope to wear down the attacker to the extent that his initial relative weakness is transformed into relative superiority, thus offering the possibility of eventually assuming the offensive and achieving positive combat results. The Franklin and Nashville Campaign of our Civil War and the El Alamein Campaign of World War II are examples.

Sometimes the commander of a numerically superior offensive force may reduce the strength of portions of his force in order to achieve decisive superiority for maximum impact on the enemy at some other critical point on the battlefield, with the result that those reduced-strength components are locally outnumbered. A contingent thus reduced in strength may therefore be required to assume a defensive posture, even though the overall operational posture of the marginally superior force is offensive, and the strengthened contingent of the same force is attacking with the advantage of superior combat power. A classic example was the role of Davout at Auerstadt when Napoleon was crushing the Prussians at Jena. Another is the role played by "Stonewall" Jackson's corps at the Second Battle of Bull Run.

4. *Flank and rear attack is more likely to succeed than frontal attack.* Among the many reasons for this are the following: there is greater opportunity for surprise by the attacker; the defender cannot be strong everywhere at once, and the front is the easiest focus for defensive effort; and the morale of the defender tends to be shaken when the danger of encirclement is evident. Again, historical examples are numerous, beginning with Hannibal's tactical plans and brilliant executions of the Battles of Lake Trasimene and Cannae. Any impression that the concept of envelopment or of a "strategy of indirect approach" has arisen either from the introduction of modern weapons of war, or from the ruminations of recent writers on military affairs, is a grave misperception of history and underestimates earlier military thinkers.

"Seek the flanks" has been a military adage since antiquity, but its significance was enhanced tremendously when the conoidal bullet of the breech-loading, rifled musket revolutionized warfare in the mid-nineteenth century. This led Moltke to his 1867 observation that the increased deadliness of firepower demanded that the strategic offensive be coupled with tactical defensive, an idea that depended upon strategic envelopment for its accomplishment. This was a basic element of Moltke's strategy in the 1870 campaign in France. Its tactical manifestations took place at Metz and Sedan; both instances in which the Germans took up defensive positions across the French line of communications to Paris, and the French commanders, forced to attack, were defeated.

5. *Initiative permits application of preponderant combat power.* The importance of seizing and maintaining the initiative has not declined in our times, nor will it in the future. This has been the secret of success of all of the great captains of history. It was as true of MacArthur as it was of Alexander the Great, Grant, or Napoleon. Some modern Soviet theorists have suggested that this is even more important now in an era of high technology than for-

merly. They may be right. This has certainly been a major factor in the Israeli victories over the Arabs in all their wars.

6. *Defender's chances of success are directly proportional to fortification strength.* To some modern military thinkers this is a truism needing no explanation or justification. Others have asserted that prepared defenses are attractive traps to be avoided at all costs. Such assertions, however, either ignore or misread historical examples. History is so fickle that it is dangerous for historians to use such words as "always" or "never." Nevertheless I offer a bold counter-assertion: never in history has a defense been weakened by the availability of fortifications; defensive works *always* enhance combat strength. At the very least, fortifications will delay an attacker and add to his casualties; at best, fortifications will enable the defender to defeat the attacker.

Anyone who suggests that breakthroughs of defensive positions in recent history demonstrate the bankruptcy of defensive posture and/or fortifications is seriously deceiving himself and is misinterpreting modern history.

One can cite as historical examples the overcoming of the Maginot Line, the Mannerheim Line, the Siegfried Line, and the Bar Lev Line, and from these examples conclude that these fortifications failed. Such a conclusion is absolutely wrong. It is true that all of these fortifications were overcome, but only because a powerful enemy was willing to make a massive and costly effort. (Of course, the Maginot Line was not attacked frontally in 1940; the Germans were so impressed by its defensive strength that they bypassed it, and were threatening its rear when France surrendered.) All of these fortifications afforded time for the defenders to make new dispositions, to bring up reserves, or to mobilize. All were intended to obstruct, to permit the defenders to punish the attacker and, above all to delay; all were successful in these respects. The Bar Lev Line, furthermore, saved Israel from disastrous defeat and became the base for a successful offensive.

7. *An attacker willing to pay the price can always penetrate the strongest defenses.* No matter how alert the defender, no matter how skillful his dispositions to avoid or mitigate the effects of surprise or the effects of flank or rear attack, a skillful attacker can always achieve at least a temporary advantage for some time at a place he has selected. This is one reason why Napoleon always endeavored to seize and retain the initiative. In the great battles of 1864 and 1865 in Virginia, Lee was always able to exploit his defensive advantage to the utmost. But Grant equally was always able to achieve a temporary superiority when and where he wished. This did not always result in a Union victory—given Lee's defensive skill—but invariably it forced Lee to retreat

until he could again impose a temporary stalemate with the assistance of powerful field fortifications. A modern example can be found in the Soviet offensive relieving Leningrad in 1943. Another was the Allied breakout from the Normandy beachhead in July and August of 1944.

8. *Successful defense requires depth and reserves.* It has been asserted that outnumbered military forces cannot afford to withhold valuable firepower from ongoing defensive operations and keep it idle in reserve posture. History demonstrates that this is specious logic and that linear defense is disastrously vulnerable. Napoleon's crossing of the Po in his first campaign in 1796 is perhaps the classic demonstration of the fallacy of linear (or cordon) defense.

The defender may have all of his firepower committed to the anticipated operational area, but the attacker's advantage in having the initiative can always render much of that defensive firepower useless. Anyone who suggests that modern technology will facilitate the shifting of engaged firepower in battle overlooks three considerations: (a) the attack can inhibit or prevent such movement by both direct and indirect means, (b) a defender engaged in a fruitless firefight against limited attacks by numerically inferior attackers is neither physically nor psychologically attuned to making lateral movements even if the enemy does not prevent or inhibit it, and (c) withdrawal of forces from the line (even if possible) provides an alert attacker with an opportunity for shifting the thrust of his offensive to the newly created gap in the defenses.

Napoleon recognized that hard-fought combat is usually won by the side committing the last reserves. Marengo, Borodino, and Ligny are typical examples of Napoleonic victories that demonstrated the importance of having resources available to tip the scales. His two greatest defeats, Leipzig and Waterloo, were suffered because his enemies still had reserves after his were all committed. The importance of committing the last reserves was demonstrated with particular poignancy at Antietam in the American Civil War. In World War II there is no better example than that of Kursk.

9. *Superior combat power always wins.* Military history demonstrates that whenever an outnumbered force was successful, its combat power was greater than that of the loser. All other things being equal, God has always been on the side of the heaviest battalions, and always will be.

In recent years two or three surveys of modern historical experience have led to the finding that relative strength is not a conclusive factor in battle outcome. As we have seen, a superficial analysis of historical combat could support this conclusion. There are a number of examples of battles won by the side with inferior numbers. In many battles, outnumbered attackers were successful.

These examples are not meaningful, however, until the comparison includes the circumstances of the battles and the opposing forces. If one takes into consideration surprise (when present), relative combat effectiveness of the opponents, terrain features, and the advantage of defensive posture, the result may be different. When all the circumstances are quantified and applied to the numbers of troops and weapons, the side with the greater combat power on the battlefield is always seen to prevail.

10. *Surprise substantially enhances combat power.* Achieving surprise in combat has always been important. It is perhaps more important today than ever. Quantitative analysis of historical combat shows that surprise has increased the combat power of military forces in those engagements in which it was achieved. Surprise has proven to be the greatest of all combat multipliers. It may be the most important of the Principles of War, it is at least as important as Mass and Maneuver.

11. *Firepower kills, disrupts, suppresses, and causes dispersion.* It is doubtful if any of the people who are today writing on the effect of technology on warfare would consciously disagree with this statement. Yet, many of them tend to ignore the impact of firepower on dispersion, and as a consequence they have come to believe that the more lethal the firepower, the more deaths, disruption, and suppression it will cause. In fact, as weapons have become more lethal intrinsically, their casualty-causing capability has either declined or remained about the same because of greater dispersion of targets. Personnel and tank loss rates of the 1973 Arab-Israeli War, for example, were quite similar to those of intensive battles of World War II, and the casualty rates in both of these wars were less than in World War I.

12. *Combat activities are always slower, less productive, and less efficient than anticipated.* This is the phenomenon that Clausewitz called "friction in war." Friction is largely due to the disruptive, suppressive, and dispersal effects of firepower upon an aggregation of people. This pace of actual combat operations will be much slower than the progress of field tests and training exercises, even highly realistic ones. Tests and exercises are not truly realistic portrayals of combat because they lack the element of fear in a lethal environment, present only in real combat. Allowances must be made in planning and execution for the effects of friction, including mistakes, breakdowns, and confusion.

13. *Combat is too complex to be described in a single, simple aphorism.* This has been amply demonstrated by the preceding paragraphs. All writers on military affairs (including this one) need periodically to remind themselves of this. In military analysis it is often necessary to focus on some particular aspect of combat. However, the results of such closely focused analysis must then be evaluated in the context of the brutal, multifarious, overlapping realities of war.

Source: Dupuy, *Understanding War*, 1–7.

Appendix 2

Dupuy's Combat Advance Rate Verities

1. *Advance against opposition requires local combat power preponderance.* In order to be able to undertake successful offensive operations, and to advance against opposition, a military force must have combat power superiority. This is simply a question of whether or not advance is possible, and has nothing to do with *rate* of advance. It should also be noted that superiority in numbers, even superiority in firepower, is not enough to assure combat power preponderance, and thus to achieve the ability to advance. For instance, a numerically inferior force, but one that is more effective in using its weapons and equipment and in coordinating its activities, can often advance against a more numerous force. The Germans demonstrated that against the Russians in World Wars I and II, as have the Israelis against the Arabs on a number of occasions in their several wars. Combat power superiority means a preponderance of power (not mere numbers) when due consideration is given not only to firepower and effectiveness, but also to the advantages that defensive posture gives to a defender, and to the effects of such factors as terrain and weather upon mobility and performance. . . .

2. *There is no direct relationship between advance rates and force strength ratios.* While preponderance of combat power is essential for an attacking military force to be able to initiate and sustain an opposed advance, a large combat power preponderance does not necessarily enable a force to advance more rapidly than is possible if the preponderance is marginal. The historical record indicates that there is a relationship, even though tenuous, between rate of advance and the *combat power* ratio (not the force strength ratio). But, there are so many other considerations affecting or modifying advance rates that combat power ratios taken alone cannot determine advance rates. There is no direct relationship between advance rates and personnel strength or force strength ratios because these ratios do not include the circumstantial factors affecting the forces.

3. *Under comparable conditions, small forces advance faster than larger forces.* One of the best examples of this verity is the pursuit of Darius III by Alexander the Great after the Battle of Arbela. Alexander, accompanied by a handful of his Companion Cavalry, quickly outdistanced even the swift cavalry contingents of his fast-moving army in this famous chase. It is not necessary

to go back 2,000 years to demonstrate this verity. The raids of Grierson and Stuart in the Civil War and the advance of German armor to the English Channel in 1940 are typical examples. . . . This verity is simply a manifestation of the effect of "friction" in war.

4. *Advance rates vary inversely with the strength of the defender's fortifications.* This refers not only to the trenches and other works that enhance the fighting capability of defenders, but also to the man-made obstacles that defenders use to strengthen those works and to enhance the degrading effects of natural terrain features. Man-made obstacles include such things as minefields, ditches, tank traps, abatises, and destroyed bridges.

5. *Advance rates are greater for a force that achieves surprise.* While perhaps it is not self-evident, it is certainly logical that surprise should have an effect upon advance rates. Surprise works in three ways to increase advance rates. First, surprise increases combat power and this makes it easier to advance and advance faster. Second, surprise enhances mobility, making advance easier and faster. Third, surprise increases the defender's vulnerability, facilitating the advance of the surpriser. Examples of the effect of surprise include Grant's advance in the Vicksburg Campaign; the Megiddo Campaign in 1918; the German blitzkriegs in Poland, France, the Balkans, and Russia; and the Sinai Campaign in 1967.

6. *Advance rates decline daily in sustained operations.* Comparing three- and four-day advance rates with one hundred–day advance rates in the examples shown earlier suggests that there is a fatigue factor that degrades sustained movement significantly. There has been no systematic analysis of this effect.

7. *Superior relative combat effectiveness increases an attacker's advance rate.* The way in which relative combat effectiveness superiority contributes to combat power, and thus to the ability to advance or to prevent advance, has been discussed. When possessed by the attacker, superior combat effectiveness confers an additional advantage, and in this situation the advance rate will be faster, for the same combat power ratio, than if the combat effectiveness of the two sides were equal.

The reason for this is that superiority in combat effectiveness reflects a combination of better leadership, better training, and higher morale, which will inevitably manifest itself in greater initiative, more imagination, and superior skill. The force with the greater effectiveness can be expected to make better use of its combat power superiority, of the terrain conditions, and the various other considerations that affect advance rates. This was demonstrated often by the Germans in World War II, as well as by the Israelis against the Arabs in their recent wars.

8. *An "all-out" effort increases advance rates at a cost in higher casualties.* For short periods of time a force with superior combat power can advance somewhat more rapidly against serious opposition than its capabilities would normally indicate, provided the commander is willing (and the troops are able) to sustain considerably greater casualties than would be the case if standard operating procedures were followed. This verity relates to the ability to move against substantial opposition and does not relate to rapid advances against limited opposition.

9. *Advance rates are reduced by difficult terrain.* This seems so obvious it is hardly worth mentioning. Yet, it demonstrates why a strength ratio or force ratio cannot be used alone to determine advance rates.

10. *Advance rates are reduced by rivers and canals.* This is also another almost-too-obvious verity. It is listed separately to assure that the discrete problem of relating river crossings to advance rates is not just lumped together with the quite different problems of coping with other variations in terrain.

11. *Advance rates vary positively with the quality and density of roads.* There will probably be no argument that road marches are facilitated by road quality and road density, but questions may be raised about what these things have to do with the movement of troops who are engaged in battle and, consequently, more likely to shun than to use roads. Two things need to be remembered. First, when opposition is light, there will be considerable use of roads by the spearheads of advancing forces, as well as by the main bodies. Second, when opposition is intense, sustained ability to move will depend in substantial part upon logistical support provided over roads.

12. *Advance rates are reduced by bad weather.* A major effect of bad weather is impaired and reduced mobility of individuals and units moving off roads. Almost as important is the effect of bad weather upon the alacrity with which individuals perform routine and assigned tasks. Clausewitz commented that the frailties and interactions of individuals create the phenomenon he called "friction of war." Friction increases when the weather is bad.

13. *Advance rates are lower at night than in daytime.* This is another verity that is perhaps self-evident. But things that appear self-evident are not necessarily remembered in the planning and simulation process. The inhibiting and delaying effects of darkness on movement must not be ignored.

14. *Advance rates are reduced by inadequate supply.* This is another verity that is self-evident, yet may be overlooked. It operates in several ways. The first and most obvious of these is related to fuel for armored, mechanized, or motorized forces. Lack of fuel can bring the movement of such a force to a complete halt, as occurred in western Europe in early September 1944. It is not only inadequacy of fuel that can slow or even halt a force. If ammunition is short, a commander will have to wait for replenishment. Even a small force not dependent upon vehicles and with adequate ammunition will have to slow down to forage, if adequate food is not delivered.

15. *Advance rates reflect interactions with friendly and enemy missions.* One reason why a force strength ratio, or even the combat power ratio cannot be used as the primary determinant of advance rates is that few commanders have either the authority or the opportunity to press an advance without constraint. Advance rates usually have to be adjusted to conform to some degree to the movements of adjacent commands. Advance rates more often than not are related to geographical objectives, and once such objectives are reached, advance will halt or the pace will slacken until new missions and/or new objectives are set.

The pace of an advance can be affected substantially by the manner in which the opposing force conducts its defense or its retrograde movement. A skillful delay is likely to slow down the attacker's advance rates more than would be expected from a straightforward comparison of the strengths and inherent capabilities of the opposing forces.

Source: Dupuy, *Understanding War*, 158–63.

Appendix 3

Dupuy's Combat Attrition Verities

1. *In the average battle, the attacker's numerical strength is about double the defender's.* This is perhaps surprising in light of general acceptance of the rule of thumb that an attacker needs a three-to-one superiority in order to be confident of success. In fact, however, it appears that an attacking commander who has a two-to-one superiority will risk a battle under such circumstances for one or more of three principal reasons; he has the initiative and thus can expect to initiate combat at a time and place of his choosing; he hopes to be able to surprise the defender, and thus magnify, or multiply, his superiority; and/or if he has confidence in the qualitative superiority of his troops or his leadership (or both), he counts on this to give him the additional margin of superiority he needs for success.

The defending commander also plays some part in a combined decision to bring about a battle under such circumstances. If the odds were three or more to one against him, he would likely try to avoid battle. With odds around two-to-one he can hope that the rule of thumb will work in his favor, that he can avoid being surprised, and that he can also make use of surprise, or superior quality of troops or leadership to achieve success.

2. *In the typical modern battle the attacker is successful more often than the defender.* In a database of 601 battles between 1600 and 1973, the attacker was successful in 366 battles, or 61%. In the most recent wars—World War II and the Arab-Israeli wars—the attacker has been successful in nearly 75% of the cases. This is logical, of course; since the attacker has the initiative, it would be surprising if he were to attack unless he believed the circumstances were conducive to victory. Further, it makes historical sense that most wars are won by the side that has been on the offensive longer and more successfully, as demonstrated by the American Civil War and World War II.

3. *Casualty rates of winners are lower than those of losers.* The casualty rates (not absolute numbers) of successful forces are almost always lower than the rates of unsuccessful opponents. This is true regardless of who is attacker and who is defender.

4. *Casualty rates of small forces are higher than those of large forces.* Writing nearly 100 years ago, American military historian Theodore Ayrault Dodge noted that this phenomenon was as evident in the battles of antiquity as it

was in the wars of the nineteenth century. Under comparative or equivalent conditions, smaller forces *always* have higher casualty rates than larger forces. This is due in part to the fact that larger forces usually have a lesser proportion of their troops exposed directly to hostile fire than do smaller forces, and in part to the effect of "friction" on larger forces. . . .

5. *More effective forces inflict casualties at a higher rate than less effective opponents.* Forces with higher combat effectiveness values have greater casualty-inflicting capability than their less effective opponents. In World Wars I and II, the Germans had higher combat effectiveness than their opponents, and they almost always had higher casualty-inflicting rates under all conditions: when they had air support; when they did not; when they were attacking; when they were defending; when they were successful; and when they were defeated. The same phenomenon is found in the casualty statistics of the Arab-Israeli wars, particularly that of 1973, where both sides won victories and suffered defeats in about equal proportion, but the Israelis had a substantially higher casualty-inflicting capability than the Arabs.

6. *There is no direct relationship between force ratios and casualty rates.* Attrition rates depend on many factors, such as weather, terrain, tactical posture, and relative combat effectiveness. Accordingly, the influence of personnel strength ratios or force strength ratios on attrition rates is reduced to a point where no clear relationship exists. Combat power ratios, which take into account the circumstances of combat, do influence attrition rates, but only due to several interacting factors.

7. *In the average modern battle the numerical casualties of attacker and defender are often similar.* This seems to be true when the combat effectiveness of the opponents does not differ markedly and the battle outcome is not an overwhelming catastrophe for the loser.

8. *Casualty rates for defenders vary inversely with strength of fortifications.* There is considerable historical evidence that, if other conditions remain unchanged, the casualty rates of defenders decrease as the strength of their fortifications increases. As Clausewitz wrote, "Defense is the stronger form of combat."

9. *Casualty rates of a surprising force are lower than those of a surprised force.* This is because the organized and determined forces of the surpriser, fully prepared for battle and given greater confidence by the knowledge that the opponent is caught unawares, perform more effectively at the moment of surprise. The forces being surprised, on the other hand, are disorganized, unprepared, and possibly demoralized, and are less effective until they recover from being surprised.

10. *In the average battle, attacker casualty rates are somewhat lower than defender casualty rates.* This is in large part because winners have lower casualty rates than losers, and attackers win more often than defenders. Also contributing is the fact that attackers achieve surprise more often than defenders, since attackers have the initiative. There is also a mathematical reason: the attacker is usually more numerous than the defender, though the numerical casualties of both sides are usually similar.

11. *In bad weather, casualty rates for both sides decline markedly.* This is because soldiers do not use their weapons as effectively in inclement weather as they do in good weather. More time is spent surviving or remaining comfortable than in bringing fire to bear on the enemy.

12. *In difficult terrain, casualty rates for both sides decline markedly.* This, too, is a reflection of the effect of environmental circumstances on the ability of troops to employ their weapons. In difficult terrain, more effort has to be used to move, and thus less effort is available for firing weapons.

13. *The casualty-inflicting capability of a force declines after each successive day in combat.* The reason for this phenomenon is not clear, although fatigue is unquestionably a factor. The reduction in capability occurs steadily while a unit is in combat, but capability is recovered fairly rapidly after short periods of rest from combat. The degradation of casualty-inflicting capability is one way in which the effect of casualties incurred on unit effectiveness can be determined and measured. More research needs to be done on this phenomenon.

14. *Casualty rates are lower at night than in daytime.* This is another example of casualty rates being related to opportunities to employ weapons effectively. There is simply less capability to acquire targets and bring fire to bear on them at night than in the daylight.

15. *Casualty rates are higher in summer than in winter.* This applies primarily to temperate climates, where the distinction between summer and winter is marked by substantial differences in the hours of daylight. The increased time for effective employment of weapons seems to be only slightly offset by the inhibiting effects of more luxuriant foliage in summer.

16. *The faster the front line moves, the lower the casualty rates for both sides.* The reason for this phenomenon, which is validated by historical experience in combat in World Wars I and II, is that troops advancing rapidly have less time to use their weapons than troops advancing slowly. When the rate of advance is rapid, more of the soldier's time is spent on the movement itself, and less time is available to fire on targets. At the same time, it is more dif-

ficult to acquire targets during rapid movement, so the defenders as well as the attackers are hit less often.

17. *Casualty rates seem to decline during river crossings.* This relationship, which needs further study, is apparently due to the fact that attackers are very largely occupied with matters other than using their weapons, and the number of exposed targets for defenders to fire at is generally smaller than usual, except at the actual crossing site.

18. *An "all-out" effort by one side raises loss rates for both sides.* This is true whether it be the attacker making an attack *à outrance* or a defender holding a position at all costs. This verity is simply a result of the fact that a commander willing to take higher losses to accomplish his mission will, in fact, incur higher losses, but will also force his opponent to fight more intensively and be more exposed.

19. *A force with greater overall combat power inflicts casualties at a greater rate than the opponent.* Combat power includes consideration of the environmental, operational, and human factors comprising the circumstances of a particular battle or engagement. A numerically inferior force in well-prepared defenses with highly mobile reserves and good morale and leadership could have greater combat power than a numerically stronger attacker. This can be true even if the attacker has higher combat effectiveness. It is the aggregate of the various factors that determines the ability to inflict casualties on the opponent.

20. *The killed-to-wounded distribution of personnel casualties in twentieth-century warfare is consistent.* About 20% of battle casualties are killed immediately. This corresponds to a wounded-to-killed ratio of 4:1. About 65% of battle casualties survive their wounds, even with minimal care. This leaves about 15% of those hit who are seriously wounded and not likely to live without medical care. The proportion of seriously wounded who survive has increased over the past century and a half from less than 5% of those hit to more than 12% due to improvements in medical evacuation and treatment.

21. *Material loss rates are related to personnel casualty rates.* People are hit in most cases when tanks, vehicles, and artillery weapons are hit. Thus, personnel casualties are caused by the same impacts that destroy and damage material. This means that there are relationships between personnel casualties and material losses that can be used to estimate the latter, given the former. These relationships vary from item to item, and they depend on battlefield density and distribution of the equipment and its relative vulnerability to damage from hostile fire.

22. *Tank loss rates are five to seven times higher than personnel casualty rates.* This applies to combined arms engagements in which armored forces make up a substantial proportion of the fighting strength on one or both sides.

23. *Attacker tank loss rates are generally higher than defender tank loss rates.* This is in relation to personnel casualty rates on the opposing sides. If the attacker's tank loss rate is about seven times that of the attacking personnel casualty rate, the defender's tank loss rate will probably be closer to five times (or even less) the defender's casualty rate.

24. *Artillery material loss rates are generally about one-tenth personnel casualty rates.* For towed guns the relationship is closer to one-twentieth. This is an observed phenomenon that applies to artillery pieces hit by enemy fire. It does not include catastrophic losses of artillery pieces due to over-run or surrender.

25. *Self-propelled artillery loss rates are about three times greater than for towed guns.* This is due to a combination of factors: large exposed target; presence of fuel and ammunition in the self-propelled gun carriages; and vulnerability of engines to damage even when the weapon is still able to fire effectively. They are also more likely to be committed under more immediately lethal combat circumstances than are towed artillery pieces. It should be noted, however, that crew loss rates are slightly lower for self-propelled guns than for towed guns.

26. *Average World War II division engagement casualty rates were 1–3% a day.* Successful divisions in western Europe lost about 1–2% casualties a day in intensive combat; losing or unsuccessful divisions lost about 2–3% a day.

27. *Attrition rates in the 1973 October War were comparable to those in World War II.* In spite of the increased lethality of weapons and the greater sophistication of military technology, personnel casualty rates and tank loss rates for engagements in the October War seem to have been approximately the same as those for both personnel and tanks in intensive battles of World War II in western Europe; they were slightly less than comparable to World War II loss rates on the Eastern Front.

28. *Casualty rates in minor hostilities after 1945 are about half those experienced in World War II.* This has been true for sophisticated forces; accurate records are not available for their opponents. The lower rates are probably due to a combination of higher CEVs, as well as to the absence of sustained artillery fire in many of these kinds of combat engagements.

Source: Dupuy, *Understanding War*, 174–80.

Notes

Preface

1. OEG dates back to 1942, when it was the wartime Naval Operations Research Group (ORG). It then continued as a Federally Funded Research and Development Center (FFRDC).

2. For a brief history see U.S. Congress, *History of the Department of Defense*. I was the author of that history.

3. For example, as of January 2016, there were only three reviews of the book on Amazon.com, and it was ranked somewhere around one million on the Amazon best-sellers rank.

4. Carl von Clausewitz (1780–1831), born in Burg, Prussia, served in the Prussian Army and briefly in the Russian Army. He was a major general in the Prussian Army. His seminal work, *On War*, was published posthumously in 1832. Baron Antoine Henri Jomini (1779–1869), born in Payerne, Switzerland, was a major in the Swiss Republic Army and a general of brigade in Napoleon's French Army. He deserted to the Russian Army in 1813, where he rose to be a full general. John Frederick Charles Fuller (1878–1966), born in Chichester, England, rose to major general after World War I but was not called back to service in World War II because of his fascist views and affiliations. See Dupuy, *Understanding War*, 9–20; Dupuy et al., *Harper Encyclopedia of Military Biography*.

1. Understanding War

1. See Lawrence, *America's Modern Wars*, for a more detailed discussion of this process.

2. The Soviet Union consisted of fifteen republics, which are now the independent nations of Russia, Ukraine, Belarus, Moldavia, Lithuania, Latvia, Estonia, Georgia, Armenia, Azerbaijan, Kazakhstan, Turkmenistan, Uzbekistan, Kirgizstan, and Tajikistan. Its capital was Moscow.

3. International Institute for Strategic Studies, *Military Balance 1974–1975*, 9. The preface was written in September 1974, so the data are current as of then. The previous issue (from September 1972) had the Soviet army at 2 million, but the same number of divisions in Eastern Europe. These are, of course, estimates made at the time by a private organization and could be in error.

4. *The Military Balance* tends to list all the tanks in a country's inventory, whether operational or with a unit, or not. So, for example, Bulgaria is listed as having five tank brigades and 2,250 tanks. At 450 tanks a brigade, something does not match up correctly here. See International Institute for Strategic Studies, *Military Balance 1974–1975*, 12.

5. International Institute for Strategic Studies, *Military Balance 1974–1975*, 18–26. Not all these forces were deployed in central Europe, and this count does include the armies of Turkey, Greece, Portugal, Norway, or Canada.

6. *Imbalance of Power*, 228. This report does use the International Institute for Strategic Studies' military balance data for some of their ground combat comparisons.

7. This was a common enough mind-set that one reporter in Iraq called the Dupuy Institute to ask about it. He was repeatedly told by serving officers that these were new missions for the U.S. Army, which from their perspective was certainly the case. From the perspective of a historian, they clearly were not.

8. Drawn from R. Filipelli, Parallel Narratives website, http://parallelnarratives.com/the-three-stages-of-maos-revolutionary-warfare/.

9. Islamic State of Iraq and the Levant, sometimes referred to as ISIS (Islamic State of Iraq and Syria).

10. They consist of the Warfare and Armed Conflict Data Base (WACCO) of 793 cases from 1898–1998, the Campaign Data Bases (CaDB) of 196 cases from 1904–91, the Large Action Data

Base (LADB) of 55 cases from 1912–73, the Division-Level Engagement Data Bases (DLEDB) of 752 cases from 1904–91, the Battalion-Level Operations Data Base (BLODB) of 127 cases from 1918–91, the Company-Level Actions Data Base (CLADB) of 98 cases from 1914–2000, the Small Action Data Base (SADB) of 5 cases from 1941–82, the Battles Data Base (BADB) of 243 cases from 1600–1900, and the Small Scale Contingency Operations Data Bases (SSCODB) of 203 cases from 1944–2001.

In addition the Dupuy Institute maintains the Battle of Britain Data Base (BOBDB), Dupuy Insurgency Spread Sheets (DISS) of 109 insurgencies from 1944–2008, the Ardennes Campaign Simulation Data Base (ACSDB), and the Kursk Data Base (KDB). These last three have been used for analysis in Lawrence, *America's Modern Wars*; Dupuy et al., *Hitler's Last Gamble*; and Lawrence, *Kursk*.

2. Force Ratios

1. Clausewitz, *On War*, 194. The original was published in German in 1832. See also appendix 1, which repeats the thirteen "timeless verities of combat" provided in Dupuy, *Understanding War*.

2. Leonhard, "Force XXI and the Theory of Winning Outnumbered."

3. See Lawrence, "A Rebuttal to Force XXI and the Theory of Winning Outnumbered." Data used were from the Dupuy Institute proprietary of the Land Warfare Data Base.

4. The original database done by HERO was the Land Warfare Data Base. See HERO, *Analysis of Factors*. This report examines 601 battles. Updates and revisions were provided in HERO, *Combat History Analysis Study Effort*.

Our version of the Land Warfare Data Base (LWDB) was slightly revised and consisted of 605 battles. There is a government-created version of the database, Combat History Analysis Study Effort, but the computerized version is incomplete and has errors in the coding. Also see Hartley, *Topics in Operations Research*, which reprints an incomplete copy of the database.

5. The number of cases from before 1915 have remained the same. Since that time we have added hundreds of cases to the databases from 1915 and later, in addition to a large number of smaller actions from 1914 on.

6. There are forty-eight battles from the period 1600–1699. In twenty-five of these, the attacker attacked while outnumbered and won in eighteen cases (there was also one draw). The engagements include eighteen battles from the Thirty Years War, nine battles from the English Civil War, five battles from the Dutch War (1672–78), eight battles from King William's War, and eight battles from other wars.

7. Clausewitz, *On War*, 361–62:

Defense appears to fall into disrepute whenever a particular style of it has become obsolete; that is what happened in the case described above [Seven Years War]. In its day this method of defense really had been superior to the attack.

If we survey the development of modern war, we find that at the beginning—in the Thirty Years War and the War of the Spanish Succession—an army's deployment and disposition was one of the main elements in a battle. It was the most important part of the plan of action. This normally worked to the advantage of the defender because his forces were deployed and in position from the start. With the troops' increased ability to maneuver, this advantage was lost, and for a time the attack gained the upper hand. The defender now sought protection behind rivers or deep valleys, or on mountains. He thus recovered a distant advantage, which lasted until the attacker became so mobile and skilled that he could venture even into rough country and attack in separate columns; which enabled him to *turn* the enemy. This led to greater and greater extension of the line of battle until it naturally occurred to the attacker to concentrate on a limited number of points and pierce the enemy's shallow position. Thus the offensive gained the upper hand for the third time, and once again the defensive had to change its methods. This is what happened in the recent wars. Forces were kept concentrated in large masses, most of them not deployed and, wherever possible, in concealed positions. The object was simply to be ready to deal with the attack as soon as its intentions became clear.

This does not entirely preclude defending one's ground in a partly passive manner, for to do so offers such decisive advantages that it is frequently done in the course of a campaign. But usually the passive defense of terrain is no longer dominant—which is all we are concerned with here.

If the offensive were to invent some major new expedient—which is unlikely in view of the simplicity and inherent necessity that marks everything today—the defensive will also have to change its methods. But it will always be certain of having the benefit of terrain, and this will generally ensure its natural superiority; for today the peculiarities of the topography and the ground have a greater effect on military action than ever.

8. See Dupuy Institute, *Measuring the Effects of Combat in Cities, Phase I*, 47–49. These were for engagements of outcome III (attack fails), outcome IV (attacker advances), and outcome V (defender penetrated). Outcome definitions are provided in chapter 8. Detailed statistics of each engagement are provided on pages 89–112 of the Phase I report.

9. See Dupuy Institute, *Measuring the Effects of Combat in Cities, Phase II*, 31–32. These were for engagements of outcome III (attack fails), outcome IV (attacker advances), and outcome V (defender penetrated). Detailed statistics of each engagement are provided on pages 103–27 of the Phase II report.

10. See Dupuy Institute, *Measuring the Effects of Combat in Cities, Phase III*, 34–36. These were for engagements of outcome III (attack fails), outcome IV (attacker advances), and outcome V (defender penetrated). Detailed statistics of each engagement are provided on pages 111–19 of the Phase III report.

11. The three failed attacks at force ratios of 2.92 to 3.89 are the U.S. 7th Infantry Division's attack on Kochi Ridge (Onaga I, II, and III) from 25 April to 3 May 1945 in the battle for Okinawa. The failed attack with a force ratio of 7.90 is the U.S. 96th Infantry Division's attack on Kakazu and Tombstone Ridges from 9–12 April 1945, also from the battle for Okinawa.

12. Clausewitz, *On War*, 195. Emphasis added.

13. Clausewitz, *On War*, 194–95.

14. Clausewitz, *On War*, 134.

3. Attacker versus Defender

1. See appendix 1 of this book.

2. Clausewitz, *On War*, 84.

3. Also see Julius Caesar, *Civil War*.

4. Human Factors

1. On Napoleon's quote in the epigraph, derived from a letter written 27 August 1808 to his brother Joseph in Spain, see Dupuy, *Understanding War*, 11.

2. Clausewitz, *On War*, 194.

3. Clausewitz, *On War*, 137. In fact Clausewitz spent little time discussing the abilities of the troops, even though he clearly considered ability part of "relevant strength." He writes in his chapter on "relevant strength":

The courage and morale of an army have always increased its physical strength, and always will. But there are periods in history when great psychological advantage was gained by superior organization and equipment; others where the same result was achieved by superior mobility. Sometimes it was a matter of novel tactics; at other times the art of war revolved around efforts to exploit terrain skillfully on large and comprehensive lines. On occasion generals have managed to gain great advantage over one another by such means. But efforts of this type have declined, making way for simpler and more natural procedures. If we take an unbiased look at the experiences of the recent wars, we must admit that those means have almost disappeared, both from the campaign as a whole and the decisive engagements, and particularly from the major battle. . . . *Today armies are so much alike in weapons, training, and equipment that there is little difference in such matters between the best and the worst of them.* (282, emphasis added)

Clausewitz obviously felt that differences between the armies he observed or studied in the Seven Years War and the Napoleonic Wars were not significant. This caused him to focus on generalship rather than other human factors. In modern wars, such as the 1991 Gulf War, armies differ in weapons, training, and experience; in fact, in most cases in the near future we will not be facing armies equal to us in weapons, training, or experience.

4. For example, see Dupuy, *Numbers, Predictions and War*, 33.

5. I would add to that list of factors "generalship," to separate it from "leadership." "Leadership" in this sense represents the training and capabilities of the noncommissioned and commissioned officers throughout the unit, which is going to be fairly consistent in an army from unit to unit. It will also be a fairly consistent positive or negative influence on a unit. On the other hand, "generalship" represents the guy at the top of the unit, making the decisions. This is widely variable; the history of warfare is populated with brilliant generals, a large number of perfectly competent ones, and a surprisingly large number of less than competent ones. Within an army, no matter the degree and competence of the officer corps or the rigor of their training, poor generals show up, and sometimes brilliant generals show up with no military training (like the politician turned general Julius Caesar).

6. Outcome I is limited action; outcome II is limited attack; outcome III is failed attack; outcome IV is attack advances; outcome V is defender penetrated; outcome VI is defender enveloped; and outcome VII is other. See chapter 8 for a more complete definition and discussion of outcomes.

5. Measuring Human Factors: Italy

1. See Dupuy, *Understanding War*, 28–30.

2. From the foreword by Charles Messenger in Rowland, *Stress of Battle*, ix. David Rowland is considered the father of British historical analysis.

3. One could argue that weapons and technology are also equally important, but the differences between weapons capabilities in conventional forces are often not as significant as the other factors.

4. These are rated 0, 1, or 2 for both the attacker and defender: (1) conceptual accomplishment, (2) geographical accomplishment, (3) block hostile mission, (4) command and staff performance, and (5) troop performance. The analyst can also assign a bonus or penalty.

5. There are some alternative metrics. One could compare total killed on both sides, although this will generate odd comparisons if one side has a lot of MIA results and a low number (underreporting) of KIA. One could also compare "total losses," which is total KIA and MIA. This metric may be useful, but it too has some problems. When a defender is overrun, a certain percentage of what would normally be WIA becomes CIA (captured in action). As such, the attacker casualties include KIA and MIA, while the defender casualties included KIA, MIA, and those WIA that could not get out of the way (which are recorded as MIA). This inflates the defender's losses relative to the attacker's when he is overrun. We decided to stay with total casualties as a measurement, as we believe this figure produces more consistent results across a wide range of engagements.

6. For example, see Dupuy, *Numbers, Predictions and War*, 95–110; Dupuy, *Understanding War*, 105–23.

7. See Dupuy, *Understanding War*, 109–17; Dupuy, *Numbers, Predictions and War*, 103–7.

8. See Dupuy, *Understanding War*, 121–23.

9. Because the database continued to be updated, some of the engagements had been corrected or modified in light of additional research.

10. See Dupuy Institute, *Capture Rate Study, Phases I & II*, 38–61; Lawrence, *Measuring Human Factors* (a briefing given at the International Society of Military Operational Researchers).

11. Zetterling, "CEV Calculations in Italy, 1943," 23.

12. The engagement at a force ratio of 4.99 is the British 46th Infantry Division's fight at Sessa Arunca from 29 October–2 November 1943. Its outcome is coded as "Attack Advances." The mission accomplishment score of the attacker is 5 and of the defender is 6, so it is determined to be a defender victory even though the attacker advanced 1.2 kilometers over the course of the five-day engagement. The defender's mission is recorded as "delay." Among the American attacks there are nine cases in the database where the outcome is recorded as "attack advances" and the winner is recorded as "defender"; there are three cases where the outcome is recorded as "attack advances" and the engagement is recorded as a draw; and there is one case where a "failed attack" is recorded as a draw. Among the British attacks there are six cases in the database where the outcome is recorded as "attack advances" and the winner is recorded as "defender" and two cases where a "failed attack" is recorded as a draw. There were seven failed UK attacks at greater than a 4 to 1 ratio; three were cases of "attack advances" where the winner was recorded as the defender, two were "limited actions" where the winner was recorded as the defender, and two were "failed attacks."

13. By "weighted average" I mean that the total attacker strength across all the engagements compared to the total defender strength across all the engagements. This usually produces a different ratio (usually lower) than if one simply averages the forty-nine different force ratios.

14. Calculated as 2.97 divided by 1.97.

15. Only one engagement is from later than June 1944, so this database represents much of the major fighting from the landing at Salerno until the conquest of Rome.

16. For example, the average U.S force ratio for successful attacks was 1.97, while for the British it was 2.97. The German average was 1.85. So 1.97/1.85 = 1.06 or a 6 percent difference. As most of the successes were against the British, maybe the calculation should be 2.97/1.85 = 1.61.

17. The engagements are all from actions by the 1st, 5th, 46th, and 56th Infantry Divisions and the 7th Armoured Division between September 1943 and June 1944. The 7th Armoured Division had between 150 and 157 main battle tanks for each of these engagements, while the average number of main battle tanks for all the British attacks was 51. The average number of main battle tanks for all the American attacks was 88.

18. Note that the engagements are coded by seven outcomes, which include these two categories, and they are also coded by winner (attacker, draw, or defender). Usually "failed attack" is a defender win and "attacker advances" is an attacker win. There are a couple of exceptions. Outcomes also include "limited action" and "limited attack," so this categorization removes these from the engagements to be considered.

19. If all the U.S. data are used, including penetrations (all seventy cases), the figures are 24,614 U.S. casualties (average of 352) versus 23,215 German casualties (average of 332). There were twenty-six cases (37 percent) in which the Americans suffered fewer losses than the defender. Because they included breakthroughs, these figures were not used for the conclusions.

20. Note that the data are not significantly different if all forty-nine cases are used. The figures are 8,542 UK casualties (average of 174) versus 5,229 German casualties (average of 107). There were seventeen cases (35 percent) in which the British suffered fewer losses than the defender.

21. For example, 1.89 casualty advantage of the Germans over the British divided by the 1.29 casualty advantage of the Germans over the Americans (1.68/1.29 = 1.30).

22. The difference between the British and the Germans being 28 percent (696/544 = 1.28).

23. Germans were 6 percent better based on mission effectiveness, 22 percent better based on nonpenetrating successful attacks, 34 percent better based on "failed attacks," 29 percent better based on "attack advances" and "failed attacks," and 8 percent better based on U.S. defense.

24. Germans were 61 percent better based on mission effectiveness, 46 percent better based on nonpenetrating successful attacks, 99 percent better based on "failed attacks," 68 percent better based on "attack advances" and "failed attacks," and 28 percent better based on UK defense.

25. Dupuy passed away in 1995, and the first analysis by the Dupuy Institute was done in 2000.

6. Measuring Human Factors: Ardennes and Kursk

1. This included six engagements not part of the Ardennes Campaign: Kasserine Pass, 19–20 February 1943; Seine River, 23–25 August 1944; and four engagements from the Westwall-Huertgen Forest Campaign, October–December 1944. There were sixty-four engagements from Ardennes in 16–31 December 1944 and one from Ardennes on 13 January 1945.

2. Some of the larger and smaller Ardennes engagements were moved to other databases, including our battalion-level engagement database. The division-level engagement database now consists of seventeen engagements from Normandy (many urban), six from the Pursuit across France, twelve from Brittany (many urban), seventeen from the Channel Ports (many urban), twenty-four from Westwall (many urban), eight from Lorraine, and fifty-seven from the Ardennes.

3. The German army consisted of ground units from the regular German Army (the Wehrmacht), the SS, and the air force (the Luftwaffe).

4. This includes thirteen engagements categorized as "defender penetrated" and one categorized as "other."

5. Not all the engagements had an outcome of "failed attack." Four were considered "attack advances" even though they scored as a draw or defender win, and five were "limited attack."

6. In table 6.4 a type IV engagement is one where the "attack advances," a type V engagement is when the defender is penetrated, and a type VI engagement is when the defender is enveloped. Not all "attack advances" are successful attacks.

7. The choice of measures fundamentally biases the numbers in favor of multiday engagements and weights the averages in favor of large engagements. There are two other metrics that could have been used for these comparisons: losses per day and percentage of losses per day. Losses per day was not chosen as a metric because the issue was comparative losses between two sides. The percentage of losses per day could have been selected, but it was felt this would give equal weight to small and large actions. A measurement weighted by size seemed to be of more value. The advantage of percentage of losses (or percentage of losses per day) is that it ties the measurement to the number of people in the engagements. As the Ardennes and Italian databases are similar in the average size of an engagement, it was felt that the two databases could be compared directly.

8. Dupuy et al., *Hitler's Last Gamble*, appendix H "German Combat Performance," 498–501.

9. They suffered an average of 264 losses on the offense while causing 672 losses, for a 2.55 to 1 exchange ratio in favor of the Germans. This was heavily influenced by two of the engagements being the 18th Volksgrenadier Division's operations in Schnee Eifel, where they were able to obtain the surrender of thousands of troops from the U.S. 106th Infantry Division. If these two engagements are removed, the numbers are 274 for the attacker and 219 for the defender, for a 1.25 to 1 exchange ratio in favor of the United States. While on the defense, they suffered 268 losses and caused 160 losses, for a 1.68 to 1 exchange ratio.

10. This analysis was based on forty-nine engagements from the LII Corps and XLVIII Panzer Corps operations in 4–18 July 1943. These were two of the five corps involved in the Army Group South's attack. Some of the other analysis of the Kursk data provided in this book is based on the expanded database of 192 engagements, covering all five corps.

11. The opposite of a force ratio of 5 to 1 is 0.2 to 1. If one takes a simple average of these two numbers, the average force ratio is 2.6 to 1, whereas the actual average should be 1.0 to 1. Therefore the "averages" for the German attacks at Kursk are calculated by summing the force ratios greater than 1 and adding 1 for every force ratio below 1, then dividing that by the sum of the inverse of the force ratios below 1 and adding 1 for every force ratio above 1. For example, if the data set consists of two 5-to-1 attacks and a 1-to-5 attack, the average force ratio is 11/7ths, or 1.57 to 1.

12. CIA should be a subset of MIA because CIA become prisoners of war.

13. The subject is also addressed in appendix 3 of Lawrence, *Kursk*.

14. AWOL is a U.S. Army administrative term that indicates any person who is missing from

duty without permission. Sometimes they turn out to be deserters. The U.S. Marine Corps uses the term Unauthorized Absence (UA).

7. Measuring Human Factors: Modern Wars

1. The similarities are particularly notable in the low-odds attacks: when the Soviets attacked (twelve cases), they did so at odds of 1.00 to 1 and had a negative loss exchange of 4.83 to 1. In their two cases the Arabs attacked at 0.96 to 1 and had a negative loss exchange of 4.91 to 1. The relationship using total force and loss ratios (weighted averages) is similar: the Soviets attacked at 1.02 to 1 and suffered losses at 3.92 to 1, while the Arabs attacked at 0.95 to 1 and suffered losses at 3.87 to 1.

Because there were only two Arab attacks, not much weight could be given to this measurement, except that the figures for all attacks match fairly closely. The Soviets attacked (eighteen cases) at 1.42 to 1 and suffered losses at a ratio of 5.63 to 1. The Arabs attacked (also eighteen cases) at 4.09 to 1 and suffered losses at 3.65 to 1. For the total force and loss ratios (weighted averages), the Soviets attacked at 1.43 to 1 and suffered losses at 6.04 to 1, and the Arabs attacked at 3.02 to 1 and suffered losses at 2.81 to 1. Because of the mismatch in force ratios, it is harder to directly compare these sets of engagements.

On the other hand, the German low-odds attacks against the Soviets (twenty-one cases) were at 0.93 to 1 and had a favorable loss exchange ratio of 0.41 to 1. The Israeli low-odds attacks against the Arabs (twenty-six cases) were at 0.92 to 1 and had a favorable loss exchange ratio of 0.43 to 1. For the weighted averages the numbers were similarly close, with the German low-odds attacks at 0.99 to 1 and the loss ratio at 0.27 to 1, while the Israeli low-odds attacks were at 0.89 to 1 and the losses at 0.28 to 1.

The statistics for all attacks also similarly matched, with the German attacks (thirty-one cases) at 1.66 to 1 with a loss ratio of 0.30 to 1, and the Israeli attacks (thirty-one cases) at 1.29 to 1 with a loss ratio of 0.46 to 1. For the weighted averages, the Germans attacked at 1.34 to 1 with a loss ratio still at 0.30 to 1, while the Israelis attacked at 1.04 to 1 with a loss ratio of 0.31 to 1. Clearly the relative combat performance between these two forces is very similar.

2. Dupuy, *Elusive Victory*, 598.

3. See the discussion in chapter 16, "A New Square Law," in Dupuy, *Understanding War*, 221–35.

4. The U.S. archival records from the Vietnam era are now open, and good data are available from the U.S. unit records, even though some of the U.S. Army record keeping is the worst we have seen in over a hundred years of records. The North Vietnamese Army and the Viet Cong did keep records, although access and exploration have been limited.

5. See Clodfelter, *Vietnam in Military Statistics*, 255, 257, 258. The estimate of 731,000 is from Clodfelter.

6. (47,357 + 254,257 + 5,193)/731,000.

7. The exchange rate is almost 4 to 1 using the data from 1966 to 28 January 1973 presented in Clodfelter, *Vietnam in Military Statistics*, 258 (44,528 U.S. battle deaths + 161,814 South Vietnamese battle deaths + 5,193 Free World battle deaths compared to 821,037 VC/NVA battle deaths). This includes no reduction in VC/NVA casualties for overcounting.

8. We do have two smaller engagements from the Falklands in our databases.

9. Twenty-five Cubans killed, 59 wounded, 638 taken prisoner; no more than 45 Grenadians killed in action, 358 wounded. See Clodfelter, *Warfare and Armed Conflicts*, 1180. Also see the Raines, *Rucksack War*, 532, which has 19 U.S. killed and 125 wounded.

10. U.S. losses were 26 killed (no count of wounded given); Panamanians suffered 65 military deaths (out of 345 deaths). See Clodfelter, *Warfare and Armed Conflicts*, 1181.

11. Using these same data and his combat model, Dupuy calculated their combat effectiveness value as around 6.

12. And we do not know how to test this outside of using a combat model structure.

13. The Dupuy Institute has updated and revised both versions of these databases.

14. They are listed in the bibliography. Some of the reports are available at www.dupuyinstitute.org.

15. See Dupuy Institute, *Soviet/Russian Influence*, done for the Office of the Secretary of Defense, Net Assessment.

16. If the invasion is dated 19 March to 1 May, 2003, then there were 135 killed and 552 wounded for the months of March and April. The wounded-to-killed ratio was 4.09 to 1. There were also troops from the United Kingdom and small contingents from Australia and Poland, in addition to Kurdish and Iraqi militias. The total forces committed were 92,000 U.S. and 20,000 allied troops.

17. This is 149 combat deaths, 145 noncombat deaths, and 849 wounded for a wounded-to-killed ratio of 5.70 to 1.

18. See chapter 19 for a more detailed explanation of this estimate.

8. Outcome of Battles

1. See appendix 3 of this book for a list of the combat attrition verities.

2. Avellino is the 509th Parachute Battalion's attack on 14–18 September 1943. The engagement was truly an outlier, being the only battalion-level engagement in this data set (600 people attacking 1,200) and the only engagement where the outcome is classified as "other," being a case where the attacker is attacking while surrounded. The remaining engagements were mostly division-level actions that fit one of the other six outcome definitions.

3. We now have that many engagements but have not redone the analysis.

4. One of the better discussions is in four articles by H. W. Beuttel published in the *International TNDM Newsletter*. See "Iranian Casualties in the Iran-Iraq War: A Reappraisal"; "Iranian Casualties in the Iran-Iraq War (1980–1988)"; "Chemical Weapons and Iranian Casualties in the Iran-Iraq War"; and "Iranian Casualties in the Iran-Iraq War: A 2010 Update."

5. See the discussion on human factors (chapter 5) in Dupuy Institute, *Capture Rate Study, Phase III*.

9. Exchange Ratios

1. Also see appendix 3 of this book.

2. U.S. Army, *Field Manual 105-5* (1958), 80.

3. Allen, *Situational Force Scoring*, 20.

4. James Graham, First Marquis of Montrose (1612–50), commanded Scottish Highlander and Irish forces in seven major battles in 1644–45, winning six of them, and was outnumbered by his opponents in all seven battles. In 1650 he fought in one additional battle, and in this case he outnumbered his opponents. He lost that battle and lost his life at age thirty-seven. Only two of those battles are in our database (Tippermuir and Kilsyth), but they both had very lopsided casualty exchanges.

5. Lanchester, *Aircraft in Warfare*, 46–60. Lanchester provided no data to support these claims but relied on an intellectual argument based on a gross misunderstanding of ancient warfare.

6. This version of the database was still being expanded at this time.

7. In particular, see Fain, "The Lanchester Equations and Historical Warfare," 73.

10. The Combat Value of Superior Awareness

1. The Battle of Kadesh appears to have been an ambush of the lead element of the Egyptian forces by the Hittites, so obviously one side did not have good situational awareness.

2. The data consisted of engagements from the following campaigns: Fall of France, 15 May 1940, with 1 case; North Africa, 11 April–17 June 1941, with 5 cases; Crete, 20–27 May 1941, with 1 case; Tunisia, 14 February–23 March 1943, with 5 cases; Salerno, 9–18 September 1943, with 14 cases; Volturno, 13 October–4 November 1943, with 39 cases; Barbara Line, 5–14 November 1943, with 15 cases; Garigliano, 2–9 December 1943, with 25 cases; Rapido-Garigliano, 20–21 January 1944, with 2 cases; Anzio, 25 January–23 February 1944, with 18 cases; Rome, 12 May–4 June 1944, with 23 cases; North Italian 13–17 September 1944, with 1 case; Kursk (LII Corps and XLVIII Pan-

zer Corps), 4–18 July 1943, with 49 cases; Kursk (ss Panzer Corps, III Panzer Corps, and Corps Raus), 4–18 July 1943, with 42 cases; Kharkov II, 12–20 February 1943, with 11 cases; Kharkov III, 7–15 March 1943, with 32 cases; and Kharkov IV, 18–23 August 1943, with 12 cases. Temporally, while these battles occur over a time span in excess of four years, 97 percent of them cover a sixteen-month period from February 1943 to June 1944. They include a mixture of nations. This is important to consider since not all armies performed the same or operated in a similar manner. In all cases one side consisted of the Germans; the opposing sides were French defending in 1 case, United States attacking in 71 cases, United Kingdom attacking in 51 cases, United States defending in 11 cases, United Kingdom defending in 15 cases, Soviets attacking in 42 cases, and Soviets defending in 104 cases.

3. Under the U.S. Fifth Army were the 3rd, 34th, 36th, and 45th Infantry Divisions and 1st Armored Division with the II and VI Corps, along with elements of the 82nd Airborne Division. Under the UK X Corps were the 46th and 56th Infantry Divisions and 7th Armoured Division (which departed for England in December 1943). The UK Eighth Army included the V and XIII Corps and the 1st, 5th, and 78th Infantry Divisions, the Indian 4th and 8th Infantry Divisions, the 2nd New Zealand Division, the 1st Canadian Infantry Division, and the 5th Canadian Armoured Division.

4. This includes the 3rd Panzer Grenadier Division, 15th Panzer Grenadier Division, 29th Panzer Grenadier Division, and 90th Panzer Grenadier Division; Hermann Göring Panzer Division, 16th Panzer Division, and 26th Panzer Division; 1st FJD; and 65th Infantry Division, 94th Infantry Division, and 305th Infantry Division ID.

5. Dupuy began work in 1962 as Trevor N. Dupuy and Associates (TNDA); the company then became the Historical Evaluation and Research Organization (HERO), then Data Memory Systems Incorporated (DMSI). These were all intellectual predecessors to the Dupuy Institute, established in 1992.

11. The Combat Value of Surprise

1. Dated 14 June 1993 and superseded by *Field Manual 3-0: Operations* on 14 June 2001, which still lists nine principles of war in paragraphs 4-33 to 4-49: objective, offensive, mass, economy of force, maneuver, unity of command, security, surprise, and simplicity. Surprise is described in paragraph 4-47: "Surprise is the reciprocal of security. Surprise results from taking actions for which an enemy or adversary is unprepared. It is a powerful but temporary combat multiplier. It is not essential to take the adversary or enemy completely unaware; it is only necessary that he become aware too late to react effectively. Factors contributing to surprise include speed, information superiority, and asymmetry." Also see appendix 1 of this book.

2. Clausewitz, *On War*, 360: "Surprise becomes effective when we suddenly face the enemy at one point with far more troops than he expected. This type of numerical superiority is quite distinct from numerical superiority in general: it is the most powerful medium in the art of war."

3. For example, see Dupuy Institute, *Capture Rate Study, Phases I & II*, appendix 10.

4. Dupuy, *Numbers, Predictions and War*, 160, 153, 155, 201.

5. Dupuy, *Attrition*, 151.

6. If based on percentage of attacker wins, the change is a 72 percent better result (86/50 = 1.72). If based on the percentage of outcomes IV–VI, the change is 26 percent better (72/57 = 1.26). If based on the change in ratio of attacker to defender scores, the difference is 61 percent (1.7456/1.0857 = 1.61). The average of these three different looks at the data is 53 percent ((1.72 + 1.26 + 1.61)/3 = 1.53).

7. We ignored the "defender much more knowledgeable" category due to the small number of data points and very extreme results and instead concentrated on the other four categories for information advantage. If based on percentage of attacker wins, the change is a 60 percent better result (80/50 = 1.60). If based on the percentage of outcomes IV–VI, the change is 21 percent worse (53/67 = 0.79). If based on the change in ratio of attacker to defender scores, the difference

is 22 percent (1.26/1.03 = 1.22). The average of these three different looks at the data is 20 percent ((1.60 + 0.79 + 1.22)/3 = 1.20).

8. The results are such that the outcomes favor the attacker as their situational awareness decreases. Just for completeness this comes out to a 23 to 50 percent change. If based on percentage of attacker wins, the change is a 40 percent better result (74/53 = 1.40). If based on the percentage of outcomes IV–VI, the change is 50 percent better (75/50 = 1.50). If based on the change in ratio of attacker to defender scores, the difference is 23 percent (.1.29/1.05 = 1.23). The average of these three different looks at the data is 38 percent ((1.40 + 1.50 + 1.23)/3 = 1.38).

9. If based on percentage of attacker wins, the change is an 80 percent better result (83/46 = 1.80). If based on the percentage of outcomes IV–VI, the change is 33 percent better (68/51 = 1.33). If based on the change in ratio of attacker to defender scores, the difference is 50 percent (1.47/0.98 = 1.50). The average of these three different looks at the data is 54 percent ((1.80 + 1.33 + 1.50)/3 = 1.54).

12. The Nature of Lower Levels of Combat

1. See appendix 3 of this book.

2. Based on a meeting in 1998 with Don Hakenson, director, Center for Unit Records Research, Records Management and Declassification Agency. Dupuy Institute, *Records Management Survey Meeting*. McLean VA: 20 October 1998, 24.

3. HERO was one of four companies Dupuy founded during the period from 1962 and 1992. The others were TNDA and DMSI, which were sometimes run concurrently with HERO, and the Dupuy Institute. All companies did the same kind of work, had some of the same staff, and were effectively direct descendants of the previous organization. For a more detailed discussion see Lawrence, "A Brief History of Trevor N. Dupuy's Organizations."

Table 12.1 is from Historical Evaluation and Research Organization, *Handbook on Ground Forces*, 75. The data presented in the report are the same as in the book, with no further detail provided. See also Historical Evaluation and Research Organization, *Historical Survey of Casualties*, report 99 (previously 97). The data for this report included 35 days of division-level combat, 82 days of regimental-level combat, and 128 days of battalion-level combat. They were all one-sided (United States in World War II) data. They report that the average daily rate of battle casualties for a division was 2.08 percent, for a regiment 3.58 percent, and for a battalion 5.56 percent (see page 86).

4. The database was part of what was used to develop the QJM database, which was later used to create the Land Warfare Data Base, which was used as the seed for the Dupuy Institute's databases.

5. Figure 12.1 is from Perez, "Exactly How the Unit Size Modifiers Are Calculated," 22.

6. Historical Evaluation and Research Organization, *Handbook on Ground Forces*, 121.

7. Historical Evaluation and Research Organization, *Casualty Estimates for Contingencies*, 21. This report was the source of some of the data in the previous table. The same data, with the numbers as percentages (reduced by a factor of 10), are provided in Dupuy, *Attrition*, 69.

8. These data are also presented in Dupuy, *Attrition*, 76, converted to percentages, but with the World War II percentage figures inserted from page 42. The data in the report are different; they are presented in table 12.3.

9. The published report was Data Memory Systems, *Quantified Judgment Model*, report 124. The actual data are in the Dupuy Institute file: TNDM-Low Intensity Combat, dated 1992, briefing no. 1660, "Simulating Combat in Low Intensity Conflict."

10. Hartley in *Topics in Operations Research* did a multiple regression model using the data from HERO's Land Warfare Data Base. The *Chairman of the Joint Chiefs of Staff Guide 3161* was a series of casualty look-up tables based on historical data. A large part of that data was provided under contract by DMSI and HERO.

11. There were also some issues with short and sharp engagements that lasted less than four hours. Converting the data to daily loss rates sometimes resulted in a very high figure. Conversely, when we modeled engagements of fewer than four hours we often underestimated loss rates.

13. The Effects of Dispersion on Combat

1. See appendix 1 of this book.

2. This work was originally done in 1996, before we divided the Land Warfare Data Base into parts based on unit size and period and before we added hundreds of additional modern engagements (post-1900). It is an earlier version of the database that is used elsewhere in this book, although there have been no changes made to the engagements before 1900 nor any additional pre-1900 engagements added. We have not updated this analysis with the more recent versions of the database that was used for the other chapters of this book, but as can be seen from the data there, the additional data would not change the pattern or results of this discussion.

3. Dupuy recommended a multiplier of 2.0 (*Numbers, Predictions and War*, 219).

4. In the original construct, for the purpose of measuring the effects of weapons, Dupuy envisioned the maximum density of an array of targets as being one man per square meter or one million men in a square kilometer. This is an improbable density figure that never occurred in the real world, although it is representative of some ancient armies' deployed phalanx formations (although they were never a kilometer deep). A dispersion of 3,000 for World War II combat means this improbable density figure is divided by 3,000 to provide a figure of 333 men per square kilometer. This construct is primarily used to explain the continued degradation in the killing effectiveness of weapons, even though the weapons' ability to kill has greatly improved. See Dupuy, *Understanding Wars*, 84; Dupuy, *Numbers, Predictions and Wars*, 28–30.

5. This is from the World War II data: (4,169 + 1,814)/2 = 2,992.

6. There were six battles from the Russo-Japanese War (1904–5) in this data set. Perhaps they should be placed at the beginning of period 3 (1912–20) rather than the end of period 2 (1816–1905).

7. In particular the work done by Dean Hartley (Oakridge) with the Land Warfare Data Base and Paul Davis (RAND).

14. Advance Rates

1. See appendix 2 of this book.

2. Historical Evaluation and Research Organization, *Opposed Rates of Advance*.

3. ATLAS was a campaign model designed in the 1960s by Research Analysis Corporation. It assigned a single score to a division in order to model corps-, army-, and theater-level engagements (as is similarly done for many commercial war games). CEM was the primary model used by the CAA from the 1970s until it was replaced a few years ago by RAND's Joint Integrated Contingency Model, which is partly based on Dupuy's work. See Davis, "The Influence of T. N. Dupuy's Research."

4. Davis, "The Influence of T. N. Dupuy's Research," i.

5. Helmbold, *Rates of Advance*. In Helmbold's defense, the QJM and TNDM also had such a construct, even though Dupuy too claimed there was no clear relationship between force ratios and advance rates.

6. See Dupuy, *Understanding War*, 154, 155; Dupuy Institute, *Capture Rate Study, Phases I & II*, 64.

7. This one used selected engagements from our databases and consisted of only 202 cases.

8. This is a somewhat mismatched data set, as the urban warfare cases have a higher average force ratio and a lower average advance rate. For more details, see chapter 16 on the effect of urban terrain on advance rates. Seven cases were removed due to incomplete data on the advance rate, leaving us with forty-three urban and conurban cases and eighty-seven nonurban cases.

9. Of these, seventy-one were from the Ardennes Campaign.

15. Casualties

1. See appendix 3 of this book.

2. Historical Evaluation and Research Organization, *Handbook on Ground Forces*, 79. This was drawn from three works by Theodore A. Dodge: *Alexander*, *Hannibal*, and *Caesar*. The rate applies only for the winners. For the losers he simply states "usual massacre."

3. Beebe and De Bakey, *Battle Casualties*, 34. This figure was created by taking an average of the ratios provided in Longmore, *Gunshot Injuries*, 588–90. Data cover various battle and war totals, from Blenheim in 1704 to the end of the Franco-Prussian War in 1871.

4. Historical Evaluation and Research Organization, *Handbook on Ground Forces*, 81; Dupuy, *Attrition*, 49. The actual figures used from *Handbook*, 205, were KIA 69,982, WIA 318,200, DOW 44,775. The killed in action figures include deaths among prisoners.

5. See Dupuy, *Understanding War*, page 178. Also see appendix 3 of this book.

6. Gulf War data from Congressional Research Service, *American War and Military Operations*.

7. The source for these figures is iCasualties.org, whose reports are mostly based on U.S. DOD reporting.

U.S. figures for Iraq killed by service are 3,294 army, army reserve, and army national guard (2,594 hostile, 700 nonhostile); 1,022 marine and marine reserve (849 and 173); 104 navy and naval reserve (64 and 40); 57 air force and air national guard (30 and 27); and 8 others (7 and 1). This is a total of 4,465 as identified by service. U.S. figures for Iraq wounded by service are 22,516 for the army, 8,622 for the marines, 637 for the navy, and 448 for the air force. This creates a wounded-to-killed ratio by force of 8.68 to 1 for the army, 10.16 to 1 for the marines, 9.95 to 1 for the navy, and 14.93 to 1 for the air force.

U.S. figures for Afghanistan killed by service are 1,613 army, army reserve, and army national guard (1,292 hostile, 321 nonhostile); 441 marine and marine reserve (373 and 73); 126 navy and naval reserve (84 and 42); 106 air force and air national guard (66 and 40); and 11 others (10 and 1). This is a total of 2,297 as identified by service. U.S. figures for Afghanistan wounded by service are 12,309 for army, 4,630 for marines, 339 for navy, and 396 for air force. This creates a wounded-to-killed ratio by force of 9.53 to 1 for the army, 12.41 to 1 for the marines, 4.04 to 1 for the navy, and 6.00 to 1 for the air force.

8. This is based on 1,462 killed and 72,807 wounded. Dupuy writes in *Attrition*, "The raw data for World War I shows a ratio of wounded-to-killed of 5.96 which is significantly higher than in most of the other wars. This is because slightly more than one-third of the total casualties, or 72,773 casualties, were caused by poison gas. However, less than 2% of the total gas casualties were killed in action, and less than 2% of the survivors of gas injuries died of their gas-related injuries" (50).

9. See U.S. Department of the Army, Office of the Surgeon General, *Textbook of Military Medicine*, 58.

10. U.S. Department of the Army, Office of the Surgeon General, *Textbook of Military Medicine*, 60, 61, 64, 65. The UK data were based on a sampling of 3,609 out of the approximately 50,000 British casualties suffered over the six-week campaign. The U.S. data came from Reister, *Medical Statistics in World War II*. The Korean War data came from Reister, *Battle Casualties and Medical Statistics*. The Vietnam War data came from S. Neel, *Medical Support of the U.S. Army*.

11. Based on rifle and small arms lethalities ranging from 0.30 to 0.39 (with the lethality figures of 0.26 and 0.49 not used).

12. Based on artillery or fragmentation lethalities ranging from 0.07 to 0.27.

13. Clodfelter, *Vietnam in Military Statistics*, 241.

14. Dupuy, *Attrition*, 58, 59. I left out the table "Causes of Died of Wounds in 20th Century Wars (U.S. only)."

15. Regarding the Soviet Army data, the number of missing declined, with 19,596 MIA in the first period and 13,205 MIA in the second period. Other analysis has shown that at least 75 percent of the missing were captured by the Germans. See Dupuy Institute, *Capture Rate Study, Phase III*.

16. The UK data are not very useful, as their overall losses were very low before 2 January.

17. But it cannot be measured statistically as the databases cover the entire population of the Ardennes Campaign and the southern portion of the Battle of Kursk. The question is whether the data from the Ardennes Campaign and the Battle of Kursk can be used to draw more general conclusions about the nature of combat.

18. German losses were 6 killed, 77 wounded, and 14 missing in the engagement "Rakovo-Novenkoye I" on 16 July 1943. They had only 1 missing (no killed and wounded) in the engagement "6th PzD Prepares to Attack" on 4 July 1943. In their defensive engagement "The 106th Infantry Division Defends" on 18 July 1943, they had 2 killed, 6 wounded, and 4 missing. In contrast, in the engagement "The 320th ID Crosses the Donets" on 5 July 1943 the attacking Germans had 254 killed, 1,207 wounded, and 202 missing.

19. Paraphrased from comments made during a meeting in Moscow in September 1995. Dr. Sverdlov was a professor at the Frunze Military Academy, a veteran of World War II, and an author.

20. The wounded-to-killed ratio was 5.51 for the 1st Brigade, 5th Infantry Division (Mechanized); 6.57 for the 1st Cavalry Division; 6.12 for the 101st Airborne Division; and 6.32 for the 23rd Infantry Division. See Bellamy and Lawrence, *Why Is Marine Combat Mortality Less*. Note that all these wounded-to-killed ratios calculated from operational records probably do not include those people who died of wounds after they left the division hospital. As we are comparing divisions with divisions, this is probably not generating a distortion in our analysis.

21. U.S. Department of the Army, Office of the Surgeon General, *Textbook of Military Medicine*, 65.

22. Data from iCasualties.org, with 1,392 killed from IEDs out of 2,745 killed through the end of April 2014.

23. See Clodfelter, *Warfare and Armed Conflicts*, 785, for World War I data. U.S. Army figures are 50,510 KIA and 193,663 WIA; USMC 2,461 KIA and 9,520 WIA. A separate compilation of U.S. Army losses shows 36,931 KIA and 13,973 DOW for a total of 50,604 battle deaths and 198,059 wounded; the wounded-to-killed ratio is 3.91, with 7.05 percent DOW (assuming the DOW are not counted among the wounded).

See Clodfelter, *Warfare and Armed Conflicts*, 958, for World War II data: U.S. Army 234,874 KIA and 565,861 WIA; USMC 19,733 KIA and 67,207 WIA. U.S. Army data included air corps data. Clodfelter, *Warfare and Armed Conflicts*, 696, lists U.S. Army Air Forces (USAAF) losses of 50,451 battle deaths and 18,447 wounded (and 39,773 POW and 9,799 MIA). These subtracted from the U.S. Army data provide the ratio for World War II without the USAAF.

See Clodfelter, *Warfare and Armed Conflicts*, 1,216, for Korean War data: U.S. Army 27,704 KIA and 77,596 WIA; USMC 4,267 KIA and 23,744 WIA.

See Clodfelter, *Warfare and Armed Conflicts*, 1,322, for Vietnam War data: U.S. Army 30,839 battle deaths and 96,811 WIA; USMC 13,053 battle deaths and 66,134 WIA (hospitalized wounded).

24. We have also done the same comparison by division for World War I and for the thirty-four divisions that were part of the American Expeditionary Force; their average wounded-to-killed ratio was 3.84. This probably included gas casualties.

25. These include the six-month-long fight on Guadalcanal (7 August 1942–7 February 1943), where the 1st Marine Division had a wounded-to-killed ratio of 2.53, the 2nd Marine Division 3.47, the Americal Division 2.54, and the 25th Infantry Division 2.03. It includes the second part of the Solomon Islands Campaign (2 July 1943–15 June 1944), where the U.S. Army on New Georgia had a ratio of 3.54, and the 3rd Marine Division on Bougainville had a ratio of 3.66. In the Gilbert Islands (November 1943) the 27th Infantry Division at Makin Island had a ratio of 2.30, while the 2nd Marine Division had a ratio of 2.05. In New Britain (15 December 1943–March 1944) the 1st Marine Division at Cape Gloucester had a ratio of 2.59, while the force as a whole had a ratio of 2.84. In the Marshall Islands (29 January–February 1944) the 7th Infantry Division at Kwajalein had a ratio of 5.95, while the 4th Marine Division at Roi-Namur had a ratio of 2.88, and the mixed army and marine force of Eniwetok had a ratio of 2.89.

The Mariana Islands consisted of three operations under the command of the V Amphibious Corps. At Saipan (15 June–July 1944) the marines had a ratio of 3.51, while the entire force had a ratio of 4.21. At Guam (21 July–10 August 1944) the marines had a ratio of 3.46, while the total forces had a ratio of 4.38. At Tinian the 2nd and 4th Marine Divisions had a ratio of 4.67.

The Palau Islands (15 September–27 November 1944) consisted of the 1st Marine Division at

Peleliu with a ratio of 4.47 and the 81st Infantry Division at Peleliu with a ratio of 5.52. The USMC ratio for all losses was 4.22; the U.S. Army's was 5.06; and the U.S. Navy's was 3.20.

See the five-volume official history for more details: Frank and Shaw, *Victory and Occupation*, 395, 587, 636–37, 797, 884.

26. Clodfelter, *Warfare and Armed Conflicts*, 931.

27. This issue was first brought to my attention by Dr. Ronald F. Bellamy (Col., USA, ret).

28. Reister, *Battle Casualties and Medical Statistics*, 4. The official total from the Adjutant General's Report shows 19,585 killed in action (including 251 killed after capture) and 79,526 wounded in action. The Adjutant General's battle casualty report shows a total of 27,704 battle deaths among U.S. Army personnel in Korea. In addition to the 19,585 killed in action (of which 251 were killed after capture), 2,034 died of wounds (including 104 who died while captured), 3,791 were declared dead from missing in action, and 2,294 died of nonbattle causes while captured or missing. See Reister, *Battle Casualties and Medical Statistics*, 4, 16.

29. Reister, *Battle Casualties and Medical Statistics*, 16.

30. Meid and Yingling, *U.S. Marine Operations in Korea*, 575.

31. Clodfelter, *Vietnam in Military Statistics*, 255. The source of his figures is Office of the Assistant Secretary of Defense (Comptroller), Directorate of Information.

32. Bellamy and Lawrence, *Why Is Marine Combat Mortality Less*.

33. Data assembled from the iCasualties.org databases.

34. The lower figure comes from comparing the marine wounded-to-killed figure to the ratio for all army divisions that served in the Pacific to the marine wounded-to-killed figure (3.41/3.22). The higher figure comes from comparing the marine figures to the army in the Pacific figures (3.41/2.62).

35. The lower figure comes from comparing the 3rd Marine Division's ratio to the average of the ratio for the 1st Cavalry and 101st Airborne Divisions (7.10/(6.57+6.12/2)). The higher figure comes from comparing the 1st Marine Division's ratio to the American Division's ratio (8.68/6.32). Those two units were certainly involved in very similar operations.

36. The lower figure comes from comparing the marine ratio from Iraq to the army's ratio from Iraq (10.16/8.68). The higher figure comes from comparing the marine ratio from Afghanistan to the army's ratio from Afghanistan (13.13/9.98). A comparison of the ratios from Fallujah (7.91/6.00) provides a figure of 32 percent.

37. See Bellamy and Lawrence, *Why Is Marine Combat Mortality Less*. While we believe this difference is primarily because of different reporting systems, it may also be due to different evacuation priorities.

38. The Adjutant General's reporting procedures excluded those superficially wounded who returned to duty from aid stations and the like without losing time, as did the Statistical Health Report after December 1944. As Beebe and De Bakey note, "Counts of wounded in the Statistical Health Report cover all men losing a day or more of time whether or not admitted to hospital, but prior to a change issued in December 1944 additional cases carded for record only (men losing no time) were also included. Procedures of The Adjutant General, however, dictated the exclusion of the living wounded who were not admitted to hospital but who did lose some time in more forward installations. Because of an apparent lack of uniform instructions as to what constituted a hospital, however, theater practice seems to have varied in this respect" (*Battle Casualties*, 7).

39. German soldiers in World War II had to spend three days in the hospital to be counted as wounded, compared to one day for the U.S. Army. This probably did not make a big change in the relative casualty count between these forces. The UK counting rules in World War II were similar to the U.S. Army's.

40. Reister, *Medical Statistics in World War II*, table 1, p. 4.

41. This was according to the Surgeon General. The Adjutant General reported 79,526 wounded. See Reister, *Battle Casualties and Medical Statistics*.

42. Actually referred to as "nonfatal wounds, hospital care not required" in table 1051 of U.S.

Department of Defense, Office of the Assistant Secretary of Defense (Comptroller), Directorate for Information, Operations and Control, 15 January 1976. For the U.S. Marine Corps the numbers were 51,399 "nonfatal wounds, hospital care required" and 37,234 "nonfatal wounds, hospital care not required."

43. Bellamy and Lawrence, *Why Is Marine Combat Mortality Less*, figure 143. For the complete definition see appendix 1 of Lawrence, "Background Paper on Wounded-to-Killed Ratios."

44. The manual also notes, "However, injuries due to the elements or to self-inflicted wounds are not to be considered as sustained in action and are thereby not to be interpreted as battle casualties. Examples of injuries not to be interpreted as battles casualties are: frostbite, 'battle fatigue,' sunstroke, heat exhaustion and diseases not verified as cases of biological warfare." *Wounded in action not evacuated* was also defined: "A term to describe all personnel wounded in action and not evacuated beyond the regimental level collecting and clearing agency." See Bellamy and Lawrence, *Why Is Marine Combat Mortality Less*, figures 139, 140, 141; appendix 1 of Lawrence, "Background Paper on Wounded-to-Killed Ratios."

45. Dr. Cole was responsible for managing the publication of the Army Green Book series, the U.S. Army's official history of World War II. He also authored or coauthored several books in the series and was later a vice president of Research Analysis Corporation. This conversation occurred in early 1989 at a meeting at DMSI. He told me that some of his British compatriots claimed the Germans counted fewer wounded because of the three-day rule mentioned earlier.

46. Table 15.30 includes all German ground forces, including SS and Paratroop units, which for administrative purposes did not report to the German Army. Data from Dupuy et al., *Hitler's Last Gamble*, 464–77 apply only to divisions and independent brigades and do not include independent attached battalions and other smaller units, headquarters, or other nondivisional units. Table 15.31 loss data were compiled from the unit records of the more than seventy divisions and corps engaged.

47. See Historical Evaluation and Research Organization, *Historical Analysis of Wartime Replacement*.

48. The Dupuy Institute conducted a survey and created a database of over 150 combat models and casualty estimation methodologies. See Dupuy Institute, *Casualty Estimation Methodologies Study*.

49. See the four capture rate studies conducted by the Dupuy Institute: (1) *Capture Rate Study, Phases I & II*; (2) *Capture Rate Study, Phase III*; (3) *Capture Rate Study: Medical Requirements for EPW, Phase IV*; and (4) *Capture Rate Study: EPWs in Small Scale Contingency Operations, Phase IV (Part 2)*.

50. Again, see the Dupuy Institute's capture rate studies.

16. Urban Legends

1. For example, McLaurin et al., *Modern Experience in City Combat*; Leitch et al., *Analysis of Casualty Rates and Patterns*; Edwards, *Mars Unmasked*; Glenn, *Heavy Matter*.

2. Glenn, *Heavy Matter*.

3. For Boulogne this was the Canadian 3rd Infantry Division attack from 17 to 23 September 1944. For Calais, the Canadian 3rd Infantry Division attack from 25 to 30 September 1944. For Dieppe, the Canadian 2nd Infantry Division attack on 1 September 1944. For Le Havre, the UK I Corps attack from 10 to 12 September 1944. For Brest, the U.S. VIII Corps attack from 26 August to 21 September 1944.

4. See Dupuy Institute, *Measuring the Effects of Combat in Cities, Phase I*.

5. A complete set of the analytical tables used to generate this summary (including the results for outcomes I, II, VI, and VII) and those following may be found in appendix 6 of the original Phase I report, which is at the Dupuy Institute website. The original report is Dupuy Institute, *Measuring the Effects of Combat in Cities, Phase I*.

6. See Dupuy Institute, *Measuring the Effects of Combat in Cities, Phase I*, appendix 6, table 2.

7. This last could be argued, and has been argued endlessly before. However, limiting the count to combat and combat support personnel, and those service and service support personnel found

in a division and its attachments, simplifies the measurement process in the DuWar DLEDB, which, after all, is a division-level database.

8. In the total data set there were some cases of zero armor losses and zero armor presence as well as an occasional simple lack of any record regarding armor. In some cases it was evident that the armor loss data included combat and noncombat (mechanical) losses as well as both destroyed and damaged vehicles. The DuWar DLEDB armor losses do not distinguish between MBT and light tanks, and the percentage of armor loss figures are based on the total tanks on hand (MBT and light tanks). However, the loss of light tanks was usually minor in any case.

9. There were seven additional engagements of the German Totenkopf SS Division that were partially completed dealing with its operations to the north of Kharkov in March. These operations were against extremely scattered and disorganized opposition and extended over a very long front. There were some problems in identifying the opposition, and more research was needed; therefore these operations were not completed. Six of them were in rolling mixed and conurban terrain and one was in rolling mixed terrain. There were also six more engagements that could have been added from the 282nd Infantry Division defensive fighting in August. Five of these were in rolling mixed and conurban terrain and one was in withdrawal through urban terrain (effectively unopposed) to rolling mixed terrain. However, they were similar in nature to the other 12 August engagements so there was not much more that could be learned from them.

10. The Dupuy Institute continued adding more Kursk engagements to the database after this effort, so that there were eventually 192. The details of these are included in my book *Kursk: The Battle of Prokhorovka*.

11. These include the seven Totenkopf SS Division engagements that occurred north of Kharkov in March. Also, late in the project we discovered that one more round of research would be required to identify all the Soviet forces facing the German 282nd Infantry Division in August. It was not deemed worthwhile to delay the project for another three months to obtain the material for these last thirteen engagements.

12. The data are provided in detail in Dupuy Institute, *Measuring the Effects of Combat in Cities, Phase II*, 12–23.

13. A complete set of the analytical tables used to generate this summary (including the results for outcomes I, II, VI, and VII) and those following may be found in appendix 5 of Dupuy Institute, *Measuring the Effects of Combat in Cities, Phase II*.

14. Again, in the total data set there were some cases of zero armor losses and zero armor presence as well as an occasional simple lack of any record regarding armor. See Dupuy Institute, *Measuring the Effects of Combat in Cities, Phase I* for additional comments.

15. This was possible because initial Japanese strengths were well defined in documents captured during and after the battle, while their losses were known to have been about 100 percent.

16. The aggregate statistics of this work are provided in Dupuy Institute, *Measuring the Effects of Combat in Cities, Phase III*, 18–21.

17. A more detailed comparison is provided in Dupuy Institute, *Measuring the Effects of Combat in Cities, Phase III*, 22–29.

18. See especially Dupuy Institute, *Measuring the Effects of Combat in Cities, Phase I*, appendix 7.

19. See Dupuy Institute, *Measuring the Effects of Combat in Cities, Phase III*, 55, for a probable explanation for this outlier.

20. See in particular Dupuy Institute, *Capture Rate Study, Phases I & II*; Lawrence, *Measuring Human Factors*.

21. See Dupuy, *Attrition*, figure 25.

22. The exception here is the Second Battle of Fallujah in 2004, where an isolated force of over one thousand Muslim guerrillas stubbornly resisted the attacking U.S. force of over ten thousand over the course of forty-six days. This case is unusual, being a large force of guerrillas fighting a last stand, very similar to what occurred on Hue in 1968. It was not unusual in that

the U.S. advance rates and loss rates were particularly low. As this case had not occurred at the time this study was done, it was not included in these data. It does provide ample confirmation for our original study.

23. This factor is noted in a number of the reports at the time and especially in NARA 106-0.3 to 106-0.4, Sixth Army, Box 2406, Historical Reports, Luzon, Combat in Manila and Report of Operations—Battle of Manila and in NARA 214-0.4 to 214-0.8, XIV Corps, Box 4623, Lessons Learned—Defense of Cities. One of these buildings—although having one entire face blown away by American firepower—refused to collapse, but instead "bent." The building then simply settled to the ground intact, but slightly off plumb. Compare this to the tendency for modern buildings to collapse when placed under the asymmetrical stress of blast loading.

24. The typical U.S. experience in World War II was that units with an approximate strength of three thousand had an average daily casualty rate of 2.6 percent; for a strength of eight hundred it was about 9.5 percent. See Dupuy, *Attrition*, figure 25.

25. This is assuming of course that the attacker is in fact capable of successful offensive operations of any kind.

26. The rationalization that the attack was intended to complete the isolation of the Egyptian Army on the east bank of the Suez Canal is specious in the extreme. They were already effectively isolated; capturing the city was simply another potential bargaining chip at the peace table.

27. Modern concrete and steel high-rise construction techniques are not very resistant to blast effects, as was seen in the destruction of the Alfred P. Murrah Federal Building in Oklahoma City in April 1995. The more recent destruction of the World Trade Center in New York City highlights other obvious problems associated with modern building design.

28. With the possible exception of the Iran-Iraq War, which generated World War I–like stagnation.

29. It may also be said that the U.S. apparently has been the only nation to fully accept the cost of deploying these new systems and technologies.

30. The highest rate was at Chinese Farm I, when the Israelis' armor loss was 24.40 percent per day.

31. Although twenty German divisions were trapped in the pocket, less than half held positions in the city and its suburbs. Soviet attacks on the forces holding in the city were apparently rare, except for periodic air and artillery bombardment. Most of the attacks on the encircled forces were on the units defending outside the city.

17. The Use of Case Studies

1. For example, see Glenn, *Combat in Hell*, 7; Glenn, *Art of Darkness*, 5, 6; Glenn, *Heavy Matter*, 17.

2. A good analytical discussion of this phenomenon is provided in Rowland, *Stress of Battle*.

3. Glenn, *Heavy Matter*, 12.

4. McLaurin et al., *Modern Experience in City Combat*, 18. Curiously, in an otherwise excellent paper, this declaration regarding casualties is unsupported by any comprehensive collection of data or analysis in their case studies. Most of the cases contain no casualty data whatsoever.

5. Leitch et al., *Analysis of Casualty Rates and Patterns*, tables 19, 20, 21. The analytical underpinnings for these estimates are data taken from three case studies: the Battle for Hue in 1968, Operation Peace for Galilee in Lebanon 1982, and the Russian military operations in Chechnya.

6. Dupuy, *Attrition*, 42. After extensive research covering some thirty-five years of study and the analysis of over 135 engagements involving U.S. divisions in the European Theater of Operations (ETO), the highest single-day divisional loss rate found remains 10 percent. The 99th Infantry Division suffered that loss on 17 December 1944 in the Ardennes. (Close rivals for that claim would be the 106th Infantry Division on 19 December and the 17th Airborne Division on 8 January 1945, both also in the Ardennes.)

7. NARA RG 407, entry 427, 302-1, 2nd Infantry Division G-1 Reports, June to December 1944, box 5978. These reports were prepared some time after the battle and are obviously more accurate than the Estimated Loss Reports found in RG 331, Records of Allied Operational and Occupation

Headquarters, World War II, SHAEF (Supreme Headquarters Allied Expeditionary Forces) Command Staff, G-1 Admin Section Decimal File 1944–45, box 38, 12th Army Group G-1 Daily Summaries and RG 407, entry 427, European Theater of Operations Theater Historian, Combat Interviews, box 24014, folder 14, Operations of the 2nd Infantry Division at Brest.

8. See Operations of the 2nd Infantry Division at Brest.

9. It may be that the losses of 10 September were more indicative of the previous fighting in the fortified belt around the city. On 9 September the rate was a very similar 0.636 percent.

10. The Brest city wall was similar in construction—masonry-faced rammed earth—and layout to that encountered by U.S. Marines during the Battle for the Citadel of Hue in Vietnam during the Tet Offensive of 1968. However, the Brest wall was about twice as thick and higher, and the Germans had improved it by constructing modern steel-reinforced concrete emplacements to guard the exterior, as well as barracks, tunnels, and other emplacements to strengthen the interior.

11. 1st Infantry Division, Office of the A.C. of S., G-1, Report of Operations for October, dated 1 November, NARA RG 407, entry 427, 301-1, June 1944 to 31 December 1948, box 5672.

12. History of the VII Corps for the period 1–31 October 1944, NARA RG 407, entry 427, 207-0.3 6 June to December 1944, box 3827.

13. That the German artillery support increased drastically from the start to the end of the battle is reported in the comments regarding the strength of the German barrages found in the American records, and in the German records as well. A German analysis noted that the number of their firing batteries increased by 13 percent from the period 1–10 October to 11–20 October and that the number of rounds they fired increased by 50 percent. See "Beurteilung der feindl. Artillerie vor dem LXXXI.A.K." (Estimate of Enemy Artillery Opposed to the LXXI Army Corps), NARA Microfilm RG 242, T314, R1597, F0246.

14. NARA RG 407, entry 427, ETO Theater Historian, Combat Interviews, box 24035, folder 84, 29th Infantry Division.

15. According to Major Weintrob, the Table of Authorized Equipment for the division psychiatrist consisted of only "a sphygmomanometer, a set of five (5) tuning forks, a percussion hammer, and an ophthalamoscope." NARA RG 407, entry 427, ETO Theater Historian, Combat Interviews, box 24035, folder 84, 29th Infantry Division.

16. Statistics on WIA returned to duty are incomplete.

17. Nonfatal battle casualties admitted in the period were 3,002, for a total of 3,554, including the combat exhaustion cases.

18. Sick cases were also referred to as "disease and non-battle injuries," a category that at the time included neuropsychiatric cases or combat exhaustion.

19. 1st Infantry Division, Office of the A.C. of S., G-1, Report of Operations, dated 1 October, 1 November, and 1 December 1944, in NARA RG 407, entry 427, 301-1, June 1944 to 31 December 1948, box 5672. Expected sick rates for September were 0.210 percent, for October 0.240 percent, and for November 0.27 percent. By this criteria the 1st Division's experience in November, when it was not engaged in major urban operations, was very high indeed. See Dupuy, *Attrition*, 57, for average sick rate experience by month for U.S. divisions in the ETO.

20. Glenn, *Heavy Matter*, 12.

21. Report on the Artillery with the VIII Corps in the Reduction of Brest, 22 August–19 September 1944, NARA RG 407, entry 427, 208-ART-0.3 to 208-ART-0.7, August 1944, box 4090.

22. Report on the Artillery with the VIII Corps in the Reduction of Brest.

23. Based on the unit of fire data in the VIII Corps Artillery reports.

24. Love, *Artillery Usage in World War II*.

25. See History of the VII Corps for the period 1–31 October 1944. Based on Love's averages for all postures, the average rate for the fifty-four 105mm and twelve 155mm howitzers would be 77.87 rounds-per-day and for an attack posture it would be 226.87 rounds-per-day.

26. History of the VII Corps for the period 1–31 October 1944.

27. History of the VII Corps for the period 1–31 October 1944.

28. VIII Corps reported that the "most effective weapons in close-in city fighting were found to be the BAR [Browning automatic rifle], the submachine gun, and the automatic carbine." "Fighting in Cities," NARA RG 407, entry 427, 208-0.3.0 to 208-0.10, box 3960.

29. At this time the infantry regiment was not authorized any submachine guns, but it had 293 pistols, 836 carbines, and 1,990 rifles.

30. "Fighting in Cities" notes that due to limited fields of fire machine guns offered little support for advancing troops and were used only to interdict enemy movement across streets.

31. "Fighting in Cities" notes that hand grenades were "essential" in urban fighting and that rifle grenades were "extensively" used.

32. See "Fighting in Cities."

33. The assumption that water consumption increases in a desert combat environment or that the consumption of hot food increases in a cold-weather environment (if conditions allow) is perfectly reasonable and may be supportable. However, the assumption that an urban environment increases consumption of food and water appears both unreasonable and unsupportable.

34. Love, *Artillery Usage in World War II*, Phase I report, 53–57.

35. NARA 214-0.3, XIV Corps, box 4621, Historical Reports, 1 May 44–15 June 1945. The composition and strength of the artillery component of XIV Corps varied considerably during the campaign. These are the most reasonable estimates of consumption based on our understanding of the daily average artillery strength of XIV Corps during the different time periods: 9 January–3 March, 16 75mm howitzers, 133.91 105mm howitzers, 53.71 155mm howitzers, and 12 155mm guns; 2 February–3 March, 24 75mm howitzers, 180 105mm howitzers, 61.2 155mm howitzers, and 12 155mm guns; 3 March–1 June, 24 75mm howitzers, 73.8 105mm howitzers, 34.6 155mm howitzers, and 2.60 155mm guns.

18. Modeling Warfare

1. For specific details see appendix G of Dupuy Institute, *Casualty Estimation Methodologies Study*.

2. See appendix A of Dupuy Institute, *Casualty Estimation Methodologies Study*. The Wilbur Payne paper is worth reading for many reasons. The building housing the CAA in Fort Belvoir, Virginia, is named after him.

3. By the Dupuy Institute in its various capture rate studies. See Dupuy Institute, *Capture Rate Study, Phases I & II*; Dupuy Institute, *Capture Rate Study: Phase III*.

4. This is not an insignificant point. To assemble and draw statistics from a set of unit records is a fairly time-consuming effort. To assemble and draw statistics from two sets of unit records takes at least twice as long. Added to that is the fact that one set will be in a different language. The real challenge, though, and what really is time-consuming, is that one then has to match up the opposing units, a more difficult task than most people envision. To date, only the Dupuy Institute has any extensive experience doing this.

5. In particular Theaterspiel used *Field Manual 101-10* as the basis for its attrition methodology. Data from *Field Manual 101-10* tables were still used in CAA's Concept Evaluation Model in the 1980s to help shape the outputs that came from the Combat Sample Generator as part of the Attrition Calibration process.

6. *Chairman of the Joint Chiefs of Staff Guide 3161*. This guide was built mostly from research provided by Dupuy's old company, DMSI. FORECAS by Christopher Blood of the Naval Health Research Center was developed from independent research on battalion logs of various U.S. Marine Corps units.

7. The .30 caliber rifle in 1944 had a value of 1 at 0–500 yards and 0.5 at 500–1,000 yards. The 1973 rifle had a value of 1 at 300 meters, 0.5 at 500 meters, and 0 at 1,000 meters. Light machine guns started with a value of 6, etc. Firepower scores did not exist for armor and field artillery in 1944 but did in later versions. The later versions evolved from the March 1944 version.

8. See Stockfisch, *Models, Data, and War*, 18–21.

9. The first mathematical ground combat models were developed by ORO in the early 1950s. In conjunction with Project ARMOR and Los Alamos, George Gamow investigated the application of electronic computers to Monte Carlo war games. He initiated project Tin Soldier "to provide a technique for the detailed analysis of military tactical doctrines and weapon design which approaches much more closely the military realism of actual battle (or at least practice maneuvers) than does the simple mathematical analysis of the past." Gamow, "Monte Carlo Method in Wargame Theory," April 1952, and Zimmerman, "The Application of Electronic Computers to Monte Carlo War Game Methods," November 1952, reprinted in Gamow and Zimmerman, *Mathematical Models for Ground Combat*.

ORO held a series of meetings in October 1952 to develop a game theory approach to tank engagements. From these meetings came a proposal for a simple game modeling tank-versus-tank combat called TATOO (Tank against Tank, Model 00). Although proposed for computer use, sample games of TATOO appear to have been played using only hand calculations. The lack of terrain representation led ORO to propose an expanded version. This requirement presumably led to the development of CARMONETTE, the first digital computer ground combat simulation, in 1953. Joseph C. Harrison Jr., "TATOO: A Tank Battle on the Digital Computer," December 1952, and W. Edward Cushan, "TOBOGGAN: Tank Battle Games," January 1953, reprinted in Clark et al., *War Gaming, Cosmogon, and Zigspiel*.

10. As of early 1965, ORO/RAC's suite of simulations included CARMONETTE at the tactical level, TACSPIEL at the division level, and THEATERSPIEL at the theater level, as well as several varieties of Quick Gaming. Richard Zimmerman, "Staff Memorandum: Speech to Trustees, 9 Jan 65 on The Spectrum of War Gaming of Ground Operations," RAC, McLean VA, February 1965.

11. Clark, *Casualties as a Measure*.

12. Clark, *Casualties as a Measure*, 34.

13. U.S. Army, *Field Manual 105-5* (1967), 128–33.

14. The two exceptions are the U.S. 106th Infantry Division in December 1944, which incidentally continued fighting after suffering more than 40 percent losses, and the Philippine Division in Bataan, which suffered 100 percent losses in one day in addition to very heavy losses in the days leading up to its surrender on 9 April 1942.

15. This was Historical Evaluation and Research Organization, *Forced Changes of Combat Posture*. The years 1954 to 1988 were not entirely quiet. See Historical Evaluation and Research Organization, *Defeat Criteria Seminar* and the significant article by Robert McQuie, "Battle Outcomes." Some of the results of the 1988 study were summarized in Dupuy, *Understanding Defeat*.

16. The 1988 study was the basis for Dupuy's *Understanding Defeat*.

17. See Dupuy Institute, *Casualty Estimation Methodologies Study*, where we actually do attempt to locate and list them all. It has been difficult to identify all combat models and find good descriptions of them. We believe we have identified at least 90 percent of them. We have managed to assemble basic descriptions on over 80 percent of those that we have identified.

18. See Dupuy Institute, *Casualty Estimation Methodologies Study*. This taxonomy was created by Dr. James Taylor and me, with comments provided by Richard Anderson, Jay Karamales, Dr. Shawn Woodford, Dr. Brian McCue, and Eugene Visco. While it is not the final word on taxonomies of casualty estimation methodologies, it is the most extensive such effort done to date.

19. To date the Dupuy Institute's capture rate study is the only example I know of a two-sided look-up table.

20. See Dupuy Institute, *Casualty Estimation Methodologies Study*, 17–20, 94–98 for a discussion of the problems with using Lanchester equations for casualty estimations of ground combat. The fundamental issue is that they have been tested multiple times against historical ground combat databases (including the Kursk Data Base and Ardennes Campaign Simulation Data Base, which I developed and managed) and so far have not been able to replicate the historical results.

21. This is in what is referred to as FM 101-10 (*Field Manual 101-10*) but at the time was the U.S. War Department's *Staff Officer's Field Manual*. I have not examined earlier usage of this but would not be surprised if the U.S. Army made use of one-sided historically based look-up tables before this.

22. U.S. Navy Lt. J. V. Chase first proposed the use of systems of equations to predict attrition, but his work was classified and never used in the industry. Lanchester's similar approach, published in late 1914, became the basis for use of differential calculus in attrition modeling.

23. Although CAA Attrition Calibration runs based on the Combat Sample Generator model could be considered another example of this.

24. This is an issue that Dupuy and many, many others have debated with the defense analytical community for a very long time. The exchange between Dupuy and Walt Hollis, undersecretary of the army (operations research), in the issue of *Armed Forced Journal* in 1986–87 is as good as any in addressing the heart of the issue. See Dupuy, "Can We Rely upon Computer Combat Simulations?" and Hollis, "Yes We Can Rely on Computer Combat Simulations." While this seemingly bitter disagreement was occurring publicly, Hollis was providing and continued to provide budget money to HERO (Dupuy's company) to develop the Ardennes Campaign Simulation Data Base for use in validating CEM, Force Concepts Evaluation Model (FORCEM), and Joint Theater Level Simulation (JTLS).

25. The need to determine the requirements for military police was part of the reason behind the Dupuy Institute's capture rate study.

26. This description is based on conversations in 1993–95 with retired Frunze Military Academy professors.

27. Shubik and Brewer, *Models, Simulations, and Games*.

28. Unlike the Dupuy Institute, they did not do the survey themselves but instead submitted a seventy-page questionnaire to 135 people and collected 132 responses. Among the models surveyed were ATLAS, CARMONETTE, CEM, TACSPIEL, and THEATERSPIEL. Eight models in our database were part of their survey.

29. Shubik and Brewer, *Models, Simulations, and Games*, 64, 69–70.

30. Stockfisch, *Models, Data, and War*, viii.

31. Stockfisch, *Models, Data, and War*, 129.

32. For example, see McQuie, "Military History"; Honig et al., *Report of the Army Models Committee*; Uhle-Wettler, "Computer Supported Studies and Military Experience"; Low, *Theater-Level Gaming and Analysis Workshop*; McEnany, "Uncertainties and Inadequacies in Theater Level Combat Analysis"; Hardison et al., *Review of Army Analysis*; Battilega and Grange, *Military Applications of Modeling*, Appendix A, "Some Critiques of Military Modeling"; Office of the U.S. Comptroller General, *Report to the Congress*; Wood, "Very Grave Suspicion"; *Army*, "In Pursuit of the Essence of War"; Dupuy, "Criticism of Combat Models Cite Unreliability of Results"; Dupuy, "Rebuttal Rebutted"; Dupuy, "Can We Rely upon Computer Combat Simulations?"; Dupuy, *Understanding War*.

33. Hollis, "Yes We Can Rely on Computer Combat Simulations."

34. The U.S. Army Concepts Analysis Agency is now called the Center for Army Analysis (CAA).

35. U.S. Department of the Army, Office of Deputy Chief of Staff, *Report of the Model Input Data and Process Subcommittee*, viii. The members of this subcommittee were the chairman, Dick Lester, Maj. David Block, Walter Clifford, Lt. Col. Matthew Difiore, Maj. David Fenimore, Col. Fred Gantzler, Brinton Harrison, Helga Knapp, Robert McConnell, Franklin McKie, John Riente, and Lt. Col. Henry Schroeder.

36. U.S. Department of the Army, Office of Deputy Chief of Staff, *Report of the Model Input Data and Process Subcommittee*, appendices D and E.

37. This was the Ardennes Campaign Simulation Data Base developed by HERO and originally managed by me.

38. Paul Berensen, Memorandum for Mike Bauman, director, TRADOC Analysis Center; Edgar Vandiver III, director, USA Concepts Analysis Agency; John McCarthy, director, U.S. Army Material Systems Analysis Activity, 21 January 1997 in *International TNDM Newsletter* 1, no. 4 (1997): 6.

39. In 1989 B. Stanley Pons of the University of Utah and Martin Fleischmann of the University of Southampton announced that they had successfully conducted an experiment that demonstrated practical cold fusion effects (fusion at room temperature, as opposed to in a nuclear reactor). As is essential in the scientific process many other scientists immediately reviewed their experiment. Failure to re-create the results disproved the claim of success.

40. This includes our own validation of the TNDM, which is discussed in chapter 19.

41. Again I have no budget figures, but I am aware that hundreds of people, especially if one counts all contractors, have been working in U.S. Army operations research in any given year.

42. The Dupuy Institute's estimate of the guerrilla war in Iraq is provided in Lawrence, *America's Modern Wars*.

43. In the ultimate irony, according to rumor, one casualty estimate overestimated the U.S. casualties in Iraq because it assumed a nasty urban fight for Baghdad.

44. The Gulf War resulted in 147 battle deaths, 236 other deaths, and 467 wounded. The Invasion of Iraq resulted in 140 fatalities (108 hostile and 32 nonhostile) and 551 wounded.

45. The United States lost 4,486 killed and 32,223 wounded in Iraq from March 2003 through 2012 and 2,301 killed and 17,674 wounded in Afghanistan from December 2001 through December 2013 (wounded count is only through September 2012). The war in Afghanistan is ongoing. The source of this data is the iCasualties.org website. The Dupuy Institute used to maintain its own separate database of these casualties and found little disagreement with the iCasualties.org figures. Total people killed from all causes in Iraq is estimated to be around 120,000 to 140,000 or higher. Iraq Body Count website reports 121,480–134,767 civilian deaths to violence, and a total of 180,000 violent deaths due to combat. I am not sure whether anyone has an estimate of total wounded. (Usually it is four to six times more.) In the past we have cross-checked the figures of Iraq Body Count, and I believe they are reasonable estimates. Total people killed from all causes in Afghanistan is probably at least half of the number killed in Iraq.

46. Morse and Kimball, *Methods of Operations Research*, 1. This revised edition (2003) was originally published in 1951 by Technology Press of MIT and John Wiley. The original volume was first published by the U.S. Navy in 1946.

19. Validation of the TNDM

1. Dupuy Institute, *TNDM: Manual*.

2. See Dupuy Institute, *Casualty Estimation Methodologies Study*, 139–44, for a list of criticisms and rebuttals to them, and a discussion of the weaknesses of the model.

3. It is unclear what these percentages specify. They are quoted from Dupuy Institute, *TNDM: General and Theoretical*, which was prepared by Trevor Dupuy. I suspect it is a measurement of the model's ability to predict winners and losers. No validation report based on this effort was ever published. Also, the validation figures seem to reflect the results after any corrections made to the model based on these tests. It does appear that the division-level validation was "incremental." We do not know if the earlier validation tests were tested back to the earlier data, but we have reason to suspect not.

4. The original QJM validation data were first published in Historical Evaluation and Research Organization, *Combat Data Subscription Service Supplement*. That effort used data from 1943 through 1973.

5. HERO published its QJM validation database in Historical Evaluation and Research Organization, *QJM Data Base*.

6. Dupuy Institute, *TNDM: General and Theoretical*.

7. This had the unfortunate effect of undervaluing World War II–era armor by about 75 percent relative to other World War II weapons when modeling World War II engagements. This left the Dupuy Institute with the compromise methodology of using the old OLI method for calculating armor (mobile fighting machines) for World War II engagements and using the new OLI method for calculating armor for modern engagements.

8. "Testimony of Col. T. N. Dupuy, USA, Ret., before the House Armed Services Committee, 13 Dec 1990," Dupuy Institute file 1-30, "Iraqi Invasion of Kuwait."

9. Dupuy, *Attrition*, 123–24.

10. See Gözel, "Fitting Firepower Score Models to the Battle of Kursk Data."

11. "Testimony of Col. T. N. Dupuy, USA, Ret., before the House Armed Services Committee."

12. "Testimony of Col. T. N. Dupuy, USA, Ret., before the House Armed Services Committee."

13. For example, the Wikipedia article on the Gulf War discusses Dupuy's estimate compared to others.

14. John P. Jumper, "In Gulf War, Precision Air Weapons Paid Off," *New York Times*, 14 July 1996, http://query.nytimes.com/gst/fullpage.html?res=9803eedb1e39f937a25754c0a960958260. The actual statement in the article is "The coalition air assault on Iraq forces in Kuwait results in fewer than 400 casualties versus Gen. H. Norman Schwarzkopf's prewar estimate of 10,000 to 20,000." The author was the deputy chief of staff, for plans and operations, U.S. Air Force, in 1996.

15. Brad Knickerbocker, "Pentagon's Quietest Calculation: The Casualty Count," *Christian Scientist Monitor*, 28 January 2003, http://www.csmonitor.com/2003/0128/p01s02-woiq.html.

16. Michael R. Gordon, "Cracking the Whip," *New York Times*, 27 January 1991, http://query.nytimes.com/gst/fullpage.html?res=9d0ceed8163ef934a15752c0a967958260.

17. Interview with Ted Koppel, *Nightline*, ABC, March 1991.

18. U.S. Casualties from https://www.va.gov/opa/publications/factsheets/fs_americas_wars.pdf. Other casualties from Clodfelter, *Warfare and Armed Conflicts*.

19. U.S. Department of Veterans Affairs, "Fact Sheet."

20. Zetterling, "CEV Calculations in Italy, 1943." See also Dupuy Institute, *Research Plan*.

21. See Gözel, "Fitting Firepower Score Models to the Battle of Kursk Data."

22. There are ten engagements in the database from six to eight days in length.

23. Not all of these studies have been posted to our website yet.

24. Combat effectiveness value is a figure used to adjust the relative combat value of one side. It represents the difference in morale, training, experience, and other intangible factors that exist in warfare. In effect, it tries to assign a value to human factors in combat. It is usually a value that you have to assign to one side, based on an understanding of these factors and their influence. Assigning a value of 1 means that both sides are at equal levels of competence in these areas, which the historical record clearly indicates is not the case.

25. More specifically there was also the 10th Panzer Brigade, which arrived on the battlefield a few days before the battle started. This brigade was supposed to command both the Gross Deutschland Panzer Regiment and the 39th Panzer Regiment, except the brigade commander had no staff and no command vehicles. Furthermore the commander of the Gross Deutschland Panzer Regiment simply ignored this arrangement and went about his own business. On the afternoon of 6 July, the commander of the brigade was put in reserve, and all the tanks of the two regiments were then assigned to the commander of the Gross Deutschland Panzer Regiment. When he was wounded, the former brigade commander took over the regiment.

26. Lawrence, "Validation of the TNDM at Battalion Level"; Lawrence, "The Second Test of the TNDM Battalion-Level Validations: Predicting Casualties."

27. Trevor N. Dupuy passed away in July 1995, and the validation was conducted in 1996 and 1997.

28. *International TNDM Newsletter* 1, no. 2: 59–61; no. 4: 17–18, 19–30; no. 5: 33–50; no. 6: 35–39. All are from 1996 and 1997.

29. For the battalion-level validation see the following, all by Lawrence: "Validation of the TNDM at Battalion Level"; "Validation of the Quantified Judgment Model"; "The First Test of the TNDM Battalion-Level Validations: Predicting the Winners"; "The Second Test of the TNDM Battalion-Level Validations: Predicting Casualties"; "Use of Armor in the 76 Battalion-level Engagements"; "The Second Test of the TNDM Battalion-Level Validations: Predicting Casualties, Final Scorecard."

For Zetterling's validation test see "CEV Calculations in Italy, 1943"; Lawrence, "Response to Niklas Zetterling's Article."

For the corps- and division-level validation see Lawrence, "Validation of the TNDM to Corps-Level Combat"; Lawrence, "Validation of the TNDM to Division-Level Combat"; Lawrence, "Summation of QJM/TNDM Validation Efforts."

All articles are in the *International TNDM Newsletter*, published by the Dupuy Institute.

20. Conclusions

1. More precisely: "This book is single-mindedly devoted to Understanding War, in the context of the significance of military history in fostering such an understanding through its contribution to a theory of combat" (Dupuy, *Understanding War*, xvii).

2. Specifically, we believe we have confirmed or validated timeless verities numbers 2 and 10, combat advance rate verities number 2, and combat attrition verities number 4 and 6.

3. We believe our work helps support timeless verities number 9, combat advance rate verities number 1, and combat attrition verities numbers 1, 2, 3, 7, 10, 20, 26, 27, and 28.

4. These are timeless verities number 1, 3, 4, 5, 6, 7, 8, 11, 12, and 13; combat advance rate verities number 3, 4, 5, 6, 7, 8, 9, 10, 11, 12, 13, 14, and 15; and combat attrition verities number 5, 8, 9, 11, 12, 13, 14, 15, 16, 17, 18, 19, 21, 22, 23, 24, and 25.

5. See Dupuy Institute, *Casualty Estimation Methodologies Study*, 270–72. In fact only four other major combat models have undergone a validation to historical data: ATLAS, CEM, JANUS, and VECTOR (and by default ORSBM). None of them has undergone more than one validation, and there are problems with some of these validation efforts.

6. It was originally going to be titled *Understanding Insurgencies*.

7. According to the International Institute for Strategic Studies, *Military Balance 2002–2003*, published in October 2002. For all practical purposes, it was much less than that.

Bibliography

Archives

Archival Research: Most of the engagements used in the analysis of combat in this book were based on unit records drawn from these archives.

Bundesarchiv (German Federal Archives), Freiburg.
Central Archive of the Russian Ministry of Defense (TSAMO), Podolsk, Moscow Region.
National Archives and Records Administration (NARA), College Park MD.
National Archive and Records Administration (NARA), Washington DC.
Public Records Office (PRO), Kew Gardens, London.

Databases Used: All the Dupuy Institute databases are built primarily from unit records drawn from various archives. Books and secondary sources used are listed in the databases but not the bibliography.

Ardennes Campaign Simulation Data Base (ACSDB) (Dupuy Institute).
Battalion-Level Operations Data Base (BLODB) (Dupuy Institute).
Battles Data Base (BADB) (Dupuy Institute).
Campaign Data Base (CADB) (Dupuy Institute).
Company-Level Action Data Base (CLADB) (Dupuy Institute).
Division-Level Engagement Data Base (DLEDB) (Dupuy Institute).
iCasualty.org databases.
Iraq Body Count: http://www.iraqbodycount.org/.
Kursk Data Base (Dupuy Institute).
Land Warfare Data Base (LWDB) (Dupuy Institute).
Large Action Data Base (LADB) (Dupuy Institute).
Small Action Data Base (SADB) (Dupuy Institute).
Small-Scale Contingency Operations (SSCO) Data Base (Dupuy Institute).

Published Works

Allen, Patrick. *Situational Force Scoring: Accounting for Combined Arms Effects in Aggregate Combat Models.* N-3423-NA. Santa Monica CA: RAND, 1992.
Anonymous. "In Pursuit of the Essence of War." *Army,* January 1984.
Battilega, John, and Judith Grange. *The Military Applications of Modeling.* Wright-Patterson AFB OH: Air Force Institute of Technology Press, 1979.
Beebe, Gilbert W., and Michael E. De Bakey. *Battle Casualties: Incidence, Mortality, and Logistic Considerations.* Springfield IL: Charles C. Thomas, 1952.
Bellamy, Ronald F., and Christopher A. Lawrence. *Why Is Marine Combat Mortality Less Than That of the Army.* N.p.: Gray and Associates, 1998.
Berensen, Paul. "Memorandum for Mike Bauman, director, TRADOC Analysis Center; Edgar Vandiver III, director, USA Concepts Analysis Agency; John McCarthy, director, U.S. Army Material Systems Analysis Activity." *International TNDM Newsletter* 1, no. 4 (1997): 6.
Beuttel, H. W. "Chemical Weapons and Iranian Casualties in the Iran-Iraq War: A Further Note and Update." *International TNDM Newsletter* 3, no. 1 (2009): 21–32.

———. "Iranian Casualties in the Iran-Iraq War: A Reappraisal." *International TNDM Newsletter* 2, no. 3 (1997): 6–17.

———. "Iranian Casualties in the Iran-Iraq War: A 2010 Update." *International TNDM Newsletter* 3, no. 2 (2010): 14–29.

———. "Iranian Casualties in the Iran-Iraq War (1980–1988): A Reappraisal, Part 2, Casualty Causes." *International TNDM Newsletter* 2, no. 4 (1998): 20–24.

Chairman of the Joint Chiefs of Staff Guide 3161: Guide to Battle Casualty Rate Patterns for Conventional Ground Forces. N.p., 15 January 1998.

Clark, Charles, et al. *War Gaming, Cosmogon, and Zigspiel.* ORO-SP-12. Baltimore MD: Operations Research Office, Strategic Division, May 1957.

Clark, Dorothy K. *Casualties as a Measure of the Loss of Combat Effectiveness of an Infantry Battalion.* Operations Research Office, Johns Hopkins University, 1954.

Clausewitz, Carl von. *On War.* Princeton NJ: Princeton University Press, 1976.

Clodfelter, Micheal. *Vietnam in Military Statistics: A History of the Indochina Wars, 1772–1991.* Jefferson NC: McFarland, 1995.

———. *Warfare and Armed Conflicts: A Statistical Reference to Casualties and Other Figures, 1618–1991.* Jefferson NC: MacFarland, 1992.

Congressional Research Service. *American War and Military Operations Casualties: Lists and Statistics.* Report. Washington DC, 13 July 2005.

Data Memory Systems. *The Quantified Judgment Model in Low Intensity Conflict Application.* Fairfax VA: Data Memory Systems, [1992].

Davis, Paul K. "The Influence of T. N. Dupuy's Research on the Treatment of Ground Combat in RAND's RSAS and JICM Models." *International TNDM Newsletter* 2, no. 4 (1998): 6–12.

Davis, Paul K., and Donald Blumenthal. *The Base of Sand Problem: A White Paper on the State of Military Combat Modeling.* N-3148-OSD/DARPA. Santa Monica CA: RAND, 1991.

Dodge, Theodore A. *Alexander.* Boston: Houghton Mifflin, 1890.

———. *Caesar.* Boston: Houghton Mifflin, 1891.

———. *Hannibal.* Boston: Houghton Mifflin, 1891.

Dupuy, T. N. *Attrition: Forecasting Battle Casualties and Equipment Losses in Modern War.* Falls Church VA: Nova, 1995.

———. "Can We Rely upon Computer Combat Simulations?" *Armed Forces Journal,* August 1987, 58–63.

———. "Criticism of Combat Models Cite Unreliability of Results." *Army,* March 1985, 16–18.

———. *Elusive Victory: The Arab Israeli Wars, 1947–1974.* 1978. Fairfax VA: HERO Books, 1984.

———. *The Evolution of Weapons and Warfare.* New York: De Capo Press, 1984.

———. *If War Comes: How to Defeat Saddam Hussein.* McLean VA: HERO Books, 1991.

———. *Numbers, Predictions and War: The Use of History to Evaluate and Predict the Outcome of Armed Combat.* Fairfax VA: HERO Books, 1985.

———. *Numbers, Predictions, and War: Using History to Evaluate Combat Factors and Predict the Outcome of Battles.* New York: Bobbs-Merrill, 1979.

———. "Rebuttal Rebutted." *Army,* September 1985, 6.

———. *Understanding Defeat: How to Recover from Loss in Battle to Gain Victory in War.* New York: Paragon House, 1990.

———. *Understanding War: History and Theory of Combat.* New York: Paragon House, 1987.

Dupuy, Trevor N., David L. Bongard, and Richard C. Anderson Jr. *Hitler's Last Gamble: The Battle of the Bulge, December 1994–January 1945.* New York: Harper Collins, 1994.

Dupuy, Trevor N., Curt Johnson, and David L. Bongard. *The Harper Encyclopedia of Military Biography.* New York: Harper Collins, 1992.

Dupuy Institute. *Capture Rate Study, Phases I & II: Final Report.* McLean VA, 6 March 2000.

———. *Capture Rate Study, Phase III: Post–World War II Capture Rates*. McLean VA, 10 November 2000.

———. *Capture Rate Study: Medical Requirements for EPW, Phase IV (Part 1)*. McLean VA, 17 November 2000.

———. *Capture Rate Study: EPWs in Small Scale Contingency Operations, Phase IV (Part 2)*. McLean VA, 27 March 2001.

———. *Casualty Estimation Methodologies Study*. Annandale VA, 25 July 2005.

———. *Conducting a Comparative Historical Perspective: Measuring the Effectiveness of the Future Combat Systems (FCS) in the Battle of Kursk*. Annandale VA, 30 May 2006.

———. *Conducting a Comparative Historical Perspective: Measuring the Effectiveness of the Future Combat Systems (FCS) in the Battle of Kursk—Corps Engagements*. Annandale VA, 15 July 2006.

———. *Measuring the Effects of Combat in Cities, Phase I*. McLean VA, 11 January 2002.

———. *Measuring the Effects of Combat in Cities, Phase II*. Annandale VA, 30 June 2003.

———. *Measuring the Effects of Combat in Cities, Phase III*. Annandale VA, 31 July 2004.

———. *Measuring the Value of Situational Awareness*. Annandale VA, May 2004.

———. *Research Plan*. Report E-3. McLean VA, 7 October 1998.

———. *Small Unit Engagement Data Base and Revised QJM Calculation Factors, Final Report*. Annandale VA, 7 June 2011.

———. *Soviet/Russian Influence on Chinese Military Doctrine*. Annandale VA, July 2003.

———. *The Tactical Numerical Deterministic Model (TNDM): A General and Theoretical Description*. McLean VA, October 1994.

———. *Tactical Numerical Deterministic Model (TNDM): Manual of Rules and Procedures (Provisional)*. McLean VA, October 1994.

Edwards, Sean J. A. *Mars Unmasked: The Changing Face of Urban Operations*. MR-1173-A. Santa Monica CA: RAND, 2000.

Estes, Kenneth W. *U.S. Marines in Iraq, 2004–2005: Into the Fray*. Washington DC: History Division, U.S. Marine Corps, 2011.

Fain, Janice B. "The Lanchester Equations and Historical Warfare: An Analysis of Sixty World War II Land Engagements." In *Combat Data Subscription Service*. Arlington VA: Historical Evaluation and Research Organization, Spring 1977.

Frank, Benis M., and Henry I. Shaw Jr. *Victory and Occupation: History of the U.S. Marine Corps Operations in World War II*. Vol. 5. N.p.: Historical Branch, G-3 Division, Headquarters, U.S. Marine Corps, 1968.

Gamow, George, and Richard Zimmerman. *Mathematical Models for Ground Combat*. ORO-SP-11. Baltimore: Operations Research Office, Strategic Division, April 1957.

Garand, George W., and Truman R. Strobridge. *Western Pacific Operations: History of the U.S. Marine Corps Operations in World War II*. Vol. 4. N.p.: Historical Division, Headquarters, U.S. Marine Corps, 1971.

Glenn, Russell W. *The Art of Darkness: Deception and Urban Operations*. MR-1132-A. Santa Monica CA: RAND, 2000.

———. *Combat in Hell: A Consideration of Constrained Urban Warfare*. MR-780-A/DARPA. Santa Monica CA: RAND, 1996.

———. *Heavy Matter: Urban Operations' Density of Challenges*. MR-1239. Santa Monica CA: RAND, 2000.

Gözel, Ramazan. "Fitting Firepower Score Models to the Battle of Kursk Data." NPGS thesis. Naval Postgraduate School, Monterey CA, 2000. https://archive.org/details/fittingfirepower00goze.

Hardison, David C., et al. *Review of Army Analysis*. N.p.: U.S. Army, April 1979.

Hartley, Dean S., III. *Topics in Operations Research: Predicting Combat Effects*. Catonsville MD: Institute for Operations Research and Management Science, 2001.

Helmbold, Robert. *Rates of Advance in Historical Land Combat Operations.* CAA-RP-90-1. Bethesda MD: U.S. Army Concepts Analysis Agency, 1990.

Historical Evaluation and Research Organization. *Analysis of Factors That Have Influenced Outcomes of Battles and War: A Data Base of Battles and Engagements.* 6 vols. Dunn Loring VA, 1983.

——. *Casualty Estimates for Contingencies: Final Report.* Vol. 1. Fairfax VA, 15 November 1985.

——. *Combat Data Subscription Service.* 8 vols. Dunn Loring VA, 1975–78.

——. *Combat Data Subscription Service Supplement.* Vol. 1, no. 3: HERO *Report 50.* Dunn Loring VA, Summer 1975.

——. *Combat History Analysis Study Effort (CHASE) Data Enhancement Study (CDES).* 5 vols. Fairfax VA, January 1986.

——. *Defeat Criteria Seminar: Seminar Papers on the Evaluation of the Criteria for Defeat in Battle.* Fairfax VA, 12 June 1987.

——. *Forced Changes of Combat Posture (Breakpoints).* Fairfax VA, 1988.

——. *Handbook on Ground Forces Attrition in Modern Warfare.* Fairfax VA, 1986.

——. *Historical Analysis of Wartime Replacement Requirements: Experience for Selected Major Items of Combat Equipment.* Vols. 1 and 2. Washington DC, 26 July 1966.

——. *Historical Survey of Casualties in Different Sized Units in Modern Combat.* Dunn Loring VA, 1982.

——. *History, Numbers and War.* 12 vols. Dunn Loring VA, 1977–81.

——. *Opposed Rates of Advance of Large Forces in Europe (ORALFORE).* Dunn Loring VA, 1972.

——. *The QJM Data Base.* 3 vols. HERO Report 100. Fairfax VA, 1985.

Hollis, Walt W. "Yes We Can Rely on Computer Combat Simulations." *Armed Forces Journal,* October 1987, 118–19.

Honig, John, et al. *Report of the Army Models Committee.* N.p.: U.S. Army, 1971.

Hough, Frank O., Verle E. Luidwig, and Henry I. Shaw Jr. *Pearl to Guadalcanal: History of the U.S. Marine Corps Operations in World War II.* Vol. 1. N.p.: Historical Branch, G-3 Division, Headquarters, U.S. Marine Corps.

Imbalance of Power: Shifting U.S.-Soviet Military Strengths. San Rafael CA: Presidio Press, 1978.

International Institute for Strategic Studies. *The Military Balance 1974–1975.* London: International Institute for Strategic Studies, 1974.

——. *The Military Balance 2002–2003.* Oxford: Oxford University Press, 2002.

Julius Caesar. *The Civil War: Together with the Alexandrian War, the African War and the Spanish War by Other Hands.* London: Penguin Books, 1967.

——. *The Conquest of Gaul.* London: Penguin Books, 1982.

Lanchester, F. W. *Aircraft in Warfare: The Dawn of the Fourth Arm.* Sunnyvale CA: Lanchester Press, 1995.

Lawrence, Christopher A. *America's Modern Wars: Understanding Iraq, Afghanistan and Vietnam.* Philadelphia: Casemate, 2015.

——. "Background Paper on Wounded-to-Killed Ratios." Unpublished manuscript, 24 May 2012.

——. "A Brief History of Trevor N. Dupuy's Organizations." *International TNDM Newsletter* 2, no. 1 (1997): 15–20.

——. "The First Test of the TNDM Battalion-Level Validations: Predicting the Winners." *International TNDM Newsletter* 1, no. 5 (1997): 33–39.

——. *Kursk: The Battle of Prokhorovka.* Sheridan CO: Aberdeen Books, 2015.

——. *Measuring Human Factors in Combat: Part of the Enemy Prisoner of War Capture Rate Study.* McLean VA: Dupuy Institute, 31 August 2000.

——. "A Rebuttal to 'Force XXI and the Theory of Winning Outnumbered.'" *International TNDM Newsletter* 2, no. 1 (1997): 35–38.

——. "Response to Niklas Zetterling's Article." *International TNDM Newsletter* 1, no. 6 (1997): 24–25.

———. "The Second Test of the TNDM Battalion-Level Validations: Predicting Casualties." *International TNDM Newsletter* 1, no. 5 (1997): 40–50.

———. "The Second Test of the TNDM Battalion-Level Validations: Predicting Casualties, Final Scorecard." *International TNDM Newsletter* 1, no. 6 (1997): 37–39.

———. "Summation of QJM/TNDM Validation Efforts." *International TNDM Newsletter* 3, no. 2 (2010): 38–41.

———. "Use of Armor in the 76 Battalion-Level Engagements." *International TNDM Newsletter* 1, no. 6 (1997): 35–36.

———. "Validation of the Quantified Judgment Model." *International TNDM Newsletter* 1, no. 2 (1996): 62–63.

———. "Validation of the TNDM at Battalion Level." *International TNDM Newsletter* 1, no. 2 (1996): 59–61.

———. "Validation of the TNDM to Corps-Level Combat." *International TNDM Newsletter* 3, no. 2 (2010): 5–9.

———. "Validation of the TNDM to Division-Level Combat." *International TNDM Newsletter* 3, no. 2 (2010): 10–13.

Leitch, R. A., H. R. Champion, and J. F. Navein. *Analysis of Casualty Rates and Patterns Likely to Result from Military Operations in Urban Environments.* Washington DC: U.S. Marine Corps, Commandant's Warfighting Laboratory, November 1997.

Leonhard, Robert R. "Force XXI and the Theory of Winning Outnumbered." *Army*, June 1996.

Longmore, T. *Gunshot Injuries.* London: Longmans Green, 1877.

Love, J. Duncan. *Artillery Usage in World War II.* 2 vols. ORO-T-375. N.p., April 1959.

Low, Lawrence J. *Theater-Level Gaming and Analysis Workshop for Force Planning, September 1977.* Report to Office of Naval Research. N.p., 1980.

McEnany, Brian R. "Uncertainties and Inadequacies in Theater Level Combat Analysis." Paper delivered at 16th U.S. Army Operations Research Symposium, n.p., 12–14 October 1977.

McLaurin, R. D., Paul A. Jureidini, David S. McDonald, and Kurt J. Sellers. *Modern Experience in City Combat.* Aberdeen Proving Ground MD: Abbot Associates, U.S. Army Human Engineering Laboratory, March 1987.

McQuie, Robert. "Battle Outcomes: Casualty Rates as a Measure of Defeat." *Army* 37 (November 1987).

———. "Military History: A Mathematical Analysis." *Military Review*, May 1970.

Meid, Pat, and James M. Yingling. *U.S. Marine Operations in Korea 1950–53.* Vol. 5: *Operations in West Korea.* Washington DC: Headquarters, U.S. Marine Corps, 1972.

Morse, Philip M., and George E. Kimball. *Methods of Operations Research.* Mineola NY: Dover, 2003.

Neel, S. *Medical Support of the U.S. Army in Vietnam 1965–1970.* Washington DC: U.S. Government Printing Office, 1973.

1994 Defense Almanac.

Office of the U.S. Comptroller General. *Report to the Congress: Models, Data and War. A Critique of the Foundation for Defense Analysis.* Washington DC, 1980.

Perez, Jose. "Exactly How the Unit Size Modifiers Are Calculated." *International TNDM Newsletter* 1, no. 3 (1996): 22–23.

Raines, Edgar F., Jr. *The Rucksack War: U.S. Army Operational Logistics in Grenada, 1983.* Washington DC: Center of Military History, 2010.

Reister, F. A. *Battle Casualties and Medical Statistics: U.S. Army Experience in the Korean War.* Washington DC: U.S. Department of the Army, Office of the Surgeon General, 1973.

———. *Medical Statistics in World War II.* Washington DC: U.S. Department of the Army, Office of the Surgeon General, 1975.

Rich, Susan. "TDI Profile: Trevor N. Dupuy." *International TNDM Newsletter* 2, no. 1 (1997): 39–40.

Rowland, David. *The Stress of Battle: Quantifying Human Performance in Combat.* London: TSO, 2006.

Shaw, Henry I., Jr., and Douglas T. Kane. *Isolation of Rabaul: History of the U.S. Marine Corps*

Operations in World War II. Vol. 2. N.p.: Historical Branch, G-3 Division, Headquarters, U.S. Marine Corps, 1963.

Shaw, Henry I., Jr., Bernard C. Nalty, and Edwin T. Turnblagh. *Central Pacific Drive: History of the U.S. Marine Corps Operations in World War II.* Vol. 3. N.p.: Historical Branch, G-3 Division, Headquarters, U.S. Marine Corps, 1966.

Shubik, Martin, and Garry D. Brewer. *Models, Simulations, and Games—A Survey.* R-1060-ARPA/RC. Santa Monica CA: RAND, May 1972.

Stockfisch, J. A. *Models, Data, and War: A Critique of the Study of Conventional Forces.* *R-1526-PR. Santa Monica CA: RAND, March 1975.

Taylor, James G. *Lanchester Models of Warfare.* 2 vols. Arlington VA: Operations Research Society of America, 1983.

Uhle-Wettler, Franz. "Computer Supported Studies and Military Experience." *Soldat und Technik*, April 1975.

U.S. Army. *Field Manual 105-5: Maneuver Control.* Washington DC, 1958.

———. *Field Manual 105-5: Maneuver Control.* Washington DC, December 1967.

———. *Field Manual 100-5: Operations.* Washington DC, 14 June 1993.

———. *Field Manual 3-0: Operations.* Washington DC, 14 June 2001.

U.S. Congress, Office of Technology Assessment. *A History of the Department of Defense Federally Funded Research and Development Centers.* Washington DC: U.S. Government Printing Office, June 1995.

U.S. Department of the Army, Office of Deputy Chief of Staff for Personnel, Office of Deputy Under Secretary of the Army Operations Research for Personnel Plans and Systems Directorate. *Report of the Model Input Data and Process Subcommittee of the Casualty Estimation Steering Committee.* Washington DC: U.S. Government Printing Office, January 1986.

U.S. Department of the Army, Office of the Surgeon General. *Textbook of Military Medicine: Warfare, Weaponry, and the Casualty.* Pt. 1, vol. 5: *Conventional Warfare Ballistic, Blast, and Burn Injuries.* Washington DC: U.S. Government Printing Office, 1991.

U.S. Department of Veterans Affairs. "Fact Sheet: America's Wars." July 2007. https://www.va.gov/opa/publications/factsheets/fs_americas_wars.pdf.

U.S. War Department. *Staff Officer's Field Manual. Pt. 2: Technical and Logistical Data.* Washington DC: Government Printing Office, 1932.

Wood, J. P. P. "Very Grave Suspicion." *Royal United Services Institute Journal*, March 1982.

Zetterling, Niklas. "CEV Calculations in Italy, 1943." *International TNDM Newsletter* 1, no. 6 (1997): 21–23.

———. *Normandy 1944: German Military Organization, Combat Power and Organizational Effectiveness.* Winnipeg, Canada: J. J. Fedorowicz, 2000.

Printed in the USA
CPSIA information can be obtained
at www.ICGtesting.com
CBHW080711010924
13956CB00013B/1012

9 781612 348865